PSYCHOLOGY
Adapted Readings

PSYCHOLOGY,
Adapted Readings,

EDITED BY

Jerome Kagan
Harvard University

Marshall M. Haith
Harvard University

Catherine Caldwell

HARCOURT BRACE JOVANOVICH, INC.
New York   Chicago   San Francisco   Atlanta

ISBN: *O-15-572560-2*

Library of Congress Catalog Card Number: 76-149096

Printed in the United States of America

ABOUT THE COVER

The structure on which the two children are climbing is in a Baltimore playground planned and built by psychiatrist Stephen M. Cohen, sculptor Stan C. Edminster, and neighborhood adults and children to fit the needs, behavior, and wishes of the children who would be using it. (Photo by Richard Linfield. Courtesy of *The Johns Hopkins Magazine.*)

ACKNOWLEDGMENTS FOR ILLUSTRATIONS

Part Opening Photographs

P. 2, Edmund B. Gerard, Life Magazine © Time, Inc.; p. 24, Monkmeyer Press Photo; pp. 48 and 382, Meryl Sussman; pp. 70 and 306, Ken Heyman; p. 92, Wide World Photos, Inc.; p. 118, Berne Greene; p. 166, Don Snyder; p. 194, Gerry Cranham/ Rapho Guillumette Pictures; p. 220, Jerome Hirsch; p. 246, Joel Peter Witkin; p. 288, Edmund Engelman; p. 334, Hanna W. Schreiber/Rapho Guillumette Pictures.

Text Figures

Fig. 3-2, from *Introduction to psychology*, 4th ed., p. 272, by Hilgard and Atkinson, copyright © 1967 by Harcourt Brace Jovanovich, Inc., (after R. M. Yerkes and S. Morgulis, "The method of Pavlov in animal psychology," *Psychological Bulletin* 6 (1909): 257–73). Figs. 6-1 and 6-2, after Wilder Penfield and Lamar Roberts, *Speech and brain mechanisms*, figs. 2 and 8, copyright © 1959 by Princeton University Press; reprinted by permission. Fig. 10-1, photograph by Theodore Polumbaum.

Preface

Ideally, a collection of readings for students of introductory psychology should be chosen from the full range of psychological literature. It should include both classic works—established landmarks in the field—and "frontier" pieces describing new research and current controversies. At the same time, the selections should be accessible to the student in content and style. They should require no more knowledge of psychology than the beginning student has, and they should be engaging and relevant to his interests.

When selections are simply reprinted, a readings book inevitably reflects some sort of compromise between scholarly importance and accessibility to the student. If the editor opts for accessibility, he must omit valuable material because it is too difficult or too detailed, giving the space instead to "readable" but peripheral, sometimes even trivial, pieces. If he chooses to stress scholarly importance, he has to include selections in which crucial issues are obscured, perhaps by elaborate statistical analyses that the student cannot follow or by theoretical discussions that are, from the student's point of view, impossibly esoteric.

Because the selections in *Psychology: Adapted Readings* were to be edited, we were able to choose them for importance and interest with little concern for the limitations usually imposed by complexity and length. Most of the thirty-five selections concern recent research and thought, but the work of such important early psychologists as James, Pavlov, and Freud is also represented. The readings range from the perennial controversy over mind and behavior that began with James and Watson around the turn of the century to very recent research, such as Allen and Beatrice Gardner's first report on their efforts to teach sign language to a chimpanzee and Bibb Latané and John Darley's series of studies, suggested by the Kitty Genovese murder, of the "apathetic" behavior of bystanders during emergencies. Three selections that may be particularly interesting to today's students are Alan Harrington's account of his first LSD trip, R. D. Laing's case study of a young schizophrenic, and Robert Coles's description of the life of a black child in a Boston ghetto.

The character of the editing differs, of course, from selection to selection. A few pieces have not been changed at all. Others have been revised to clarify technical terminology, to remove puzzling allusions to earlier research, and to shorten detailed descriptions of experimental equipment, methodology, and statistical techniques. Still others have been substantially rewritten, usually in order to reduce a very long article or several chapters from a book to manageable length. Overall, our aim has been to bring the material within the range of the beginning student's understanding by sharpening the basic focus of a selection and by substituting layman's language for technical terms. We have tried to do this without distorting the author's intent or obliterating his writing style. William James retains his Victorian phraseology, for example; B. F. Skinner, his asperity; Lewis Terman, his slightly old-fashioned charm.

The readings present varying, sometimes opposing, points of view toward fourteen major psychological topics. Each part is introduced by a headnote that discusses the topic in question and explains the significance of the selections that follow. Most of the readings support and elaborate points made in introductory textbooks; others will, we hope, extend students' thinking in new directions.

For their helpful comments on our choice of readings, we thank Neil A. Carrier, Southern Illinois University; Melvin H. Marx, University of Missouri; Robert B. McCall, Fels Research Institute; Allen Parducci, University of California, Los Angeles; and Sidney I. Perloe, Haverford College. And, of course, we are most grateful to the authors of the selections, both for allowing us to include their material and for reviewing our adaptations for substantive accuracy.

JEROME KAGAN
MARSHALL M. HAITH
CATHERINE CALDWELL

Contents

PSYCHOLOGY
Adapted Readings

The Beginnings
of Modern
Psychology

Twentieth-century American psychology began with the work of a great nineteenth-century man, William James. Around 1875, James opened a small demonstration laboratory at Harvard University, the first psychology laboratory established in the United States. Fifteen years later, in 1890, he published his classic textbook, *Principles of Psychology*, which begins with a classic definition: "Psychology is the science of mental life." Based on James's lectures to introductory psychology classes at Harvard, *Principles of Psychology* discusses almost every major topic in contemporary psychology, including memory, perception, emotion, instinct, consciousness, and the activity of the brain. It is still widely read, not only for its historical importance but for James's extraordinary perceptiveness and clarity of thought.

Before James's time (1848–1910), virtually all work in psychology was done in Europe, chiefly by men whose interests and methods were more philosophical than scientific. Most European psychologists relied on the introspective method: they asked their subjects to look into their own minds—to introspect—and try to describe the contents and progression of their thoughts.

James attacked the introspective method on several grounds. He considered it unreliable and tedious, and he thought it misleading in its implications about the way human behavior actually develops. In James's opinion, behavior is determined primarily by the goals we adopt, and both the goals we choose and the ways we try to reach them are strongly affected by the demands of the environment. This view of human behavior parallels James's convictions as a philosopher. Pragmatism, the American philosophical movement that he helped found, says that philosophical ideas should not be formulated and evaluated completely in the abstract. Instead, it stresses their practical consequences for life in the real world.

James's emphasis on a close relationship between human behavior and the environment shows the influence of Charles Darwin's theory of evolution. James saw the psychological development of a person throughout his lifetime, rather like the biological development of species from generation to generation, as a series of attempts to adapt to environment. However, whereas Darwin allotted plants and animals a relatively passive, purposeless role in their own evolution, James saw man as a dynamic agent who does much to determine what his own experience will be.

"On Attention," drawn from *Principles of Psychology*, reflects James's conviction that man actively determines his own experience. People choose, consciously or unconsciously, which things they will attend to; attention serves as a screen, admitting only a few of the many stimuli available at a given time. As you sit in a classroom, you may listen to what the lecturer is saying or watch what the person beside you is doing, but you probably will not notice the smudges on the window, the ticking of the watch on your wrist, or the pressure of the belt around your waist. This example concerns sensory stimuli, but selective attention also operates in mental processes. When you are concentrating on what you will include in a paper, you do not think at the same time about how you will pay your bills or what route you will take to your next class. If you do, your attention has shifted, and you are no longer thinking about the paper.

The nature of attention and the mechanisms that guide it were important psychological topics during James's time and today, once again, they are hotly debated issues. However, attention fell from favor as a subject of study shortly after James's death and was neglected for several decades, chiefly as the result of John Watson and the rise of behaviorism.

John Watson (1878–1958) was even more impatient than James with the endless arguments of European philosopher-psychologists about the internal workings of men's minds. Watson believed that James's emphasis on analyzing man's behavior in terms of adaptation to the environment, known as functional analysis, was a step in the right direction. But he thought that James had not gone far enough. Attention, consciousness, mental states—such subjects, important to James, were too "mentalistic" for Watson.

When "Psychology as the Behaviorist Views It" was published in 1913, it caused a tremendous stir, and it has become one of the most famous articles in psychology's vast literature. Watson argued that psychologists should leave introspection and the subjective analysis of men's minds to philosophy and concentrate exclusively on behavior that can be observed and recorded by objective methods. Behaviorism, the school of psychology based on Watson's ideas, has attracted many psychologists over the last fifty years and has played a crucial role in the development of the field as a whole. One sign of its impact is that James's definition of psychology as "the science of mental life" is seldom used today; instead, the standard short definition states that psychology is "the science of behavior."

Another aspect of Watson's work, though not discussed in "Psychology as the Behaviorist Views It," should be mentioned because of its importance in contemporary thought, both within and outside psychology. Watson was convinced that experience, not inherited characteristics, is the main determinant of human behavior —that a child's abilities and personality traits develop chiefly as the result of interaction between the child and the people and things around him rather than unfolding in ways that are predetermined from birth. In favoring the nurture side of the so-called nature-nurture controversy, Watson adopted an optimistic position. If man's behavior is not genetically fixed but rather develops through experience, then change for the better is possible. Many current social and educational programs, such as preschools for disadvantaged children, are statements of faith in Watson's argument.

1

On Attention

WILLIAM JAMES

Everyone knows what attention is. It is the focusing of the mind on one of several possible objects or trains of thought. It implies a mental withdrawal from some things in order to deal effectively with others.

The opposite of attention is the confused, dazed, scatterbrained state that in French is called *distraction*. We are all familiar with distraction. Most people probably fall into it several times a day. In the back of our minds we know what we ought to be doing: getting up, dressing, answering the person who has spoken to us, trying to take the next step in reasoning something out. But somehow we cannot start. Every moment we expect lethargy to depart, since we know no reason why it should stay. But it continues until—also without reason that we can discover—something enables us

ON ATTENTION Adapted from *The principles of psychology*. New York: Henry Holt, 1890, and Dover, 1950.

to gather ourselves together. Then we blink and shake our heads, and the background idea becomes effective. The wheels of life go round again.

This is the awakening of attention. One object comes into the focus of consciousness; others are temporarily suppressed. The awakening may come about either because of a stimulus from outside or because of some unknown inner alteration. Attention amounts to a concentration on one single object to the exclusion of all else—a selective attention to that object.

Attention and Experience

Strangely, so obvious a state as attention has received hardly any notice from English psychologists. The motive for ignoring it is clear enough. These psychologists are bent on showing how the contents of the mind are pure products of experience, and experience is supposed to be something simply given to a passive organism.

But the moment one thinks of the matter, one sees the falseness of defining experience simply as the presence to the senses of an outward order. Millions of items in the environment are present to my senses but never become part of my experience. Why? Because they have no interest for me. *My experience is what I attend to.* Only the items that I notice shape my mind. Without selective interest experience is utter chaos.

An empiricist like Spencer, for example, regards the mind as completely passive clay upon which experience rains down. The clay will be marked most deeply where the drops fall thickest, and in this way the shape of the mind is molded. If this were true, a family of dogs bred for generations in, say, the Vatican ought to become accomplished connoisseurs of sculpture. But surely an eternity of seeing the statues would leave a dog as unappreciative as it was at first, because the dog lacks an original interest to knit his discrimination onto.

These writers have ignored the glaring fact that subjective interest, may, by laying a weightier finger on particular items of experience, so accent them as to give infrequent associations far more power to shape our thought than the most frequent ones have. Interest makes experience more than experience makes interest.

How Many Things
Can We Attend To at Once?

The question of how broad a span of consciousness we have has often been asked. The number of things we can attend to at one time is altogether indefinite and depends on the power of the individual intellect, on the form of the apprehension, and on what the things are. When the things must be apprehended by the senses, the number that can be attended to at once is small. Sir William Hamilton writes:

> If you throw a handful of marbles on the floor, you will find it difficult to view at once more than six, or seven at most, without confusion. But if you group them into twos or threes or fives, you can comprehend as many groups as you can units, because the mind considers the groups only as units—it views them as wholes and throws their parts out of consideration (Hamilton, 1860–61).

Such observations, however, decide nothing at all about attention itself. Instead they measure in part the distinctness of our vision and in part the strength of the associations a person makes between seen arrangements of objects and the names of numbers. Each number-name is a way of grasping a group of objects as one total object. In a total object, all the parts converge in one concept. But when the object before us breaks into parts not connected with each other, it becomes harder to apprehend all the parts at once. The mind tends to let go of one while it attends to another.

If the question of how many ideas or things we can attend to at once means how many entirely disconnected systems or processes of conception can go on simultaneously, the answer is: not easily more than one but perhaps two, or even three, if the processes are very habitual. When the processes are not habitual and are therefore less automatic, as in the story of Julius Caesar dictating four letters while he wrote a fifth, there must be rapid oscillation of the mind from one process to another.

The Effects of Attention

The remote effects of attention are incalculable. The practical and theoretical life of the whole species, as well as of individual beings, results from the selection that the habitual direction of attention involves. Our experience is determined by what we choose to attend to; by the ways in which we attend to things, we control the sort of universe we think we live in.

The immediate effects of attention are to make us (1) perceive, (2) conceive, (3) distinguish, and (4) remember—all better than we otherwise could—both more things in succession and each thing more clearly. Attention also (5) shortens reaction time.

Perceiving and conceiving. Most people would say that a sensation attended to becomes stronger than it otherwise would be. When we listen for a certain note in a chord, the one we attend to sounds a little louder and more emphatic than the others. When we mentally break a series of monotonous strokes into a rhythm by accentuating every second or third stroke, the one on which the stress of attention is laid seems to become stronger as well as more emphatic. Similarly, every artist knows how he can make a scene in his imagination appear warmer or colder in color according to the way he sets his attention. If for warm, he soon begins to see the red color start out of everything; if for cold, the blue.

But the intensification seems never to lead the judgment astray. Just as we rightly perceive and name the same color under different lights and the same sound from different distances, so we seem to make an allowance for the varying amounts of attention with which objects are viewed. Were this not so, we would not be able to note intensities: weak impressions would become stronger by the very fact of being observed. As Stumpf says:

> I should not be able to observe faint sounds at all, but only such as appeared to me of maximal strength, or at least of a strength that increased with the amount of my observation. In reality, however, I can, with steadily increasing attention, follow a diminuendo perfectly well (Stumpf, n.d.).

Distinguishing. There is no question whatever that attention increases the clearness of all that we perceive with our senses or conceive in our minds. Clearness, as produced by attention, means distinctness from other things and internal analysis or subdivision. These are essentially products of intellectual discrimination, which involves the perceiving, comparing, and remembering of various relationships. Attention itself does not distinguish and analyze, however. The most we can say is that it is a precondition for doing so.

Remembering. An object once attended to will remain in the memory, whereas one inattentively allowed to pass will leave no traces. Whether certain states of mind are unconscious or, rather, states to which no attention has been paid and which are therefore forgotten is a question that remains to be resolved.

Shortening reaction time. Reaction time is shorter when a person concentrates his attention on an expected movement rather than on an expected signal. In a series of experiments conducted by Münsterberg, the five fingers were used to react with, and the reactor had to use a different finger for each of several signals. For example, when a word in the nominative case was called out he responded with his thumb, for the dative he used another finger; similarly, towns, rivers, beasts, plants, elements, or poets, musicians, philosophers, and so on were assigned to different fingers, so that when a word from these classes was mentioned a particular finger, and no other, had to indicate the reactor's awareness of the class the word belonged to. In a second series of experiments the reactor had to answer aloud questions such as "Name an edible fish," "Name the first drama of Schiller," "Which is greater, Hume or Kant?" and "Which letter comes later in the alphabet, the letter L or the first letter of the most beautiful tree?" Even in this series, which required more intellectual activity than the first, the speed of reaction was much quicker—seldom more than a fifth of a second—when the reactor turned his attention in advance toward the answer; when he concentrated on the question, the reaction time was from four to eight times longer.

One must bear in mind that in these two series of experiments the reactor knew in advance the kind of question he was to receive and, consequently, the sphere within which the answers lay. When, by contrast, the attention was kept on the question and not on the possible reply, the entire process of answering had to be gone through after the question had been heard. No wonder the time was prolonged. The results beautifully illustrate the way in which expectant attention prepares the motor centers and shortens the work that a stimulus has to perform on them.

The Nature of the Attentive Process

Two physiological processes immediately suggest themselves in connection with the nature of the attentive process. They are (1) sensorial adjustment: adjustment of the sensory organs; and (2) ideational preparation: mental expectations about the object to which attention is paid.

The muscles that guide the sense organs are adjusted most energetically in sensorial attention. But there are good grounds for believing that intellectual attention, attention to the *idea* of a physical object, is also accompanied by some degree of excitement of the sense organs to which the object appeals. Since in mature life we never attend to anything without our interest in it being derived to some extent from its association with other objects, the two processes probably coexist in all our attentive acts.

These two points must now be proved in more detail. *Sensorial adjustment* obviously takes place when we attend to physical things. When we look or listen we involuntarily adjust our eyes and ears and turn our head and body as well; when we taste or smell we adjust the tongue, lips, and respiration to the object; in feeling a surface we move the fingers in a suitable way. In all these acts, besides making relevant involuntary muscular contractions of a positive sort, we inhibit other movements that might interfere with the result. We close our eyes in tasting, sometimes hold our breath in listening, and so on. The result is a more or less massive organic feeling that attention is going on.

In intellectual attention, somewhat surprisingly, similar feelings of activity occur. Fechner was the first, I believe, to analyze these feelings and discriminate them from the stronger ones just mentioned. He writes:

> When we transfer attention from objects of one sense to those of another, we have an indescribable feeling of altered *direction* or differently localized tension. We feel a strain forward in the eyes, one directed sidewise in the ears, increasing with the degree of attention and changing according as we look at an object carefully or listen to something attentively. We speak accordingly of *straining the attention*. The difference is most plainly felt when the attention oscillates rapidly between eye and ear, and the feeling localizes itself with most decided difference in regard to the various sense organs, according as we wish to discriminate a thing delicately by touch, taste, or smell.

> But now I have, when I try to recall vividly a picture of memory or fancy, a feeling perfectly analogous to that which I experience when I want to apprehend a thing keenly by eye or ear. This analogous feeling is very differently localized. While in sharpest possible attention to real objects the strain is plainly forward, the case is different in memory or fancy, for here the feeling withdraws entirely from the external sense organs and seems rather to take refuge in that part of the head which the brain fills. If I wish, for example, to recall a place or person it will arise before me with vividness not according as I strain my attention forward but rather in proportion as I, so to speak, retract it backwards (Fechner, 1889).

It has been said that we may attend to an object on the periphery of the visual field without turning the eyes toward it. Teachers notice the acts of children at whom they appear not to be looking. In general, women train their peripheral visual attention more than men. Usually, as is well known, no object lying in the marginal portions of the field of vision can catch our attention without at the same time "catching our eye." Practice, however, enables us with effort to attend to a marginal object while keeping the eyes still. The object under these circumstances never becomes perfectly distinct—the place of its image on the retina makes distinctness impossible—but, as anyone can satisfy himself by trying, we become more vividly conscious of it than we were before the effort was made.

This leads us to the second feature of the attentive process: *ideational preparation*. The effort to attend to an object on the periphery of the visual field, such as the marginal region of a picture, is nothing more or less than the effort to form as clear an idea as possible of what is portrayed. The idea comes to the aid of the sensation and makes it more distinct. It comes with effort, and that effort is the remaining part of what we know as our attention's strain. This inward reproduction, this mental anticipation of the thing we attend to, is present in all acts of attention.

It must of course be present when the attention is of the intellectual variety: then the thing attended to is nothing but an idea, an inner reproduction or concept. However, it is also present in sensorial attention. For example, in Figure 1-1, where the form of the figures is ambiguous, we can make the change from one apparent form to the other by imagining strongly the form we wish to see. Similarly, in a drawing where certain lines form an object that has no connection with what the picture ostensibly represents (or in an inkblot whose apparently abstract form conceals a meaningful shape) we may not be able to see the hidden object for a long time; but once we have seen it we can attend to it whenever we like because our imagination has a mental duplicate of it. In the meaningless French words *pas de lieu Rhone que nous*, who can recognize immediately the English "paddle your own canoe"? But who that has once noticed it can fail to have it arrest his attention again? When waiting for a distant clock to strike, our mind is so filled with its image that at every moment we think we hear the longed-for or dreaded chime. So of an awaited footstep. Every stir in the wood is for the hunter his game,

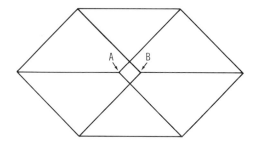
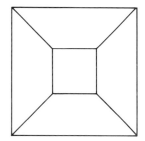

FIGURE 1-1

The transparent figure on the left looks different when the viewer imagines that Point A is closest to him and Point B is farthest away from him than when he imagines that Point A is farthest away and Point B is closest. The figure on the right changes in a similar way, depending on whether the viewer imagines the inner square to be closer to him or farther away than the outer square.

for the fugitive his pursuers. Every bonnet in the street is momentarily taken by the lover to enshroud the head of his idol. The image in the mind is the attention; the *preperception* is half of the perception of the looked-for thing. It is for this reason that men have eyes only for the aspects of things that they have already been taught to see.

A third part of the attentive process is the inhibition of irrelevant movements and ideas. This seems, however, to be a feature of voluntary attention rather than of all attention, and it need not particularly concern us now. Noting merely the intimate connection between attention on the one hand and perception, imagination, discrimination, and memory on the other, let us draw a few practical conclusions.

The practical conclusions concern teaching. First, to strengthen attention in children who care nothing for the subject they are studying and let their wits go woolgathering, interest must be derived from something that the teacher associates with the task—a reward or punishment, if nothing less external comes to mind. Ribot says:

> A child refused to read; he is incapable of keeping his mind fixed on the letters, which have no attraction for him, but he looks with avidity upon the pictures contained in a book. "What do they mean?" he asks. The father replies, "When you can read, the book will tell you." After several colloquies like this, the child resigns himself and falls to work, first slackly, then the habit grows, and finally he shows an ardor that has to be restrained. This is a case of the genesis of voluntary attention. An artificial and indirect desire has to be grafted on a natural and direct one. Reading has no immediate attractiveness, but it has a borrowed one, and that is enough (Ribot, 1889).

Second, take the mind-wandering that may trouble us while reading or listening to a speech. If attention is the reproduction of a sensation from within, it should deepen one's attention to the words if one forms the habit not of reading merely with the eye or of listening merely with the ear but of articulating the words to oneself. Experience shows that this is the case. I can keep my wandering mind a great deal more closely upon a conversation or a lecture if I actively echo the words to myself than if I simply hear them. A number of my students report that the same is true of them. (However, repetition of this sort does not confer the meaning of what is said; it only keeps the mind from wandering into other channels. The meaning sometimes comes, as it were, in beats at the ends of sentences or in the midst of words that were mere words until then.)

Third, a teacher who wishes to engage the attention of his class must knit new ideas onto things the class already knows, that is, onto things of which it has preperceptions. The old and familiar is readily attended to by the mind and helps hold the new. Of course it is in every case a very delicate problem to know which familiar thing to use. Psychology can only lay down the general rule.

Inattention

Having spoken of attention, let me add a word about inattention. We do not notice the ticking of the clock, the noise of the city streets, or the roar of the brook near the house, and even the din of a foundry or factory will not mingle with the thoughts of its workers if they have been there long enough. When we first put on spectacles, the bright reflections they give of windows and so on are very disturbing, but in a few days we ignore them altogether. The pressure of our clothes and shoes, the beating of our hearts and arteries, our breathing, certain constant bodily pains, habitual odors, tastes in the mouth—all these are examples of unchanging sensations that we are not conscious of.

The cause of this unconsciousness is not merely the blunting of the sense organs. If the sensation were important we should notice it well enough, and we can at any moment notice it by throwing our attention expressly on it, provided it has not become so inveterate that inattention to it is ingrained in our very constitution. And even in these cases, a real effort at observation will, with patience, soon give us command of the impression. Inattentiveness must therefore be a habit grounded on more than mere sensory fatigue.

Helmholtz has formulated a general law of inattention: we ignore all impressions that are valueless to us as signs by which to discriminate things. At most, such impressions fuse with others into an aggregate effect. The odors that are part of the taste of such foods as meat, fish, cheese, butter, and wine do not come to our attention as odors. The various muscular and tactile feelings that make up what we perceive as wet, elastic, doughy, and so forth are not singled out separately for what they are. They have formed connections in the mind that are difficult to break; they are parts of processes that differ altogether from the processes of catching the attention.

How can impressions that are not needed by the intellect be thus shunted off from all relation to the rest of consciousness? Müller has made a plausible reply to this question. He begins:

> When we first come out of a mill or factory in which we have re-
> mained long enough to get used to the noise, we feel as if something were

lacking. Our total feeling of existence is different from what it was when we were in the mill. A friend writes to me, "I have in my room a little clock which does not run quite twenty-four hours without winding. In consequence of this, it often stops. So soon as this happens, I notice it, whereas I naturally fail to notice it when going. When this first began to happen, I suddenly felt an undefined uneasiness or sort of void without being able to say what was the matter. Only after some consideration did I find the cause in the stopping of the clock" (Müller, n.d.).

That the stopping of an unfelt stimulus may itself be felt is a well-known fact. The sleeper in church wakes when the sermon ends; the miller does the same when his wheel stands still. Müller suggests that impressions that come to us when the thought centers are preoccupied with other matters may be blocked, or prevented from invading those centers, and may then overflow into lower paths of discharge. And he further suggests that if the process recurs often enough in response to a particular stimulus, the sidetrack created will become so deep that it is used no matter what may be going on in the centers above.

Müller's suggestion leads to another. It is a well-known fact that persons striving to keep their attention on a difficult subject will resort to meaningless movements such as pacing the room, drumming the fingers, playing with keys or a watch chain, scratching the head, pulling the mustache, jiggling the foot, and so on. There is an anecdote of Sir Walter Scott's in which a boy rises to the head of his class by cutting a button off the usual head boy's jacket, a button the boy was in the habit of twirling in his fingers during the lesson. With it gone, the owner's power of recitation also departed.

The purpose of much of this activity is unquestionably to release emotional excitement during anxious and concentrated thought. But may it not also be a means of drafting off all irrelevant sensations of the moment, thus keeping the attention more exclusively concentrated on its inner task? I offer the suggestion for what it is worth; the connection of the movements themselves with the continued effort of attention is certainly a genuine and curious fact.

REFERENCES

Fechner, G. T. *Elemente der Psychophysik* [Elements of psychophysics].
    Leipzig: Breitkopf & Härtel, 1889.

Hamilton, Sir William. *Lectures on metaphysics and logic*, Lecture 14.
    4 vols. Edinburgh: W. Blackwood & Sons, 1860–61.

Müller, G. E. *Zur Theorie der sinnlichen Aufmerksamkeit* [Toward a theory of sensorial attention].

Ribot, T. A. *Psychologie de l'attention* [The psychology of attention]. 1889.

Stumpf, C. *Tonpsychologie* [Psychology of sound].

2

Psychology
as the Behaviorist
Views It

J O H N   B .   W A T S O N

The time seems to have come when psychology must discard all
reference to consciousness, when it should no longer pretend that
it is making mental states the object of observation. We have become
so enmeshed in speculative questions about the mind and the nature
of conscious content that I, as an experimental psychologist, feel
something is wrong with our premises and the types of problems
that develop from them.

There is no longer any guarantee that we all mean the same thing
when we use the same words. One psychologist will state that the
attributes of a visual sensation are quality, extension, duration, and
intensity. Another will add clearness. Still another, order. I doubt
that any one psychologist can describe what he means by "visual
sensation" in a set of statements that will be agreed to by three other
psychologists of different training. For another example, take the

PSYCHOLOGY AS THE BEHAVIORIST VIEWS IT   Adapted from *Psychological Review*
20 (1913).

question of the number of isolable visual sensations. Is there an extremely large number of color sensations or only four—red, green, yellow, and blue? If we say that every just-noticeable difference in color is a simple sensation, then the number of sensations is so large and the conditions for obtaining them so complex that the concept of sensation is useless. On the other hand, the claim that there are only four color sensations also has its drawbacks. Yellow, while psychologically simple, can be obtained by superimposing red and green spectral rays on the same surface.

Titchener, who has fought a valiant fight for a psychology based on introspective reports of internal experience, feels that differences of opinion on matters such as the number of sensations and their attributes are perfectly natural in the present undeveloped state of psychology. While I admit that every growing science is full of unanswered questions, I wonder how anyone can confidently believe that there will ever be more uniformity than there is now on such questions. I firmly believe that, unless the introspective method is discarded, psychology will still be divided two hundred years from now on whether intensity is an attribute of color, and on whether there is a difference in "texture" between image and sensation, and on hundreds of other similar questions.

Psychologists' views on other mental processes are just as chaotic. Are we agreed on what feeling is? One man states that feelings are attitudes. Another finds them to be groups of organic sensations. Still another says they are elements that are separate from, but rank equally with, sensations.

My quarrel is not only with structural psychologists like Titchener. The last fifteen years have seen the growth of what is called functional psychology, which emphasizes the biological significance of conscious processes rather than the introspective, subjective analysis of conscious states. I have done my best to understand the difference between functional psychology and structural psychology. Instead of clarity, confusion grows upon me. The terms "sensation," "perception," "affection," "emotion," and "volition" are used as much by the functionalist as by the introspectionist. But the functionalist adds the word "process" after each term as if in some way to remove the corpse of content and leave function in its place. Surely if these concepts are elusive from the standpoint of content they are even more deceptive when viewed as functions, especially when function is ascertained by means of introspection.

I was surprised and pleased some time ago to open Pillsbury's book and see psychology defined as the science of behavior. Another book calls it the science of mental behavior. When I saw these promising statements, I thought: Here we surely have two books written along unusual lines. In each case, however, the "science of behavior" idea is dropped after a few pages, and one finds the conventional treatment of sensation, perception, imagery, and so forth, along with certain shifts in emphasis that serve to give the author's personal imprint.

This leads me to the point at which I should like to make my argument constructive. I believe *behaviorism* is the only consistent and logical functionalism. I believe we can write about psychology defining it as Pillsbury does and never going back on the definition—never using the words "consciousness," "mental states," "mind," "content," "introspectively verifiable." It can be done in terms of stimulus and response, habit formation, and the like. Furthermore, I believe it is really worthwhile to make that attempt now.

The psychology that I should attempt to build up would start with the observable fact that men and animals alike make adjustments to their environment by means of hereditary equipment and learned habits. The adjustments may be adequate, or they may be so close to inadequate that the organism barely maintains its existence. Second, certain stimuli lead the organism to make each adjustment response. In a completely worked out system of psychology, the responses can be predicted if the stimuli are known. These statements are crass and raw in the extreme, yet hardly more raw and less realizable than the ones that appear in the psychology books of the day.

I can better illustrate my point by choosing an everyday problem that anyone might meet in the course of his work. Some time ago I was called on to make a study of certain species of birds. Until I went to Tortugas I had never seen these birds alive. When I arrived I found the animals doing some things that seemed to work very well in their environment and other things that seemed unsuited to the birds' type of life. First I studied the responses of the group and later those of individual birds. In order to investigate the relationship between habits and hereditary responses, I took young birds and reared them myself. I was able to note the order of the appearance of hereditary adjustments and their complexity, and later the beginnings of habit formation.

Had I been called on to examine the aborigines of Australia, I should have found the problem more difficult—the types of responses called forth by physical stimuli would have been more varied, and the number of effective stimuli larger—but I would have gone about my task the same way. In the main, my aim in all such work is to gain an accurate knowledge of adjustments and the stimuli that call them forth. My ultimate goal is to learn general and particular methods by which I can control behavior.

If psychology follows the plan I suggest, the educator, physician, jurist, and businessman can use our data in practical ways as soon as we are able to obtain them experimentally. Ask any physician or jurist today whether scientific psychology plays a part in his daily routine and you will hear him deny it. I think he will be right. One of my earliest dissatisfactions with psychology was that there was no realm of application for the principles being worked out in the laboratory.

What gives me hope that the behaviorist's position is defensible is the excellent health of certain branches of psychology that have already partially withdrawn from the parent, experimental psychology, and have become less dependent on introspection. Experimental pedagogy, the psychology of drugs, the psychology of advertising, legal psychology, the psychology of tests, and psychopathology are all vigorous fields.

These are sometimes called practical or applied psychology. Surely there was never a worse misnomer. At present these fields are truly scientific: they look for broad generalizations that will lead to the control of human behavior. For example, experimental pedagogy attempts to find out by experimentation whether a series of stanzas can be memorized more easily if the whole is learned at once or if each stanza is learned separately. But experimenters do not try to apply their findings; the application is up to teachers. In legal psychology we test the effects of the passage of time on the reliability of a witness's report. But again, whether the results are ever applied depends on lawyers and judges.

When a pure psychologist says that he is not interested in such questions because they relate to applications of psychology, he shows his failure to understand the scientific aim of the problems and his indifference to a psychology that concerns itself with human life. The only fault I find with "applied" disciplines of psychology is that much of their material is stated in terms of introspection. A statement in terms of objective results would be far more valuable. There is never reason for appeal to be made to consciousness or for introspective data to be sought during an experiment and published in the results.

In experimental pedagogy especially one can see the desirability of keeping all results purely objective. If this is done, work on learning in human beings will be directly comparable with work on learning in animals. For example, using rats as subjects, Ulrich at Johns Hopkins has obtained certain findings on effort in learning. He is prepared to give comparative results on the effectiveness of having the animal work at a problem once a day, three times a day, or five times a day; on whether it is better to have the animal learn only one problem at a time or three simultaneously; and so on. We need similar experiments on men, and we care as little about their conscious processes during the experiments as we do about such processes in rats.

I am more interested at present in showing the necessity for uniformity in experimental procedures and in the statement of results of human and animal study than in developing my ideas about changes in the scope of human psychology. To illustrate, let us consider for a moment the problem of identifying the range of visual stimuli to which an animal responds. We put our animal in a situation where he will learn to respond to one of two colored lights. We feed him at one light and punish him at the other. In a short time the animal learns to go to the light at which he is fed. At this point questions arise that I may phrase in two ways. I may choose the psychological way and ask whether the animal sees the two lights as I do, as two distinct colors, or as the colorblind do, as two grays of different brightness. On the other hand, I may phrase the question behaviorally: Is the animal responding on the basis of the difference in wavelengths between the two stimuli or on the basis of the difference in intensity? The behaviorist does not think of the animal's response in terms of his own experience with colors and grays. Furthermore, he is as much interested in comparing the rat's spectrum with the chick's as with man's.

There is hardly a problem in human vision that is not also a problem in animal vision: the limits of the spectrum, threshold values, flicker, and so on. Every one is capable of being worked out by behavioral methods. Many are being worked out at the present time.

I feel that all work on the senses can be consistently carried forward along the lines I have suggested for vision. Our results will, in the end, give an excellent picture of the function of each organ. The anatomist and the physiologist may take our data and show, on the one hand, the structures that are responsible for these responses, and, on the other, the physicochemical relations that are involved in the reactions of nerve and muscle.

Memory, too, can be studied behaviorally. Indeed, nearly all the methods used today in the study of memory yield the type of results I am arguing for; the problem is that other matters claim a larger part of the experimenter's interest. For example, consider experiments in which a series of nonsense syllables is presented to a human subject for memorization. What ought to receive the emphasis are the rapidity of habit formation, the errors, the peculiarities in the form of the learning curve, the persistence of habits formed in the course of the experiment, the relation of these habits to those formed when more complex material is used, and so on. However, at present the subject is asked to explain and elaborate on his performance after introspection, so that the experimenter can contemplate the internal mental machinery used in learning, recall, memory, and forgetting—instead of identifying the human's observable ways of shaping his responses to meet the problems presented by the extremely complex environment into which he is thrown, or showing the similarities and differences between man's methods and those of animals.

The situation is somewhat different in the study of more advanced behavior such as reasoning, judgment, imagination, and conception. At present, the only statements we have of them concern content. Our minds have been so warped by the fifty-odd years devoted to the study of states of consciousness that we can see problems only one way. We ought to meet the situation squarely and say that we are not able to carry forward investigations along all these lines by the methods now in use. I should like to repeat that the introspective method has reached a dead end. But as behavioral methods become better developed, it will be possible to undertake investigations of increasingly complex forms of behavior. Problems that must be laid aside now can be raised again later, to be viewed from a new vantage point in more concrete settings.

If the approach I suggest is adopted will there remain in psychology a world of pure psychics, to use Yerkes' term? I confess I do not know. The plan that I favor leads to the ignoring of consciousness in the sense that the term is used by psychologists today. I have virtually denied that this realm of psychics is open to experimental investigation, and I do not wish to go further into the problem here because it leads inevitably into metaphysics.

In conclusion, I suppose I must confess to a deep bias. I have devoted nearly twelve years to experimentation on animals. It is natural that I should drift into a theoretical position that harmonizes with my experimental work. Possibly I have put up a straw man and have been fighting that. Certainly the position I advocate is weak enough at present and can be attacked from many standpoints. Yet I still feel that the considerations I have urged should have a wide influence on the type of psychology developed in the future. What we need to do is make behavior, not consciousness, the objective point of attack. Surely there are enough problems in the control of behavior to keep us all working many lifetimes without ever allowing us time to think of consciousness as such.

Conditioning

Try to imagine how much a newborn baby has to learn in order to acquire the behavior of a normal adult. Maturation and physical growth will account for part of his development, of course, but very little human behavior emerges automatically. Almost all abilities, from basic skills like walking and speaking to advanced ones like flying a plane and getting along with the opposite sex, have to be learned. People develop through experience—they learn.

Some psychologists believe that there are only two kinds of learning: classical conditioning and operant conditioning. Classical conditioning was discovered by Ivan Pavlov, author of the first selection in this part, and operant conditioning by B. F. Skinner, author of the second selection. Pavlov worked with dogs, Skinner with pigeons; as you read, try to think of examples of human behavior that is learned in the ways they describe.

A Russian physiologist and psychologist, Pavlov (1849–1936) made history with his work on classical conditioning, which won him the Nobel Prize in 1927. His research is summarized in his book *Conditioned Reflexes*. "The Salivary Reflex in Dogs," which comes from that book, describes some of the basic principles of classical conditioning. They are fairly straightforward, and Pavlov's contemporaries found them a welcome relief from the complicated, philosophical explanations of behavior offered by Sigmund Freud and others.

As Pavlov used it, the word "conditioning" meant association—association between an event that under ordinary circumstances triggers a reflex, such as the presence of food in a dog's mouth, which triggers the salivary reflex, and an event that normally does not set off that reflex, such as the sound of a beating metronome. Pavlov found that if the metronome was started just before food was put in the dog's mouth, eventually the sound of the metronome alone would make the dog salivate. After frequently experiencing the two events together—the sound of the metronome and the presence of food in the mouth—the dog came to associate the two; thus the salivary reflex became a conditioned response to the metronome.

In the last section of "The Salivary Reflex in Dogs," Pavlov compares the brain to a telephone switchboard. He suggests that by means of associations formed through experience the brain connects stimuli and conditioned responses much as a switchboard connects two telephones. The brain-as-switchboard idea, very useful at the time it was formulated, is now outmoded. Today, psychologists seeking a machine with which to compare the human brain tend to choose the computer.

Recently, when some 220 chairmen of psychology departments were asked to name the most influential men in contemporary psychology, B. F. Skinner came out far ahead of everyone else. Skinner is a strict behaviorist, in the tradition of John Watson. He and his followers have shown that very complex sequences of behavior can be learned through operant conditioning, and many educational innovations, including teaching machines and programed textbooks, are based on its principles.

In "Pigeons in a Pelican," Skinner describes a training program for pigeons that he ran during the Second World War. Using operant conditioning, he taught the birds to guide missiles toward their targets by pecking at an image on a screen. The plan met with considerable resistance in Washington—officials found it hard to believe that the pigeons were as reliable as Skinner's data proved them to be—and it was never put into operation. However, the work did influence the mechanical guidance systems devised later and, as Skinner says, it taught him a great deal about pigeons.

The basic law of operant conditioning is that behavior which is reinforced, or rewarded, tends to recur. Conversely, behavior that is not reinforced tends to die out. If a pigeon is given a grain of food every time it pecks a white disk and never given food when it pecks anything else, it will peck the white disk more and more often and other things less and less often. Though simple, this teaching technique is not as simple as it sounds. For best results, behavior must be reinforced *immediately:* the pigeon must associate the grain with pecking and not with, say, pulling its head away from the disk. Furthermore, once the pigeon has learned to peck the disk, the reinforcement schedule must be changed in order to keep the bird pecking at the highest and steadiest rate possible. The best way to teach new behavior is to reinforce it every time it occurs, but the best way to keep it going, once learned, is to reinforce it only once in a while. Through the careful control of reinforcement schedules, Skinner was able to train his pigeons to peck hundreds of times for just a few grains of food.

Skinner is a controversial as well as an influential figure. He has no doubt, for example, that man is a machine, though he admits that the machine is highly complex and, at present, poorly understood. Words used to describe so-called human characteristics, such as "consciousness," "will," and "thought," he considers vague attempts at description that will someday give way to more precise, more mechanical terminology. The real question, he has said, is not whether men can build a computer that thinks but whether men themselves do.

Some people find Skinnerian psychology reassuring, because it suggests that behavior is more flexible and more controllable —more susceptible to programing—than they had supposed. Others find it alarming, because it conjures up visions of 1984. In response, Skinnerians sometimes point out that the pressing problem is not to decide whether operant conditioning *should* be used to modify behavior but to discover the ways it in fact *does* so, with or without our approval, in our daily life.

3

The Salivary Reflex
in Dogs

I V A N   P A V L O V

The activity of an animal's nervous system must be regarded as based on *inborn reflexes:* hereditary and automatic reactions by the animal to certain outside stimuli. But in animals high on the evolutionary scale, inborn reflexes alone are not enough to maintain life. If the cerebral cortex in the brain of a dog is severely damaged, the animal soon dies, despite the fact that all its inborn reflexes continue to operate. Thus one must study the activities of the brain as well as those of the lower parts of the nervous system in order to understand the complex relationship between an animal and its environment that everyday existence demands.

In performing such studies in our laboratory we have used purely objective methods, treating the activities of the brain as physiological

THE SALIVARY REFLEX IN DOGS Adapted from *Conditioned reflexes: An investigation of the physiological activity of the cerebral cortex.* Translated and edited by G. V. Anrep. Oxford: The Clarendon Press, 1927. Used by permission of The Clarendon Press, Oxford.

facts and avoiding all speculation about subjective states. We have also avoided analogies between the consciousness of men and that of animals. In this way we hope to bring the study of the brain into line with studies conducted in other branches of natural science.

In the part of our investigations that I shall describe here, we studied in dogs a reflex that occurs every day in the life of all animals: the food, or alimentary, reflex. This reflex has two components, the secretion of saliva that starts the digestive processes and the motor response in which the animal tries to get hold of the food and eat it. We confined our experiments almost entirely to the secretion response, taking motor reactions into account only when there were special reasons to do so.

Since we needed to measure the amount of saliva secreted under different circumstances, all the dogs were subjected to a minor operation before the experiments began. The opening of the salivary duct, normally inside the mouth, was surgically moved to the outside of the dog's cheek or to the underside of its chin. The saliva could then be collected in a small glass funnel and measured, in drops of exactly equal volume, by an electrical recording device that produced tracings like those shown in Figure 3-1. The complete experimental set-up is shown in Figure 3-2.

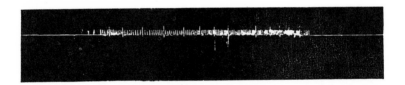

FIGURE 3-1

Two tracings that record salivation in response to musical tones. The top tracing records a dog's response to a tone lasting 30 seconds. The tone began at the first downward mark and ended at the second. The third mark shows the point at which food was presented to the dog. In all, the tracing shows 68 drops of saliva. The bottom tracing is a similar record, but the tone continued for 60 seconds, during which the 123 drops were collected.

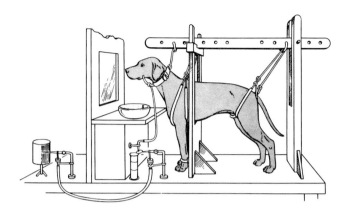

FIGURE 3-2

Measuring the salivation reflex. The dog's salivary duct is connected to
the tube in its cheek. The saliva flows through the tube into a glass con-
tainer and activates the device shown lower-left, which records the exact
amount of saliva secreted.

It was essential to eliminate irrelevant stimuli and to allow only those
stimuli that could be entirely controlled by the experimenter to reach
the animal. At first we thought it would be enough simply to isolate the
experimenter in a research chamber with the dog, but this precaution
proved wholly inadequate. The experimenter, no matter how still he tried
to be, was himself a constant source of stimuli. His slightest movement—
blinking the eyes, breathing, changes in posture, and so on—all acted as
stimuli that could damage the experiments by making exact interpretation
of the results impossible. In addition, the footfalls of passers-by, chance
conversations, even shadows cast through the windows into the room,
could set up disturbances in the animal's brain that might invalidate the
experiments.

To eliminate disturbing factors like these, a special laboratory was
built in Petrograd at the Institute of Experimental Medicine. The building
was surrounded by an isolating trench, and each research room was par-
titioned with soundproof material into two compartments, one for the
animal and the other for the experimenter.

Reflexes: Inborn and Conditioned

I shall introduce the principles identified in our research by means
of several demonstrations.

DEMONSTRATION 1

A dog stands in the experimental compartment, its salivary glands relatively inactive. A metronome begins to beat. Nine seconds later, the dog starts to secrete saliva. In 45 seconds, 11 drops are collected.

In this demonstration the activity of the salivary gland has been called into play by a sound—a stimulus quite different from the one that normally activates the food reflex. Through *conditioning*, the sound of the metronome had been associated with food; now the two signals, the beating of the metronome and the food, produce the same reaction in the animal. This is an example of a reaction that involves the brain. A brain-damaged dog could not have been conditioned to respond with salivary secretion to any sound.

DEMONSTRATION 2

Food is shown to a dog, but the animal is not allowed to take it into its mouth. The secretion of saliva begins after 5 seconds, and 6 drops are collected in 15 seconds.

The effect of seeing the food is the same as that observed after the sound of the metronome began. And, like the sound of the metronome, the sight and smell of food do not themselves trigger an inborn salivary reflex. Instead, they trigger a reflex *acquired* by the animal in the course of its existence.

The fact that salivary secretion in response to the sight and smell of food is an acquired reflex rather than an inborn reflex is shown by Zitovich's experiments with puppies. The puppies were taken away from their mother after birth and fed for a considerable time only on milk. When they were a few months old, Zitovich showed them some solid food—bread or meat. No secretion of saliva followed. Only after the puppies had eaten bread and meat on several occasions did the sight or smell of the food lead to salivation.

DEMONSTRATION 3

Food is placed in a dog's mouth. Salivary secretion begins in 1 or 2 seconds.

The secretion is brought about by the action of the food on the mucous membranes of the mouth and tongue; the response is an *inborn* reflex. This demonstration and the preceding one show why a brain-damaged dog can die of starvation in the midst of plenty. The dog will eat only if food chances to come into contact with its mouth or tongue. These demonstrations also show the elementary and primitive nature of inborn reflexes.

We are now in a position to appreciate the importance of stimuli that serve as signals to the brain. Whereas the salivary reflex, which is triggered by the presence of food in the mouth, functions in every dog from birth, the signal reflex that operates in response to the sight and smell of food (like the one that, after conditioning, operates in response to the sound of the metronome) develops *after* birth.

This leads to the question of how new reflex mechanisms are formed. The development of a new reflex is inevitable under a given set of physiological conditions. The conditions have nothing to do with the subjective states of the dog. Signal reflexes proceed according to rigid laws and are in every sense a part of the *physiological* activity of living beings.

I have called this group of reflexes *conditioned reflexes* to distinguish them from inborn, or unconditioned, reflexes. The term "conditioned" is apt, I think, because both the formation and the maintenance of new reflexes do depend on very many conditions. Conditioned reflexes are common, everyday phenomena. In man, they are often called habits.

Concerning the precise conditions under which a new conditioned reflex is created, the main requirement is that the conditioned stimulus (the sound of the metronome), initially a neutral stimulus that has no effect on the reflex action, must overlap in time with the unconditioned stimulus (food). The dog in Demonstration 1, for instance, had been stimulated by the sound of the metronome and then immediately presented with food on several occasions, until the sound alone activated the salivary glands.

The mild defense reflex set off when an objectionable substance is put in a dog's mouth can also be conditioned. A little acid solution brings about a definite response without conditioning: the dog tries to get rid of the acid, shaking its head violently, opening its mouth, and moving its tongue. At the same time, the animal produces a large amount of saliva to wash away the acid. If another stimulus (again it could be the sound of a metronome) is used with the acid often enough, that stimulus alone will cause the defense reaction in the dog.

Although the first requirement for the formation of a conditioned reflex is the coincidence in time of the neutral stimulus (sound) and the unconditioned stimulus (food), it is not enough that the two stimuli overlap. For the neutral stimulus to become a conditioned stimulus, it must begin *before* the unconditioned stimulus. Otherwise—if the food is presented before the metronome begins to beat—the conditioned reflex cannot be established at all.

Generalization
and Discrimination

After one musical tone has been established as a conditioned stimulus, similar tones spontaneously affect the animal the same way. Likewise, if touching a certain area of skin is made a conditioned stimulus, touching nearby areas will cause the conditioned reaction as well, although the reaction may be weaker. This spontaneous development of accessory reflexes I have called the *generalization of stimuli*.

In the world outside the laboratory, occurrences of a stimulus usually vary in strength and quality. For example, the sound of an owl's wings is a conditioned stimulus that in field mice regularly evokes a defense reaction, flight, even though the sound varies in pitch, strength, and tone depending on a number of factors. In such instances, generalization of stimuli is important for the animal's safety.

In other instances, generalization has only a limited or temporary significance and is eventually replaced by more precise, more specialized connections. This is called the *discrimination of stimuli*. We can produce the discrimination of stimuli, or the specialization of a conditioned reflex, in the laboratory by rewarding, or reinforcing, responses to a particular stimulus but never reinforcing responses to similar but not identical stimuli.

The Cerebral Cortex
as a Switchboard

The cerebral cortex is the medium through which conditioned reflexes are established. All conditioned reflexes must be represented in one or another specific group of brain cells. One group of cells must be connected with one activity of the organism, another group with another activity; perhaps one group facilitates an activity and another inhibits it. Thus we can think of the cerebral cortex as an extremely complicated switchboard.

Despite the complexity of the switchboard, there are always large spaces available for the development of new connections. Furthermore, points on the cortex that are already involved in one conditioned activity often change their physiological role and become connected with another activity of the animal. The idea of representing the cortex as a switchboard is in accord with current anatomical and physiological teachings. However, the final resolution of the many delicate problems the idea presents is a complex and difficult matter.

4

Pigeons in a Pelican

B . F . S K I N N E R

This is the history of a crackpot idea, born on the wrong side of the tracks intellectually speaking but eventually raised to a sort of middle-class respectability. It is the story of a proposal to use living organisms to guide missiles—of a research program during the Second World War called Project Pigeon and its peacetime continuation at the Naval Research Laboratory called ORCON, from the words "organic control."

Man has always made use of the sensory abilities of animals, because they are more acute than his own or more convenient. Sometimes little or no training is necessary. The watchdog probably hears better than his master and, in any case, listens while his master sleeps; as a detecting system, the dog comes supplied with an alarm— he need not be taught to announce the presence of an intruder. At

PIGEONS IN A PELICAN Adapted from *American Psychologist* 15 (1960). Used by permission of the author.

other times, training is quite explicit. In the seeing-eye dog the repertoire of learned signaling responses is so elaborate that communication between dog and master resembles the verbal interchange between man and man.

The detecting and signaling systems of animals have special advantages for use in guiding explosive devices toward the targets they are to destroy. Homing systems for guided missiles have now been developed that sense and signal the position of a target by responding to radiation, noise, radar reflections, and so on, but these have not always been available. In any case, animals are cheaper, more compact, and, in particular, very good at responding to visual patterns. Animals are used not because they are more sensitive than men—after all, the kamikaze pilots of Japan did very well—but because they are expendable.

The ethical question of our right to convert a lower creature into an unwitting hero is a peacetime luxury. There were bigger questions to be answered in the late thirties. A group of men had come into power who promised and eventually accomplished the greatest mass murder in history. In 1939 the city of Warsaw was laid waste in an unprovoked bombing, and the airplane emerged as a new and horrible instrument of war against which only the feeblest defenses were available.

The Pelican

Project Pigeon was conceived against this background. It was to be tested first in an air-to-ground missile called the Pelican. The name is a useful reminder of the state of the missile in America at that time: the mechanisms of the missile took up so much space that there was no room for explosives, hence its resemblance to the pelican, whose "beak can hold more than its belly can." My title is perhaps now clear.

At the University of Minnesota in the spring of 1940 the capacity of the pigeon to steer toward a target was tested with a moving hoist. The pigeon, held in a jacket (as shown in Figure 4-1) and harnessed to a block, could move only its neck and head. By moving its head in appropriate directions, the bird could operate a control system to ascend, descend, and travel from side to side. The whole system, mounted on wheels, was pushed across a room toward a bull's-eye on the far wall. During the approach the pigeon raised or lowered itself and moved from side to side in such a way as to reach the wall in a position that allowed it to eat grain from the center of the bull's-eye. The pigeon learned to reach its target no matter what the starting position, even during fairly rapid approaches.

The experiment was shown to several scientists engaged in early defense activities for the Office of Scientific Research and Development, in Washington. The result was the first of a long series of rejections. The project would probably have been abandoned had it not been for a young man whose last name I have ungratefully forgotten, but whose first name —Victor—we hailed as a hopeful sign. Victor walked into the Department of Psychology at Minnesota one day in the summer of 1942 looking for an animal psychologist. He had a scheme for installing a dog in an antisubmarine torpedo in order to steer the torpedo toward its goal, and he wanted a statement from an animal psychologist that it would work. Though understandably surprised to learn of our work with pigeons, he seized on it eagerly as support for his plan. He approached a number of companies in Minneapolis, but his project was rejected by everyone. However, one company, General Mills, asked for more information about our work with pigeons. We described the project and presented the available data to Arthur D. Hyde, vice-president in charge of research. The company was not looking for new products, but Hyde thought that it might, as a public service, sponsor the development of the pigeon system to a point at which a government agency could be persuaded to take over.

FIGURE 4-1
Thirty-two pigeons, jacketed for testing.

Training the Pigeons

We moved into the top floor of a flour mill in Minneapolis and set to work on further improvements. It had been difficult to induce our pigeons to respond to a distant target. Their natural pursuit behavior was not appropriate to the characteristics of a missile, and they started working dangerously late in the descent. A new system was therefore designed, in which the image of various targets was projected on a screen. The pigeon was held near the screen and, with a few grains released onto a plate, was reinforced for pecking at the image on the screen. The signal that guided the missile was to be picked up from the point of contact of screen and beak.

We began to study the pigeon's reactions to various patterns and to develop steady rates of response through the use of appropriate schedules of reinforcement. We trained pigeons to track a target continuously for a matter of minutes without reinforcement, to follow a variety of land and sea targets, to neglect large patches intended to represent clouds or flak, to concentrate on one target while another was in view, and so on. We found that a pigeon could hold the missile on a particular street intersection in an aerial map of a city. Through appropriate schedules of reinforcement it was possible to maintain longer uninterrupted runs than could conceivably be required by a missile.

We also undertook a more serious study of the pigeon's behavior. We ascertained optimal conditions of food deprivation, studied the effects of special reinforcements (for example, pigeons were said to find hemp seed particularly delectable), tested the effects of energizing drugs and increased oxygen, and so on. We found that pigeons could be induced to peck so energetically that the base of the beak became inflamed. We investigated the effects of temperature extremes, of changes in atmospheric pressure, of increased carbon dioxide pressure, of increased and prolonged vibration, and of noises such as pistol shots. We investigated optimal conditions for the quick development of discriminations and began to study the pigeon's reactions to patterns, testing for generalization from a test figure to the same figure upside down, in different sizes and colors, and against different backgrounds.

We made a demonstration film and renewed our contact with the Office of Scientific Research and Development. An observer was sent to Minneapolis, and on the strength of his report we were given an opportunity to present our case in Washington in February, 1943. At that time we were offering a homing device capable of reporting with an on-off signal the orientation of a missile toward various visual patterns. Its capacity to respond to pattern was, we felt, our strongest argument, and the fact that the device used only visible radiation (the same form of information available to the human bombardier) made it superior to the radio-controlled missiles then under development because it was resistant to jamming. Our film had some effect. Other observers were sent to Minneapolis to see the demonstration itself, and the pigeons, as usual, behaved beautifully. One of them held the supposed missile on a street intersection in the aerial map for five minutes—the target would have been lost if the pigeon had paused for a second or two. The observers returned to Washington, and two weeks later we were asked to supply data on (1) the population of pigeons in the United States (fortunately, the Census Bureau had some figures) and (2) the accuracy with which pigeons struck a point on a plate. There were many arbitrary conditions to be taken into account in measuring the latter, but we supplied possibly relevant data. At long last, in June, 1943, the Office of Scientific Research and Development awarded a modest contract to General Mills to "develop a homing device."

At that time we were given some information about the missile the pigeons were to steer. The Pelican was a wing-steered glider still under development and not yet successfully guided by any homing device. It was being tested on a target consisting of a stirrup-shaped pattern bulldozed out of the sandy soil near the New Jersey coast. The white lines of the target stood out clearly against brown and green cover. Color photographs were taken from various distances and various angles, and the accuracy of the reproductions was checked by flying over the target.

Because of security restrictions we were given only very rough specifications of the signal to be supplied to the controlling system in the Pelican. It was no longer to be simply on-off; if the missile was badly off target, an especially strong correcting signal was needed. But further requirements were left mainly to our imagination. The General Mills engineers were equal to this difficult assignment. With what now seems like unbelievable speed, they designed and constructed a system giving a graded signal. A lens in the nose of the missile, shown in Figure 4-2, threw an image on a plate within reach of the pigeon, which was located in a pressurized chamber. Four air valves resting against the edges of the plate were jarred open momentarily as the pigeon pecked. When the missile was on target, the pigeon pecked the center of the plate and all valves admitted equal amounts of air. But if the image moved as little as a quarter of an inch off-center, as if the missile were very slightly off-target, the pigeon's peck was also off-center, and more air was admitted by the valves on one side. This resulted in appropriate correcting orders.

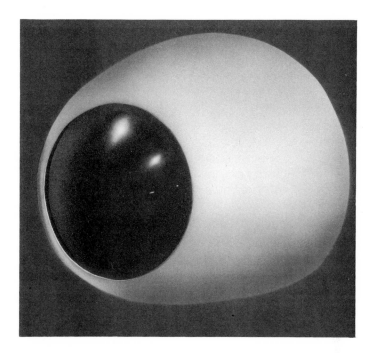

FIGURE 4-2
Nose of the missile called The Pelican, showing lenses.

The device required no materials in short supply, was relatively fool-proof, and delivered a graded signal. It had another advantage. By this time we had begun to realize that a pigeon was more easily controlled than a physical scientist serving on a committee. It was very difficult to convince the latter that the former was an orderly system. We therefore multiplied the probability of success by designing a multiple-bird unit. There was adequate space in the nose of the Pelican for three pigeons, each with its own lens and plate. An average signal could easily be generated. The majority vote of three pigeons offered an excellent guarantee against momentary pauses and aberrations.

The General Mills engineers also built a simulator designed with the steering characteristics of the Pelican insofar as these had been communicated to us. When the three-bird nose was attached to the simulator, the pigeons could be put in full control and the adequacy of the signal tested under pursuit conditions. Targets were moved back and forth across the far wall of a room at prescribed speeds and in given patterns of oscillation, and the tracking response of the whole unit was studied quantitatively.

Another Rejection

By December, 1943, less than six months after the contract was awarded, we were ready to report to the Office of Scientific Research and Development. Observers visited the laboratory and watched the simulator under the control of a team of three birds follow a target about a room. They also reviewed our tracking data. The only questions that arose were the inevitable consequence of our lack of information about the signal required to steer the Pelican. As it turned out, we had not chosen the best values in collecting our data, and in January, 1944, the Office of Scientific Research and Development refused to extend the General Mills contract. The reasons given seemed to be due to misunderstandings or, rather, to lack of communication. We had already collected further data with new settings of the instruments, and these were submitted in a request for reconsideration.

We were given one more chance. We took our new data to the radiation lab at the Massachusetts Institute of Technology for examination by specialists working on the Pelican controls. To our surprise the scientist whose task it was to predict the usefulness of the pigeon signal said that according to his equations our device could not possibly yield the signals we reported. We knew, of course, that it had done so. We examined the inconsistency and traced it to the fact that, in pecking an image near the edge of the plate, the pigeon strikes a glancing blow; hence the air admitted at the valves is not linearly proportional to the displacement of the target. This could be corrected in several ways, but it was our understanding that in any case the signal was adequate to control the Pelican. Indeed, one authority, on looking at graphs of the performance of the simulator, exclaimed, "This is better than radar!"

Two days later, encouraged by our meeting at MIT, we reached the summit. We were to present our case to a committee of the country's top scientists. The hearing began with a brief report by the scientist who had discovered the "inconsistency" in our data, and to our surprise he still regarded it as unresolved. He predicted that the signal we reported would cause the missile to "hunt" wildly and lose the target. Fortunately another scientist was present who had seen the simulator performing under excellent control and who could confirm our report of the facts. But reality was no match for mathematics.

The basic difficulty, of course, lay in convincing a dozen distinguished physical scientists that the behavior of a pigeon could be adequately controlled. We had hoped to score on this point by bringing with us a demonstration. We used a small black box with a round translucent window in one end. A slide projector placed some distance away threw on the window an image of the New Jersey target. In the box was a pigeon—a pigeon which, incidentally, had at that time been harnessed for thirty-five hours. The pigeon behaved perfectly, pecking steadily and energetically at the image of the target as it moved about the plate. One scientist with an experimental turn of mind put his hand between the image and intercepted the beam from the projector. The pigeon stopped instantly. When the image again appeared, pecking began within a fraction of a second and continued at a steady rate.

It was a perfect performance, but it had just the wrong effect. The spectacle of a living pigeon carrying out its assignment, no matter how beautifully, simply reminded the committee of how utterly fantastic our proposal was. I will not say that the meeting was marked by unrestrained merriment, for the merriment was restrained. But it was there, and it was obvious that our case was lost.

Hyde closed our presentation with a brief summary: we were offering a homing device unusually resistant to jamming, capable of reacting to a wide variety of target patterns, requiring no materials in short supply, and so simple to build that production could be started in thirty days. He thanked the committee, and we left. As the door closed behind us, he said to me, "Why don't you go out and get drunk!"

Official word soon came: "Further prosecution of this project would seriously delay others which in the minds of the division would have more immediate promise of combat application." Possibly the reference was to a particular combat application at Hiroshima a year and a half later, when it looked for a while as if the need for accurate bombing had been eliminated for all time. In any case we had to show for all our trouble only a loftful of curiously useless equipment and a few dozen pigeons with a strange interest in a feature of the New Jersey coast. The equipment was scrapped, but thirty of the pigeons were kept to see how long they would retain the behavior they had been taught.

In the years that followed there were faint signs of renewed interest. Winston Churchill's personal science advisor, Lord Cherwell, learned of the project and "regretted its demise." A scientist who had some contact with the project during the war and who evidently assumed that its classified status was not to be taken seriously made a good story out of it for the *Atlantic Monthly*, changing names to protect the innocent.

Other uses of animals began to be described. The author of the *Atlantic*

Monthly story also published an account of a plan to release thousands of "incendiary bats," each carrying a small fire-bomb with a time control, over enemy cities. The bats would take refuge, as is their custom, under eaves and in other out-of-the-way places, and shortly thereafter thousands of small fires would break out. The scheme was never used because it was feared that it would be mistaken for germ warfare and might lead to retaliation in kind. Another story circulating at the time told how the Russians had trained dogs to blow up tanks. A Swedish proposal to use seals to achieve the same end with submarines was not successful, apparently because the required training was never achieved. I cannot vouch for the authenticity of probably the most fantastic story of this sort, but it ought to be recorded. The Russians were said to have trained sea lions to cut mine cables. A complicated device attached to the sea lion included a motor-driven cable cutter, a tank full of small fish, and a device that released a few fish into a muzzle covering the sea lion's head. In order to eat, the sea lion had to find a mine cable and swim alongside it until the cutter was automatically triggered, at which point a few fish were released from the tank into the muzzle. After a certain number of cables had been cut, both the energy of the cutting mechanism and the supply of fish were exhausted. Then the sea lion received a special stimulus, to which it responded by returning to its home base for special reinforcement and reloading.

ORCON

The story of our own venture has a happy ending. With the discovery of German accomplishments in the field of guided missiles, feasible homing systems suddenly became very important. Franklin V. Taylor of the Naval Research Laboratory in Washington heard about our project and asked for further details. As a psychologist Taylor appreciated the special capacity of living organisms to respond to visual patterns and was aware of recent advances in the control of behavior. More important, he was a skillful practitioner of a kind of control that our project had conspicuously lacked: he knew how to approach the people who determine the direction of research. He showed our demonstration film so often that it was completely worn out—but to good effect, for support was eventually found for a thorough investigation of "organic control" under the general title ORCON.

Taylor also enlisted the support of engineers in obtaining a more effective report of the pigeon's behavior. A new study took place: the plate upon which the image of the target was thrown was given a semiconducting surface, and the tip of the bird's beak was covered with a gold electrode. A single contact with the plate sent an immediate report of the location of the target to the controlling mechanism. The work that went into this system contributed to the so-called Pickoff Display Converter, developed as part of the Naval Data Handling System, which makes it no longer necessary for a radar operator to report verbally the location of a point on the screen. Like the pigeon, he has only to touch the point with a special contact instrument. (He holds it in his hand.)

At the Naval Research Laboratory in Washington the responses of pigeons were studied in detail. Average peck rate, average error rate, average hit rate, and so on were recorded under various conditions. The tracking behavior of the pigeon was analyzed with methods similar to those used with human operators. Pattern perception was studied, including generalization from one pattern to another. A simulator was constructed to test the pigeon's ability to control navigation toward an actual target, such as a ship at sea seen from a plane approaching at six hundred miles an hour, by responding to images of the approach to the target shown on film. A few frames of a film showing the approach to a ship are shown in Figure 4-3.

The publications from the Naval Research Laboratory that report this work provide a serious evaluation of the possi-

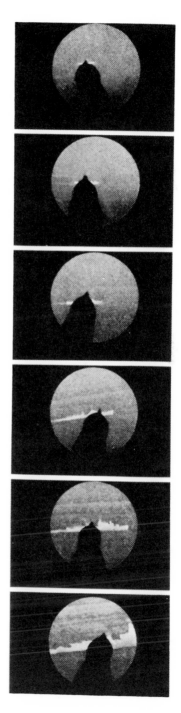

FIGURE 4-3

Frames from a simulated approach to a ship at six hundred miles per hour.

bilities of organic control. Although in simulated tests a pigeon occasionally loses a target, its tracking characteristics are surprisingly good. Moreover, in the seven years since the last of these reports, a great deal of information has been acquired. The color vision of the pigeon is now well understood and the maintenance of behavior through scheduling of reinforcement has been drastically improved. Tests made with the birds retained from the old Project Pigeon showed that even after six years of inactivity a pigeon will immediately and correctly strike a target to which it has been conditioned and will continue to respond for some time without reinforcement.

The use of living organisms in guiding missiles is, it seems fair to say, no longer a crackpot idea. A pigeon is an extraordinarily subtle and complex mechanism capable of performances that at the moment can be equaled by electronic equipment only of vastly greater weight and size, and the animal can be put to reliable use through the principles that have emerged from an experimental analysis of its behavior.

But this vindication of our original proposal is perhaps the least important result. Something happened during the brief life of Project Pigeon that has taken a long time to be appreciated. The practical task before us created a new attitude toward the behavior of organisms. We had to maximize the probability that a given form of behavior would occur at a given time. We could not enjoy the luxury of observing one variable while allowing others to change in what we hoped was a random fashion. Our task forced us to emphasize experimental control, and its success in revealing orderly processes gave us an exciting glimpse of the superiority of laboratory practices over verbal (and some kinds of mathematical) explanations.

The Crackpot Idea

One virtue of crackpot ideas is that they breed rapidly and their progeny show extraordinary mutations. Everyone is talking about teaching machines nowadays, but Sidney Pressey can tell you what it was like to have a crackpot idea in that field forty years ago. His self-testing devices and self-scoring test forms now need no defense, and psychomotor training devices have also achieved a substantial respectability. This did not, however, prepare the way for devices to be used in verbal instruction —that is, in the kinds of teaching that are the principal concern of our schools and colleges. Even five short years ago that kind of instruction by machine was still in the crackpot category. (I can quote official opinion to that effect from high places.)

There is a direct genetic connection between teaching machines and Project Pigeon. We had been forced to consider the mass education of pigeons. True, the scrap of wisdom we imparted to each was small, but the required changes in behavior were similar to those that must be brought about in vaster quantities in human students. The techniques of shaping behavior and of bringing it under stimulus control that were used on the top floor of that flour mill in Minneapolis needed only a detailed reformulation of verbal behavior to be directly applicable to education.

I am sure there is more to come. In the year after the termination of Project Pigeon I wrote *Walden Two*—a utopian picture of a properly engineered society. Some psychotherapists might argue that I was suffering from personal rejection and simply retreated to a fantasied world where never was heard a discouraging word. But another explanation is, I think, equally plausible. That piece of science fiction was a declaration of confidence in a technology of behavior. Call it a crackpot idea if you will; it is one in which I have never lost faith. I still believe that the same kind of wide-ranging speculation about human affairs, supported by studies of compensating rigor, will make a substantial contribution toward that world of the future in which, among other things, there will be no need for guided missiles.

Memory

Try to remember a significant event from your childhood, perhaps the day you first saw your younger brother or sister or the day you started school. Remember as much as you can about the event, and then ask yourself how you did it. Did you reconstruct the episode from a few isolated shreds, such as a mental picture of your mother holding the child and a sensation in your stomach that reminds you of emotions you felt at the time, knitting the shreds together by imagining what the rest of the experience must have been? Or did one vivid image seem to reactivate the memory of a longer chain of events, which came to your mind without effort once the image had occurred to you?

A memory is a psychological record of the past that can be called up in the present. But what kind of record, and how is it brought to mind? The two selections in this part, one by Frederic C. Bartlett and the other by Wilder Penfield, come to very different conclusions on these questions.

In "On Remembering," Bartlett takes the position that memory is *constructive*. According to Bartlett, a person bases his memories on past experience and builds from there. But what he remembers is influenced not only by his past experience but by his personal needs, emotions, and present circumstances. Bartlett used a new technique in his work on memory: he asked people to read stories (in this article, a short folk tale) and then reproduce them after varying amounts of time had passed. Most earlier psychologists, because they wanted to study memory as an isolated phenomenon uncontaminated by the influence of experience, asked their subjects to memorize lists of nonsense words—POV, JUK, ZAX—and other meaningless material. Bartlett argued that the principles which govern the remembering of meaningless material may not hold true for more coherent memories. By asking his subjects to read and reproduce stories, he was able to study not only how long their memory of the stories lasted but what kind of thing each person remembered most and least accurately. Most important, his technique allowed him to analyze the changes his subjects made in the remembered stories—the material they added and the purpose it seemed to serve.

Wilder Penfield, author of "The Interpretive Cortex," is a neurosurgeon. He found that when an electrode touched a particular area in a patient's brain during surgery (performed with a local anesthetic, so that the patient was conscious throughout), the electrical currents seemed to reactivate the patient's memory of past events or to change his interpretation of present ones. Penfield's patients did more than remember episodes; they seemed to reexperience them. If a patient remembered a walk in the park, the event seemed to unfold again, at the same pace as it had originally and with great vividness, so that he could see the trees swaying in the breeze and smell the lilacs in the park even though he knew he was in an operating room. One woman remembered a song she had heard at a particular time in the past. The memory was so fully "there" in the present that she thought a phonograph record was being played on the other side of the room.

Penfield concluded that past experience may be stored in the brain in much the same way that sound is stored on tape, ready to be released in response to the proper stimulus. He suggests that the still-unidentified part of the brain in which memories are stored may be connected with the interpretive cortex by pathways of nerve cells, neural connections along which electrical impulses pass in order to activate detailed records of the past.

The constructive view of memory described by Bartlett and the tape-recorder theory of memory suggested by Penfield seem to be incompatible. However, they may apply to different kinds of memory. Much current research on memory is addressed to the question of whether remembering is one activity or a catch-all word used to describe several distinct phenomena. For example, short-term memory (the remembering of very recent events) and long-term memory (distant ones) seem to operate quite differently, and different processes may be involved in remembering names, faces, episodes, ideas, and feelings. Experimental data on these possibilities are being gathered both by behavioral scientists and by biochemists, who are looking for changes experience seems to bring about in the cells of the brain.

5

On Remembering

FREDERIC C. BARTLETT

When we say that we remember a sequence of events, we seldom, if ever, mean that we have exactly duplicated it in our minds. In the thousands of cases of remembering that I have collected, exact recall is very rare. Generally, a person asked to retell a story he has read begins hesitantly, goes back and forth between doubt and satisfaction as he proceeds, and moves ahead with more confidence after he is well along. Thus remembering appears to be far more a matter of construction than one of simple reproduction.

The purpose of the experiment that I shall describe was to observe normal processes of remembering, which usually have this constructive character. They include such features as condensation, elaboration, and invention. I used a story rather than nonsense material, such as lists of meaningless syllables, because nonsense material lends itself to rote memorization and offers little opportunity for constructive remembering.

ON REMEMBERING Adapted from *Remembering*. New York: Cambridge University Press, 1932. Used by permission of the author and the publisher.

Each subject read the story to himself twice. Then, after different periods of time had passed, he was asked to reproduce what he had read. The first attempt at reproduction usually took place fifteen minutes after the subject had finished reading; the amount of time between the first reproduction and later ones varied from days to years. The experiment called for several reproductions instead of just one so that I could gain information about the types of change remembered material undergoes with the passage of time.

The story that the subjects read was a North American folk tale, adapted from a translation by Franz Boas. The tale is as follows:

The War of the Ghosts

One night two young men from Egulac went down to the river to hunt seals, and while they were there it become foggy and calm. Then they heard war cries, and they thought: "Maybe this is a war party." They escaped to the shore, and hid behind a log. Now canoes came up, and they heard the noise of paddles, and saw one canoe coming up to them. There were five men in the canoe, and they said:

"What do you think? We wish to take you along. We are going up the river to make war on the people."

One of the young men said: "I have no arrows."

"Arrows are in the canoe," they said.

"I will not go along. I might be killed. My relatives do not know where I have gone. But you," he said, turning to the other, "may go with them."

So one of the young men went, but the other returned home.

And the warriors went on up the river to a town on the other side of Kalama. The people came down to the water, and they began to fight, and many were killed. But presently the young man heard one of the warriors say: "Quick, let us go home. That Indian has been hit." Now he thought: "Oh, they are ghosts." He did not feel sick, but they said he had been shot.

So the canoes went back to Egulac, and the young man went ashore to his house, and made a fire. And he told everybody and said: "Behold I accompanied the ghosts, and we went to fight. Many of our fellows were killed, and many of those who attacked us were killed. They said I was hit, and I did not feel sick."

He told it all, and then he became quiet. When the sun rose he fell down. Something black came out of his mouth. His face became contorted. The people jumped up and cried.

He was dead.

I chose this particular story for four reasons. First, it represents a level of culture and a social environment very different from those of my subjects. Therefore it offered good material for transformation and constructive remembering. Second, some of the incidents described are not connected with each other in any obvious way, and I wanted to see how my subjects would deal with the lack of rational order. Third, the end of the story might easily be seen as involving the supernatural, and I wished to discover how the subjects would cope with this. Finally, the dramatic character of some of the events in the tale seemed likely to arouse fairly vivid visual imagery.

I was particularly interested in studying how the visual imagery aroused by the tale would affect the remembering process. In an earlier experiment, I had found that my subjects fell naturally into two classes: those who relied primarily on visual images and those whose memories were determined chiefly by language cues. Subjects in the second group, the "vocalizers," appeared to use a complex and indirect method of recall and to lack confidence in their descriptions—except when, as happened occasionally, they became aware of a visual image. At that time they immediately seemed more sure of themselves. The "visualizers," on the other hand, were consistently confident in their attitude even when their memories were inaccurate. I wanted to find out whether the maxim "seeing is believing" would hold true for my new group of subjects as well. The ways in which four subjects remembered the story are described and discussed below.

Subject 1:
Two Typical Reproductions

Twenty hours after he read the story, Subject 1 produced the following reproduction:

The War of the Ghosts

Two men from Edulac went fishing. While thus occupied by the river they heard a noise in the distance.

"It sounds like a cry," said one, and presently there appeared some men in canoes who invited them to join the party on their adventure. One of the young men refused to go, on the ground of family ties, but the other offered to go.

"But there are no arrows," he said.

"The arrows are in the boat," was the reply.

He thereupon took his place, while his friend returned home. The party paddled up the river to Kaloma, and began to land on the banks of the river. The enemy came rushing upon them, and some sharp fighting ensued. Presently someone was injured, and the cry was raised that the enemy were ghosts.

The party returned down the stream, and the young man arrived home feeling none the worse for his experience. The next morning at dawn he endeavored to recount his adventures. While he was talking something black issued from his mouth. Suddenly he uttered a cry and fell down. His friends gathered round him.

But he was dead.

The changes the subject made are typical: the story has been shortened considerably, mainly by omissions; it is somewhat more coherent and logical than the original version; the style is more modern and journalistic. For example, Subject 1 substitutes "refused to go, on the ground of family ties" for "I will not go along. I might be killed. My relatives do not know where I have gone" and "feeling none the worse for his experience" for "They said I was hit, and I did not feel sick." The more familiar "boat" replaces "canoe" once, and hunting seals becomes merely "fishing." The main point about the ghosts, who were the young man's allies, not his opponents, is entirely misunderstood.

Eight days later, Subject 1 remembered the story as follows:

The War of the Ghosts

Two young men from Edulac went fishing. While thus engaged they heard a noise in the distance. "That sounds like a war cry," said one, "there is going to be some fighting." Presently there appeared some warriors who invited them to join an expedition up the river.

One of the young men excused himself on the ground of family ties. "I cannot come," he said, "as I might get killed." So he returned home. The other man, however, joined the party, and they proceeded in canoes up the river. While landing on the banks the enemy appeared and were running down to meet them. Soon someone was wounded, and the party discovered that they were fighting against ghosts. The young man and his companion returned to the boats, and went back to their homes.

The next morning at dawn he was describing his adventures to his friends, who had gathered round him. Suddenly something black issued from his mouth, and he fell down uttering a cry. His friends closed around him, but found that he was dead.

The changes in the first reproduction now seem to be more marked. The story has become still more concise, still more coherent. The lack of arrows, which the young man gave as his first reason for not joining the war party in the original tale and as his second reason in Subject 1's first reproduction, has now dropped out completely. On the other hand, a part of the other excuse, "I might get killed," now comes back into the story, although it was left out of the first version. It is perhaps odd that the friend, after returning home, seems suddenly to come back into the story when the young man is wounded, but this kind of confusion of connected incidents is common in remembering.

Subject 2:
Rationalization of the Ghosts

Fifteen minutes after reading the original tale, Subject 2 offered the following first reproduction:

The Ghosts

There were two men on the banks of the river near Egulac. They heard the sound of paddles, and a canoe with five men in it appeared, who called to them, saying: "We are going to fight the people. Will you come with us?"

One of the two men answered, saying: "Our relations do not know where we are, and we have not got any arrows."

They answered: "There are arrows in the canoe."

So the man went, and they fought the people, and then he heard them saying: "An Indian is killed, let us return."

So he returned to Egulac, and told them he knew they were Ghosts.

He spoke to the people of Egulac, and told them that he had fought with the Ghosts, and many men were killed on both sides, and that he was wounded, but felt nothing. He lay down and became calmer, and in the night he was convulsed, and something black came out of his mouth.

The people said:

"He is dead."

The most interesting feature of this reproduction is the attempt to deal with the ghosts. The subject volunteered, "At first I thought there was something supernatural about the story. Then I saw that Ghosts must be a class or a clan name. That made the whole thing more comprehensible."

In fact, from the outset the subject clearly missed the real point about the ghosts, although he makes them central in his version of the story. The reproduction is a beautiful illustration of the strong tendency to rationalize, common to all my subjects. Whenever anything appeared incomprehensible or queer, it was either omitted or explained. Rarely was this rationalization the effect of conscious effort; more often, the subject made the change without suspecting what he was doing. In this case, he made the ghosts the central part of the story. They alone remained in the title. They were always written with a capital G—a true case of unwitting transformation that solved a special problem. Then came the specific explanation, "Ghost is a clan name," and the whole difficulty disappeared. Subject 2 was extremely well satisfied with his version, just as the visualizers in the earlier experiments seemed to be contented with their work.

The satisfaction persisted, and two weeks later the Ghosts had become more prominent still. The story was remembered thus:

The Ghosts

There were two men on the banks of a river near the village of Etishu(?). They heard the sound of paddles coming from upstream, and shortly a canoe appeared. The men in the canoe spoke, saying: "We are going to fight the people: will you come with us?"

One of the young men answered, saying: "Our relations do not know where we are; but my companion may go with you. Besides, we have no arrows."

So the young man went with them, and they fought the people, and many were killed on both sides. And then he heard shouting: "The Indian is wounded; let us return." And he heard the people say: "They are the Ghosts." He did not know he was wounded, and returned to Etishu(?). The people collected round him and bathed his wounds, and he said he had fought with the Ghosts. Then he became quiet. But in the night he was convulsed, and something black came out of his mouth.

And the people cried:

"He is dead."

By now the young man's antagonists up the river are definitely made to say that the people he is helping are the Ghosts (that is, members of the Ghost clan). The Indian becomes more of a hero and is the center of interest at the end, when, for the first time, his wounds are "bathed." The Indian's ignorance of his wound, a point that had worried this subject in his earlier reproduction, comes back into the main body of the story but appears to be attributed merely to general excitement. In fact, the supernatural element has almost entirely been dropped.

This ingenious rationalization of the ghosts is a clear instance of how a special interest can produce an unrealized distortion in remembered material. The subject was a keen student of anthropology who later carried out much important fieldwork, particularly on the topics of kinship names and clan systems.

Rationalization was illustrated in practically every series of reproductions, but the rationalizations used varied greatly from case to case. The particular form adopted depended on individual special interests, as in the "Ghost clan" instance just described, or on some fact of personal experience, or on individual attitude.

Here, for example, is *The War of the Ghosts*, as recalled by one subject six months after the original reading. (No title was given.)

Four men came down to the water. They were told to get into a boat and to take arms with them. They inquired "What arms?" and were answered "Arms for battle." When they came to the battlefield they heard a great noise and shouting, and a voice said: "The black man is dead." And he was brought to the place where they were, and laid on the ground. And he foamed at the mouth.

From this short version all unusual terms, all proper names, all mention of the supernatural, have disappeared. But the most interesting point is the treatment of the troublesome "something black" that concludes the original story. "Black" was transferred to the man and so made perfectly natural, while "foamed at the mouth" is obviously a rationalization of the original "Something black came out of his mouth."

Subject 3:
Ghosts as Ghosts

The preceding reproductions can be compared with a short series obtained from Subject 3, a native of northern India, who was on a very different educational plane from that of the rest of my subjects. He was a man of considerable intelligence but ill trained, from the point of view of an English university, and ill adapted to the environment in which he was living. He was impressionable, imaginative, and high-strung. He first reproduced the story as follows:

Story

There were two young men, and they went on the riverside. They heard war cries, and said: "There is a war of the ghosts." They had no arrows. They saw a canoe, and there were five men in it. They said: "The arrows are in the canoe." The war of the ghosts begins. Many were killed. There was one young man who was hit, but did not become sick. He heard that the Indian was wounded. He came back to his village in the canoe. In the morning he was sick, and his face contracted. Something black came out of his mouth, and they cried: "He was dead."

The subject seemed very excited. He said that he clearly visualized the whole scene; especially vivid were some Indians with feathers on their heads. The story is very short and jerky and lacks style. The ghosts made a tremendous impression on this subject.

Two weeks later the following version was obtained:

Story

There were two ghosts. They went on a river. There was a canoe on the river with five men in it. There occurred a war of ghosts. One of the

ghosts asked: "Where are the arrows?" The other said: "In the canoe."
They started the war and several were wounded, and some killed. One
ghost was wounded but did not feel sick. He went back to the village in
the canoe. The next morning he was sick and something black came out
of his mouth, and they cried: "He is dead."

The ghosts appear to have strengthened their hold on the story during
the interval; they have entirely displaced the two young men. If anything,
this narrative is even less coherent than the first reproduction.

After another month the subject tried again:

Story

There were ghosts. There took place a fight between them. One of them
asked: "Where are the arrows?" The other said: "They are in the
canoe." A good many of the combatants were wounded or killed. One
of them was wounded, but did not feel sick. They carried him to his
village some miles away by rowing in the canoe. The next day something
black came out of his mouth and they cried: "He is dead."

The first part of the story has completely disappeared, and it is now
entirely a matter of a fight between ghosts. The dominant detail seems
to have overshadowed nearly all the rest. To the subject himself, this
version of the tale seemed clear enough, but compared with the versions
by other subjects it is very jerky and disconnected.

Subject 4:
Constructive Remembering

Finally, I will record a reproduction obtained six and a half years
after the original reading. The subject had given only one previous reproduction, immediately after reading the story. The earlier version included
the usual features: some abbreviation, a little modernization of the style,
and a comment to the effect that the "something black" must have been
the man's soul, "after the ancient Egyptian belief."

When I unexpectedly met this man again six and a half years later, he
volunteered to try to remember the story. He recalled it in steps, with
some hesitation, but on the whole with surprising ease. I will give his
version exactly as he wrote it.

1. Brothers.
2. Canoe.
3. Something black from mouth.
4. Totem.

5. One of the brothers died.
6. Cannot remember whether one slew the other or was helping the other.
7. Were going on journey, but why I cannot remember.
8. Party in war canoe.
9. Was the journey a pilgrimage for filial or religious reasons?
10. Am now *sure* it was a pilgrimage.
11. Purpose had something to do with totem.
12. Was it on a pilgrimage that they met a hostile party and one brother was slain?
13. I think there was some reference to a dark forest.
14. Two brothers were on a pilgrimage, having something to do with a totem, in a canoe, up a river flowing through a dark forest. While on their pilgrimage they met a hostile party of Indians in a war canoe. In the fight one brother was slain, and something black came from his mouth.
15. Am not confident about the way brother died. May have been something sacrificial in the manner of his death.
16. The cause of the journey had *both* something to do with a totem, and with filial piety.
17. The totem was the patron god of the family and so was connected with filial piety.

Subject 4 was very pleased and satisfied with the result of his effort, and indeed, considering the time that had passed since he first saw the story, his version is remarkably accurate and detailed. There is a good deal of invention, and it was about his inventions that he was most pleased and most certain. The totem, the filial piety, the pilgrimage—these he regarded as his most brilliant recaptures, and he was almost equally sure of the dark forest, once it had come in. Although the ghost element of the original seems to have been omitted completely, it is somehow active, helping to produce elaborations in the form of the totem, filial piety, a mysterious forest, and a sacrificial death.

The remembered stories I have quoted all involved constructive rather than merely reproductive memory. Subject 1, like many others, made the story more coherent and modernized its phrasing. Subject 2 rationalized the ghosts by making them into a Ghost family or clan. Subject 3, by contrast, magnified the supernatural element and allowed it to dominate his story. Subject 4's version is full of rationalizations and explanations, and most of his running comments were aimed at making the chain of events as coherent as possible. Built up step by step by combining memory fragments and inventions, this last version is the best example of all of constructive remembering.

6

The Interpretive Cortex

WILDER PENFIELD

There is an area on the surface of the human brain where electrical stimulation can produce an experience of past events. It is as though a wire recorder or a strip of film with sound track had been set in motion within the brain. The sights and sounds, and the thoughts, of a former day pass through the mind again. The purpose of this article is to describe the area of the brain from which this neuron record of the past can be activated and to suggest what contribution it may make to the normal functioning of the brain.

Man's brain differs from the brain of other mammals mostly in the large size of the cerebral cortex, the surface of the part of the brain called the cerebrum, which is divided into two halves, the left and the right hemispheres. The cerebral cortex of man, also referred to as gray matter, is so vast that it could never be contained

THE INTERPRETIVE CORTEX Adapted from *Science* 129 (June 26, 1959):1719–25. Used by permission of the author and the American Association for the Advancement of Science.

within the human skull if it were not folded and refolded upon itself, forming a very large number of fissures and convolutions. About 65 percent of the neurons, or nerve cells, in the brain are hidden in them, below the surface.

A side view of the brain, showing the left cerebral hemisphere, is presented in Figure 6-1. Although only the left hemisphere is shown, there is an "interpretive" area on the cerebral cortex of both the left and the right temporal lobes. It is from the interpretive areas, and from only those areas, that electrical stimulation during surgery has occasionally produced psychical responses. They can be classified as (1) experiential responses and (2) interpretive responses.

Experiential Responses

Occasionally, during an operation performed on a patient under local anesthesia, gentle electrical stimulation of the interpretive cortex, left or right, has caused the conscious patient to become aware of some previous experience. The experience seems to be picked at random from the patient's past. It comes back to him in great detail. He is suddenly

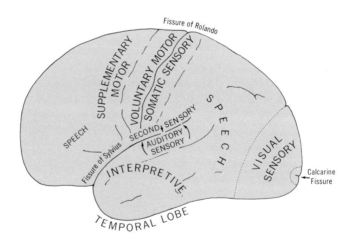

FIGURE 6-1

Side view of the left cerebral hemisphere, showing the location of areas responsible for various functions. The hallucinations and illusions described in the text were caused by applying an electrode to points in the area labeled "interpretive."

aware again of things he paid attention to some time ago. The recollection stops suddenly when the electrical current is switched off. Here are some examples of experiential response to electrical stimulation.

One patient observed, when the electrode touched the temporal lobe, "There was a piano over there and someone playing. I could hear the song, you know." When the cortex was stimulated again, without warning and at about the same point, the patient remembered a different experience. "Someone is speaking to another. He mentioned a name, but I could not understand it . . . It was like a dream." Again the point was restimulated without the patient's knowledge. He said quietly, "Yes, 'Oh, Marie, Oh, Marie!' Someone is singing it." On the fourth application of the electrode, he heard the same song again and said it was "the theme song of a radio program." When the electrode was then applied to another point, the patient said, "Something brings back a memory. I can see Seven-Up Bottling Company—Harrison Bakery." He was evidently seeing two of Montreal's large neon advertisements. The surgeon then warned him that he was about to apply the electrode again, said "Now," but did not stimulate. The patient (who has no way of knowing when the electrode is applied unless he is told, since the cortex itself is without sensation) replied promptly, "Nothing."

A second patient heard an orchestra playing a melody while the electrode was held in place. The music stopped when the electrode was removed. It came again when the electrode was reapplied. On request, the patient hummed the tune, accompanying the orchestra, while the electrode was held in place. Over and over again, restimulation at the same spot produced the same popular song. The music always seemed to begin at the same place and to progress at the same tempo. All efforts to mislead the patient failed. She believed that a phonograph was being turned on in the operating room on each occasion and stoutly asserted her belief during a conversation some days after the operation.

When an electrode was applied to the right temporal lobe of another patient, a boy, he heard his mother talking to someone on the telephone. The stimulus was repeated without warning, and he heard his mother again in the same conversation. When the electrode was applied again after a lapse of time, he said, "My mother is telling my brother he has got his coat on backwards. I can just hear them." The surgeon asked the boy whether he remembered this happening. "Oh, yes," he said, "just before I came here." Asked whether the experience seemed like a dream, he replied, "No, it is like I go into a daze."

A fourth patient cried out in astonishment when the electrode was applied. "Yes, doctor, yes, doctor. Now I hear people laughing—my friends in South Africa!" He explained his surprise by saying that though he knew he was on an operating table in Montreal, he seemed to be laughing with two of his cousins, whom he had left behind on a farm in South Africa.

Interpretive Responses

Instead of an experiential response, which involves a reliving of past events, stimulation of the interpretive area of the brain may produce a quite different response. The patient discovers that he has somehow changed his interpretation of what he is seeing, hearing, or thinking at the moment. For example, he may exclaim that his present experience seems familiar, as though he had seen, heard, or thought it before. He realizes that this must be a false interpretation. Or things may seem suddenly strange, absurd. Sights or sounds may seem distant or faint, or they may come unexpectedly close and seem loud. One patient may feel suddenly afraid, as if his environment were threatening him, and he may feel possessed by a nameless dread or panic. Another patient may say he feels lonely, aloof, or as if he were observing himself from a distance.

Under normal circumstances, anyone may make such interpretations of the present, and the interpretations serve him as guides to action and reaction. But for the interpretations to be accurate guides, they must be based on previous, comparable experience. It is conceivable, therefore, that the recall mechanism activated during an experiential response and the mechanism activated during an interpretive response are parts of a single, more general mechanism.

Which Part of the Brain Does What?

In 1861, Paul Broca showed that the destruction of a certain small part of the left cerebral hemisphere in man affected only the power of speech. It was soon realized that this was the *speech area* of man's dominant hemisphere (the left, in most people). In 1870, Fritsch and Hitzig applied an electric current to the cortex of one hemisphere of a lightly anesthetized dog and caused the legs on the opposite side to move. Thus the *motor area* of the cortex was discovered. After that, the discovery of brain areas responsible for behavior became a research target for many clinicians and experimentalists. It soon became evident that separate areas of the cortex were involved in the voluntary control of the limbs, and in the sensations of vision, sound, smell, and touch.

Before considering further the portion of the cortex that I call interpretive, a part of the brain to which neurologists had previously assigned no special function, let us turn briefly to the workings of the better-understood motor and sensory areas. It has been demonstrated that a bundle of efferent (outgoing) nerve fibers runs down from the motor area of the cortex through the lower brain stem and the spinal cord and on out to the muscles. Afferent (incoming) nerve tracts have also been found to carry impulses in the other direction, from the eye, ear, nose, skin, and body into separate sensory areas of the cortex. These processes are illustrated in Figure 6-2.

The activity of the brain depends on the movement within it of transient electrical impulses. The changing patterns formed by these paths of passing energy make possible the changing content of the mind. The patterns are never quite the same from one moment to the next; neither is the content of the mind.

The streams of electrical impulses that pass through the sensory areas of the cortex seem to differ from one another only in timing and pattern.

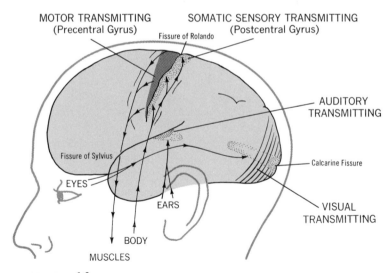

FIGURE 6-2

Sensory and motor areas of the brain. The sensory areas are stippled, and the pathways to them from eyes, ears, and body are indicated by entering arrows. The motor cortex is indicated by dark shading, and the nerve tract running out from it toward the muscles is indicated by emerging arrows. The part of the cortex that covers the primary visual reception area is shown by vertical lines.

The visual stream passes from the eyes to the visual cortex and then to a target below the cortex, whereas the auditory stream passes from the ears to the auditory cortex and on to a target below the cortex. When a surgeon artificially stimulates a portion of the sensory cortex, what must happen is that he sends a current along the next "piece of road" to a subcortical destination. When the electrode is applied to the visual cortex, the patient reports colors, lights, and shadows that move and take on crude outlines. Applied to the auditory cortex, it causes him to hear a ringing or hissing or thumping sound. When applied to the postcentral gyrus, shown in Figure 6-2, it produces a tingling sensation or a false sense of movement. Thus sensation is produced by the passage inward of electrical impulses. When the electrode is applied to the motor area of the cortex, movement is produced by the passage of impulses outward to the muscles.

Psychical responses to electrical stimulation, as distinguished from sensory and motor responses, have been elicited from parts of the cortex labeled "interpretive" in Figure 6-1. They have never been produced by stimulation in other areas. There are, of course, other large areas of cortex that are neither sensory nor motor in function. Although they seem to be associated in some way with psychical processes, they do not seem to function in response to so simple a stimulus as the application of an electrode.

Epilepsy

In epileptics, psychical phenomena of the sort we produced in the operating room are often the first sign that a seizure is about to occur. They seem to initiate the fit. Indeed, one aim of our research was to locate the part of the brain responsible for epileptic attacks so that, if it could be spared, it could be removed.

The first suggestion that psychical phenomena were associated with the part of the cortex I am calling interpretive came about as the result of research on epilepsy. Nineteenth-century clinicians had recognized that the start of epileptic attacks was characterized by what they called an "intellectual aura." J. H. Jackson later substituted the expression "dreamy states," which he said resembled the states sometimes experienced by healthy people as a feeling of "reminiscence" (Taylor, 1931). His patients mentioned "dreamy feelings," "dreams mixed up with present thoughts," "double consciousness," a feeling "as if I went back to all that occurred in my childhood," "silly thoughts." Jackson did not attempt to classify these states, as I have done in describing them as experiential and interpretive, but he did discover that they were produced in the area of the cortex that I call interpretive.

Brief reference may be made to a specific case, an epileptic patient in whom electrical stimulation produced the first responses recognized as psychical. She was a girl of sixteen, admitted in 1936 to the Montreal Neurological Institute complaining of epileptic attacks. Each attack was ushered in by the same hallucination. It was a little dream, she said, in which an experience from early childhood was reenacted, always the same train of events. She would then cry out with fear and run to her mother. Occasionally this was followed immediately by a major convulsive seizure.

During surgery, under local anesthesia, we tried to set off the dream by a gentle electrical stimulus in the right temporal lobe. The attempt was successful: the "little dream" occurred. Stimulation at other points on the temporal cortex produced sudden fear without the dream. At still other points, stimulation caused her to say that she saw "someone coming toward me." At another point, she said she heard the voices of her mother and her brothers.

Since that time, although practically all areas of the cerebral cortex have been stimulated and studied in more than a thousand brain operations, psychical responses of the experiential or interpretive variety have been produced only from the interpretive cortex.

It seems reasonable to classify psychical seizures (epileptic dreamy states) and psychical responses to electrical stimulation in the same way, as experiential or interpretive. *Experiential* psychical seizures are reenactments of past experiences, hallucinations in which there is an awareness of experiences from the past without complete loss of awareness of the present. *Interpretive* psychical seizures, by contrast, focus on present experience or the emotions related to it.

The most common interpretive responses and seizures are (1) recognition (*déjà vu*)—the illusion that things seen, heard, or thought are familiar; (2) visual illusion—the illusion that things seen are changing, as coming nearer, growing larger; (3) auditory illusion—the illusion that things heard are changing, as coming nearer, growing louder, changing tempo; (4) illusional emotion—the emotion of fear or, less often, loneliness, sorrow, or disgust.

The Interpretive Cortex and Memory

What, then, is the function of the interpretive cortex? We may say, first of all, that the interpretive cortex has something to do with a mechanism that can reactivate a vivid record of the past. It also has something to do with a mechanism than can bring about a reflex interpretation of the present. However, to conclude that here is the mechanism of memory would be unjustified.

What a man remembers when he makes a voluntary effort is apt to be a generalization. If this were not so, he might be hopelessly lost in detail. A man may summon a song to mind at will. He hears it then in his mind, not all at once but advancing phrase by phrase. He may sing it or play it too, and one would call this memory.

On the other hand, the experiential responses I have described are detailed reenactments of a single experience. Such experiences soon slip beyond the range of voluntary recall. If a patient hears music in response to the electrode, he hears it in one particular strip of time. That time runs forward again at the original tempo, and he hears the orchestration or sees the player at a piano "over there." These are details he would have thought forgotten.

A vast amount of work remains to be done before the mechanisms of memory, and how and where the recording takes place, are understood. This record is not laid down in the interpretive cortex, but it is kept in a part of the brain that is intimately connected with it.

The way the interpretive cortex seems to be used in remembering can be suggested by an example. After years of absence you meet, by chance, a man whose very existence you had forgotten. On seeing him, you may be struck by a sudden sense of familiarity even before you have time to "think." A signal seems to flash into consciousness to tell you that you have seen the man before. You watch him as he smiles, moves, and speaks, and the sense of familiarity grows stronger. Then you remember him. You may even recall his name. The sight and the sound of the man have given you instant access, through some reflex, to the record of a past in which this man played some part. The opening of this forgotten record was subconscious, not a voluntary act. You would have known him even against your will. Although he was a forgotten man a moment before, suddenly you can summon the record in such detail that you notice small changes—a new slowness to his gait, a new line about the mouth. If the man had been a source of danger to you when you knew him, you might have felt fear as well as familiarity before you had time to remember why. The fear, like the sense of familiarity, would have been a signal resulting from a subconscious comparison of present with past experience.

"Consciousness," said William James, "is never quite the same in successive moments of time. It is a stream forever flowing, forever changing." The stream of changing states of the mind that James described so well does flow constantly through each man's waking hours, leaving a record in the brain.

Transient electrical impulses, moving through the circuits of the nervous system, leave a path that can be followed again. The pattern of this pathway, from neuron to neuron along each nerve-cell body, fiber, and junction, is the recorded pattern of each man's past. A steady stream of electrical pulses applied through an electrode to points in the interpretive cortex causes a stream of excitation to flow from the cortex to the place where past experience is recorded. This stream of excitation acts as a key to the past.

Under normal circumstances, the interpretive cortex must make some functional contribution to comparison of the present with related past experience. The combination and comparison of present experience with similar past experience must call for remarkable scanning of the past and classification of similarities. How that scanning and classification process is carried out remains to be seen; for now, the term "interpretive cortex" will serve to identify at least part of the contribution that appears to be made by that particular portion of the brain.

REFERENCE

Taylor, J., ed. *Selected writings of John Hughlings Jackson.* On epilepsy and epileptiform convulsions, vol. 1. London: Hodder and Stoughton, 1931.

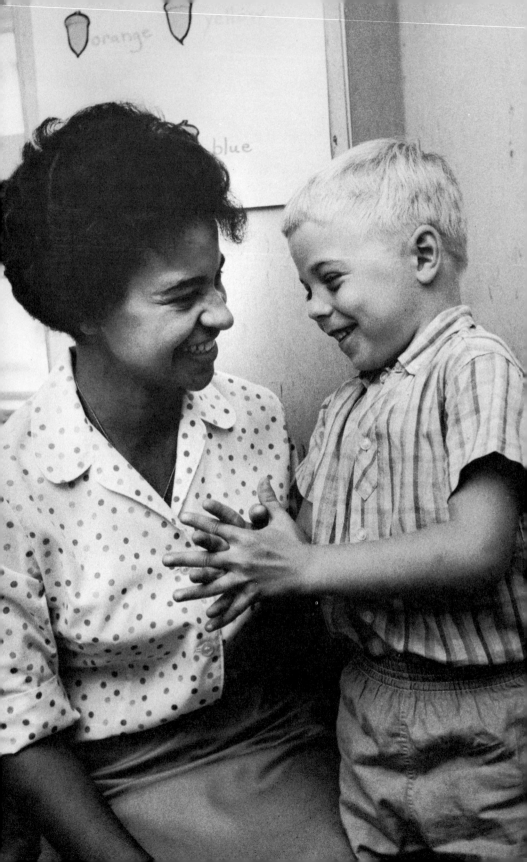

Efficiency
in Learning

The description of learning in Pavlov's and Skinner's articles emphasized the basic principles of classical and operant conditioning. These principles assert that behavior is built up from a series of environmental experiences and give little attention to the internal psychological state of the learner. James and Bartlett, by contrast, stressed the active role an individual takes in determining his own experience and memories. Psychologists working in that tradition sometimes condemn conditioning theory as mechanistic, on the ground that it fails to recognize the effect of attitudes and other internal processes on learning.

If you give several people the same task to learn, they will probably learn it differently—at different rates of speed, with different degrees of accuracy, and often by different methods. Some of the reasons for these differences are discussed in "Memorizing, Recoding, and Perceptual Organization," by Mary D. Allan, and "Mechanization in Problem Solving: A Case of Rigid Behavior," by Abraham S. Luchins.

When a person is asked to memorize a fairly large amount of meaningless material, he imposes a structure on it that makes it psychologically meaningful to him and therefore easier to learn. Allan analyzes the strategies people devised in memorizing the order of letters in a scrambled deck of twenty-six alphabet cards. All the subjects broke the unorganized material into smaller, more manageable units. They grouped the letters in different ways, one person remembering the two-card sequence Q V because it reminded him of Queen Victoria and another having no trouble with Q V F because it was part of a code he had used in the Navy. In the second half of her experiment, Allan compares the efficiency of the "whole method," in which the subjects went through the whole pack of twenty-six cards at once, and the "part method," in which they learned the cards in five small packets prepared by the experimenter, working on only one packet at a time. The whole method worked considerably better, apparently because it allowed each subject to organize the material in the way that was most meaningful to him. Allan concludes that a kind of internal recoding takes place when people are presented with more material than they can learn easily. She suggests that there may be a basic organizational activity of the human nervous system that does for the mind roughly what a computer programer does for his machine when he organizes many bits of information into chunks the computer can "understand."

Although a learning strategy is helpful only when it suits the task at hand, people often continue to use a particular problem-solving method when it no longer applies. A rat that learns a roundabout route through a maze to a food box usually takes the same route even when the experimenter opens a gate to a shorter, more direct path. Similarly, a person who learns to solve a problem in a certain way may continue to use that method on other, similar-looking problems, even when an easier, faster method is available and, indeed, even when the first one fails to work at all. This type of behavior is the subject of Luchins's "Mechanization in Problem Solving: A Case of Rigid Behavior."

People approach problems in ways that vary from very flexible (each problem is seen as unique, to be solved by a method devised especially for the occasion) to very rigid (many quite different problems are attacked with one habitual strategy) whether it works or not. Luchins examined the variations in rigidity shown by several groups of people on a series of arithmetic problems, in an attempt to identify the factors that increase and decrease rigidity. He found, for example, that both anxiety and boredom tend to heighten rigidity, whereas interest with little tension contributes to flexibility. He also discovered that the age and sex of the problem-solver affect rigidity. In conclusion, he points out several factors common in public school classrooms that enhance rigidity and suggests some changes teachers could make to encourage greater flexibility in children.

7

Memorizing, Recoding,
and Perceptual Organization

MARY D. ALLAN

Memorizing, in one form or another, plays an important part in all formal learning. When what is to be memorized is long and complicated, most people break it up into manageable portions, usually of a length that can be repeated correctly from immediate memory. They learn each fragment and then put the fragments together.

There is a limit to the amount of material that the immediate memory can cope with. For example, seven digits is the most that the average adult can repeat without error on the first try. However, if bits of material are grouped in certain ways, larger amounts can be learned in one try. For example, you can remember a large number of letters if they are grouped as meaningful words or sentences rather than scrambled in a meaningless order.

MEMORIZING, RECODING, AND PERCEPTUAL ORGANIZATION. Adapted from *British Journal of Psychology* 52 (1961). Used by permission of the author and the British Psychological Society.

Miller (1956) has suggested that a concept from electronics, limited channel capacity, may be useful for understanding the human memory. Electronics engineers who deal with machines of limited channel capacity know that what is limited is the number of items that can be processed at any one time, not the amount of information each item conveys. Thus the capacity of a machine can be increased by recoding "bits" of information into "chunks," each chunk carrying as much data as possible. The assumption is that if the limitation on a machine's channel capacity is number of items, then a machine can process chunks as easily as it can bits.

The question is, Does the human memory increase its capacity by recoding the information it is presented with? If so, what sort of coding system is used? One way to find out is to keep bombarding human subjects with more bits of information than their minds can immediately absorb and see what happens.

The plan of our investigation was to overload the human communication channel by asking subjects to memorize a long, random series of letters. By this method we hoped to find out whether a basic activity of the human nervous system—perhaps similar to chunking—would reveal itself.

Experiment 1:
A Scrambled Alphabet

The first experiment was carried out at the Applied Psychology Unit, Cambridge University. The subjects were five National Servicemen from the British Navy, all with above-average intelligence ratings.

Their task was to learn the alphabet in random order as it appeared in a pack of twenty-six cards. Twenty-six items of ungrouped material are far more than the memory can normally absorb at once, and we wanted to see what would happen if the subjects were asked to make repeated attempts to absorb the whole sequence, without breaking it up into manageable portions. (It should be mentioned that the purpose of the experiment was *not* to find the most efficient way to memorize nonsense material but to see what happens when memory is strained beyond its power of immediate absorption. For this reason, we made no attempt to compare the performance of the five experimental subjects with that of a control group.)

The sequence of letters that had to be learned was:

N A J S T W H I D Q V F Z C E P G O K B X R Y L M U

Each letter was printed on a separate card. The subjects were told that the pack of cards given them contained the twenty-six letters of the alphabet all jumbled up; they were instructed to take the pack in one hand, to turn the cards over one by one while saying the letters out loud, and to try without strain to note the order in which they turned up. The subjects went through the pack at the rate of about one card per second. When each man had gone through the pack, he was asked to call out the letters in the correct order as nearly as he could remember it.

As soon as he had finished, he was asked to begin the procedure again, with the cards in the same order. He went through the pack a second time, turning each card over as before, saying the letters aloud, and reporting the order as he remembered it. He continued the repetitions until he had learned the whole pack correctly.

In order to get the whole sequence right it took the five subjects five, four, six, three, and four trials. Their performances had certain characteristics in common, and these shared features will be illustrated through a detailed discussion of the first subject, who went through the cards five times in order to memorize the sequence correctly. Table 7-1 shows what he said on each trial.

TABLE 7-1

Original sequence	N A J S T W H I D Q V F Z C E P G O K B X R Y L M U
Trial 1	N A J H I Q U
Trial 2	N A J S T H I D Q V F G L M U
Trial 3	N A J S T W H I D Q V F Z C E L X G P R Y L M U
Trial 4	N A J S T W H I D Q V F Z C E P G O K B Y R L M U
Trial 5	All correct

This subject started off by saying, "Well, it ends with U and starts with N A J." Apart from that he could remember very little. On the second trial, he again fixed the beginning and the end of the series: "It ends with L M U and begins with N A J S." This time he was somewhat more successful in filling in intermediate sequences.

For the remaining trials he began at the beginning and, in a rather jerky fashion, recalled long sequences fairly correctly. It was obvious that he was recalling the material in small groups. Without being told to do so, he had started by making a sort of schema and fixing limits. Then he grouped the intervening material into small units and tried to place them correctly—hence the jerky performance.

The rest of the subjects behaved similarly; all of them tried to organize the material into manageable units. Frequently the units were meaningful: most subjects recognized H I D as a word and O K as a slang expression, and C E P reminded one subject of a car registration number. Another remembered Q V F because it is a code used in the Navy, whereas someone else saw the Q V instantly as Queen Victoria. The groupings, however, were entirely individual. One subject had been trained as a Morse code operator. He was used to receiving Morse code in five-letter groups, and for him a five-letter group was a perceptual unit. It took him only three trials to memorize the twenty-six-letter sequence.

Recoding: Bits into Chunks

The concept of recoding is very helpful in explaining this exercise in learning. It could be said that two kinds of recoding took place: *categorical recoding*, in which the letters were grouped together and translated into meaningful units, and *ordinal recoding*, in which the units were assigned a position in the sequence as a whole. The final step consisted in building bridges with the left-over material—that is, with the material that the subject could not codify and thus found most difficult to master.

Obviously success in this exercise depends on how many bits of information a subject is able to encode into a chunk. With our nonsense sequence of letters, most subjects could translate the letters into meaningful units of only two or three. The Morse code operator required fewer trials than the others because he could see a group of any five letters as a unit.

The final part of the experiment had a dramatic quality that never failed to impress the subjects themselves. After each subject had learned the order of the letters, he was asked to say them in reverse order. Not only could all the subjects do this; they could also begin at any point in the sequence and go forward or backward as directed. These accomplishments were not limited to the original experimental group. Later on, various other people of both sexes learned sequences of jumbled letters in the manner described above, and in every case they were able to give the letters in the reverse order on request, without further learning.

As has already been stated, the purpose of this study was to observe what subjects would do if forced to strain the memory beyond its power of immediate absorption. What most subjects did first was become exasperated with the task. After one try, they wanted either to accept defeat and go no further or to divide the cards into small groups that could be learned easily one at a time. But when they went on as instructed, there emerged a pattern or structure created by the subjects themselves. The letters grouped themselves into units that the subjects found easy to handle, and each unit was assigned a place in the total structure. As the material became·more manageable, the subjects' anxiety disappeared, and most showed satisfaction with the learned task. To their surprise, the final result was not a piece of rote learning but a structure of their own creation within which they could move backward or forward with equal ease.

There was undoubtedly a perceptual element in the way each subject organized the material to be memorized. That is, the groups into which each man combined the individual letters depended on which and how many letters he perceived as forming some sort of meaningful unit. The subjects were not told to chunk the jumbled alphabet; they did so on their own, and in their own ways. This was the way the human organism, left to itself, processed more than it could absorb. This fact suggests that what we set out to discover may be perceptual organization, an activity spontaneously undertaken by the nervous system under certain conditions of stress.

Sir Frederic Bartlett, who was interested in our experiment and in this interpretation of it, suggested that we consider another question: "Will efforts toward perceptual organization be made if the communication channel is functioning below capacity, or only when it is overloaded?" Our second experiment was an attempt to find an answer to this question.

Experiment 2:
Whole Method versus Part Method

In this experiment, the subjects were five airmen, again all National Servicemen with above-average intelligence ratings. The task for each subject was to memorize two twenty-six-letter sequences by two different methods.

The first method was the *whole method*, the one used in Experiment 1. The subjects were asked to treat the twenty-six letters as a whole, going through the pack of cards one at a time, saying each letter aloud, and then attempting to recall the entire sequence. The only difference from Experiment 1 was that we did not stop when the subject had learned the material. He went through the cards and recited the letters eight times, even if he did not need that many trials to memorize the order.

The second method was the *part method*. In this case the twenty-six letters were given to the subjects already divided up into five packets, four of them containing five cards and one containing six. Each packet was memorized separately, the subjects reading out the five or six letters and recalling them from immediate memory. This was done eight times, so that the subjects had eight trials on each group of letters before going on to the next. Finally, the subjects were asked to recall the full sequence of twenty-six letters by putting the memorized parts together.

The two sequences of letters were as follows:

V R O D X C U M J H B S Z L I W T P A E Y Q K N G F

K P Z C O N A L J X F Q T S M R Y W B U V G E I H D

Each subject learned one sequence by the whole method, then the other sequence by the part method. Using the whole method, all subjects succeeded in memorizing the sequences correctly within eight trials. Using the part method, none of the subjects was able to memorize the sequences after the same amount of practice. Table 7-2 gives details of the final, eighth recall session for the part method.

T A B L E 7-2

Original sequence	V R O D X	C U M J H	B S Z L I	W T P A E	Y Q K N G F
Subject 1	V X	C U M J H	R T		
Subject 2	V R O D	C U M J H			Y Q K N G F
Subject 3	V R U D X	O U M J H	S B Z L I	W P T Q F	Y Q K N G F

Original sequence	K P Z C O	N A L J X	F Q T S M	R Y W B U	V G E I H D
Subject 4	Z C O	N V X			V G E I H D
Subject 5			Q T S	W H I U D	E I

As this record makes clear, none of the subjects could correctly repeat the sequence by putting the parts together, although all of them could correctly repeat the order of the cards in the other pack after the same amount of practice by the whole method.

Perceptual Organization as a Form of Recoding

The subjects in Experiment 1, forced to absorb a long sequence of disconnected information, tried to organize the material into meaningful units, which they built into a structure. In other words, they tried to create a pattern. However, most subjects showed exasperation and frustration on the first trials and would have liked either to abandon the task because of the discomfort of stress or to divide the sequence into portions that could be memorized easily by rote. Yet when the whole method of learning was compared to the part method, we found that although it was more stressful at the beginning, it was more efficient. It seems, then, that when only five or six letters are processed at a time—that is, when the memory is not overloaded—spontaneous perceptual organization does not have a chance to occur.

What these exercises in memorizing suggest is that perceptual organization is a form of recoding, an activity that occurs under certain kinds of stress. The Gestaltists, by concentrating on the way things appear and by minimizing the role of experience, have made it difficult to view perception as an activity in which we engage. Thanks to their work, we know a great deal about the laws of dynamic wholes, but we know little about the laws of dynamic structuring by which those wholes are formed. If there are such laws, perhaps one of them relates to this matter of overloading the human communication channel, and perhaps it concerns the efficient packaging of data into perceptual units—chunks, if you will—that can be processed by a channel of limited capacity.

REFERENCES

Miller, G. A. The magical number seven, plus or minus two: some limits in our capacity for processing information. *Psychological Review* 63 (1956): 81–97.

Woodworth, R. S. *Experimental psychology*. London: Methuen, 1938.

8

Mechanization

in Problem Solving:

A Case of Rigid Behavior

ABRAHAM S. LUCHINS

For both theoretical and practical reasons, psychologists and other social scientists are interested in behavior that persists even though any usefulness it once had is long since gone. Why do people hold onto one pattern or thought or activity when another, more efficient pattern is available? Why do they repeat behavior that is destructive and self-defeating? Persistence in a behavior pattern can be funny or merely annoying, as when a person stumbles over a chair because he forgets he is in a motel instead of his own bedroom or cannot find his car at the parking lot because he took the bus that day. It can also be serious and even tragic, as when childlike behavior, mannerisms, or fears become neuroses or psychoses in adulthood or

MECHANIZATION IN PROBLEM SOLVING: A CASE OF RIGID BEHAVIOR Adapted from *Rigidity of behavior: A variational approach to the effect of "Einstellung,"* by Abraham S. Luchins and Edith Hirsch Luchins. Eugene: University of Oregon Books, 1959. Used by permission of Abraham S. Luchins and the publisher.

when outmoded prejudices and customs obstruct needed changes in the behavior and institutions of social groups.

The study of rigid behavior that I shall describe here involved a series of arithmetic problems presented to thousands of people under various conditions. Our aim was to find out how differences in the conditions, such as tension or lack of tension in the testing room, and differences in the people, such as age and sex, would affect the flexibility with which they approached the problems. Since we studied rigidity in problem-solving behavior specifically, our findings are perhaps particularly relevant to the teaching techniques used by schools. One aim of modern education, it is said, is to educate children in such a way that while they build a repertoire of useful patterns of thinking and acting, they do not become mechanized robots.

The Basic Experiment

The first problem in the series we gave our subjects was as follows: Suppose you have two jars, one that holds 29 quarts of liquid and one that holds 3 quarts. Using the two jars, you are to obtain 20 quarts of water. There are no graduated marks on the jars; all you know is that one holds 29 quarts and the other holds 3. How would you solve the problem? The solution is to fill the 29-quart jar and then bail out the extra nine quarts by using the other, 3-quart jar three times.

The rest of the series consisted of ten similar problems, shown on the left in Table 8-1. I suggest you try them yourself. Cover the two right-hand columns of the table (which give solutions) and allow yourself two and a half minutes on each problem. If you have not solved a problem when the time is up, go on to the next one. Any or all three jars in each problem may be used. Please do not continue reading until you have done the problems, keeping track of your solutions in any way you choose.

Now, did you notice that Problems 2 through 6 can all be solved the same way? In each case, you can begin by filling Jar B and then remove the excess water by filling Jar A once and Jar C twice. This procedure leaves in Jar B the correct amount of water. The method of solution can be summarized as an equation: $B - A - 2C$. Did you use this method in Problems 2 through 6? Did you use it to solve any of the later problems?

The last five problems, Problems 7 through 11, can be solved in somewhat simpler ways than $B - A - 2C$, as shown in the Solution column of Table 8-1. However, $B - A - 2C$ does work, at least on Problems 7, 8, 10, and 11. It does not work on Problem 9.

TABLE 8-1

The basic experiment.

Problem	Given jars with these capacities (in quarts)			Obtain	Solution	Alternate solution
	JAR A	JAR B	JAR C			
1		29	3	20 quarts	B − 3C	None
2	21	127	3	100	B − A − 2C	B − 9C
3	14	163	25	99	B − A − 2C	None
4	18	43	10	5	B − A − 2C	None
5	9	42	6	21	B − A − 2C	2C + A
6	20	59	4	31	B − A − 2C	B − 7C
7	23	49	3	20	A − C	B − A − 2C
8	15	39	3	18	A − C	B − A − 2C
9	28	76	3	25	A + C	None
10	18	48	4	22	A + C	B − A − 2C
11	14	36	8	6	A − C	B − A − 2C

The simpler way to solve Problems 7, 8, 10, and 11 is called the *direct method*. The formula that solves Problems 2 through 6 is called the *set method*, because it is a habit, or set, that the problem-solver forms in doing these problems. A person who uses the set method to solve Problems 7 and 8 does not necessarily show rigid behavior, but he does show a certain susceptibility to habit. One purpose of Problem 9, which cannot be solved by the B − A − 2C method, is to break the set; a person who fails that problem and proceeds with the set method on Problems 10 and 11 is behaving rigidly—continuing to use a method that has become not only inefficient but, on Problem 9, ineffective.

Did you perhaps use the set method throughout, overlooking the direct alternative in Problems 7, 8, 10, and 11 and failing Problem 9? If so, you did what most people who try the series do. Early in our investigation we asked 1,039 people to do the eleven problems while 970 others, the control group, did only Problems 7 through 11. In the experimental group, which did all the problems, 83 percent of the subjects used the set method (the B − A − 2C procedure) on Problems 7 and 8, and 64 percent failed Problem 9. In the control group, which had no opportunity to form the habit of using the B − A − 2C method, virtually everyone used the direct method on Problems 7 and 8 and only 5 percent failed Problem 9. We have given the eleven problems to thousands of other subjects over the years. In every group, most people stick to the set method and ignore the direct one, even when the set method fails them at Problem 9.

Stress and Rigidity

Most psychological theories hold that people's behavior becomes more rigid when they are anxious, tense, or frustrated, and it is widely accepted that frustrating and anxiety-provoking situations should be avoided in child training, teaching, psychotherapy, and other attempts to change behavior. To test these assumptions, we decided to investigate the influence of frustration and anxiety on the ways people solve the water-jar problems just described.

STRESSFUL CONDITIONS

In one experiment we tried to create anxiety in our subjects by presenting the water-jar problems as a speed test. We told the children in elementary school classes that they would be timed and asked them to work as fast as they could, since speed would be taken into account in scoring. They were also told that their principal and teachers would examine the papers and that their report-card marks and grade placement would be influenced by the test scores. While the children were working, the experimenter expressed astonishment that they had not finished yet, claimed they were very slow, and said that children in lower grades usually finished in less time.

There were many strained and even tearful faces in the seven classes that took the speed test. After it was over, the children spoke of having been worried, upset, and afraid. Some said all they could think of was subtraction and hurrying. Some hoped never again to have to take such a test.

The children's solutions to the problems showed marked rigidity. Of 98 children, only 2 used the direct method of solving Problems 7 through 11 and only 3 were able to solve Problem 9. Many children tried to apply the set method $(B - A - 2C)$ to Problem 9, writing $76 - 28 - 3 - 3$ equals 25 (the number of quarts called for in the problem), even though $76 - 28 - 3 - 3$ actually equals 42. To state the results in percentages, 98 percent of the children in the speed-test groups used the set method on Problems 7 through 11 and 97 percent of them failed Problem 9. By contrast, only 70 percent of the children in control groups, which worked under neutral, nonstressful conditions, used the set method on Problems 7 through 11, and only 58 percent failed Problem 9.

The problems were also given as a speed test to eight college classes. The students were told that the test was part of an intelligence test, and the fact that they were being timed was emphasized. There was a large clock on the wall and an array of stopwatches on the experimenter's desk; in addition, the minutes were recorded on the blackboard as they passed. Several times during the experiment the experimenter remarked impatiently that elementary school children usually worked faster.

In contrast to the rather carefree atmosphere that was usual when college students tried the problems under neutral conditions, there was now considerable tension. Subjects later reported that they had felt anxious, nervous, under strain. When the papers were examined, we found that 93 percent of these students had used the set method on Problems 7 through 11, as compared with 82 percent of the students tested under neutral conditions. The difference on Problem 9 was even more striking: 84 percent of the students in the speed-test groups failed to solve it, as compared with 56 percent in the control groups.

It should be mentioned that speed itself did not produce rigidity. In some classes, the first student to hand in his paper had direct solutions to every problem. It was seeing others hand in their papers, some subjects later admitted, that intensified their fear and nervousness. That is, it was not speed alone that increased rigidity but the person's reaction to the emphasis on speed.

RELAXED CONDITIONS

In the speed-test experiments, we stressed that a test was being given and that a student might get a poor grade on it. Students who took part in these experiments, as we have seen, were concerned about how well they would do and said they felt worried, upset, and afraid. If subjects were relaxed—if we could persuade them not to regard the experiment as a test and not to be anxious about their performance—would rigidity disappear?

In an attempt to answer this question, we enlisted the services of several students in an undergraduate psychology class. Each of them asked a fellow student, in a casual and offhand manner, "Please do me a favor and help me check these problems that I have to use in the lab tomorrow." The problems were then presented one at a time, with the usual two and a half minutes allowed for each. Afterward, the subjects were interviewed about their reactions to the task. On the basis of the interviews, we chose for examination only the work of the 20 subjects who seemed to have the most relaxed, carefree, casual attitude toward the problems. They did not consider the problems a test and seemed unconcerned about how their performance would affect their status in the class.

Of these 20 subjects, 70 percent used the set method instead of the direct one on Problems 7 and 8, and 35 percent failed Problem 9. Those who failed Problem 9 did not regard it as a failure; they thought there was something wrong with the problem, and some seemed pleased to have helped a fellow student catch a problem that did not "check." These results, together with those obtained from the speed-test groups and from the control groups, which worked under neutral conditions, are shown in Table 8-2. It is clear that the relaxed, carefree atmosphere did weaken—although by no means destroyed—behavioral rigidity.

TABLE 8-2

The effects of stress and relaxation on rigidity in college students.

Conditions	Percentage who used set method on Problems 7–11	Percentage who failed to solve Problem 9
Stressful	93	84
Neutral	82	56
Relaxed	70	35

These findings seem to suggest that the way to avoid rigidity and foster desirable changes in behavior is to get rid of frustration and anxiety. However, things are not quite that simple. The relaxed subjects who thought they were helping a fellow student check problems for the lab were not so relaxed that they were indifferent, uncritical, or unwilling to get involved in the problems. Other relaxed subjects who did seem to have such attitudes—for example, people who were quite conceited about their arithmetical ability and regarded the problems as child's play—tended to use the set method and fail Problem 9 more often than the average for their groups. Apparently their extreme self-assurance led them to repeat the set method automatically instead of facing the requirements of each problem.

It appears that both very low and high anxiety foster rigidity, while a small amount of anxiety works against it. This is fairly understandable when one considers that a person who is not at all anxious or frustrated may see no reason to change or even to reflect on his behavior. Change is an adjustment brought about by disequilibrium—by a sense that things are out of balance, not as they should be. If a person senses no disequilibrium, he is not likely to rock the boat.

Individual Differences

In the ten years or so since the water-jar problems were devised, the series has often been used in connection with personality testing as a measure of general rigidity. That is, rigid behavior in solving the problems has been seen not merely as part of the person's response to something about the testing situation, such as whether the atmosphere is tense or relaxed, but as a reflection of his personality. With this point of view in mind, let us review some findings on the performances of people who differ in age and sex.

AGE

Most theories of personality state that there is a relationship between age and rigidity. However, some say that rigidity increases with age while others say it decreases. In the main, our findings support the increase-with-age theory, but they also suggest that the relationship is not a simple one.

As we mentioned earlier, the behavior of a person who uses the set method to solve Problems 7 and 8 is not necessarily rigid, since the set method is only slightly more awkward than the direct one and, in addition, it works. What the use of the set method on those problems shows is that the problem solver is susceptible to habit—that he has a *potential* for rigidity. According to our data, older people are more likely to use the set method on Problems 7 and 8 than younger ones. Susceptibility to set, then, does increase with age in a straightforward and consistent manner.

Behavioral rigidity, as distinguished from susceptibility to set, is measured chiefly by Problem 9. At that point in the series the old method of solution does not work; the person who cannot find a new one has been, so to speak, locked into his habit. When we reviewed our data on the way various groups of subjects dealt with Problem 9, the following findings emerged.

1. Young children were less rigid (that is, less likely to fail to solve Problem 9) than older children.
2. Young adults (mean age 21) were less rigid than older children and less rigid than middle-aged adults (mean age 43).
3. Middle-aged adults (mean age 37) were less rigid than older adults (mean age 61).

The group that seems to be out of step here is the older children. They show more rigidity than younger children, and also more rigidity than young adults. One might expect older children to show *less* rigidity on our series of problems than younger ones, on the ground that their greater familiarity with arithmetic would help them in the task. That hypothesis is not borne out by our data and could be abandoned, except that we then face the problem of explaining why rigidity declines between late childhood and early adulthood. Perhaps the performance of the older children is influenced by their experience with drill and repetition at school—more extensive experience than that of younger children and not yet in the past, as it is with young adults. We shall return later to the idea that drill and repetition discourage flexibility.

SEX

In general, boys showed less rigid behavior on the water-jar problems than girls. Among college men and women the same trend consistently appeared, although the differences were not large. Another experimenter found men and women equally susceptible to habit, as measured by the use of the set method on Problems 7 and 8, but women more rigid than men, as indicated by failure at Problem 9 (Guetzkow, 1951).

It seems highly unlikely that the difference in behavioral rigidity between males and females is due to some inherited, biological difference between the sexes. To assume it is would be to overlook the many instances in which females do not show rigid behavior, and the instances in which males show much rigidity.

We venture an explanation based on observations we made in the elementary school classes of the children tested. The social atmosphere in the classrooms tended to be rather autocratic. The teacher demanded blind confidence and dependency; restraint, pedantry, passivity, and submissiveness were desired traits; free initiative was not encouraged. It is fairly obvious how such an atmosphere might foster habitual and perhaps rigid responses.

We would expect that a person, of whichever sex, who had learned to behave in a submissive, dependent way would show more rigidity in problem solving than one who had been encouraged to think and act on his own. And the people who are taught submissiveness are likely to be girls. In our society, submissiveness and dependency are associated with females—indeed, they are traits that are often considered feminine and rarely, if ever, called masculine. Thus girls are more likely to be offered opportunities to learn submissiveness and dependency and also to seize them, believing that by doing so they are learning to be girls.

Controlling Mechanized Behavior

The discussion so far has suggested a number of ways in which rigid, mechanized behavior can be enhanced or minimized. It is well to remember, however, that the psychological question of *how* to control behavior cannot be separated from the ethical question of *why* we wish to control behavior. Any attempt to control behavior implies a desire to work toward one kind of man rather than some other kind. For example, one might wish to work toward *Homo sapiens*, a thinking, rational being, or toward *Homo mechanicus*, a robotlike mechanism.

Assuming that *Homo sapiens* is preferable, should we try to eliminate all automatic behavior? I think not. Mechanized habits equip a person with fast, ready responses to everyday situations. If a person had to think about each response and make a decision in every situation, he would be much like the centipede who stopped to analyze his leg movements and ended up immobile in a ditch. However, the uncritical application of habits is likely to produce serious difficulties. Habits can be tools, but they can also be prisons. This is something that those who believe in a *Homo sapiens* model of man will want to avoid.

Our findings suggest a number of ways to avoid the indiscriminate application of habits. To limit the discussion, let us consider only what schools might do. First, educators should perhaps keep in mind that genuine problem solving is different from the uncritical application of a method to a problem. Applying a method uncritically merely gives a person practice in the use of the method. Genuine problem solving, by contrast, requires the making of decisions. In a series of tasks, each one must be faced as a new situation, another occasion for decision making. If there are no decisions to be made, there is no problem.

Telling students to apply a designated method or process to a "problem," as in isolated drill, removes a major opportunity for decision making. Moreover, if students are told to use a particular method or response, they may be less likely to study the problem as a whole, in its context. Hence they may not learn to distinguish between situations in which a given method or response applies and situations in which it does not. Isolated drill is often used at school to teach arithmetical skills, and this may help account for the fact that some children and adults, although they know how to add, subtract, multiply, and divide, do not know which they should do unless the problem explicitly tells them. They seem not to have grasped the relationship between a process, on the one hand, and, on the other, the area in which it is useful. Drill may teach *how* a process, skill, or habit should be applied, but it does not teach *where* it should be applied. In addition to practicing various processes, then, students should be given more opportunities to select the process that is appropriate to a particular task.

Many of our subjects were surprised to learn that there was more than one method of solving the water-jar problems. Their experience in school had apparently been limited mainly to problems that were presented as solvable by one, and only one, method. Yet outside the classroom it is not uncommon to find a problem that can be solved by more than one method (or by none), or by a method that leads to several answers. Experience in school with problems that are solvable by various methods may help students see a distinction between methods and the solutions to which they lead; in addition, such a teaching approach may show students that the conscious selection of a method is one step in problem solving. It may also help students realize that of the several ways to solve a problem some ways are more efficient than others.

Schools, then, should perhaps show more interest in processes as contrasted with the results of the processes. Emphasis on the end product is characteristic of "objective tests" in which one's score is based not on the process that led to the answer but merely on the answer. A suitable process may, through a minor error, lead to an incorrect final answer; a correct final answer can sometimes be obtained through incorrect or invalid reasoning. It may even be worthwhile to acquaint students with problems that have been proved to be unsolvable in order to help combat the assumption that each problem has one, and only one, solution.

Our speed-test experiments indicate the possible bad effect on thinking of extreme ego involvement, tenseness, and fear. The findings point to a need for reevaluation of the instantaneous responses demanded in some classrooms and on many tests. Our results imply that the nature of the prevailing social atmosphere may have a strong influence on whether a person meets problems with robotlike habits, even when they are inappropriate, or faces problems freely and engages in reasoned decision making.

Finally, some children showed an absolute confidence in their teacher, often a kind of blind trust akin to unthinking submission, that would not seem conducive to genuine problem solving. In extreme cases this attitude amounted to the belief that what the teacher said (or seemed to say) was correct, that one should do just what the teacher did, and that there was no reason for individual initiative. Such an attitude, when transferred to the experimenter in our investigation (who was regarded as a teacher by most children), may have encouraged the children to copy blindly the illustrated method for solving the water-jar problems. Perhaps the children assumed that they had to use this method because the experimenter had demonstrated it on Problem 1 or because he wanted them to use it. A distinction should be drawn between respect for authority, on the one hand, and unquestioning submission and sheeplike following, on the other. The latter ought to be avoided if genuine problem solving is the objective.

These suggestions for controlling mechanized behavior can be adapted to contexts other than schools. (Both in school situations and elsewhere their fruitfulness will, of course, have to be tested by observation and research.) For example, parents can help combat uncritical application of habits by not demanding blind obedience, by not putting a premium on speedy responses, by avoiding a tense social atmosphere, by providing varied opportunities for genuine problem solving, and by explaining to a child the distinction between decisions that are and are not his to make.

In summary, our findings offer some guidelines for maximizing the advantages of habits while minimizing their disadvantages in personal and social functioning. Educators, parents, psychologists—all can play roles in developing an individual who will face problems constructively rather than act from force of habit, who will use habits as tools without becoming a slave to habits, and who will so well master habits that they do not master him.

R E F E R E N C E

Guetzkow, H. An analysis of the operation of the set in problem solving behavior. *Journal of Genetic Psychology* 45 (1951): 219–44.

Perception

Through perception, we organize and interpret the evidence available to our senses. Perception depends, first of all, on the characteristics of a physical stimulus. If you close your eyes and someone puts sugar in your mouth, the sweet taste and granular texture will probably tell you what it is. Perception also depends on the sensory abilities of the person who does the perceiving. If he is colorblind, he may see no difference between a green tie and a red one. A somewhat more difficult idea to grasp is that the feelings and emotions of the perceiver may also affect what he sees, hears, and feels. A woman may perceive a man she wants to go out with as strikingly attractive; after she has gone out with him, his looks may seem simply average. His physical appearance has not changed and neither has her sensory ability, but her reactions have altered her perception of his appearance.

One way to appreciate the importance of perceptual experience in everyday life is to do without it for a while. It is a rare person who has not wished at one time or another that he could spend hours, even days, lying quietly in bed with no one to bother him and nothing to do. In "Sensory Deprivation: A Case Analysis," Jack H. Mendelson and his colleagues describe a study that approximated those conditions as nearly as possible. All visual, auditory, tactile, and other stimuli were reduced to a minimum, and the subjects' task was simply to relax and do nothing.

As it turns out, hardly a more distressing situation exists. Instead of enjoying the peace and quiet, subjects deprived of sensory stimuli report difficulty in concentrating, disorganized thought, loss of time sense, spatial disorientation, and hallucinations. Many subjects ask to end such sensory deprivation experiments long before their scheduled time is up. The two men described in "Sensory Deprivation: A Case Analysis" were able to hold out for only a few hours. Mendelson and his colleagues report the reactions of the two subjects in some detail and suggest some relationships between their responses to sensory deprivation and their psychological histories.

Except for people confined in iron lungs or marooned on desert islands, overstimulation is a more likely problem than understimulation. Before sensory deprivation was studied, many psychologists believed that much of man's behavior was aimed at reducing stimulation to the lowest possible point. It now appears that an intermediate amount of stimulation is best, and that under- as well as overstimulation puts stress on an organism and reduces the efficiency of its behavior. Proper functioning seems to require a continual flow of information from the environment.

Richard Held and Alan Hein, authors of "The Role of Movement in the Development of Visually Guided Behavior," have carried out a number of studies on the *kind* of information from the environment that normal functioning requires, and on how that information affects the plasticity (changeability) of perceptions. In one experiment, Held and Hein had several people wear distorting glasses that made things appear to be several inches to the right of where they actually were. At first, when the subjects reached for objects, they reached too far to the right, but in time they adapted to the distortion and could pick things up normally. When they took the glasses off, they went through another period of readjustment. Until they had moved about without wearing the glasses for a while, they aimed too far to the *left*.

Held and Hein saw a connection between their finding in the vision-distortion experiment with human subjects and studies by other experimenters of kittens raised under different conditions of deprivation. These studies had shown that kittens raised in a lighted and patterned environment but prevented from moving about freely in it did poorly on tests of behavior guided by vision. Kittens permitted to move about but deprived of all visual stimulation except light also did poorly on the tests. Held and Hein found these studies difficult to interpret because they did not include the effects of active movement by an organism through an environment rich in visual stimulation. They theorized that infants' development of behavior guided by vision, such as coordination of hand and eye in reaching, requires not only the presence of visual stimulation but experience moving around in the environment.

In "The Role of Movement in the Development of Visually Guided Behavior," Held and Hein report the experiment they conducted to test their hypothesis. They reared kittens in such a way that all of them saw the same things but only half of them controlled their movement through the environment. The results suggest that physical interaction with the environment, in the form of self-produced movement, plays a vital role in the development of perception.

Since all animals have a common evolutionary history, many principles of behavior discovered in studies with lower animals also hold true for man. But one cannot assume that they will, and it is sometimes very difficult to test the findings of animal studies with human beings. For example, an experimenter cannot raise a human infant in the dark, as he can a chick or a kitten, in order to study the effects of early experience on visual perception.

One way to get around this problem is to study human adults who have very different cultural backgrounds. In "Cultural Differences in the Perception of Geometric Illusions," Marshall H. Segall, Donald T. Campbell, and Melville J. Herskovits describe an experiment of this type. They investigated the effects of experience on perception by comparing the susceptibility of people from vastly different physical and cultural environments—urban and rural, advanced and primitive—to visual illusions. One might suppose that sophisticated city-dwellers from technologically advanced cultures would be less likely to be fooled by optical illusions of all types, but this is not the case. Instead, they are less susceptible to some kinds of visual illusion and more susceptible to others. The reason seems to lie in variations in the visual characteristics of the surroundings of people from different societies, and in related variations in their habitual inferences about what a certain arrangement of visual stimuli represents.

9

Sensory Deprivation:

A Case Analysis

JACK H. MENDELSON

PHILIP E. KUBZANSKY

P. HERBERT LEIDERMAN

DONALD WEXLER

PHILIP SOLOMON

One kind of research on sensory deprivation is aimed at identifying *general relationships* between a reduction in the amount of information a person receives through his senses and changes in his behavior. A second approach, the one used in the experiment described below, examines in considerable detail the *individual responses* people have to sensory deprivation. Its aim is to suggest hypotheses rather than to test them. This type of research is intensive: it allows the investigator to study complex relationships among the many variables that affect an individual's reactions to sensory deprivation.

SENSORY DEPRIVATION: A CASE ANALYSIS Adapted by permission of the publisher from Philip Solomon *et al.*, *Sensory Deprivation*. Cambridge, Mass.: Harvard University Press. Copyright, 1961, by the President and Fellows of Harvard College. Used by permission of Jack H. Mendelson and the publisher. This selection originally appeared under the title "Physiological and psychological aspects of sensory deprivation—a case analysis."

Each of the twelve men who took part in the experiment was asked to lie on his back in a tank-type respirator (iron lung), as shown in Figure 9-1. The motor of the respirator ran constantly, producing a dull sound that masked any others in the room, but the vents of the respirator were left open so that the subject breathed for himself. Comfortable but rigid cylinders held his arms and legs, and he could not see any part of his body—only the front of the tank and the blank white walls and ceiling of the room. The air temperature was constant, and the lighting was low and unvarying. The subject could drink eggnog from a feeding tube at any time; bedpans and urinals were given on demand.

The subjects were told that the purpose of the study was to see what happens to normal people when they are placed in a tank-type respirator but breathe for themselves. We asked them to move as little as possible and said that an observer would always be present, though they would

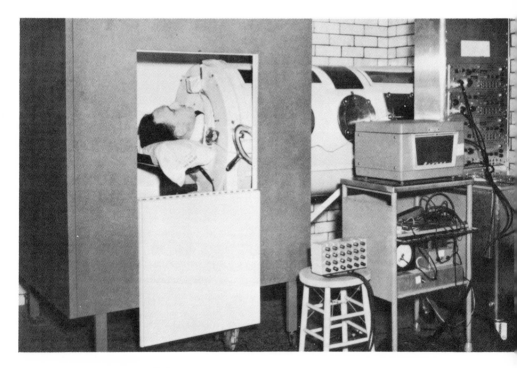

FIGURE 9-1

Each man lay on his back in a tank-type respirator. He breathed for him self, but he was deprived of virtually all sensory stimuli.

not be able to see him and he would not speak. The experiment would last for thirty-six hours unless a subject wanted to end it earlier.

While each subject was in the iron lung, the sounds he made were taped, and his sleep patterns and general motor activity were noted. Equipment in an adjoining room kept a running record of his pulse and his brain waves.

After each subject had left the respirator, he was interviewed at length about himself and about his feelings, fantasies, preoccupations, and experiences of time and space orientation during the experiment. A week or so later he returned for a series of five personality tests, including the Thematic Apperception Test (in which the person being tested makes up stories about ambiguous pictures) and the Minnesota Multiphasic Personality Inventory. To insure objectivity, the tests were administered and scored by psychologists who had not been involved in earlier parts of the experiment.

Here is how two men (out of a total of twelve) reacted to their experience in the respirator. These two were chosen because of the completeness of their records and because, despite some similarities in their personalities, their responses to sensory deprivation were quite different.

Subject 1

This man, a twenty-six-year-old, white, single professional-school student, spent six hours in the respirator before ending the experiment. At the beginning he was awake, alert, and comfortable. The changes in his pulse rate, sleep patterns, and motor and verbal behavior over the next six hours are graphed in Figure 9-2.

The subject's normal pulse rate was 70, and it showed little change during his first hour in the respirator except for a small drop in the last fifteen minutes. From then until the beginning of the fifth hour, his pulse remained fairly steady and low; he dozed from time to time; and his motor activity, though it showed a slight, steady increase, stayed low. The record for the two hours preceding his decision to leave the experiment was quite different. The subject stayed wide awake; his pulse went rapidly up and down; his motor activity, especially during the sixth hour, increased.

As for verbal behavior, this subject began to talk as soon as the experiment began and continued to speak for most of the first hour. Then verbalization dropped off, began to rise again, and by the end of the experiment was almost as high as it had been at the beginning. Three speech samples are given below, one recorded at the start of the experiment, one

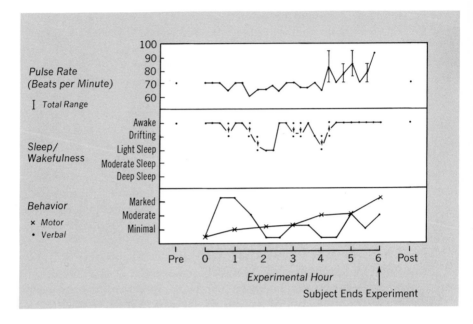

FIGURE 9-2

The record of the pulse rate, sleep pattern, and motor and verbal activity of Subject 1. He remained fairly calm until the fourth hour; from then on, he was wide awake and his pulse went rapidly up and down.

in the middle, and one at the end. Note that the subject's main concerns seem to be social isolation, an uncertainty about time, the lack of cues for orienting himself in time, and his prolonged immobility.

After the subject had settled down in the respirator he said:

> It's difficult to talk in here, it seems, with the situation sort of ambiguous. You're not really quite alone and yet not really with anybody. And I think as it progresses, and I fall into thinking of the situation one way or the other, it will be easier to speak. So far, the sensations are pretty much realizations of total aloneness. There is nothing to think about, except what you brought in with you in your own head. Perhaps I can think of this like writing a letter, perhaps that would be more easy. But then, of course, I'll be playing a role in response to somebody on the other end, maybe not. Not even an awareness of time in here. I wonder how I'm going to know what time it is.

> Motor is an interesting thing. It's the only sensation really external to myself. Before it went on I was listening to the cars. I had forgotten it

would be turned on and I was already using the cars as a reference point to outside. With the motor on it's almost impossible to hear anything, I think. It gives a sensation of movement. I think there is a lot of this situation to that little Laika in the rocket. I feel like I'm in a rocket. In a rocket, I know you wouldn't feel any sensation of motion. You would have no gravity. It's something like that. Maybe a one-man submarine.

It's a good time to know poetry, for one's self. That wouldn't really be quite cricket either. Some people say they lie down just to think things over. Just stay awake and think, which is what I could be doing now. But I never do that much, though, anyway. Hmmm. It's difficult to think in the abstract. Without anything really to think about—as a problem, or anyone to catch you up, refute you, argue back. I never have been able to think without thinking in words or arguments, or writing.

At the beginning of the second hour, just after awakening from a period of drowsiness, the subject said:

I didn't know where I was for a moment. I don't know what woke me up, either. I wasn't really asleep, though. Dozed, I guess. I wonder what you're supposed to do in here if you develop an itch? I haven't had to put up with that yet, though. Saying anything that comes to my mind, the next thing I know I haven't even said anything. I don't know if I've been thinking or what. I guess I was almost asleep. I don't think I was dreaming. It's comfortable in here anyway, I guess. Except for these cardboard things—you can't bend your arms much or nothing. I'm not even hungry. It must be lunch time—about that. And I didn't have anything to eat since breakfast. And I'm not hungry.

At the end of the sixth hour, the subject asked to end the experiment:

I'm a picture of a mixture of embarrassment and irritation. I find the thought coming more and more powerfully that I want to get out, that I want to stop, yet I don't want to either, for some reason. Some feeling of embarrassment, some feeling that I haven't been here very long, that I should be able to go on with this. It comes unbidden—I just can't lie here with my back stiff much longer. My hands are getting sweaty. It's really becoming a struggle now. Very difficult to avoid asking—out. I don't think that I'll probably be able to do it much longer. Talking about it seems to help somewhat, though. My hands are still sweaty. More so. It sort of comes up like a wave. Almost comes to my lips. Unbidden. The whole thing—to be able to get out—to bend over—my back—then in another minute I can control it. How long, I don't know. The desire to move becomes almost overpowerful—overpowering. I can't talk so straight. At moments it's really panicky.

O.K., Doctor, I've had enough, I think. Doctor, you'd better let me out, I guess. I could last a while longer, but I don't know—my back—it's pretty bad. I think you had better open it up. I'm getting very restless—thrashing, etc. It would just be a matter of minutes, anyway. Although it would probably seem like hours. I'd just as soon not carry it to—I don't know what would happen, but I'd just as soon not. My lips are dry and every muscle seems to be sweating.

During the psychiatric interview that followed the experiment, this subject seemed uncertain of himself and almost distraught. His anxiety was particularly clear from the way he spoke: verbosely, with all feelings and thoughts described in great detail. He said he was always tense and had frequent mood swings, and he also mentioned occasional short periods of inappropriate laughter that puzzled him.

He was very critical of his father's values but thought that he and his mother saw the world in the same way. As a child, he had often had headaches and stomach aches. He still bit his nails and, though he hid it, was very afraid of dentists and amusement park rides.

Despite considerable intelligence, the subject had never been a good student. He decided to enter professional school only because he did well on an aptitude test, and his work there had been poor. He had trouble concentrating, he said, and felt he did not have "the right mind for it." He was preoccupied with daydreams about his future, in which he imagined himself as a successful professional man who worked with the weak and suffering and counseled younger people to model themselves after him.

He had little interest in women. In his two sustained heterosexual relationships, he had let the women dominate him. However, he related fairly well to people who sought him out and who saw him as a sympathetic and perceptive listener.

Some days later, the subject returned for psychological testing, which confirmed and supplemented the impressions of the psychiatric interviewer. The subject seemed to be a bright, self-conscious, intellectualizing young man with an overwhelming sense of failure, confusion, and aimlessness. His manner was at times pathetic and self-pitying, at other times cynically and sarcastically critical. In dealing with people, he seemed to feel that more was demanded of him than he could deliver, though others might see him as intelligent, sensitive, and reasonably effective. He viewed authority figures as controlling, overly demanding, and lacking in wisdom and benevolence. His fantasies, though rich and heroic in their proportions, sometimes had a threatening, ominous quality. He seemed to think heterosexuality unattainable for him and to expend little effort in that direction, though there was some closeness in his relationships with his peers. He saw himself as an often sullen, drifting person who had been unable to find a comfortable niche in the world but maintained a moderately adequate and stable pattern of dealing with people and problems.

The significance of this personality material in relation to the subject's behavior and physiological responses during the experiment will be commented on after we have described Subject 2.

Subject 2

This man was a twenty-five-year-old, white, single college graduate. He spent three and a half hours in the respirator. As Figure 9-3 shows, his pulse rate, sleep pattern, and verbal and motor behavior during that time were quite unlike those of the first subject.

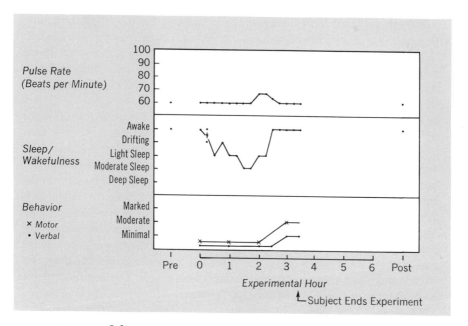

FIGURE 9-3

The record of the pulse rate, sleep pattern, and motor and verbal activity of Subject 2. This subject slept for most of his first two hours in the respirator, perhaps in an attempt to avoid the stress of the situation. An hour and a half after he woke up, he ended the experiment.

This subject's normal pulse rate was 60. It stayed at that level for the first two hours, which the subject spent mostly dozing and sleeping. He moved hardly at all during that time, and his verbalizations consisted of repeated attempts to get a response from the observer by calling "Hey, Doc." During the third hour, his pulse rate rose as he woke up, and he began to move around more and talk a little. Thirty minutes after the fourth hour started, he asked to end the experiment.

When the tank was opened, he lay for two or three minutes without moving or speaking. His face was immobile and somber; his shoulders and arms seemed to have lost their strength and muscle tone. He looked as if he no longer had the capacity for voluntary movement, and he did not try to leave the tank until the experimenter told him to.

We learned later that this subject had some strange experiences while he was in the respirator. He did not report all of them during the psychiatric interview just after his release from the respirator, but he did say that when he woke up, just before asking to be let out, he did not know where he was or what time it was. He imagined that the observer had left the room and that the sides of the tank were pressing in on him. Although he knew how to open the respirator, he had the frightening thought that if fire broke out he would not be able to release himself. While he was thinking about that, he looked up and saw a dead insect (which really was there) on the back of a wooden screen near his head. As he watched the insect, he thought he saw a gray curtain descend over the top-center of his visual field.

The day after the experiment, the subject sought out an acquaintance of his, a member of the Psychiatric Service at a college. He was perspiring heavily, hyperactive, and obviously in great need of discussing the experiment. He talked to the psychiatrist for several hours, stressing two bizarre experiences that were very real to him and had led him to doubt his sanity. Early in the experiment, he said, he took a sip of eggnog. It tasted good, but he thought that bacteria were being produced in the eggnog trapped in the feeding tube. He imagined that he was being poisoned and that his body had begun to produce a counterpoison as an antidote. A short time after the dead-insect/gray-curtain incident, he went on, he had been frightened to see rays of light coming toward his face from the microphone of the tape recorder.

The general impression of the psychiatrist from the service was that the subject had some paranoid tendencies but was functioning well in most respects. During later sessions, the subject seemed completely recovered and showed no residual difficulties connected with his participation in the experiment.

In talking with our interviewer right after the experiment, the subject did not mention the bacteria in the feeding tube or the rays of light coming from the microphone. He seemed cooperative and eager to give an impression of masculine competence. He spoke in an authoritative, somewhat condescending manner.

However, he told the interviewer that he had always been unsure of himself, especially with women. As a child his friends teased him, but now they turned to him for advice, which pleased him. He saw himself as superior to his peers in some cultural and aesthetic areas and in social graces, but he was less sure of himself intellectually and physically. An expert marksman, he commented that if he were ever permanently disabled in combat he thought he would kill himself. When he smoked cigarettes his thoughts regularly turned to lung cancer, and when he was in a hospital building shared by tuberculosis patients he was afraid he would catch the disease. One of his hobbies was photography, but he would let himself be photographed only as part of a large group. He explained this by referring to members of the FBI, who avoid having their pictures taken so that they cannot be identified.

The subject said that both he and his father were unstable and subject to depression, though outsiders considered his father a wonderful, cheery person. He thought his father had not devoted enough time to him. He was concerned about his responsibilities to his mother and was eager to be a good, dutiful son. In his relationships with authority figures he showed either hostility or overidentification.

Psychological tests of this subject showed him as an extremely defensive individual who presented the façade of an active, assertive person. He aspired to intellectual and social achievements but expressed great doubt about his ability to succeed. Confronted by failure, he wanted to flee or to avoid the problem at hand by intellectualizing the issues. At such times he would become quite anxious, demand reassurance, and try rigidly to control his feelings, which he feared might overwhelm him. Under this pressure he might lapse into arbitrary or, at times, even irrational thinking.

Parental figures appeared to him as powerful, controlling, and punitive. On the one hand he expressed great respect for authority and strong need for approval, while at the same time he feared that approval was unattainable; thus he felt rejected. Underlying his feelings of rejection were marked resentment and anger that he tried hard to restrain. He masked his dependence on and resentment of authority behind a façade of poise and assertiveness that, however, became brittle under stress.

Comparison of the Two Subjects

Subject 1 responded to the experimental situation with a rising and changeable pulse rate, increasing motor activity, and considerable verbalization. Subject 2, however, showed no significant changes in pulse rate, slept during most of the experimental period, and talked and moved very little until thirty-five minutes before he ended the experiment.

In comparing the personalities of the two subjects, as inferred from their behavior in the respirator and from the psychiatric interviews and psychological tests, we got the impression that Subject 1 was self-conscious, introspective, and involved in chronic self-searching, whereas Subject 2 was guarded, defensive, and relatively unable to look into himself without considerable fear and anxiety. Both were trying to establish masculine identities, but they were using different methods. Subject 1 adopted an aloof, critical, "sour grapes" approach to life and related to people and problems in an intellectualized manner. Subject 2 aspired to high status and independence and had at the same time a compelling need for other people. He did not recognize or accept his strong underlying resentment of authority figures. Subject 1 thus seemed to have a better understanding of himself than Subject 2, or at least to be more willing to accept the possibility that he might not achieve his fantasied goals. Subject 2 became anxious and rigid in loosely structured situations—situations in which rules and procedures were vague and he was called on to give free reign to his imagination.

Subject 1 reacted to his confinement in the respirator with a seeming release of his tensions through verbalization and motor activity. His psychiatric history indicated that his usual defense patterns were rationalization, fantasy formation, repression, and counterphobic reactions, and the experimental situation brought out similar patterns. Subject 2 tried to deny his tensions—and succeeded, until they broke through in the form of claustrophobia, severe immobilization, and panic. As we learned later on, his reactions to isolation were in line with his usual defenses: denial, projection, and unrealistic distortion. Thus the stress of the experiment mobilized each subject's characteristic defense mechanisms.

As was mentioned earlier, case studies often suggest hypotheses that can then be tested in other research. The reactions of the two subjects described here suggest, for example, a relationship between the speed with which a person responds to stress and the effectiveness of his adjustment to it. The first subject began to react to his situation immediately, while the second responded hardly at all until just before he ended the experiment. His hallucinations, passivity when released from the respirator, and prolonged later anxiety all suggest that though he spent less time in the tank than the first subject, he was more acutely affected by the experience. This more severe disturbance on the part of the delayed responder is consistent with the findings of other research on various kinds of stress, including grief, battle fatigue, and chronic schizophrenia.

A second question raised by these two subjects is, Why, and in what way, is sensory deprivation so stressful? Our first subject was quite articulate about this, mentioning social isolation, difficulties in abstract thinking and in maintaining coherence, and restriction of movement, which he held responsible for his physical discomfort toward the end of the experiment. For both subjects, restriction of movement seemed especially difficult to bear. This is particularly interesting in view of the fact that severely paralyzed polio patients sometimes suffer hallucinations.

The precise connection between restraint of movement and hallucinations is not known, but it seems that the psychological effects of immobility depend partly on the unconscious meaning that restriction has for a person. Our first subject made it clear that his decision to end the experiment was not a rational one. He tried to resist, to talk himself out of it, but the need to escape became overpowering. The psychological urgency was reflected physiologically in the subject's acute restlessness, dry lips, and sweating. By the time he did ask to leave, he was in a state of near-panic. The second subject also showed acute stress in which unconscious factors played a part. As long as he could avoid the lack of structure inherent in the situation by sleeping, he was all right. But when he woke up he soon became extremely frightened. His hallucinations at that point were almost surely related to his disturbed personality. In both cases, it seems that physical immobility, combined with the monotonous environment and social isolation, reduced the capacity for rational thinking and permitted latent, largely unconscious material to emerge.

10

The Role of Movement
in the Development
of Visually Guided Behavior

RICHARD HELD
ALAN HEIN

Since the publication of D. O. Hebb's *The Organization of Behavior* in 1949, there has been considerable renewed interest among experimental psychologists in how exposure to the environment affects the development of an animal's capacity for perception of space and his ability to move around in it. The most common experimental approach to this question has been to subject newborn animals to some sort of environmental deprivation or restriction and to note the effects on the animals' sensorimotor development. A second approach uses adult subjects and assesses the effects of environmental change on abilities they have already developed.

One finding in the second type of experiment is that human adults

THE ROLE OF MOVEMENT IN THE DEVELOPMENT OF VISUALLY GUIDED BEHAVIOR
Adapted from *Journal of Comparative and Physiological Psychology* 56 (1963). Used by permission of the authors. This article originally appeared under the title "Movement-produced stimulation in the development of visually guided behavior."

can compensate fully and exactly for rearrangements of visual elements only if they are allowed to experience the rearranged environment through their own natural movements (Hein and Held, 1958; Held, 1955; Held and Bossom, 1961; Mikaelian and Held, in press). For instance, if a human adult's vision is distorted by a prism, he cannot adjust to the distortion and bring his hand-eye coordination back to its former level unless he is allowed to move his hand while viewing it. Simply viewing the hand is not enough.

It is our thesis that the development of normal sensorimotor coordination during infancy is also dependent on self-produced movement. However, an alternate theory holds that changes in sensory stimulation alone are sufficient for normal development. For example, Riesen and Aarons (1959) permitted kittens to see light and patterns but not to move about freely in the environment. Riesen (1961) explained certain behavioral deficits that appeared later by suggesting that the visual stimulation available to the kittens was not varied enough. We agree that variation in visual stimulation is essential to the development of normal coordination in young animals. We would add that variation in visual stimulation can be effective in avoiding these deficits only when self-produced movement brings it about.

In order to test these alternate theories, we designed an experiment using ten pairs of kittens as subjects. Exactly the same visual stimulation was available to both kittens in each pair, but only one of the two controlled its own movement through the visual environment. The apparatus used in the experiment is shown in Figure 10-1. It consisted of a large cylinder, the inside walls covered with vertical stripes of black and white masking tape, set on a rough masonite floor. In the center of the cylinder was a piece of equipment that supported a harness (for the active, or walking, kitten) on one side and a gondola (for the passive, or riding, kitten) on the opposite side. The riding kitten could not walk or otherwise control the movement of its gondola, but the visual stimulation it received was equivalent in amount and kind with the stimulation received by the walking kitten. The kittens could not see each other, and their neck yokes made it impossible for them to see their own paws and bodies.

The ten pairs of kittens were divided into two groups. The procedures used differed slightly for the two groups. The eight pairs of kittens in Group 1 were reared in total darkness from birth until they were well developed enough so that one member of the pair could move itself and its partner in the apparatus. At this point (when the kittens were between eight and twelve weeks old), the pair began using the apparatus for three hours a day. The two pairs of kittens in Group 2, by contrast, were reared in total darkness from birth to only two weeks of age. From two

FIGURE 10-1
Both kittens see the same things, but only one can control its movements through the visual environment.

to ten weeks, they were allowed to see the lighted laboratory for three hours a day but not to move about in it. At ten weeks, they began using the apparatus for three hours a day, just like the kittens in Group 1.

At several points during the experiment we performed various tests of the kittens' visually guided behavior. The two most important tests were the visually guided paw-placement test and the visual-cliff test.

Visually Guided Paw-placement Test (Riesen, 1961). The experimenter holds the kitten in his hands so that its head and forelegs are free. Then he moves the kitten slowly forward and down toward the edge of a table. A normally reared kitten extends its paws as it approaches the table edge, showing visual anticipation of contact.

Visual-cliff Test (Walk and Gibson, 1961). A visual cliff is an experimental device consisting of a horizontal plate of glass with a "deep" and a

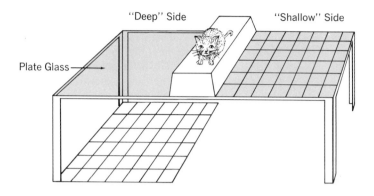

FIGURE 10-2

The visual cliff. A normal animal will descend from the platform to the shallow side and avoid the deep side.

"shallow" side, as illustrated in Figure 10-2. On the deep side, a piece of patterned material is placed 30 inches below the surface of the glass. On the shallow side, a piece of the same patterned material is attached to the bottom of the glass. The line that separates the two sides is covered by a narrow platform a few inches high. An animal placed on the platform can descend to the glass on either side; normally reared kittens choose the shallow side.

Each day, after the pairs of kittens in both groups had spent three hours in the apparatus, they were given the paw-placement test six times. The pairs of kittens in Group 1 proceeded to six tests on the visual cliff on the first day that either kitten in a pair passed the paw-placement test by extending its paws as the experimenter moved it toward the table top. The next day, both kittens in the pair were again given both tests six times. Then the passive kitten was put in a lighted room for 48 hours, with no restrictions on its movement, and retested.

The testing procedure for Group 2 was somewhat different. As with Group 1, the active kitten in each pair was tested on the visual cliff immediately after its first successful performance on the paw-placement test. However, the passive kitten was not tested on either paw placement or the visual cliff until it had spent a total of 126 hours, at 3 hours a day, riding in the gondola.

The results of the experiment are summarized in Table 10-1. The left-hand column shows the number of hours in the apparatus that was required for one kitten in each pair to develop the paw-placement response. In every case, the first kitten to give the correct response was the active

TABLE 10-1

Results of visually guided paw-placement and visual-cliff tests. All the active kittens passed the paw-placement test but their passive partners did not; thus the times given in the left-hand column are for the active kittens only. On the visual-cliff test, the active kittens behaved normally on all twelve trials, whereas the passive kittens seemed not to discriminate between the shallow and deep sides.

	Visually guided paw-placement test: hours in apparatus before one kitten passed test	*Visual-cliff test: descents to shallow side/deep side*	
Kittens in Group 1		*Active kitten*	*Passive kitten*
Pair 1	33	12/0	6/6
2	33	12/0	4/8
3	30	12/0	7/5
4	63	12/0	6/6
5	33	12/0	7/5
6	21	12/0	7/5
7	9	12/0	5/7
8	15	12/0	8/4
Kittens in Group 2			
Pair 1	30	12/0	6/6
2	33	12/0	8/4

one; after the same number of hours in the apparatus, none of the passive partners showed visually guided paw placement. The right-hand column shows how the kittens responded to their first twelve trials on the visual cliff. All the active kittens in both groups behaved like normally reared kittens: They chose the shallow side of the visual cliff every time. The passive kittens in Group 1, which tried the visual-cliff test on the same day as their active partners, showed no evidence that they could tell the shallow and deep sides apart. After 48 hours of freedom in the lighted room, however, they performed normally on the visual cliff; they also passed the paw-placement test. The passive kittens in Group 2, even after 126 hours of exposure to visual stimulation while riding in the gondola, failed to display visual paw placement and did not behave normally on the visual cliff.

These results confirm the theory that visual stimulation alone is not enough for the development of visually guided behavior. Self-produced movement, with simultaneous visual feedback, is essential. As was mentioned earlier, human adults cannot adjust fully to changes in the visual environment unless they are permitted to relearn visual-motor coordination through self-produced movement. Our results demonstrate that experiments on the effects of environmental deprivation during infancy and on environmental rearrangement during adulthood are complementary: Visual-motor coordination develops normally only when variation in the visual environment is brought about by the animal's own movement.

REFERENCES

Hein, A., and Held, R. Minimal conditions essential for complete relearning of hand-eye coordination with prismatic distortion of vision. Paper read at the Eastern Psychological Association, Philadelphia, 1958.

Held, R. Shifts in binaural localization, after prolonged exposures to atypical combinations of stimuli. *American Journal of Psychology* 68 (1955): 526–48.

Held, R., and Bossom, J. Neonatal deprivation and adult rearrangement: Complementary techniques for analyzing plastic sensory-motor coordinations. *Journal of Comparative and Physiological Psychology* 54 (1961): 33–37.

Mikaelian, H., and Held, R. Two types of adaptation to an optically-rotated visual field. *American Journal of Psychology*, in press.

Riesen, A. H. Studying perceptual development using the technique of sensory deprivation. *Journal of Nervous and Mental Diseases* 132 (1961): 21–25.

Riesen, A. H., and Aarons, L. Visual movement and intensity discrimination in cats after early deprivation of pattern vision. *Journal of Comparative and Physiological Psychology* 52 (1959): 142–49.

Walk, R. D., and Gibson, E. J. A comparative and analytical study of visual depth perception. *Psychological Monographs: General and Applied* 75 (1961).

11

Cultural Differences

in the Perception

of Geometric Illusions

MARSHALL H. SEGALL
DONALD T. CAMPBELL
MELVILLE J. HERSKOVITS

This study concerns the responses of people from European and non-European cultural backgrounds to optical illusions. The illusions were contained in drawings of two types of geometric figures, one type composed of acute and obtuse angles and the other type of right angles. There were clear differences among the Europeans and the non-Europeans in susceptibility to the two types of illusion. This finding suggests the existence of learned habits of perception that vary from culture to culture. It therefore supports the idea that we perceive shapes and other spatial relationships in ways that are learned through experience rather than determined by heredity—that is, it supports the nurture side of the so-called nature-nurture question.

CULTURAL DIFFERENCES IN THE PERCEPTION OF GEOMETRIC ILLUSIONS Adapted from *Science* 139 (February 22, 1963): 769–71. Copyright 1963 by the American Association for the Advancement of Science. Used by permission of Marshall H. Segall, Donald T. Campbell, and the American Association for the Advancement of Science.

Our experimental equipment consisted of thirty-nine drawings, each a variation on one of the basic figures shown in Figure 11-1. Over a six-year period (1956–62) the drawings were shown to a total of 1,878 people from seventeen different groups:

1. Fourteen non-European groups in twelve locations in Africa and one in the Philippines. The groups ranged in size from 46 to 344 and included children as well as adults.
2. Three "European" groups: a group of 44 South Africans of European descent, living in Johannesburg, a group of 30 undergraduates at Northwestern University, and a house-to-house sample of 208 residents of Evanston, Illinois.

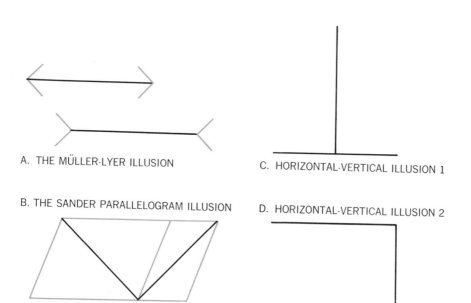

A. THE MÜLLER-LYER ILLUSION

B. THE SANDER PARALLELOGRAM ILLUSION

C. HORIZONTAL-VERTICAL ILLUSION 1

D. HORIZONTAL-VERTICAL ILLUSION 2

FIGURE 11-1

The four optical illusions on which the drawings used in the experiment were based. The lines to be compared are shown here in black. Which looks longer? In A and B, many people think the lines on the left are longer than the ones on the right; in C and D, many think the vertical lines are longer than the horizontal ones.

When a drawing was shown to a subject, his task was simply to indicate which of the two lines he thought was longer. The difference in the length of the lines varied from drawing to drawing. For example, in one drawing of the Müller-Lyer illusion (figure A) both lines were the same length; in another drawing the line on the right was very slightly longer than the one on the left; in a third, the line on the right was considerably longer; and so on. This made it possible to determine how much longer the line on the right had to be, compared to the one on the left, before a person susceptible to the illusion would see the two lines as equal.

After the responses had been collected, they were scored according to the number of times a subject was taken in by each illusion, that is, chose as longer the line that most people overestimate. We computed the mean score on each illusion for the seventeen experimental groups, and these and other findings were submitted to several types of statistical analysis.

The analysis showed that the three European groups (the South Africans, the Northwestern students, and the Evanston residents) were more likely to be fooled by the acute- and obtuse-angle illusions (figures A and B) than the non-European groups. On the right-angle illusions (figures C and D), by contrast, the Europeans did better than most non-European groups. Interestingly, however, a few non-European groups were even less susceptible to the right-angle illusions than the European groups were.

More than fifty years ago, research done by Rivers (1901) also indicated that non-Western peoples were less susceptible to the Müller-Lyer parallelogram illusion and more susceptible to the horizontal-vertical illusion than a group of Englishmen were. Since non-Europeans perform better than Europeans on one type of illusion and generally worse on the other, Rivers' findings and ours do not indicate that susceptibility to illusion is more likely among "primitive" than among "civilized" peoples. Instead, the evidence seems to point to cultural differences in visual inference systems—in habitual ways of viewing things—that are learned in response to different visual environments.

The environments in which most Americans and Europeans live include a great many rectangular objects, from buildings and windows to television screens and books. People who are used to such an environment may tend to interpret acute and obtuse angles drawn on a two-dimensional surface as if they represented rectangular objects in three-dimensional space. For example, they may see a parallelogram as a rectangle extending away from them, like a football field seen from the twenty-yard line. Accustomed to inferring the "real" length of lines that are foreshortened by perspective in three-dimensional figures such as buildings, they make similar (but incorrect) inferences about lines in two-dimensional figures such as a drawing of a parallelogram.

Similarly, the susceptibility of non-Europeans to the horizontal-vertical illusions can perhaps be traced to a habit of interpreting vertical lines as extensions away from the observer on a horizontal plane. For example, figures C and D might be interpreted as representing the intersection of two roads or paths on a plain, in which case the vertical line might be assumed to be longer than it looks. People who live where the terrain is open and flat would be more likely to form this perceptual habit than people who live in cities. However, people who live in cities and towns probably see more foreshortened vertical lines (hallways, street intersections) than those who live in rain forests or canyons. This may explain why a few non-European groups in our sample were even less likely than the Europeans to be fooled by horizontal-vertical illusions.

However, our purpose here is not to isolate the environmental features that account for our findings. It is to report the existence of cultural differences in susceptibility to geometric illusions and to point out that they seem to be based not on heredity but on differences in learned visual habits.

REFERENCE

Rivers, W. H. R. Vision. *Reports of the Cambridge anthropological expedition to the Torres Straits.* Edited by A. C. Haddon. Vol. 2, Part 1. Cambridge: The University Press, 1901.

Language
and Thinking

The physiology, problem-solving ability, and other characteristics of some animals have led psychologists to suspect that, with proper training, they might learn to talk. Chimpanzees, for example, are sociable and highly imitative, and they exchange simple messages with other chimps through noises and gestures. They also show an understanding of symbols that is promising for language learning. A chimp can learn to put poker chips into a vending machine in order to get food, which requires making a mental connection between the poker chip and the food similar to the mental connection a person makes between a word and the thing it represents. Yet so far no chimpanzee, even when raised as if it were a human infant, has managed to learn to say more than a few "words."

Under natural conditions, chimpanzees vocalize very little, but they use their hands a great deal. Thus R. Allen Gardner and Beatrice T. Gardner, authors of "Teaching Sign Language to a Chimpanzee," reasoned that a manual language might be more appropriate to chimps than a vocal one. Instead of trying to teach spoken words to their chimpanzee, a female named Washoe, they trained her in the manual sign language of the deaf. The program was remarkably successful. In twenty-two months, Washoe acquired a vocabulary of over thirty signs—seven times larger than the vocabulary of her nearest competitor, who was taught human speech. Moreover, Washoe used the signs in some remarkably "human" ways. She demonstrated the fairly advanced language-learning processes called *differentiation* and *transfer:* she learned to sign "flower" for flowers but not for other things with odors (differentiation) and to sign "key" not only for the particular key used to teach her the sign but for all keys (transfer). She combined signs into meaningful, sentence-like units (the sign for "gimme" followed by the sign for "tickle" means "I want to be tickled") and also formed new compound words (a three-sign unit, "open-food-drink," stands for "refrigerator").

The second article in this section, "How Shall a Thing Be Called?" by Roger Brown, concerns language learning in human infants. Brown asks a simple but profound question: When a mother (or another adult) names an object for a child, how does she decide which word to use? When a child holds up a dime, is his mother more likely to say "dime" than "coin" or "money"? Since short, concrete words are thought to be easiest for children to understand, one might suppose that the mother's choice would be based on the length and abstractness of the different labels that could be used. If a child points to a spoon, his mother will probably use the short, concrete word "spoon" instead of the longer, more abstract word "silverware." On the other hand, she will probably call the food on the plate "fish" rather than "bass" or "perch," even though these words are more specific than "fish" and just as short.

Brown concludes that although length and abstractness do influence the mother's choice, the most important factor is her estimate of which word will be most useful to the child in his everyday dealings with the world. Without being aware of it, the mother knows that it is useful for a child in our culture to know the difference between a spoon and a fork but not necessary that he be able to tell bass from perch. In another society, say one in which eating tools are rarely used and fish is an important food, mothers might use a single, general word for spoons and forks but teach children specific names for different kinds of fish. Thus the words adults use to label things for their children can be seen as part of a larger socialization process intended to prepare the child for participation in the existing adult society.

In the final article, "Toward a Theory of Creativity," Philip W. Jackson and Samuel E. Messick address a perennial problem in psychology—defining creativity—from an unusual angle. Instead of analyzing the characteristics of creative *people*, they attempt to identify the properties of creative *products*. They describe four properties that highly creative products (scientific discoveries as well as works of art) seem to possess: unusualness, appropriateness, power to make us see reality in a new way, and condensation of meaning. Corresponding to these four properties, they suggest, are four standards by which creative products tend to be judged, four aesthetic responses that they usually elicit from viewers, and four personality tendencies that may characterize those who make creative products.

12

Teaching Sign Language

to a Chimpanzee

R . A L L E N   G A R D N E R

B E A T R I C E   T .   G A R D N E R

The extent to which another species might be able to use human language is a classical problem in comparative psychology. One approach to this problem is to consider the nature of language, the processes of learning, the neural mechanisms of learning and of language, and the genetic basis of these mechanisms, and then, while recognizing certain gaps in what is known about these factors, to attempt to arrive at an answer by dint of careful scholarship. An alternative approach is to try to teach a form of human language to an animal. We chose the latter alternative and, in June 1966, began training an infant female chimpanzee, named Washoe, to use the gestural language of the deaf. Within the first twenty-two months of training it became evident that we had been correct in at least one major aspect of method, the use of a gestural language. Addi-

TEACHING SIGN LANGUAGE TO A CHIMPANZEE   Reprinted from *Science* 165 (August 15, 1969): 664–72. Copyright 1969 by the American Association for the Advancement of Science. Used by permission of the authors and the American Association for the Advancement of Science.

tional aspects of method have evolved in the course of the project. These and some implications of our early results can now be described in a way that may be useful in other studies of communicative behavior. Accordingly, in this article we discuss the considerations which led us to use the chimpanzee as a subject and American Sign Language (the language used by the deaf in North America) as a medium of communication; describe the general methods of training as they were initially conceived and as they developed in the course of the project; and summarize those results that could be reported with some degree of confidence by the end of the first phase of the project.

Preliminary Considerations

THE CHIMPANZEE AS A SUBJECT

Some discussion of the chimpanzee as an experimental subject is in order because this species is relatively uncommon in the psychological laboratory. Whether or not the chimpanzee is the most intelligent animal after man can be disputed; the gorilla, the orangutan, and even the dolphin have their loyal partisans in this debate. Nevertheless, it is generally conceded that chimpanzees are highly intelligent, and that members of this species might be intelligent enough for our purposes. Of equal or greater importance is their sociability and their capacity for forming strong attachments to human beings. We want to emphasize this trait of sociability; it seems highly likely that it is essential for the development of language in human beings, and it was a primary consideration in our choice of a chimpanzee as a subject.

Affectionate as chimpanzees are, they are still wild animals, and this is a serious disadvantage. Most psychologists are accustomed to working with animals that have been chosen, and sometimes bred, for docility and adaptability to laboratory procedures. The difficulties presented by the wild nature of an experimental animal must not be underestimated. Chimpanzees are also very strong animals; a full-grown specimen is likely to weigh more than 120 pounds (55 kilograms) and is estimated to be from three to five times as strong as a man, pound-for-pound. Coupled with the wildness, this great strength presents serious difficulties for a procedure that requires interaction at close quarters with a free-living animal. We have always had to reckon with the likelihood that at some point Washoe's physical maturity will make this procedure prohibitively dangerous.

A more serious disadvantage is that human speech sounds are unsuitable as a medium of communication for the chimpanzee. The vocal apparatus of the chimpanzee is very different from that of man (Bryan, 1963). More important, the vocal behavior of the chimpanzee is very different from that of man. Chimpanzees do make many different sounds, but generally vocalization occurs in situations of high excitement and tends to be specific to the exciting situations. Undisturbed, chimpanzees are usually silent. Thus, it is unlikely that a chimpanzee could be trained to make refined use of its vocalizations. Moreover, the intensive work of Hayes and Hayes (1951) with the chimpanzee Viki indicates that a vocal language is not appropriate for this species. The Hayeses used modern, sophisticated, psychological methods and seem to have spared no effort to teach Viki to make speech sounds. Yet in six years Viki learned only four sounds that approximated English words. (Dr. Hayes also informed us that Viki used a few additional sounds which, while not resembling English words, were used for specific requests.)

Use of the hands, however, is a prominent feature of chimpanzee behavior; manipulatory mechanical problems are their forte. More to the point, even caged, laboratory chimpanzees develop begging and similar gestures spontaneously (Yerkes, 1943), while individuals that have had extensive contact with human beings have displayed an even wider variety of communicative gestures (Hayes and Hayes, 1955; Kellogg and Kellogg, 1967; Kellogg, 1968). In our choice of sign language we were influenced more by the behavioral evidence that this medium of communication was appropriate to the species than by anatomical evidence of structural similarity between the hands of chimpanzees and of men. The Hayeses point out that human tools and mechanical devices are constructed to fit the human hand, yet chimpanzees have little difficulty in using these devices with great skill. Nevertheless, they seem unable to adapt their vocalizations to approximate human speech.

Psychologists who work extensively with the instrumental conditioning of animals become sensitive to the need to use responses that are suited to the species they wish to study. Lever-pressing in rats is not an arbitrary response invented by Skinner to confound the mentalists; it is a type of response commonly made by rats when they are first placed in a Skinner box. The exquisite control of instrumental behavior by schedules of reward is achieved only if the original responses are well chosen. We chose a language based on gestures because we reasoned that gestures for the chimpanzee should be analogous to bar-pressing for rats, key-pecking for pigeons, and babbling for humans.

AMERICAN SIGN LANGUAGE

Two systems of manual communication are used by the deaf. One system is the manual alphabet, or finger spelling, in which configurations of the hand correspond to letters of the alphabet. In this system the words of a spoken language, such as English, can be spelled out manually. The other system, sign language, consists of a set of manual configurations and gestures that correspond to particular words or concepts. Unlike finger spelling, which is the direct encoding of a spoken language, sign languages have their own rules of usage. Word-for-sign translation between a spoken language and a sign language yields results that are similar to those of word-for-word translation between two spoken languages: the translation is often passable, though awkward, but it can also be ambiguous or quite nonsensical. Also, there are national and regional variations in sign languages that are comparable to those of spoken languages.

We chose for this project the American Sign Language (ASL), which, with certain regional variations, is used by the deaf in North America. This particular sign language has recently been the subject of formal analysis (Stokoe, Casterline, and Croneberg, 1965; McCall, 1965). The ASL can be compared to pictograph writing in which some symbols are quite arbitrary and some are quite representational or iconic, but all are arbitrary to some degree. For example, in ASL the sign for "always" is made by holding the hand in a fist, index finger extended (the pointing hand), while rotating the arm at the elbow. This is clearly an arbitrary representation of the concept "always." The sign for "flower," however, is highly iconic; it is made by holding the fingers of one hand extended, all five fingertips touching (the tapered hand), and touching the fingertips first to one nostril then to the other, as if sniffing a flower. While this is an iconic sign for "flower," it is only one of a number of conventions by which the concept "flower" could be iconically represented; it is thus arbitrary to some degree. Undoubtedly, many of the signs of ASL that seem quite arbitrary today once had an iconic origin that was lost through years of stylized usage. Thus, the signs of ASL are neither uniformly arbitrary nor uniformly iconic; rather the degree of abstraction varies from sign to sign over a wide range. This would seem to be a useful property of ASL for our research.

The literate deaf typically use a combination of ASL and finger spelling; for purposes of this project we have avoided the use of finger spelling as much as possible. A great range of expression is possible within the limits of ASL. We soon found that a good way to practice signing among ourselves was to render familiar songs and poetry into signs; as far as we can judge, there is no message that cannot be rendered faithfully (apart from the usual problems of translation from one language to another). Technical terms and proper names are a problem when first introduced, but within any community of signers it is easy to agree on a convention for any commonly used term. For example, among ourselves we do not finger-spell the words *psychologist* and *psychology*, but render them as "think doctor" and "think science." Or, among users of ASL, "California" can be finger-spelled but is commonly rendered as "golden playland." (Incidentally, the sign for "gold" is made by plucking at the earlobe with thumb and forefinger, indicating an earring—another example of an iconic sign that is at the same time arbitrary and stylized.)

The fact that ASL is in current use by human beings is an additional advantage. The early linguistic environment of the deaf children of deaf parents is in some respects similar to the linguistic environment that we could provide for an experimental subject. This should permit some comparative evaluation of Washoe's eventual level of competence. For example, in discussing Washoe's early performance with deaf parents we have been told that many of her variants of standard signs are similar to the baby-talk variants commonly observed when human children sign.

WASHOE

Having decided on a species and a medium of communication, our next concern was to obtain an experimental subject. It is altogether possible that there is some critical early age for the acquisition of this type of behavior. On the other hand, newborn chimpanzees tend to be quite helpless and vegetative. They are also considerably less hardy than older infants. Nevertheless, we reasoned that the dangers of starting too late were much greater than the dangers of starting too early, and we sought the youngest infant we could get. Newborn laboratory chimpanzees are very scarce, and we found that the youngest laboratory infant we could get would be about two years old at the time we planned to start the project. It seemed preferable to obtain a wild-caught infant. Wild-caught infants are usually at least eight to ten months old before they are available for research. This is because infants rarely reach the United States before they are five months old, and to this age must be added one or two months before final purchase and two or three months for quarantine and other medical services.

We named our chimpanzee Washoe for Washoe County, the home of the University of Nevada. Her exact age will never be known, but from her weight and dentition we estimated her age to be between eight and fourteen months at the end of June, 1966, when she first arrived at our laboratory. (Her dentition has continued to agree with this initial estimate, but her weight has increased rather more than would be expected.) This is very young for a chimpanzee. The best available information indicates that infants are completely dependent until the age of two years and semidependent until the age of four; the first signs of sexual maturity (for example, menstruation, sexual swelling) begin to appear at about eight years, and full adult growth is reached between the ages of twelve and sixteen (Goodall, 1965; Riopelle and Rogers, 1965). As for the complete lifespan, captive specimens have survived for well over forty years. Washoe was indeed very young when she arrived; she did not have her first canines or molars, her hand-eye coordination was rudimentary, she had only begun to crawl about, and she slept a great deal. Apart from making friends with her and adapting her to the daily routine, we could accomplish little during the first few months.

LABORATORY CONDITIONS

At the outset we were quite sure that Washoe could learn to make various signs in order to obtain food, drink, and other things. For the project to be a success, we felt that something more must be developed. We wanted Washoe not only to ask for objects but to answer questions about them and also to ask us questions. We wanted to develop behavior that could be described as conversation. With this in mind, we attempted to provide Washoe with an environment that might be conducive to this sort of behavior. Confinement was to be minimal, about the same as that of human infants. Her human companions were to be friends and playmates as well as providers and protectors, and they were to introduce a great many games and activities that would be likely to result in maximum interaction with Washoe.

In practice, such an environment is readily achieved with a chimpanzee; bonds of warm affection have always been established between Washoe and her several human companions. We have enjoyed the interaction almost as much as Washoe has, within the limits of human endurance. A number of human companions have been enlisted to participate in the project and relieve each other at intervals, so that at least one person would be with Washoe during all her waking hours. At first we feared that such frequent changes would be disturbing, but Washoe seemed to adapt very well to this procedure. Apparently it is possible to provide an infant chimpanzee with affection on a shift basis.

All of Washoe's human companions have been required to master ASL and to use it extensively in her presence, in association with interesting activities and events and also in a general way, as one chatters at a human infant in the course of the day. The ASL has been used almost exclusively, although occasional finger spelling has been permitted. From time to time, of course, there are lapses into spoken English, as when medical personnel must examine Washoe. At one time, we considered an alternative procedure in which we would sign and speak English to Washoe simultaneously, thus giving her an additional source of informative cues.

We rejected this procedure, reasoning that, if she should come to understand speech sooner or more easily than ASL, then she might not pay sufficient attention to our gestures. Another alternative, that of speaking English among ourselves and signing to Washoe, was also rejected. We reasoned that this would make it seem that big chimps talk and only little chimps sign, which might give signing an undesirable social status.

The environment we are describing is not a silent one. The human beings can vocalize in many ways, laughing and making sounds of pleasure and displeasure. Whistles and drums are sounded in a variety of imitation games, and hands are clapped for attention. The rule is that all meaningful sounds, whether vocalized or not, must be sounds that a chimpanzee can imitate.

Training Methods

IMITATION

The imitativeness of apes is proverbial, and rightly so. Those who have worked closely with chimpanzees have frequently remarked on their readiness to engage in visually guided imitation. Consider the following typical comment of Yerkes:

> Chim and Panzee would imitate many of my acts, but never have I heard them imitate a sound and rarely make a sound peculiarly their own in response to mine. As previously stated, their imitative tendency is as remarkable for its specialization and limitations as for its strength. It seems to be controlled chiefly by visual stimuli. Things which are seen tend to be imitated or reproduced. What is heard is not reproduced. Obviously an animal which lacks the tendency to reinstate auditory stimuli —in other words to imitate sounds—cannot reasonably be expected to talk. The human infant exhibits this tendency to a remarkable degree. So also does the parrot. If the imitative tendency of the parrot could be coupled with the quality of intelligence of the chimpanzee, the latter undoubtedly could speak (Yerkes and Learned, 1925).

In the course of their work with Viki, the Hayeses devised a game in which Viki would imitate various actions on hearing the command "Do this" (Hayes and Hayes, 1952). Once established, this was an effective means of training Viki to perform actions that could be visually guided. The same method should be admirably suited to training a chimpanzee to use sign language; accordingly we have directed much effort toward establishing a version of the "Do this" game with Washoe. Getting

Washoe to imitate us was not difficult, for she did so quite spontaneously, but getting her to imitate on command has been another matter altogether. It was not until the sixteenth month of the project that we achieved any degree of control over Washoe's imitation of gestures. Eventually we got to a point where she would imitate a simple gesture, such as pulling at her ears, or a series of such gestures—first we make a gesture, then she imitates, then we make a second gesture, she imitates the second gesture, and so on—for the reward of being tickled. Up to this writing, however, imitation of this sort has not been an important method for introducing new signs into Washoe's vocabulary.

As a method of prompting, we have been able to use imitation extensively to increase the frequency and refine the form of signs. Washoe sometimes fails to use a new sign in an appropriate situation, or uses another, incorrect sign. At such times we can make the correct sign to Washoe, repeating the performance until she makes the sign herself. (With more stable signs, more indirect forms of prompting can be used— for example, pointing at, or touching, Washoe's hand or a part of her body that should be involved in the sign; making the sign for "sign," which is equivalent to saying "Speak up"; or asking a question in signs, such as "What do you want?" or "What is it?") Again, with new signs, and often with old signs as well, Washoe can lapse into what we refer to as poor "diction." Of course, a great deal of slurring and a wide range of variants are permitted in ASL as in any spoken language. In any event, Washoe's diction has frequently been improved by the simple device of repeating, in exaggeratedly correct form, the sign she has just made, until she repeats it herself in more correct form. On the whole, she has responded quite well to prompting, but there are strict limits to its use with a wild animal—one that is probably quite spoiled, besides. Pressed too hard, Washoe can become completely diverted from her original object; she may ask for something entirely different, run away, go into a tantrum, or even bite her tutor.

Chimpanzees also imitate, after some delay, and this delayed imitation can be quite elaborate (Hayes and Hayes, 1952). The following is a typical example of Washoe's delayed imitation. From the beginning of the project she was bathed regularly and according to a standard routine. Also, from her second month with us, she always had dolls to play with. One day, during the tenth month of the project, she bathed one of her dolls in the way we usually bathed her. She filled her little bathtub with water, dunked the doll in the tub, then took it out and dried it with a towel. She has repeated the entire performance, or parts of it, many times since, sometimes also soaping the doll.

This is a type of imitation that may be very important in the acquisition of language by human children, and many of our procedures with Washoe were devised to capitalize on it. Routine activities—feeding, dressing, bathing, and so on—have been highly ritualized, with appropriate signs figuring prominently in the rituals. Many games have been invented which can be accompanied by appropriate signs. Objects and activities have been named as often as possible, especially when Washoe seemed to be paying particular attention to them. New objects and new examples of familiar objects, including pictures, have been continually brought to her attention, together with the appropriate signs. She likes to ride in automobiles, and a ride in an automobile, including the preparations for a ride, provides a wealth of sights that can be accompanied by signs. A good destination for a ride is a home or the university nursery school, both well stocked with props for language lessons.

The general principle should be clear: Washoe has been exposed to a wide variety of activities and objects, together with their appropriate signs, in the hope that she would come to associate the signs with their referents and later make the signs herself. We have reason to believe that she has come to understand a large vocabulary of signs. This was expected, since a number of chimpanzees have acquired extensive understanding vocabularies of spoken words, and there is evidence that even dogs can acquire a sizable understanding vocabulary of spoken words (Warden and Warner, 1928). The understanding vocabulary that Washoe has acquired, however, consists of signs that a chimpanzee can imitate.

Some of Washoe's signs seem to have been originally acquired by delayed imitation. A good example is the sign for "toothbrush." A part of the daily routine has been to brush her teeth after every meal. When this routine was first introduced Washoe generally resisted it. She gradually came to submit with less and less fuss, and after many months she would even help or sometimes brush her teeth herself. Usually, having finished her meal, Washoe would try to leave her highchair; we would restrain her, signing "First, toothbrushing, then you can go." One day, in the tenth month of the project, Washoe was visiting the Gardner home and found her way into the bathroom. She climbed up on the counter, looked at our mug full of toothbrushes, and signed "toothbrush." At the time, we believed that Washoe understood this sign but we had not seen her use it. She had no reason to ask for the toothbrushes, because they were well within her reach, and it is most unlikely that she was asking to have her teeth brushed. This was our first observation, and one of the clearest examples, of behavior in which Washoe seemed to name an object or an event for no obvious motive other than communication.

Following this observation, the toothbrushing routine at mealtime was altered. First, imitative prompting was introduced. Then as the sign became more reliable, her rinsing-mug and toothbrush were displayed prominently until she made the sign. By the fourteenth month she was making the "toothbrush" sign at the end of meals with little or no prompting: in fact she has called for her toothbrush in a peremptory fashion when its appearance at the end of a meal was delayed. The "toothbrush" sign is not merely a reponse cued by the end of a meal; Washoe retained her ability to name toothbrushes when they were shown to her at other times.

The sign for "flower" may also have been acquired by delayed imitation. From her first summer with us, Washoe showed a great interest in flowers, and we took advantage of this by providing many flowers and pictures of flowers accompanied by the appropriate sign. Then one day in the fifteenth month she made the sign, spontaneously, while she and a companion were walking toward a flower garden. As in the case of "toothbrush," we believed that she understood the sign at this time, but we had made no attempt to elicit it from her except by making it ourselves in appropriate situations. Again, after the first observation, we proceeded to elicit this sign as often as possible by a variety of methods, most frequently by showing her a flower and giving it to her if she made the sign for it. Eventually the sign became very reliable and could be elicited by a variety of flowers and pictures of flowers.

It is difficult to decide which signs were acquired by the method of delayed imitation. The first appearance of these signs is likely to be sudden and unexpected; it is possible that some inadvertent movement of Washoe's has been interpreted as meaningful by one of her devoted companions. If the first observer were kept from reporting the observation and from making any direct attempts to elicit the sign again, then it might be possible to obtain independent verification. Quite understandably, we have been more interested in raising the frequency of new signs than in evaluating any particular method of training.

BABBLING

Because the Hayeses were attempting to teach Viki to speak English, they were interested in babbling, and during the first year of their project they were encouraged by the number and variety of spontaneous vocalizations that Viki made. But, in time, Viki's spontaneous vocalizations decreased further and further to the point where the Hayeses felt that there was almost no vocal babbling from which to shape spoken language. In planning this project we expected a great deal of manual "babbling," but during the early months we observed very little behavior of this kind. In the course of the project, however, there has been a great increase in manual babbling. We have been particularly encouraged by the increase in movements that involve touching parts of the head and body, since these are important components of many signs. Also, more and more frequently, when Washoe has been unable to get something that she wants, she has burst into a flurry of random flourishes and arm-waving.

We have encouraged Washoe's babbling by our responsiveness; clapping, smiling, and repeating the gesture much as you might repeat "goo goo" to a human infant. If the babbled gesture has resembled a sign in ASL, we have made the correct form of the sign and have attempted to engage in some appropriate activity. The sign for "funny" was probably acquired in this way. It first appeared as a spontaneous babble that lent itself readily to a simple imitation game—first Washoe signed "funny," then we did, then she did, and so on. We would laugh and smile during the interchanges that she initiated, and initiate the game ourselves when something funny happened. Eventually Washoe came to use the "funny" sign spontaneously in roughly appropriate situations.

Closely related to babbling are some gestures that seem to have appeared independently of any deliberate training on our part, and that resemble signs so closely that we could incorporate them into Washoe's repertoire with little or no modification. Almost from the first she had a begging gesture—an extension of her open hand, palm up, toward one of us. She made this gesture in situations in which she wanted aid and in situations in which we were holding some object that she wanted. The ASL signs for "give me" and "come" are very similar to this, except that they involve a prominent beckoning movement. Gradually Washoe came to incorporate a beckoning wrist movement into her use of this sign. In Table 12-1 we refer to this sign as "come-gimme." As Washoe has come to use it, the sign is not simply a modification of the original begging gesture. For example, very commonly she reaches forward with one hand (palm up) while she gestures with the other hand (palm down) held near her head. (The result resembles a classic fencing posture.)

Another sign of this type is the sign for "hurry," which, so far, Washoe has always made by shaking her open hand vigorously at the wrist. This first appeared as an impatient flourish following some request that she had made in signs; for example, after making the "open" sign before a door. The correct ASL for "hurry" is very close, and we began to use it often, ourselves, in appropriate contexts. We believe that Washoe has come to use this sign in a meaningful way, because she has frequently used it when she, herself, is in a hurry—for example, when rushing to her nursery chair.

INSTRUMENTAL CONDITIONING

It seems intuitively unreasonable that the acquisition of language by human beings could be strictly a matter of reiterated instrumental conditioning—that a child acquires language after the fashion of a rat that is conditioned, first, to press a lever for food in the presence of one stimulus, then to turn a wheel in the presence of another stimulus, and so on until a large repertoire of discriminated responses is acquired. Nevertheless, the so-called "trick vocabulary" of early childhood is probably acquired in this way, and this may be a critical stage in the acquisition of language by children. In any case, a minimal objective of this project was to teach Washoe as many signs as possible by whatever procedures we could enlist. Thus, we have not hesitated to use conventional procedures of instrumental conditioning.

Anyone who becomes familiar with young chimpanzees soon learns about their passion for being tickled. There is no doubt that tickling is the most effective reward that we have used with Washoe. In the early months, when we would pause in our tickling, Washoe would indicate that she wanted more tickling by taking our hands and placing them against her ribs or around her neck. The meaning of these gestures was unmistakable, but since we were not studying our human ability to interpret her chimpanzee gestures, we decided to shape an arbitrary response that she could use to ask for more tickling. We noted that, when being tickled, she tended to bring her arms together to cover the place being tickled. The result was a very crude approximation of the ASL sign for "more." (See Table 12-1.) Thus, we would stop tickling and then pull Washoe's arms away from her body. When we released her arms and threatened to resume tickling, she tended to bring her hands together again. If she brought them back together, we would tickle her again. From time to time we would stop tickling and wait for her to put her hands together by herself. At first, any approximation to the "more" sign, however crude, was rewarded. Later, we required closer approximations and introduced imitative prompting. Soon, a very good version of the "more" sign could be obtained, but it was quite specific to the tickling situation.

In the sixth month of the project we were able to get "more" signs for a new game that consisted of pushing Washoe across the floor in a laundry basket. In this case we did not use the shaping procedure but, from the start, used imitative prompting to elicit the "more" sign. Soon after the "more" sign became spontaneous and reliable in the laundry-basket game, it began to appear as a request for more swinging (by the arms)—again, after first being elicited with imitative prompting. From this point on, Washoe transferred the "more" sign to all activities, including feeding. The transfer was usually spontaneous, occurring when there was some pause in a desired activity or when some object was removed. Often we ourselves were not sure that Washoe wanted more until she signed to us.

The sign for "open" had a similar history. When Washoe wanted to

TABLE 12-1

Signs used reliably by chimpanzee Washoe within twenty-two months of the beginning of training. The signs are listed in the order of their original appearance in her repertoire. (See text for the criterion of reliability and for the method of assigning the date of original appearance.)

Signs	Description	Context
Come-gimme	Beckoning motion, with wrist or knuckles as pivot.	Sign made to persons or animals, also for objects out of reach. Often combined: "come tickle," "gimme sweet," etc.
More	Fingertips are brought together, usually overhead. (Correct ASL form: tips of the tapered hand touch repeatedly.)	When asking for continuation or repetition of activities such as swinging or tickling, for second helpings of food, etc. Also used to ask for repetition of some performance, such as a somersault.
Up	Arm extends upward, and index finger may also point up.	Wants a lift to reach objects such as grapes on vine, or leaves; or wants to be placed on someone's shoulders; or wants to leave potty-chair.
Sweet	Index or index and second fingers touch tip of wagging tongue. (Correct ASL form: index and second fingers extended side by side.)	For dessert; used spontaneously at end of meal. Also, when asking for candy.
Open	Flat hands are placed side by side, palms down, then drawn apart while rotated to palms up.	At door of house, room, car, refrigerator, or cupboard; on containers such as jars; and on faucets.
Tickle	The index finger of one hand is drawn across the back of the other hand. (Related to ASL "touch.")	For tickling or for chasing games.
Go	Opposite of "come-gimme."	While walking hand-in-hand or riding on someone's shoulders. Washoe usually indicates the direction desired.
Out	Curved hand grasps tapered hand; then tapered hand is withdrawn upward.	When passing through doorways; until recently, used for both "in" and "out." Also, when asking to be taken outdoors.
Hurry	Open hand is shaken at the wrist. (Correct ASL form: index and second fingers extended side by side.)	Often follows signs such as "come-gimme," "out," "open," and "go," particularly if there is a delay before Washoe is obeyed. Also, used while watching her meal being prepared.

Signs	Description	Context
Hear-listen	Index finger touches ear.	For loud or strange sounds: bells, car horns, sonic booms, etc. Also, for asking someone to hold a watch to her ear.
Toothbrush	Index finger is used as brush, to rub front teeth.	When Washoe has finished her meal, or at other times when shown a toothbrush.
Drink	Thumb is extended from fisted hand and touches mouth.	For water, formula, soda pop, etc. For soda pop, often combined with "sweet."
Hurt	Extended index fingers are jabbed toward each other. Can be used to indicate location of pain.	To indicate cuts and bruises on herself or on others. Can be elicited by red stains on a person's skin or by tears in clothing.
Sorry	Fisted hand clasps and unclasps at shoulder. (Correct ASL form: fisted hand is rubbed over heart with circular motion.)	After biting someone, or when someone has been hurt in another way (not necessarily by Washoe). When told to apologize for mischief.
Funny	Tip of index finger presses nose, and Washoe snorts. (Correct ASL form: index and second fingers used; no snort.)	When soliciting interaction play, and during games. Occasionally, when being pursued after mischief.
Please	Open hand is drawn across chest. (Correct ASL form: fingertips used, and circular motion.)	When asking for objects and activities. Frequently combined: "Please go," "Out, please," "Please drink."
Food-eat	Several fingers of one hand are placed in mouth. (Correct ASL form: fingertips of tapered hand touch mouth repeatedly.)	During meals and preparation of meals.
Flower	Tip of index finger touches one or both nostrils. (Correct ASL form: tips of tapered hand touch first one nostril, then the other.)	For flowers.
Cover-blanket	Draws one hand toward self over the back of the other.	At bedtime or naptime, and, on cold days, when Washoe wants to be taken out.
Dog	Repeated slapping on thigh.	For dogs and for barking.
You	Index finger points at a person's chest.	Indicates successive turns in games. Also used in response to

TABLE 12-1   (*Continued*)

Signs	*Description*	*Context*
		questions such as "Who tickle?" "Who brush?"
Napkin-bib	Fingertips wipe the mouth region.	For bib, for washcloth, and for Kleenex.
In	Opposite of "out."	Wants to go indoors, or wants someone to join her indoors.
Brush	The fisted hand rubs the back of the open hand several times. (Adapted from ASL "polish.")	For hairbrush, and when asking for brushing.
Hat	Palm pats top of head.	For hats and caps.
I-me	Index finger points at, or touches, chest.	Indicates Washoe's turn, when she and a companion share food, drink, etc. Also used in phrases, such as "I drink," and in reply to questions, such as "Who tickle?" (Washoe: "you"); "Who I tickle?" (Washoe: "Me.")
Shoes	The fisted hands are held side by side and strike down on shoes or floor. (Correct ASL form: the sides of the fisted hands strike against each other.)	For shoes and boots.
Smell	Palm is held before nose and moved slightly upward several times.	For scented objects: tobacco, perfume, sage, etc.
Pants	Palms of the flat hands are drawn up against the body toward waist.	For diapers, rubber pants, trousers.
Clothes	Fingertips brush down the chest.	For Washoe's jacket, nightgown, and shirts; also for our clothing.
Cat	Thumb and index finger grasp cheek hair near side of mouth and are drawn outward (representing cat's whiskers).	For cats.
Key	Palm of one hand is repeatedly touched with the index finger of the other. (Correct ASL form: crooked index finger is rotated against palm.)	Used for keys and locks and to ask us to unlock a door.
Baby	One forearm is placed in the crook of the other, as if cradling a baby.	For dolls, including animal dolls such as a toy horse and duck.
Clean	The open palm of one hand is passed over the open palm of the other.	Used when Washoe is washing, or being washed, or when a companion is washing hands or some other object. Also used for "soap."

get through a door, she tended to hold up both hands and pound on the door with her palms or her knuckles. This is the beginning position for the "open" sign. (See Table 12-1.) By waiting for her to place her hands on the door and then lift them, and also by imitative prompting, we were able to shape a good approximation of the "open" sign, and would reward this by opening the door. Originally she was trained to make this sign for three particular doors that she used every day. Washoe transferred this sign to all doors; then to containers such as the refrigerator, cupboards, drawers, briefcases, boxes, and jars; and eventually—an invention of Washoe's—she used it to ask us to turn on water faucets.

In the case of "more" and "open" we followed the conventional laboratory procedure of waiting for Washoe to make some response that could be shaped into the sign we wished her to acquire. We soon found that this was not necessary; Washoe could acquire signs that were first elicited by our holding her hands, forming them into the desired configuration, and then putting them through the desired movement. Since this procedure of guidance is usually much more practical than waiting for a spontaneous approximation to occur at a favorable moment, we have used it much more frequently.

Results

VOCABULARY

In the early stages of the project we were able to keep fairly complete records of Washoe's daily signing behavior. But, as the amount of signing behavior and the number of signs to be monitored increased, our initial attempts to obtain exhaustive records became prohibitively cumbersome. During the sixteenth month we settled on the following procedure. When a new sign was introduced we waited until it had been reported by three different observers as having occurred in an appropriate context and spontaneously (that is, with no prompting other than a question such as "What is it?" or "What do you want?"). The sign was then added to a checklist in which its occurrence, form, context, and the kind of prompting required were recorded. Two such checklists were filled out each day, one for the first half of the day and one for the second half. For a criterion of acquisition we chose a reported frequency of at least one appropriate and spontaneous occurrence each day over a period of fifteen consecutive days.

In Table 12-1 we have listed thirty signs that met this criterion by the end of the twenty-second month of the project. In addition, we have listed four signs ("dog," "smell," "me," and "clean") that we judged to be stable, despite the fact that they had not met the stringent criterion before the end of the twenty-second month. These additional signs had, nevertheless, been reported to occur appropriately and spontaneously on more than half of the days in a period of thirty consecutive days. An indication of the variety of signs that Washoe used in the course of a day is given by the following data: during the twenty-second month of the study, twenty-eight of the thirty-four signs listed were reported on at least twenty days, and the smallest number of different signs reported for a single day was twenty-three, with a median of twenty-nine. (The development of Washoe's vocabulary of signs is being recorded on motion-picture film. At the time of this writing, thirty of the thirty-four signs listed in Table 12-1 are on film.)

The order in which these signs first appeared in Washoe's repertoire is also given in Table 12-1. We considered the first appearance to be the date on which three different observers reported appropriate and spontaneous occurrences. By this criterion, four new signs first appeared during the first seven months, nine new signs during the next seven months, and twenty-one new signs during the next seven months. We chose the twenty-first month rather than the twenty-second month as the cutoff for this tabulation so that no signs would be included that do not appear in Table 12-1. Clearly, if Washoe's rate of acquisition continues to accelerate, we will have to assess her vocabulary on the basis of sampling procedures. We are now in the process of developing procedures that could be used to make periodic tests of Washoe's performance on samples of her repertoire. However, now that there is evidence that a chimpanzee can acquire a vocabulary of more than thirty signs, the exact number of signs in her current vocabulary is less significant than the order of magnitude—fifty, one hundred, two hundred signs, or more—that might eventually be achieved.

DIFFERENTIATION

In Table 12-1, column 1, we list English equivalents for each of Washoe's signs. It must be understood that this equivalence is only approximate, because equivalence between English and ASL, as between any two human languages, is only approximate, and because Washoe's usage does differ from that of standard ASL. To some extent her usage is indicated in the column labeled "Context" in Table 12-1, but the definition of any given sign must always depend upon her total vocabulary, and this has been continually changing. When she had very few signs for specific things, Washoe used the "more" sign for a wide class of requests. Our only restriction was that we discouraged the use of "more" for first requests. As she acquired signs for specific requests, her use of "more" declined until, at the time of this writing, she was using this sign mainly to ask for repetition of some action that she could not name, such as a somersault. Perhaps the best English equivalent would be "do it again." Still, it seemed preferable to list the English equivalent for the ASL sign rather than its current referent for Washoe, since further refinements in her usage may be achieved at a later date.

The differentiation of the signs for "flower" and "smell" provides a further illustration of usage depending upon size of vocabulary. As the "flower" sign became more frequent, we noted that it occurred in several inappropriate contexts that all seemed to include odors; for example, Washoe would make the "flower" sign when opening a tobacco pouch or when entering a kitchen filled with cooking odors. Taking our cue from this, we introduced the "smell" sign by passive shaping and imitative prompting. Gradually Washoe came to make the appropriate distinction between "flower" contexts and "smell" contexts in her signing, although "flower" (in the single-nostril form) (see Table 12-1) has continued to occur as a common error in "smell" contexts.

TRANSFER

In general, when introducing new signs we have used a very specific referent for the initial training—a particular door for "open," a particular hat for "hat." Early in the project we were concerned about the possibility that signs might become inseparable from their first referents. So far, however, there has been no problem of this kind: Washoe has always been able to transfer her signs spontaneously to new members of each class of referents. We have already described the transfer of "more" and "open." The sign for "flower" is a particularly good example of transfer, because flowers occur in so many varieties, indoors, outdoors, and in pictures, yet Washoe uses the same sign for all. It is fortunate that she has responded well to pictures of objects. In the case of "dog" and "cat" this has proved to be important because live dogs and cats can be too exciting, and we have had to use pictures to elicit most of the "dog" and "cat" signs. It is noteworthy that Washoe has transferred the "dog" sign to the sound of barking by an unseen dog.

The acquisition and transfer of the sign for "key" illustrates a further point. A great many cupboards and doors in Washoe's quarters have been kept secure by small padlocks that can all be opened by the same simple key. Because she was immature and awkward, Washoe had great difficulty in learning to use these keys and locks. Because we wanted her to improve her manual dexterity, we let her practice with these keys until she could open the locks quite easily (then we had to hide the keys). Washoe soon transferred this skill to all manner of locks and keys, including ignition keys. At about the same time, we taught her the sign for "key," using the original padlock keys as a referent. Washoe came to use this sign both to name keys that were presented to her and to ask for the keys to various locks when no key was in sight. She readily transferred the sign to all varieties of keys and locks.

Now, if an animal can transfer a skill learned with a certain key and lock to new types of key and lock, it should not be surprising that the same animal can learn to use an arbitrary response to name and ask for a certain key and then transfer that sign to new types of keys. Certainly, the relationship between the use of a key and the opening of locks is as arbitrary as the relationship between the sign for "key" and its many referents. Viewed in this way, the general phenomenon of transfer of training and the specifically linguistic phenomenon of labeling become very similar, and the problems that these phenomena pose for modern learning theory should require similar solutions. We do not mean to imply that the problem of labeling is less complex than has generally been supposed; rather, we are suggesting that the problem of transfer of training requires an equally sophisticated treatment.

COMBINATIONS

During the phase of the project covered by this article we made no deliberate attempts to elicit combinations or phrases, although we may have responded more readily to strings of two or more signs than to single signs. As far as we can judge, Washoe's early use of signs in strings was spontaneous. Almost as soon as she had eight or ten signs in her repertoire, she began to use them two and three at a time. As her repertoire increased, her tendency to produce strings of two or more signs also increased, to the point where this has become a common mode of signing for her. We, of course, usually signed to her in combinations, but if Washoe's use of combinations has been imitative, then it must be a generalized sort of imitation, since she has invented a number of combinations, such as "gimme-tickle" (before we had ever asked her to tickle us), and "open-food-drink" (for the refrigerator—we have always called it the "cold box").

Four signs—"please," "come-gimme," "hurry," and "more"—used with one or more other signs, account for the largest share of Washoe's early combinations. In general, these four signs have functioned as emphasizers, as in "please-open-hurry" and "gimme-drink-please."

Until recently, five additional signs—"go," "out," "in," "open," and "hear-listen"—accounted for most of the remaining combinations. Typical examples of combinations using these four are "go-in" or "go-out" (when at some distance from a door), "go-sweet" (for being carried to a raspberry bush), "open-flower" (to be let through the gate to a flower garden), "open-key" (for a locked door), "listen-eat" (at the sound of an alarm clock signaling mealtime), and "listen-dog" (at the sound of barking by an unseen dog). All but the first and last of these six examples were inventions of Washoe's. Combinations of this type tend to amplify the meaning of the single signs used. Sometimes, however, the function of these five signs has been about the same as that of the emphasizers, as in "open-out" (when standing in front of a door).

Toward the end of the period covered in this article we were able to introduce the pronouns "I-me" and "you," so that combinations that resemble short sentences have begun to appear.

Concluding Observations

From time to time we have been asked questions such as, "Do you think that Washoe has language?" or "At what point will you be able to say that Washoe has language?" We find it very difficult to respond to these questions because they are altogether foreign to the spirit of our research. They imply a distinction between one class of communicative behavior that can be called language and another class that cannot. This in turn implies a well-established theory that could provide the distinction. If our objectives had required such a theory, we would certainly not have been able to begin this project as early as we did.

In the first phase of the project we were able to verify the hypothesis that sign language is an appropriate medium of two-way communication for the chimpanzee. Washoe's intellectual immaturity, the continuing acceleration of her progress, the fact that her signs do not remain specific to their original referents but are transferred spontaneously to new referents, and the emergence of rudimentary combinations all suggest that significantly more can be accomplished by Washoe during the subsequent phases of this project. As we proceed, the problems of these subsequent phases will be chiefly concerned with the technical business of measurement. We are now developing a procedure for testing Washoe's ability to name objects. In this procedure, an object or a picture of an object is placed in a box with a window. An observer, who does not know what is in the box, asks Washoe what she sees through the window. At present, this method is limited to items that fit in the box; a more ingenious method will have to be devised for other items. In particular, the ability to combine and recombine signs must be tested. Here, a great deal depends upon reaching a stage at which Washoe produces an extended series of signs in answer to questions. Our hope is that Washoe can be brought to the point where she describes events and situations to an observer who has no other source of information.

At an earlier time we would have been more cautious about suggesting that a chimpanzee might be able to produce extended utterances to communicate information. We believe now that it is the writers—who would predict just what it is that no chimpanzee will ever do—who must proceed with caution. Washoe's accomplishments will probably be exceeded by another chimpanzee, because it is unlikely that the conditions of training have been optimal in this first attempt. Theories of language that depend upon the identification of aspects of language that are exclusively human must remain tentative until a considerably larger body of intensive research with other species becomes available.

Summary

We set ourselves the task of teaching an animal to use a form of human language. Highly intelligent and highly social, the chimpanzee is an obvious choice for such a study, yet it has not been possible to teach a member of this species more than a few spoken words. We reasoned that a spoken language, such as English, might be an inappropriate medium of communication for a chimpanzee. This led us to choose American Sign Language, the gestural system of communication used by the deaf in North America, for the project.

The youngest infant that we could obtain was a wild-born female, whom we named Washoe, and who was estimated to be between eight and fourteen months old when we began our program of training. The laboratory conditions, while not patterned after those of a human family (as in the studies of Kellogg and Kellogg and of Hayes and Hayes), involved a minimum of confinement and a maximum of social interaction with human companions. For all practical purposes, the only verbal communication was in ASL, and the chimpanzee was maximally exposed to the use of this language by human beings.

It was necessary to develop a rough-and-ready mixture of training methods. There was evidence that some of Washoe's early signs were acquired by delayed imitation of the signing behavior of her human companions, but very few, if any, of her early signs were introduced by immediate imitation. Manual babbling was directly fostered and did increase in the course of the project. A number of signs were introduced by shaping and instrumental conditioning. A particularly effective and convenient method of shaping consisted of holding Washoe's hands, forming them into a configuration, and putting them through the movements of a sign.

We have listed more than thirty signs that Washoe acquired and could use spontaneously and appropriately by the end of the twenty-second month of the project. The signs acquired earliest were simple demands. Most of the later signs have been names for objects, which Washoe has used both as demands and as answers to questions. Washoe readily used noun signs to name pictures of objects as well as actual objects and has frequently called the attention of her companions to pictures and objects by naming them. Once acquired, the signs have not remained specific to the original referents but have been transferred spontaneously to a wide class of appropriate referents. At this writing, Washoe's rate of acquisition of new signs is still accelerating.

From the time she had eight or ten signs in her repertoire, Washoe began to use them in strings of two or more. During the period covered by this article we made no deliberate effort to elicit combinations other than by our own habitual use of strings of signs. Some of the combined forms that Washoe has used may have been imitative, but many have been inventions of her own. Only a small proportion of the possible combinations have, in fact, been observed. This is because most of Washoe's combinations include one of a limited group of signs that act as combiners. Among the signs that Washoe has recently acquired are the pronouns "I-me" and "you." When these occur in combinations the result resembles a short sentence. In terms of the eventual level of communication that a chimpanzee might be able to attain, the most promising results have been spontaneous naming, spontaneous transfer to new referents, and spontaneous combinations and recombinations of signs.

REFERENCES

Bryan, A. L. *Current Anthropology* 4 (1961): 297.

Goodall, J. *Primate behavior.* Edited by I. DeVore. New York: Holt, Rinehart and Winston, 1965.

Hayes, K. J. Personal communication.

Hayes, K. J., and Hayes, C. *Journal of Comparative and Physiological Psychology* 45 (1952): 450.

Hayes, K. J., and Hayes, C. *Proceedings of the American Philosophical Society* 95 (1951): 105.

Hayes, K. J., and Hayes, C. *The new human primates and human evolution*. Edited by I. A. Gavan. Detroit: Wayne University Press, 1955.

Kellogg, W. N. *Science* 162 (1968): 423.

Kellogg, W. N., and Kellogg, I. A. *The ape and the child*. New York: Hafner, 1967. (Originally published New York: McGraw-Hill, 1933.)

McCall, E. A. Thesis. University of Iowa, 1965.

Riopelle, A. J., and Rogers, C. M. *Behavior of nonhuman primates*. Edited by A. M. Schrier, H. F. Harlow, and F. Stollnitz. New York: Academic Press, 1965.

Stokoe, W. C., Casterline, D., and Croneberg, C. G. *A dictionary of American Sign Language*. Washington, D.C.: Gallaudet College Press, 1965.

Warden, C. J., and Warner, L. H. *Quarterly Review of Biology* 3 (1928): 1.

Yerkes, R. M. *Chimpanzees*. New Haven: Yale University Press, 1943.

Yerkes, R. M., and Learned, B. W. *Chimpanzee intelligence and its vocal expression*. Baltimore: Williams & Wilkins, 1925.

13

How Shall a Thing
Be Called?

ROGER BROWN

The most deliberate part of first-language teaching is the business
of telling a child what each thing is called. We ordinarily speak of
the name of a thing as if there were just one, but in fact, of course,
every referent has many names. The dime in my pocket is not only
a *dime*. It is also *money*, a *metal object*, a *thing*, and, moving to
subordinates, it is a *1952 dime*, in fact a *particular 1952 dime* with a
unique pattern of scratches, discolorations, and smooth places. When
such an object is named for a very young child how is it called? It
may be named *money* or *dime* but probably not *metal object, thing,
1952 dime*, or *particular 1952 dime*. The dog out on the lawn is
not only a *dog* but is also a *boxer*, a *quadruped*, an *animate being*; it
is the *landlord's dog*, named *Prince*. How will it be identified for a
child? Sometimes it will be called a *dog*, sometimes *Prince*, less often

HOW SHALL A THING BE CALLED? Reprinted from *Psychological Review* 85
(1958). Used by permission of the author and the American Psychological
Association.

a *boxer*, and almost never a *quadruped*, or *animate being*. Listening to many adults name things for many children, I find that their choices are quite uniform and that I can anticipate them from my own inclinations. How are these choices determined and what are their consequences for the cognitive development of the child?

Adults have notions about the kind of language appropriate for use with children. Especially strong and universal is the belief that children have trouble pronouncing long names and so should always be given the shortest possible names. A word is preferable to a phrase and, among words, a monosyllable is better than a polysyllable. This predicts the preference for *dog* and *Prince* over *boxer*, *quadruped*, and *animate being*. It predicts the choice of *dime* over *metal object* and *particular 1952 dime*.

Zipf (1935) has shown that the length of a word (in phonemes or syllables) is inversely related to its frequency in the printed language. Consequently the shorter names for any thing will usually also be the most frequently used names for that thing, and so it would seem that the choice of a name is usually predictable from either frequency or brevity. The monosyllables *dog* and *Prince* have much higher frequencies according to the Thorndike-Lorge list (1944) than do the polysyllables *boxer*, *quadruped*, and *animate being*.

It sometimes happens, however, that the frequency-brevity principle makes the wrong prediction. The thing called a *pineapple* is also *fruit*. *Fruit* is the shorter and more frequent term, but adults will name the thing *pineapple*. Similarly they will say *apple*, *banana*, *orange*, and even *pomegranate;* all of them longer and less frequent words than the perfectly appropriate *fruit*. Brevity seems not to be the powerful determinant we had imagined. The frequency principle can survive this kind of example, but only if it is separated from counts like the Thorndike-Lorge of over-all frequency in the printed language. On the whole the word *fruit* appears more often than the word *pineapple* (and also is shorter), but we may confidently assume that, when pineapples are being named, the word *pineapple* is more frequent than the word *fruit*. This, of course, is a kind of frequency more directly relevant to our problem. Word counts of general usage are only very roughly applicable to the prediction of what will be said when something is named. What we need is referent-name counts. We don't have them, of course, but if we had them it is easy to see that they would improve our predictions. Bananas are called *banana*, apples *apple*, and oranges *orange* more often than any of them is called *fruit*. The broad frequency-brevity principle predicts that *money* and *dime* will be preferred to *metal object*, *1952 dime*, and *particular 1952 dime*, but it does not predict the neglect of the common monosyllable *thing*. For this purpose we must again appeal to imagined referent-name counts, according to which dimes would surely be called *dime* or *money* more often than *thing*.

While the conscious preference for a short name can be overcome by frequency, the preference nevertheless affects the naming act. I have heard parents designate the appropriate objects *pineapple, television, vinegar,* and *policeman;* all these to children who cannot reproduce polysyllabic words. Presumably they use these names because that is what the referents are usually called, but the adult's sense of the absurdity of giving such words to a child is often evident. He may smile as he says it or remark, "That's too hard for you to say, isn't it?"

Some things are named in the same way by all adults for all children. This is true of the apple and the orange. Other things have several common names, each of them used by a specifiable group of adults to specifiable children. The same dog is *dog* to most of the world and *Prince* in his own home and perhaps on his own block. The same man is a *man* to most children, *policeman* to some at some times, *Mr. Jones* to the neighborhood kids, and *papa* to his own. Referent-name counts from people in general will not predict these several usages. A still more particular name count must be imagined. The name given a thing by an adult for a child is determined by the frequency with which various names have been applied to such things in the experience of the particular adult. General referent-name counts taken from many people will predict much that the individual does, but, for a close prediction, counts specific to the individual would be needed.

The frequencies to which we are now appealing have not, of course, been recorded. We are explaining imagined preferences in names by imagined frequencies of names. It is conceivable, certainly, that some of these specific word counts might be made and a future naming performance independently predicted from a past frequency. Probably, however, such frequencies will never be known, and if we choose to explain particular naming performances by past frequencies we shall usually have to infer the frequency from the performance.

Beyond the Frequency Principle

A frequency explanation is not very satisfying even when the appeal is to known frequencies. The question will come to mind: "Why is one name more common than another?" Why is a dog called *dog* more often than *quadruped* and, by some people, called *Prince* more often than *dog?* Perhaps it just happened that way, like driving on the right side of the road in America and on the left in England. The convention is preserved but has no justification outside itself. As things have worked out, coins are usually named by species as *dime, nickel,* or *penny* while the people we know have individual names like *John, Mary,* and *Jim.* Could it just as easily be the other way around? Might we equally well give coins proper names and introduce people as types?

The referent for the word *dime* is a large class of coins. The name is equally appropriate to all members of this class. To name a coin *dime* is to establish its equivalence, for naming purposes, with all other coins of the same denomination. This equivalence for naming purposes corresponds to a more general equivalence for all purposes of economic exchange. In the grocery one dime is as good as another but quite different from any nickel or penny. For a child the name given an object anticipates the equivalences and differences that will need to be observed in most of his dealings with such an object. To make proper denotative use of the word *dime* he must be able to distinguish members of the referent category from everything else. When he learns that, he has solved more than a language problem. He has an essential bit of equipment for doing business. The most common names for coins could not move from the species level to the level of proper names without great alteration in our nonlinguistic culture. We should all be numismatists preparing our children to recognize a particular priceless 1910 dime.

Many things are reliably given the same name by the whole community. The spoon is seldom called anything but *spoon,* although it is also a piece of *silverware,* an *artifact,* and a *particular ill-washed restaurant spoon.* The community-wide preference for the word *spoon* corresponds to the community-wide practice of treating spoons as equivalent but different from knives and forks. There are no proper names for individual spoons because their individuality seldom signifies. It is the same way with pineapples, dimes, doors, and taxicabs. The most common name for each of these categorizes them as they need to be categorized for the community's nonlinguistic purposes. The most common name is at the level of usual utility.

People and pets have individual names as well as several kinds of generic name. The individual name is routinely coined by those who are disposed to treat the referent as unique, and is available afterwards to any others who will see the uniqueness. A man at home has his own name to go with the peculiar privileges and responsibilities binding him to wife and child. But the same man who is a one-of-a-kind *papa* to his own children is simply a *man* to children at large. He is, like the other members of this large category, someone with no time to play and little tolerance for noise. In some circumstances, this same man will be given the name of his occupation. He is a *policeman* equivalent to other policemen but

different from *bus drivers* and *Good Humor men*. A policeman is someone to "behave in front of" and to go to when lost. To the kids in the
neighborhood the man is *Mr. Jones*, unique in his way—a crank, bad
tempered, likely to shout at you if you play out in front of his house.
It is the same way with dogs as with people. He may be a unique *Prince*
to his owners, who feed and house him, but he is just a *dog* to the rest
of the world. A homeless dog reverts to namelessness, since there is none
to single him out from his species. Dimes and nickels have much the same
significance for an entire society, and their usual names are fixed at this
level of significance. People and pets function uniquely for some and in
various generic ways for others. They have a corresponding variety of
designations, but each name is at the utility level for the group that uses
it. Our naming practices for coins and people correspond to our nonlinguistic practices, and it is difficult to imagine changing the one without
changing the other.

The names provided by parents for children anticipate the functional
structure of the child's world. This is not, of course, something parents
are aware of doing. When we name a thing there does not seem to be any
process of choice. Each thing has its name, just one, and that is what we
give to a child. The one name is, of course, simply the usual name for us.
Naming each thing in accordance with local frequencies, parents unwittingly transmit their own cognitive structures. It is a world in which
Prince is unique among dogs and *papa* among men, *spoons* are all alike
but different from *forks*. It may be a world of *bugs* (to be stepped on),
of *flowers* (not to be picked), and *birds* (not to be stoned). It may be a
world in which *Niggers*, like *spoons*, are all of a kind. A division of caste
creates a vast categorical equivalence and a correspondingly generic name.
Mr. Jones and *Mr. Smith* do not come out of racial anonymity until their
uniqueness is appreciated.

Adults do not invariably provide a child with the name that is at the
level of usual utility in the adult world. An effort is sometimes made to
imagine the utilities of a child's life. Some parents will, at first, call every
sort of coin *money*. This does not prepare a child to buy and sell, but
then he may be too young for that. All coins are equivalent for the very
young child in that they are objects not to be put into the mouth and not
to be dropped down the register, and *money* anticipates that equivalence.
A more differentiated terminology can wait upon the age of store-going.
Sometimes an adult is aware of a child's need for a distinction that is not
coded in the English lexicon. A new chair comes into the house and is not
going to be equivalent to the shabby chairs already there. A child is permitted to sit on the old chairs but will not be permitted on the new one.
A distinctive name is created from the combinational resources of the

language. *The new chair* or *the good chair* is not to be assimilated to *chairs* in general.

Eventually, of course, children learn many more names for each thing than the one that is most frequent and useful. Sometimes a name is supplied in order to bring forward an immediately important property of the referent. A child who starts bouncing the coffee pot needs to be told that it is *glass*. Sometimes a name is supplied to satisfy the child's curiosity as to the place of a referent in a hierarchy of categories. Chairs are *furniture* and so are tables; carrots are a *vegetable* but apples are not. Probably, however, both children and adults make some distinction among these various names. *The* name of a thing, the one that tells what it "really" is, is the name that constitutes the referent as it needs to be constituted for most purposes. The other names represent possible recategorizations useful for one or another purpose. We are even likely to feel that these recategorizations are acts of imagination, whereas the major categorization is a kind of passive recognition of the true character of the referent.

The Child's Concrete Vocabulary

It is a commonplace saying that the mind of a child is relatively "concrete" and the mind of an adult "abstract." The words "concrete" and "abstract" are sometimes used in the sense of subordinate and superordinate. In this sense a relatively concrete mind would operate with subordinate categories and an abstract mind with superordinate categories. It is recorded in many studies of vocabulary acquisition (e.g., Smith, 1926; International Kindergarten Union, 1928) that children ordinarily use the words *milk* and *water* before the word *liquid;* the words *apple* and *orange* before *fruit; table* and *chair* before *furniture; mamma* and *daddy* before *parent* or *person;* etc. Very high-level superordinate terms like *article, action, quality,* and *relation,* though they are common in adult speech (Thorndike and Lorge, 1944), are very seldom heard from preschool children (International Kindergarten Union, 1928). Presumably this kind of vocabulary comparison is one of the sources of the notion that the child's mind is more concrete than the mind of the adult. However, the vocabulary of a child is not a very direct index of his cognitive preferences. The child's vocabulary is more immediately determined by the naming practices of adults.

The occasion for a name is ordinarily some particular thing. In the naming it is categorized. The preference among possible names seems to go to the one that is most commonly applied to the referent in question. That name will ordinarily categorize the referent so as to observe the equivalences and differences that figure in its usual utilization. There are not many purposes for which all liquids are equivalent or all fruits, furniture, or parents; and so the names of these categories are less commonly used for denotation than are the names of categories subordinate to them. It is true that words like *article, action, quality* and *relation* are rather common in adult written English, but we can be sure that these frequencies in running discourse are not equaled in naming situations. Whatever the purposes for which all articles are equivalent, or all actions or qualities, they are not among the pressing needs of children.

It is not invariably true that vocabulary builds from concrete to abstract. *Fish* is likely to be learned before *perch* and *bass; house* before *bungalow* and *mansion; car* before *Chevrolet* and *Plymouth* (Smith, 1926). The more concrete vocabulary waits for the child to reach an age where his purposes differentiate kinds of fish and makes of cars. There is much elaborately concrete vocabulary that is not introduced until one takes courses in biology, chemistry, and botany. No one has ever proved that vocabulary builds from the concrete to the abstract more often than it builds from the abstract to the concrete. The best generalization seems to be that each thing is first given its most common name. This name seems to categorize on the level of usual utility. That level sometimes falls on the most concrete categories in a hierarchy (proper names for significant people), and vocabulary then builds toward the more abstract categories (names for ethnic groups, personality types, social classes). Utility sometimes centers on a relatively abstract level of categorization (fish) and vocabulary then builds in both directions (perch and vertebrate). Probably utility never centers on the most abstract levels (thing, substance, etc.), and so probably there is no hierarchy within which vocabulary builds in an exclusively concrete direction.

In the literature describing first-language acquisition (McCarthy, 1946) there is much to indicate that children easily form large abstract categories. There are, to begin with, the numerous cases in which the child overgeneralizes the use of a conventional word. The word *dog* may, at first, be applied to every kind of four-legged animal. It sometimes happens that every man who comes into the house is called *daddy*. When children invent their own words, these often have an enormous semantic range. Wilhelm Stern's (Stern and Stern, 1920) son Günther used *psee* for leaves, trees, and flowers. He used *bebau* for all animals. Lombroso (Werner, 1948) tells of a child who used *qua qua* for both duck and water and *afta* for drinking glass, the contents of a glass, and a pane of glass. Reports of this kind do not suggest that children are deficient in abstracting ability. It even looks as if they may favor large categories.

There are two extreme opinions about the direction of cognitive development. There are those who suppose that we begin by discriminating to the limits of our sensory acuity, seizing each thing in its uniqueness, noting every hair and flea of the particular dog. Cognitive development involves neglect of detail, abstracting from particulars so as to group similars into categories. By this view abstraction is a mature rather than a primitive process. The contrary opinion is that the primitive stage in cognition is one of a comparative lack of differentiation. Probably certain distinctions are inescapable; the difference between a loud noise and near silence, between a bright contour and a dark ground, etc. These inevitable discriminations divide the perceived world into a small number of very large (abstract) categories. Cognitive development is increasing differentiation. The more distinctions we make, the more categories we have and the smaller (more concrete) these are. I think the latter view is favored in psychology today. While there is good empirical and theoretical support (Lewin, 1935; Lashley and Wade, 1946; Gibson and Gibson, 1955) for the view that development is differentiation, there is embarrassment for it in the fact that much vocabulary growth is from the concrete to the abstract. This embarrassment can be eliminated.

Suppose a very young child applies the word *dog* to every four-legged creature he sees. He may have abstracted a limited set of attributes and created a large category, but his abstraction will not show up in his vocabulary. Parents will not provide him with a conventional name for his category, e.g., *quadruped;* but instead will require him to narrow his use of *dog* to its proper range. Suppose a child calls all elderly ladies *aunt.* He will not be told that the usual name for his category is *elderly ladies* but, instead, will be taught to cut back *aunt* to accord with standard usage. In short, the sequence in which words are acquired is set by adults rather than children, and may ultimately be determined by the utility of the various categorizations. This will sometimes result in a movement of vocabulary toward higher abstraction and sometimes a movement toward greater concreteness. The cognitive development of the child may nevertheless always take the direction of increasing differentiation or concreteness.

The child who spontaneously hits on the category four-legged animals will be required to give it up in favor of dogs, cats, horses, cows, and the like. When the names of numerous subordinates have been mastered, he may be given the name *quadruped* for the superordinate. This abstraction is not the same as its primitive forerunner. The schoolboy who learns the word *quadruped* has abstracted from differentiated and named subordinates. The child he was abstracted through a failure to differentiate. Abstraction after differentiation may be the mature process, and abstraction from a failure to differentiate the primitive. Needless to say, the abstractions occurring on the two levels need not be coincident, as they are in our quadruped example.

Summary

Though we often think of each thing as having a name—a single name—in fact, each thing has many equally correct names. When some thing is named for a child, adults show considerable regularity in their preference for one of the many possible names. This paper is addressed to the question: "What determines the name given to a child for a thing?" The first answer is that adults prefer the shorter to the longer expression. This gives way to the frequency principle. Adults give a thing the name it is most commonly given. We have now come full circle and are left with the question, "Why is one name for a thing more common than another?"

It seems likely that things are first named so as to categorize them in a maximally useful way. For most purposes Referent A is a spoon rather than a piece of silverware, and Referent B a dime rather than a metal object. The same referent may have its most useful categorization on one level (*Prince*) for one group (the family) and on another level (*dog*) for another group (strangers). The categorization that is most useful for very young children (*money*) may change as they grow older (*dime* and *nickel*).

With some hierarchies of vocabulary the more concrete terms are learned before the abstract; probably the most abstract terms are never learned first, but it often happens that a hierarchy develops in both directions from a middle level of abstraction. Psychologists who believe that mental development is from the abstract to the concrete, from a lack of differentiation to increased differentiation, have been embarrassed by the fact that vocabulary often builds in the opposite direction. This fact need not trouble them, since the sequence in which words are acquired is not determined by the cognitive preferences of children so much as by the naming practices of adults.

REFERENCES

Gibson, J. J., and Gibson, E. J. Perceptual learning: Differentiation or enrichment? *Psychological Review* 62 (1955): 32–41.

International Kindergarten Union. *A study of the vocabulary of children before entering the first grade.* Baltimore: Williams & Wilkins, 1928.

Lashley, K. S., and Wade, M. The Pavlovian theory of generalization. *Psychological Review* 53 (1946): 72–87.

Lewin, K. *A dynamic theory of personality.* New York: McGraw-Hill, 1935.

McCarthy, D. Language development in children. *Manual of child psychology.* Edited by L. Carmichael. New York: Wiley, 1946, 477–581.

Smith, M. E. An investigation of the development of the sentence and the extent of vocabulary in young children. *University of Iowa Studies in Child Welfare* 3 (1926).

Stern, C., and Stern, W. *Die Kindersprache* [Children's language]. Leipzig: Barth, 1920.

Thorndike, E. L., and Lorge, I. *The teacher's word book of 30,000 words.* New York: Bureau of Publications, Teachers College, Columbia University, 1944.

Werner, H. *Comparative psychology of mental development.* Chicago: Follett, 1948.

Zipf, G. K. *The psycho-biology of language.* Boston: Houghton Mifflin, 1935.

14

Toward a Theory
of Creativity

P H I L I P   W .   J A C K S O N
S A M U E L   E .   M E S S I C K

The ultimate concern of the psychologist is the human mind and its inventions. Although there are many ways to describe man's mental complexity, the terms "intelligence" and "creativity" enjoy a special prominence both in the layman's language and in professional discussions. It is clear that a considerable amount of meaning is concentrated in the two words; however, it is not clear precisely what their meanings are or how they differ from each other.

In attempting to gather data on the difference between creativity and intelligence, psychologists have demonstrated that tests requiring unusual responses involve somewhat different abilities than do conventional tests of intelligence. But as Golann (1963) has pointed

TOWARD A THEORY OF CREATIVITY Adapted from *Journal of Personality* 33 (1965). Used by permission of the authors and the Duke University Press. This article originally appeared under the title "The person, the product, and the response: Conceptual problems in the assessment of creativity."

out: "Intelligence is not performance on a test; creativity is more than test performance or being judged creative. What is needed for the understanding of the relationship between creativity and intelligence is not only data but conceptual reorganization as well."

Evaluating Intellectual Performance: "Correct" versus "Good"

People are continually informed that they have done well or poorly on tasks. Although the evaluations take almost as many forms as the behavior being judged, they can be crudely classified into two overlapping groups. On the one hand are judgments having to do with the "correctness," or "rightness," of a person's performance. These evaluations deal with the degree to which certain objective and logical criteria have been satisfied. They tend to be categorical—to admit only one answer or one set of solutions and to exclude all others as incorrect. On the other hand are judgments having to do with the "goodness," or "worth," of a person's performance. These evaluations deal with the degree to which certain subjective criteria have been satisfied. The criteria of goodness tend to be continuous—to admit a wide range of responses that vary in acceptability. Although the two classes of evaluations overlap (and some kinds of behavior are evaluated in both ways), they are nonetheless distinguishable, and the distinction between them has important implications for our concept of the difference between intelligent and creative behavior. In the simplest terms, intelligent responses are *correct* and creative responses are *good*.

Many current tests of creative ability fail to distinguish between correct responses and good responses. Take as an instance the Remote Association Test developed by Mednick (1962). In this test the subject is presented with three words, such as "rat," "blue," and "cottage," and told to supply a fourth word to serve as a link between them. For the example given the answer is "cheese." It is argued that this answer reflects creativity because it is both "remote" and "useful," at least in the sense of meeting the requirements of the question. We would insist that the answer reflects intelligence because it is correct. Mednick also maintains that the answer 7,363,474 to the question "How much is 12 and 12?" is original but not creative because it is not useful. What seems more important, however, is that it is wrong. As we use the term "creative," there *are* no creative or uncreative answers to the question "How much is 12 and 12?," only correct or incorrect answers.

This is not to suggest that logical criteria are applied primarily to scientific products whereas artistic products are evaluated by less-than-logical standards. A piano solo can be as incorrect as a solution to a mathematical equation, and a scientific theory can be as good as a great novel. A poet's attempt to write a sonnet may be both incorrect and poor, as may an engineer's design for a bridge.

Before a test can be devised that successfully measures creativity, we must be able to distinguish a creative product from a correct response. We need a new definition of "creative" product. Mednick includes usefulness as a criterion of creativeness because he realizes, as do most researchers in this field, that unusualness or originality is not enough. These qualities do take us beyond the confines of correctness in evaluating intellectual performance. But the identification of the unusual is only a first step in trying to understand the good. Let us consider that first step in some detail and then attempt to identify some other properties of creative products.

How Do We Recognize Creative Products?

UNUSUALNESS AND APPROPRIATENESS

No matter what other qualities a thing may have, we generally insist that it be unusual before we are willing to call it creative. Indeed, unusualness and creativeness are so tightly joined in our thinking that the two concepts are sometimes treated as synonyms. Unusualness has become the most common and, in some of our current paper-and-pencil tests of creativity, the *only* measure of creativeness.

Unusualness is seldom defined in terms of all members of a general class, such as all paintings in existence, but in terms of a greatly restricted subset. When we say, for example, that a child's painting represents three-dimensional space in an unusual way, our standard of comparison probably includes other paintings by children but excludes paintings by adults. When we consider the many classes to which a thing can belong, it becomes apparent that its rareness depends on what it is compared with. The same object can be unique or common, depending on the frame of reference. Clearly, the choice of an appropriate group against which to judge a creative work is of utmost importance in applying the standard of unusualness. That is, infrequency is decided by reference to *norms*, which thus serve as a standard for evaluating unusualness.

Although the judgment of unusualness is a logical first step in evaluating creativeness, products designated as creative on this basis alone would make a strange collection. They would include a substantial number of things that are simply bizarre or odd. Somehow the mere oddities must be weeded out. This task requires the application of a second criterion, *appropriateness*. Appropriateness alone cannot be used as a criterion of creativeness because appropriateness without unusualness is merely cliché. But asking whether unusual products are appropriate helps eliminate from a collection of possibly creative things those that are simply absurd.

To be appropriate, a thing must fit its *context*. It must make sense in light of the demands of the situation and the desires of the person who produced it. Further, in the case of complex products, the internal elements of the work must blend together. There are both internal and external criteria of appropriateness, and quite different critical stances arise from an emphasis on one or the other.

At fairly low levels of creative production, the criterion of appropriateness is not too difficult to apply. For example, if a creativity test asks a person to think of different uses for a paper clip and he answers, "Eat it," the inappropriateness of his response is obvious. If a person is asked to write captions for cartoons and responds by giving the names of colors, again there is little question about the inappropriateness of his reaction. Note, though, that both these responses would probably be unusual, if not unique.

As products become more complex, however, and more responsive to the needs of the producer than to the demands of the situation, the determination of appropriateness becomes more complex. There are times, of course, when the judgment is still fairly easy to make. It does not require much aesthetic training to realize that the meter of a poem beginning "Death is here / Death is there / Death is lurking everywhere" is inappropriate to the theme. Yet to judge the appropriateness of the meter of a poem that is more stylistically and thematically complex may require detailed examination by highly trained persons. Even then they may disagree, and there is always the chance that the poet, or another reader, may dispute the judgment.

As the term is used in judging creative products, appropriateness deals with much more than the logical fit of the product within its context or of the product's elements with one another. At times a product violates conventional logic but somehow manages to hang together and have a logic of its own. Illustrations of this phenomenon abound in modern art and literature, and also in "nonbooks" like Jerry Rubin's *Do It*. Thus, although the judgmental standard for evaluating the appropriateness of a product is its context, the context is psychological as well as logical. It includes the producer's intentions as well as the demands of the situation.

Finally, appropriateness is a continuous quality. It exists in degrees rather than completely or not at all. In its lower forms, we recognize appropriateness in a product that merely bears a clear relation to the demands of the situation or to the intentions of its producer. In its higher forms, we marvel at the way the product reflects more subtle influences as well. At low levels of appropriateness we speak of a product as "about right," given its sources, the purpose of its maker, and the like. At higher levels we speak of a product as "just right." Indeed, at the very highest level of appropriateness we may experience a sense of recognition: it is so right that it looks almost familiar. A *New York Times* critic once described such products as having "the handprint of necessity upon them instead of the quickly tarnished sheen of the merely novel." When a person comes upon these "handprints of necessity," he may feel as if his expectations have been fulfilled, when what has really happened is that the product has made him aware of what his expectations should have been. To quote Bruner (1957), "What makes something obvious is that at last we understand it."

THE POWER TO TRANSFORM REALITY

Even among products that are both unusual and appropriate, some are surely at a higher level of creative excellence than others. One property present in some products but absent, or less obvious, in others is *power to transform reality*. Some objects combine elements in ways that defy tradition and yield a new perspective, forcing us to see reality in a new way. These products involve transformation of material or ideas to overcome conventional constraints. The transformation power of a product serves as a third criterion of creativeness. Just as the unusualness of a product is judged by norms and its appropriateness by context, the transformation power of a product is judged by the strength and nature of the constraints that are transcended.

The power to transform what we think we know is a more difficult criterion to define than unusualness or appropriateness. At first glance it might seem to be nothing more than an extreme example of unusualness. But it is unusualness with a difference—an unusualness that attacks conventional ways of thinking about things or viewing objects. In its most dramatic form a transformation involves a radical shift in approach to a subject—the kind of shift caused, for example, by Copernicus's theory that the earth revolves around the sun and by Freud's theory of the unconscious.

The difference between a merely unusual product and a product that transforms reality may be approached in another way. Things are often unusual in a purely quantitative sense: the most or the least, the largest or the smallest. Products that are unusual in this "record-breaking" sense need not, and usually do not, qualify as transformations. Transformations are not merely improvements. Rather, they are new forms.

There is a further distinction between an object that transforms and one that is merely new. If the power to transform depended only on devising a new combination of elements, almost any unique collection of things would qualify. Mechanical techniques for supplying these unique combinations could be devised, like the method of the popular writer who is said to have obtained the plots of his novels by spinning a set of wheels containing adjectives, nouns, verbs, and the like. Generally, however, these new combinations do not qualify as transformations because they terminate rather than generate thought. They are the occasion for surprise and laughter, but not for reflection and wonder.

The possibility just mentioned—that the presence of a transformation may be determined in part by its effect on the person who confronts the creative product—raises an interesting question. Do the other two criteria, unusualness and appropriateness, also have distinguishable effects on the person who experiences them? That is, are there types of aesthetic response that somehow parallel the criteria of creativeness? Let us put aside for a moment the search for characteristics of creative products and focus on how the characteristics we have already discussed might strike the observer. The development of the discussion so far is summarized in Table 14-1, which lists the three properties of creative products and the standards by which each property is judged.

TABLE 14-1

Property	Judgmental standard
unusualness	norms
appropriateness	context
power to transform reality	constraints

THE IMPACT OF THE PRODUCT

An unusual object, event, or idea characteristically evokes *surprise* in the observer. The unusual is attention-getting, it "catches our eye," its unexpectedness may shock or amaze us. By definition we cannot be prepared for it, except in a very general way. The impact of first exposure creates surprise and requires a period of adaptation during which the unusual object or event is assimilated into the observer's experience.

A person's reaction to the unusual is greatest right after exposure to the object and diminishes rapidly as time goes on. Although surprise may occur more than once in response to the same object, later exposures never quite match the impact of the first. Objects and events whose value comes almost solely from their unusualness, such as freaks in side shows and *New Yorker* cartoons, rarely warrant continued viewing.

The quality of appropriateness calls forth a reaction that we will call *satisfaction*. It is akin to a general feeling of comfort. The satisfaction would seem to have two major sources. First, there is a recognition that the demands of the creator, the material, and the external context have been met and that, as was mentioned before, the response is not only right but just right. There is an inevitability about it. Second, there is a recognition that the product is complete or sufficient. The first source of satisfaction focuses on quality (on how *well* demands are met); the second source of satisfaction focuses on quantity (on how *fully* demands are met). The satisfied observer's reactions to these two considerations are "just right" and "enough."

Bruner describes something close to the meaning intended here in his discussion of what he considers the prime property of a creative act—effective surprise. He states, "What is curious about effective surprise is that it need not be rare or infrequent or bizarre and is often none of these things. Effective surprises . . . seem rather to have the quality of obviousness to them when they occur, producing a shock of recognition, following which there is no longer astonishment" (Bruner, 1962).

Products with the power to transform reality are likely to be *stimulating* to the observer. The primary value of such products is that they change the observer's way of perceiving or thinking about his world. The unusual requires him to assimilate the product, to include it in his world, but a transformation requires him to revise his world. The newness lies not only in the product itself but in the changed environment that the product has caused. A product with the power to transform reality is something like a stone dropped in a pond. To a person standing on the bank the object of interest is not the stone, which quickly disappears from sight, but the waves it produces. A transforming object invites the viewer to move out, intellectually, in new directions—it stimulates him to consider its consequences.

In review, the first three criteria of creativeness—unusualness, appropriateness, and transformation power—may be the source of three types of aesthetic response: surprise, satisfaction, and stimulation. The possibility that different types of aesthetic response can be isolated gives rise to two important questions that can only be posed here. First, can the aesthetic responses themselves be used to indicate the presence of the qualities that give rise to them? Can we, for example, take a reaction of surprise to indicate the existence of unusualness? The second question is whether the aesthetic responses are unique to the observer or whether they also appear in the creator himself. Obviously the creator also judges his own product, yet his judgment need not (and does not) always agree with the verdict of an outside judge.

Let us now return to the criteria of creativeness and ask what needs to be added to the three that have already been suggested.

CONDENSATION OF MEANING

Unusualness, appropriateness, and power to transform reality characterize many of the things we are willing to call creative. They can be found in products from very different sources—from the scientist and the philosopher as well as from the craftsman and the artist. Yet there is another important quality that does not seem to be covered by these criteria. This quality, which appears in some highly creative products, is *condensation*.

Novelty wears out quickly. The history of fad and fashion is, in essence, an elaborate documentation of the short life and relativity of unusualness. In striking contrast to the temporary appeal of novel objects is the endurance of the greatest creative achievements of man. These we continually reexamine and reexperience.

Things that bear close and repeated examination are those that do not reveal their whole meaning on first consideration. They offer something new each time we experience them, whether they are great works of art or highly developed scientific theories. They have about them an intensity and a concentration of meaning that call for continued contemplation.

Because confusion and disorder also compel the observer's attention as he tries to make sense out of what he sees, it is necessary to distinguish between condensation and chaos. The chief difference is that a unified and coherent meaning is derived from condensation, whereas unrelated and irrelevant meanings are derived from disorder. An assortment of debris gathered in a junkyard and the ordered arrangement of the same material by an artist serve to illustrate the distinction being made here. Any meaning derived from the random assortment of junk is fortuitous, obtained either from a chance association between the pieces of junk or from irrelevant associations that the material has for the viewer. By contrast, the ordered arrangement, if it is worthy of artistic notice, has more meaning than can be understood at first glance. The color and shape of the objects, their texture, their placement, and their original function all combine to enhance their aesthetic appeal.

In the highest forms of creative condensation, simplicity and complexity come together. What at first appears simple turns out on closer inspection to have only an apparent simplicity. Conversely, that which at first seems complex is found to have a hidden simplicity that binds together its many elements. Some of Robert Frost's poems illustrate well the use of the simple to represent the complex. The reverse situation, in which complexity cloaks a hidden simplicity, occurs frequently in musical works, such as those by Bach; repeated listening is often required before the major themes and their variations become apparent.

A product characterized by condensation of meaning can be apprehended, analyzed, and interpreted in many different ways—intellectually or emotionally, in images or in ideas. It may be interpreted differently by different people or by the same person on different occasions. Such a product has *summary power*—the capacity to contain within it the essential elements for many insights and interpretations. Summary power is thus a standard by which condensation of meaning can be judged.

Before leaving this discussion of condensation, an additional point should be mentioned. The ambiguity and complexity of the four criteria of creativeness increase as we go from unusualness to condensation. If the meaning of unusualness seems clearer than the meaning of condensation, it is partly because condensation is a more complex idea than unusualness. As it is used here, the word "complex" means not only "obscure and complicated" but "difficult to judge." Judgments of transformation and condensation are more difficult to make than judgments of unusualness and appropriateness; there are more differences in viewpoint, and agreement is harder to reach, even within one school of thought.

Having added a fourth property of creative products, condensation of meaning, we return to a consideration of aesthetic responses. What is the effect of this new criterion on the observer? So far he has been surprised by unusualness, satisfied by appropriateness, and stimulated by the transforming qualities of creative products. The question now is, How will he react when he confronts a product of high condensation, one that has many levels of meaning? A condensed product is an object worth pondering; it should be examined slowly, carefully, and repeatedly. In a word, the observer is called upon to *savor* a condensation.

The surprise, the satisfaction, and the stimulation that characterize responses to other aspects of creativeness are also present in the response to condensation, but there is an important difference: these other responses are enduring and intensified. Surprise occurs not only on the first encounter but on later ones as new and unusual aspects of the product are discovered; satisfaction deepens with repeated exposure as the appropriateness of each element in the product is more fully revealed; stimulation is enriched as each new reaction to the product builds on those that preceded it. It is this continued freshness of the product and of the response to it that makes an object worth savoring.

With the addition of condensation to the list of properties and of savoring to the list of aesthetic responses, we complete our discussion of creative products and appreciative reactions. They are outlined, together with the standards by which the properties of creative objects are judged, in Table 14-2.

TABLE 14-2

Property	Judgmental standard	Aesthetic responses
unusualness	norms	surprise
appropriateness	context	satisfaction
power to transform reality	constraints	stimulation
condensation of meaning	summary power	savoring

It may be that the creative person has a set of personal qualities that corresponds, so to speak, to the properties of creative products. These qualities could be seen as inclining the person toward the creation of products that have the properties mentioned. A person who is inclined to produce the unusual can be thought of as highly *original*. A person whose products are appropriate is probably very *sensitive* to the demands of his environment and to the subtleties of the material with which he is working. Products that have the power to transform reality seem to reflect *flexibility*—a fluidity of intellect and intuition that allows the producer to toy with ideas, attitudes, and objects in ways that violate tradition. The fourth property of creative products, condensation of meaning, is extremely complex, and it is difficult to find a single word to describe the person apt to produce condensations. The word that comes closest to being appropriate, in our opinion, is *poetic*.

Our scheme is at best an incomplete outline. In order to be useful in the assessment of creativity, it must be elaborated more fully and also supported by empirical studies. In addition, it is well to remember that theories of creativity are themselves creative products. As such, they must abide by the very laws that they are designed to unearth. This realization makes us reluctant to prescribe what is yet to be done, for the day we are sure how to construct a theory of creativity will be the day we are sure how to construct a poem.

REFERENCES

Bruner, J. S. The conditions of creativity. *Contemporary approaches to creative thinking.* Edited by H. E. Gruber, G. Terrell, and M. Wertheimer. New York: Atherton Press, 1962.

Bruner, J. S. What social scientists say about having an idea. *Printers' Ink Magazine* 260 (1957): 48–52.

Golann, S. E. Psychological study of creativity. *Psychological Bulletin* 60 (1963): 548–65.

Mednick, S. A. The associative basis of the creative process. *Psychological Review* 69 (1962): 220–32.

Physiological Bases
of Behavior

Innumerable chemical changes are constantly occurring in the body: nerve cells fire in the brain and spinal cord, digestive juices turn starch into sugar, glands secrete fluids that make other glands secrete fluids, and so on. Man is, as it were, a walking test tube. When he takes in yet another chemical in the form of a powerful drug, such as LSD, the effects can be so strong and so widespread that his perceptions of himself and the world around him are almost totally changed. In "LSD: A Novelist's Personal Experience," Alan Harrington describes his first experience with LSD, which he took during a research project run several years ago by Timothy Leary and Richard Alpert. Harrington reports dramatic changes in his thoughts and emotions and very striking distortions of his visual surroundings: "The universe cracked into bright globules and separated; then I was in little pieces. . . ." The extent to which his perceptions of the outside world were intertwined with his subjective feelings is a healthy reminder that different processes such as sensation, emotion, and thought, though usually studied separately, are experienced together and are triggered by common physiological mechanisms.

In "The Effects of Hemisphere Deconnection on Conscious Awareness," Roger W. Sperry describes what happens to human perceptions and behavior when communication between the right and left halves of the brain is prevented by cutting the nerve connections that join the two hemispheres. Sperry began working on hemisphere deconnection in an attempt to find a surgical cure for epilepsy. He discovered that severing the connections between the brain hemispheres greatly reduced the frequency and severity of epileptic seizures without much apparent damage to his patients' daily behavior. However, more detailed investigation showed that the two hemispheres—the left, which controls not only the movement of the right side of the body but the verbal processes of speaking and writing, and the nonverbal right hemisphere—live independent existences after such surgery. In a sense, the patients had two minds. Sperry's research has contributed much to our scientific knowledge of the brain by helping identify the activities controlled by both sides of the brain and those controlled by only one. It also has interesting implications for our philosophical view of consciousness and the mind.

The concluding selection in the part, "Environmental Stimulation of the Reproductive System of the Female Ring Dove," by Dale Lott, Susan D. Scholz, and D. S. Lehrman, concerns the intricate interaction between internal chemical changes and external environmental stimuli in the control of behavior. In reading this article, it is helpful to keep in mind an important difference between the sexual behavior of man and that of animals lower on the evolutionary scale. The neocortex, the thinking and feeling part of man's brain, plays a very large part in human sexual behavior. Animals lower on the evolutionary scale are much less dependent on their brains and much more dependent on hormones secreted by their sex glands than man, and their sex lives seem far more "automatic" than man's. In human beings, no clear relationship between the time of ovulation in the female—a hormonal event—and the tendency of male and female to have intercourse has ever been established. In rats, by contrast, mating occurs only on the one day in five when the female rat ovulates. On that day she will mate with any male and any male will mate with her; on other days males are not attracted and she does not accept them.

Scientists who study birds have noted that they mate, lay eggs, and engage in sex-related activities such as nest-building at about the same time that certain hormonal changes take place in the female. This observation led some people to believe that the hormonal changes *caused* the sexual behavior—that the female bird, like the female rat, mates and reproduces merely because internally regulated messages from her glands tell her it is time to do so. In a series of studies on the ring dove, D. S. Lehrman challenged this simplistic notion. He identified a chain of events, called a *sequentially dependent chain* because the links must follow each other in a prescribed order, that includes not only hormones but stimuli from the environment: hormone ⟶ sensitivity to environmental stimulus ⟶ behavior ⟶ second hormone, and so on. The selection by Lehrman and his colleagues describes a study of the part played in the female ring dove's reproductive behavior by two outside stimuli, the presence of a courting male and sounds from the surrounding colony of doves.

15

LSD:

A Novelist's Personal Experience

ALAN HARRINGTON

In April I had my first experience with one of the consciousness-expanding substances—or as most physicians prefer to call them, "hallucinogenic drugs." A twelve-hour session under the influence LSD-25 dispatched me on a trip through the cosmos inside my head. LSD enables everyone to become an astronaut of himself. During this flight beyond time into the depths of consciousness, each of us can explore an inward universe filled with both violent and peaceful revelations.

I am no pioneer. Thousands of people have been research subjects before me—have ingested LSD, psilocybin, and mescaline, not to mention raw mushrooms and cactus buttons—and they have had

LSD: A NOVELIST'S PERSONAL EXPERIENCE Reprinted from *LSD: The consciousness-expanding drug.* Edited by D. Solomon. New York: Putnam, 1964. Used by permission of the author and International Famous Agency, Inc. Copyright © 1963 by HMH Publishing Co., Inc. This article originally appeared in *Playboy* (1963) under the title "A visit to inner space."

similar visions and psychic shocks. But I find the accounts of these witnesses intimidatingly beautiful. They are decorated with elevated perceptions and high philosophy. The voyages seem considerably more splendid
than mine. Gorgeous flowers and jewels, knights in armor and Moorish
castles must not be intended for everyone, at least not during the first
session. According to Gerald Heard, the greater the ego the more severe
will be the period of terror under LSD. Before the sublime moments can
come the ego must give up and, willingly or not, break apart. For those
who resist this process, the temporary "dying" can be a hellish passage.
It was that way for me—I must have been so concerned with hanging onto
ego that I missed a great deal of the beauty. (But once the dying was over
with I ascended to the top of the universe like everybody else.)

I would like to report my experience in some detail—not for the reason
that it will be filled with brighter colors than any other, but because most
accounts of the LSD voyage strike me as being either circumspect or
rarefied, and even evasive. The writers don't seem to be telling what happened to them really. They just soar away on their beautiful new wings.
Their memories read like an old Fitzpatrick travelogue, with the sun sinking in the west among lovely islands. Inner space isn't like that. It is a
glorious but sometimes frightening continuum and has a madhouse quality, a little like *Alice in Wonderland*.

.   .   .

Medically certified as being in good health, I kissed my wife good-bye
and picked up my notebook and tape recorder. She and I were nervous.
After twelve years we were going through a period of tension, being
frequently at odds and just not connecting. We had heard Timothy Leary
say that a session with one of the consciousness-expanding drugs had on
occasion helped to "save marriages." The people involved did not go
through the initial experience together but met hours afterward when
whoever took the voyage began to come back down from it, so this time
I went out with Ralph, one of the two psychologists who would be with
me, and my wife stayed on the other side of town.

It was eight o'clock at night. We walked along the dark avenue toward
the apartment where we would have the session. Arthur was already
there. He would remain back, "on the ground"; in other words, take no
LSD tonight. My companion on the voyage would be Ralph, the tall
and solemn young man now walking with me. As we walked along he
explained that the virtue of transcendental living, including the LSD
experience, was that it encouraged "up-leveling out of your hangups."
Although gentle in manner, he had a quick, attacking mind. If he tended
to be grave, he was also funny. I must say that his vocabulary conveyed

a sort of detachment. He said at various times: "my projector discovers
. . . ," "according to my viewing screen . . . ," and that to achieve
internal freedom "you've got to change your lenses and look at life in a
new way."

We arrived at the apartment, joining Arthur there. A lively and incisive
young man of about thirty, a teacher, he also radiated that perplexing
good will that I had encountered among all of Timothy Leary's colleagues. While they were in the kitchen preparing the materials, I opened
up my small Japanese tape recorder and hung the microphone on the back
of a chair. I had only fifteen minutes' worth of tape but trusted that an
interesting flow of talk would be obtained from that. I also had five newly
sharpened pencils. I laid out memo pads around the room. They had
printed on top, in large red letters, "DON'T FORGET." Ralph smiled
and said, "That may turn out to be a huge cosmic joke before the evening
is over."

Arthur had put a match to the paper, kindling, and logs in front of me
and now the fire blazed up. He lit the candles on the mantel. Feeling still
and watchful, I looked up through a big skylight at the stars and waited.
The candles smoked and somebody put on a record. It was music I had
brought: Charlie Byrd's "Bossa Nova Pelos Passaros." A record you especially like is part of the comfortable "set and setting," but Charlie Byrd's
guitar turned out to be much more than that—a melodic link to life when
I desperately needed it.

Arthur placed cushions on the rug. Ralph, my fellow voyager, came
in with the cocktail. It looked something like a Gibson. It was slightly bitter but pleasing. I sloshed water in the glass and drank down the last traces
of the LSD material. We took off at nine-thirty. It was strange to imagine
that in twenty minutes or so I would start to take leave of my senses as I
ordinarily used them. I taped Arthur's instructions:

"There are two things to remember. During the experience you're
going to come to choice points. When you reach them, imagine that you
can go up or downstream. Go downstream always if you can. Just go
with it. Second, if you get hung up, always trust your partner. You can
trust this cat. If you feel that you're going too far out, move toward your
partner. Stay with Ralph."

He said: "I'll be in the next room. Call, and I'll be right here. Remember
that. Have a good voyage."

"Why do you keep saying to trust him?" I asked.

"Paranoia," Arthur said. "You'll probably be suspicious of him. Maybe
of me. That's part of it. But now that you know, you can watch for it."

When Arthur left the room Ralph lay back on his couch. Looking uncomfortable for the only time during the night, he said: "If you don't like me . . . this can happen at some point . . . feel free to say so."

He stretched out and closed his eyes. "Our biggest choice," he murmured, "will probably be whether to keep our eyes open or not." Some minutes later his voice said: "Muddy water let stand still soon will become clear." I said nothing to him. Every now and then I uttered a few self-conscious phrases for the benefit of the tape recorder, and then switched it off. Nervously the soloing cadet, his own Walter Schirra, waited for the moment when he would cut out of time. The veteran traveler dozed. I worried about the wax gathering on the rim of the candlestick. It would soon begin to drop onto the mantel. Somebody in the hall changed the Charlie Byrd record, flipping it over.

It began with a salty taste in my mouth, and my vision started to become prismatic. (One's pupils actually dilate and appear to be the size of quarters.) There was a pressure in my head. The curtains seemed to billow. There might be somebody behind them. The air crackled silently. I had a feeling of colored musical notes floating about, and the scene, I can remark now, was quite like a Klee drawing. I felt a bit queasy, but it passed. The music was louder and the guitar strings beautifully separated. Ralph was looking at me, and I began to laugh. I was going to flip on my tape recorder! What a ridiculous, hilarious thing to do! Why not, though?

"Why not?" Ralph said, and we both laughed. I couldn't stop. Everything that I could think about was insanely and pitifully funny. The world. The universe. All the poor sweet pitiful people I knew. Myself. What a scene! Filled with noble, ridiculous people! The world, the world!

This reaction which is Cosmic Laughter was different from any way of laughing I had known. It came out of me as though propelled by a force much larger than the person laughing. It came right up from the center of my being. The force continued throughout the major part of the experience, no matter what I was feeling. It resembled both a mild and sustained electric shock passing through the body and spirit, and a mild and incomplete and continuing orgasm. A throbbing and rhythmic current, which for want of a fresh image—and one is no longer afraid of being banal—could be described as the life force, shakes you, as if you might be aboard or bestride, or being carried along with, the force that penetrates and then fills all being.

On tape a man may be heard breaking up. His voice becomes noticeably higher-pitched and breathless. Then into the laughter comes a new sound, of fear. The voice trembles. The same force projected through me an enormous grief over the Cosmic Joke. (Timothy Leary has remarked: "The ones who begin laughing always feel the terror later. They realize that the joke is on them.") I wept and sobbed, occasionally laughing. Even now, listening to the tape, I feel sorry for the individual as though it were somebody else.

The machine captured outcries from beyond despair, and frantic attempts of the man to keep himself together, to summon his intelligence and apply it against the grief that has come over him. "Oh, God . . . This is awful! . . . Oh . . . Oh . . . I didn't realize it would be so physical. This stuff won't let you go! . . . Oh . . . My God, what have I done?" Suddenly the predicted hostility comes forth. "Why are *you* so peaceful?" I demand of my fellow voyager. "How can you stretch out and smile while I suffer? Why am *I* the only one to suffer?" Then in a small voice, "I guess there are others. They suffer too."

"Yes . . ." murmured my partner, lying with his arms folded, cruising in space. He had explained that there were storage places in eternity where a traveler could park himself, watching, ready to help the neophyte passing through the turbulent area.

"This is awful. God . . . I want to get back."

"Swing with it!"

It was Arthur's voice. I saw him through air that seemed to have turned to jelly.

"Swing with it? Okay! Sure. That's right. Ha! Ha! But it's hard. I wonder if I can stand up. Shall I try?"

"Why not?" said Ralph, eyeing me compassionately over his folded arms.

"There. You see. I did it. I can walk. But I don't know why I did it. What's the point?"

We laughed but then I heard strange music.

"What's that? I didn't bring that. It's religious music! It must be yours! Is it real? No, no, it's on a record."

I have an aunt near Boston who doesn't speak to anyone in her family. Whenever she disapproves of what a person has done she stops speaking to him. It's very simple. She believes that a person should never be praised because if he's done well that is what he should do. Only his inadequacies are worthy of comment. This aunt's face appeared on the back of a leather chair opposite me, frowning and malevolent. But curiously enough I felt sorry for her, and on tape my voice says mildly: "Well, she has a right to be there. She shouldn't be so disapproving though."

I realize that personal revelations may be of no great interest, and that they will turn out to be embarrassing and tedious if wallowed in, but for the record, I burst out with confessions to Arthur, "back there" in reality, having taken nothing. A young writer named Barry Hughart, who has had some experience with truth drugs such as sodium pentathol, says that the subject typically passes through three phases—fear of homosexuality, confessions of phoniness, and a desire to go home to mother.

In this LSD experience there was no specific homosexual feeling; in fact, I have not heard of any intensified sexual desire, or arousal to action, occurring under the influence of the material. (I have a suspicion that this whole business can, if one wants to play it that way, become a substitute for direct sexual activity, because there is an over-all increase in sensuousness, but this is diffuse and random.)

I would say that the experience has a "mess around" quality involving physical expression of affection. Especially if the voyager is in distress, his companion may reach out and hold him tenderly, saying: "It's all right!" and the afflicted traveler in this situation, if his ego is still there, may think: "Now wait a minute . . . what's this?" Similarly, when a girl participates in any of the roles we have been talking about there will be the same embracing by way of consolation or—to use the adjective properly—Platonic affection, as the subjects move through various stages of the voyage; it's not like the listlessness felt in an opium pad, and it is ten miles from being an orgy, but the connection among all the people in the group is more involved than it would be at a cocktail party—that's for sure.

The confession of phoniness will sound trivial, but it was a matter of terror to me, absolute terror, that I was boring. The sum total of me in the universe was *boring*.

The voice on tape sobs: "I'm boring. Oh, Jesus, so *boring*," etc., until finally Arthur's voice replies with some annoyance: "Yes, as a matter of fact, you are boring," and the absolution, or whatever it was, made that panic go away.

The next confession, beginning at this point and recurring for the next few hours, was that I loved and desperately wanted my wife. This was a surprise to everyone, including ourselves, because as I said we had been through a bad time together. But under LSD it is impossible to fake anything: she was my connection with life.

Someone commented later: "Well, what's so surprising about two people who have been together for twelve years having a bond between them?"

Nothing, I suppose, except that the bond can be buried in the details of everyday living; it can be forgotten; the bond can be taken for granted and become boring if you let it, but just the same over the years it may still be the main cable attaching you to life. During the parts of the LSD torment when an ego is being shredded, you know who your friends are.

When time and space were disappearing I called to her. The only other link to remembered things was the beautiful progression of chords from Charlie Byrd's guitar.

The physical world I could see had begun slowly to come apart. No cubic inch of space had to do with any other. Everything in my field of vision turned into bright jelly. There was no time and place, nothing but a flow. I got up and waded through the room, making my way unsteadily. Around me the music, the fire, and the candle dripping, the lights of nearby buildings, all combined and flowed. Yet I could see Ralph and Arthur watching me, and I saw my own situation with terrible clarity. I had gone too far out and couldn't get back! I called to Ralph, remembering what Arthur had said in the beginning: ". . . if you get hung up, always move toward your partner." I did, crying: "Help me. I want to get back!"

The jelly before my eyes separated. The universe cracked into bright globules and separated; then I was in little pieces, about not to exist anymore, and being borne away on something like a jet stream, and this was the stream Arthur had mentioned, streaming unconsciousness that one was supposed not to fight. Let the ego die. Go with it—but I fought upstream all the way. Ralph caught my hand and said: "Go with it!" But I said: "Get me out. I want to go home. Where is she?" They were like people trying to help me in my envelope of flowing air, not being able to do anything but sympathize. But we could see each other with amazing clarity all this time. They were making notes on me! Arthur had a chart.

"Help me get back!"

Arthur stepped close to me and said: "There's no way you can shorten this. You've got to go through every stage. You've got to go all the way. Just let go!"

I ran to look at my watch to see how much time had gone by, and how much longer I would be in this, but my eyes were so dilated that I couldn't see the numbers or the hands, and then I forgot what time *was*. The candle was dripping on the mantel, and I pointed to what was happening, and Arthur placed a saucer underneath the candlestick, but where had the universe gone? I'd find it. I would walk out!

The foregoing, by the way, is attended by a great deal of shouting and sobbing. If the subject is having quite a bit of trouble the neighbors will be alarmed. For this reason LSD sessions should be held in top-floor apartments, remote places, or rooms with thick walls. Otherwise, if somebody should call the police or the janitor, the uninvited visitors would observe a hollering madman on the floor, and there would be too much explaining to do. Also, the session must be carefully guarded by the psychologist who has stayed back, because the soul in disorder can become panicky and decide, as I did, to leave the premises. They have a dim recollection of "home" somewhere, like the world, and feel that if they can "go out there" everything will be all right. But unfortunately there is no world anymore, and if they should get out in it there would be panic in the streets for certain, and the possibility of embracing an oncoming car, or something like that. The intended departure is easily blocked by the psychologist in charge. A subject, so far as I know, will not be violent in this phase, having no place to stand from which to launch a violent act, either physical or mental, since he's not even sure that he exists. The conception of self varies from one moment to the next, and this is the agony.

In the next room a telephone call went to my wife, one of many during the evening. "He's having a bad time. Yes, really bad. He won't give up his ego. He refuses to die," the caller said with irritation. "He's fighting it. Well, the bigger they are the harder they fall. What? I'm speaking of egos. You know, he's calling for you. Yes, you. You're the only person he wants."

"Calling for *me?*"

"Yes. I don't know. Neurotic dependency . . . that's love. What's the difference?"

"Is he the one making all that noise?"

"Yes, he still won't get up."

"He's schizoid enough as it is. I know I shouldn't have let him do it. He's probably having awful memories. Oh, yes. When he was a baby he's supposed to have had a nurse who did something or other. Ask him. . . ."

The only square thing that happened during the evening was when they came running in, as I rolled around on the floor trying to avoid going downstream, and yelled in my ear: "Do you remember a nurse? Did she do anything? . . ."

I didn't know what he was talking about. There was no nurse, no desire to top Oedipus, no wish to kill my poor father. None of these people were on the scene at any time. The LSD voyage goes out far beyond one's small private history. My trip was back through the cycle of being, which—if Jung's collective unconscious really exists, as I could now swear that it does—is the recurring history of you and me, all of us.

The ego can stand out against the universe for just so long, and then it lets go and "dies," going downstream. But at some point there must occur the ride into the hell of ego, a passage through glowing coils which plant endless bright circles in the mind. Far from home, far into inner space, the voyager can no longer be helped by his serene companion who cruises compassionately alongside the frightened speck of ego. The huge melancholy eyes watch from the couch. The brotherly hand is outstretched but ignored, and the ego travels in no time, no space, no dimension like an astronaut flung out too far who will never return until time bends back on itself to his real, dear home, and if it were not for the remote stroke of the guitar he would perish utterly in this immense void.

Arthur offered me the pulp of an orange. The schizophrenic presence accepted it, huddling cold in his jacket, then sweating with the heat from the fire, shivering, and gasping for breath.

Meanwhile the fleck of existence performed every act it had never dreamed of performing. While the body in the living room constantly changed positions, during which at various time it was fetal, crawling and sucking its thumb, the speck was pushed by a tremulous current into a lotus of naked bodies, and diving in, was folded into the universe, as if the universe was making love to itself. The speck then flew to the top of all things, and saw in every direction what was and will be. The Enduring Situation was this:

In space an endless power station, plugged and electrical, with a current pulsing through every part of it. This structure, resembling a playground jungle gym, was the totality of all being. Individual living beings attached, in stasis, made up the structure. The relationship of each being to the whole was somehow religious and also sexual.

Thereafter the speck whirled down a great glowing tract, experienced a terrific pressure, as if its mass were built up intolerably, and reentering was thrust down, labored, felt a collar, and burst clear of the ordeal.

I rested on the couch, with the colored musical notes still floating in the air around me, and I was shivering and saying: "I want to go home now. Where is she?"

Ralph smiled and informed me from the rug: "You're only a third of the way through."

"No!" I said. "I won't go back there."

It wouldn't be necessary. The death-and-rebirth phase was passed. Now we were on a plateau, the philosophical plateau, from which one can take off again or come back down. We talked about games and the love-preventing monster of ego—which was the view of yourself as opposed to identity, your self in action. We talked about the highest good being play, and the word "play." For instance, you don't work the piano. The monotheistic religions had converted play to puritanical "work," the duty of ego. I said: "What do you want to do with your life, Ralph?" and he replied: "I'm in the Buddha-making business." We discussed Norman Brown's concept built out of Freud that Time and History were forms of neurosis. We mentioned people making time and making history. I knew an advertising man who came to New York to sell space and ended up buying time.

Arthur, who had been asleep, came in and we talked. I said something, I forget what, and he got up hurriedly and left. I thought I had offended him.

"I've betrayed him in some way," I said. "I've always been a Judas."

"A thread of paranoia running through the universe," Ralph mused. "Live out that fantasy if you feel it."

"I've never known how to live."

"You just get up in the morning and do the best you can."

A man came jauntily into the room. He looked at me in a manner that was both kindly and amused.

"How do you feel, Alan?"

"Fine now. But it was terrible."

He said: "Now you know what it's like to suffer ego loss."

I answered: "My ego loss was so catastrophic that it doesn't matter."

Timothy Leary threw back his head and laughed. He sat down alongside me on the couch. He clapped me on the back offering a swallow of ginger beer and a bite from an apple. Ralph sat on the rug with his hands clasped over his knees. The phone rang. It was a long-distance call for Leary.

I had a perception that Judas was a writer who had sold the rights to Jesus' life story, and whether he wrote him up or delivered him to the orthodox authorities was the same. I had the impression that we were all recurring characters and that Timothy Leary through the centuries had always been offering something like LSD to people, Arthur had always been helping him, and Ralph had forever taken witnesses on the voyage.

On the phone Timothy Leary said: "That wasn't very cool of you, was it?"

When he put down the receiver we talked some more. He told a story: In an experiment with psilocybin, not his own, the subject had been a young electronic engineer. He went into a panic, and his traveling companion was unable to calm him down. The psychologist in charge happened to be in the bathroom. He called to his wife, who was drying dishes in the kitchen: "Straighten him out, will you?" She dried her hands and went into the living room. The distressed engineer cried out: "I want my wife!" and she put her arms around him, murmuring: "Your wife is a river, a river, a river!" "Ah!" he said more quietly. "I want my mother!" "Your mother is a river, a river, a river!" "Ah, yes," sighed the engineer, and gave up his fight, and drifted off happily, and the psychologist's wife went back to her dishes.

"You feel like going home?" Leary smiled.

"Yes. But I don't know if I can make it."

"You can do anything," he said. "Better than you ever did. You feel that something big physically has happened to you. You feel violence in your system. The drug doesn't cause that. It's in you all the time. Your cells are exploding with energy. There's more electrical energy in a cluster of cells in your body than Con Edison can produce. LSD isn't causing your eyeballs to see new things. It's just helping you to pick up on them."

Ralph and I went back to my house, and my wife held out her arms to me, and she looked as good as a piece of apple pie. Still nervously crackling with energy I fell into bed. My wife made us steak and potatoes, and we drank some beer, and we were joking together. The walls were as holey as cheese, and still billowing around me; the colored musical notes floated by, but not so many of them. Small, throbbing currents still moved through my body, but I was coming down. I could read the paper. I happened to look at Leonard Lyons' column in the New York *Post*. Though my LSD reaction was waning, I felt the old cosmic laughter that had started, it seemed ages ago, in the apartment with the skylight. Mr. Lyons' items seemed as insanely and pitifully funny as any in the universe. There was one:

> A. E. Hotchner, the adapter of Ernest Hemingway's stories, has a home in Westport. In Connecticut car owners are permitted to have four letters on their license plates. . . . Hotchner owns two cars. One has plates marked "HOTC," and the other "HNER." When the cars are parked side by side, the plates spell out his name.

I fell out of bed laughing, and contemplated this item for several minutes. I sat and pondered other paragraphs between the dotted lines:

> . . . Frank Sinatra's Youth Center near Nazareth soon will be ready for occupancy. . . .

and

> Cleopatra will give screen credits to Plutarch and Suetonius. "They were clever fellows, those two," said Darryl Zanuck of the ancient historians, "but they didn't know a thing about residuals."

The musical notes jumped, the walls bellied, and the small shudders of electricity were fading. I studied the melancholy countenance atop this column of ego. I saw the chronicler as a gallant little man running through time, carrying a handful of threads and presenting them to people and running on.

I thanked Ralph for being my companion, and for his help on the voyage, and we said good-bye to him. My wife brought me a cup of tea. I remembered something a prisoner treated by Timothy Leary's group had said after his first psilocybin experience was over: "My whole life came tumbling down and I was sitting happily in the rubble."

16

The Effects
of Hemisphere Deconnection
on Conscious Awareness

ROGER W. SPERRY

This article is a report on studies my colleagues and I have been conducting of some neurosurgical patients in Los Angeles, all advanced epileptics who underwent brain surgery because their convulsions could not be controlled by medication. The surgery was extreme: so far as I know, the most nearly complete severing of the connections between the left and right halves of the brain ever attempted in man.

The first patient on whom the surgery was tried had been having epileptic seizures for more than ten years, and his convulsions had grown worse and worse despite treatment. At the time of the operation he was averaging two serious attacks a week and had begun to have severe seizures (a type that can be fatal) every few months. In the five and a half years since surgery, the man has had not a

THE EFFECTS OF HEMISPHERE DECONNECTION ON CONSCIOUS AWARENESS Adapted from *American Psychologist* 23 (1968). Used by permission of the author.

single major convulsion. He has been able to take less medication, and his overall sense of well-being has increased. The second patient, a housewife and mother in her thirties, has also been free of seizures since surgery, which took place more than four years ago.

The excellent outcome in these two apparently hopeless, last-resort cases has led to the use of the surgery on nine more people to date. Although the epileptic seizures have not completely vanished in all nine, the results on the whole have been beneficial.

The therapeutic success of the operation, however, is a matter for my medical colleagues, Philip J. Vogel and Joseph E. Bogen. My own work has been confined entirely to the functional outcome of surgically disrupting all direct communication between the two hemispheres of the brain—that is, to the behavioral and psychological effects of hemisphere deconnection.

No major collapse of mentality or personality was anticipated as a result of surgery. In fact, we wondered at first whether we would find any behavioral change in our patients. Many symptoms have been found in "split-brain" studies of animals, but earlier research on human beings with hemisphere deconnections almost as complete as those of our patients seemed to indicate no important changes in behavior, as long as no other brain damage had occurred.

In a general way, our research confirms those earlier observations. Remarkable though it may seem, severing the neural connections between the brain hemispheres results in virtually no apparent change in the patient's ordinary behavior. If, however, appropriate tests are used, one can demonstrate that the surgery has a dramatic effect on the patient's behavior—and this is in contradiction to reports based on the earlier studies.

The Doubling of Conscious Awareness

When you split the brain in half anatomically, you do not divide its functions in half. Since both hemispheres perform many of the same activities, it is perhaps more appropriate to think of the brain's functions as being doubled than as being halved. For example, there is an apparent doubling of most types of conscious awareness. Instead of having a single, unified stream of consciousness, the patients act as if they have two independent streams of conscious awareness, one in each half of the brain. Each half of the brain seems to be out of contact with the mental experiences of the other. That is, each hemisphere seems to have its own separate

FIGURE 16-1

Apparatus for studying vision, touch, language, and other behavior in patients whose brain hemispheres have been surgically separated. The setup makes it possible to study one sense at a time—to test the patient's sense of touch while his vision is blocked off—and one side of the body at a time.

and private sensations, its own perceptions, its own concepts, its own impulses to act—and also its own chain of memories—which cannot be recalled by the other hemisphere.

The presence of two minds in one body, as it were, is one of the most striking results of the operation. It can be demonstrated with many kinds of tests, but for convenience I will refer to only one testing setup, as shown in Figure 16-1. This setup allows us to test the patient's use of his right and left hands and legs with vision blocked off, and to test the right and left halves of the visual field, separately or together. In our patients, as in people whose hemispheres are intact, everything seen on the left side of the visual field by either eye is registered in the right hemisphere of the brain and vice versa, as shown in Figure 16-2.

In one type of vision test used with our patients, pictures are projected onto one side of the screen shown in Figure 16-1 while the patient watches, using only one eye. Each picture appears for no more than a tenth of a second—too little time for the patient to get it into the other half of the visual field by moving his head or eye. The results show that our patients have not one visual world but two separate ones. For example, a patient who has identified a picture shown on one side of the

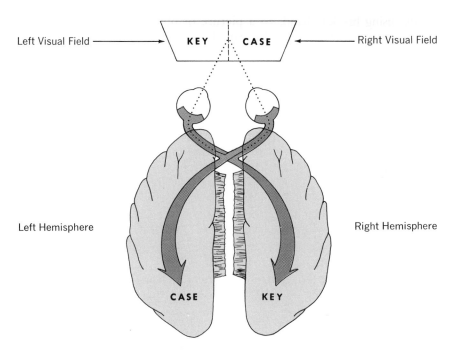

FIGURE 16-2
Things seen to the left of center with either eye are carried to the right hemisphere of the brain and vice versa.

screen will recall having seen it only if it reappears on the same side as before. If it reappears in the other half of the visual field, the patient responds as if he had not seen it before. In other words, things seen through one hemisphere are registered and remembered quite separately from things seen through the other hemisphere. Each brain hemisphere has its own train of visual images and memories.

The separate existence of two visual inner worlds also reveals itself in tests that require speech or writing. The brain center for speech and writing is located in the dominant brain hemisphere—the left hemisphere, in right-handed people. When a picture appears in the right half of the visual field and is transmitted to the left (dominant) hemisphere, the patient is able to describe what he saw in speech or writing. When the same picture is shown on the left and hence transmitted to the right hemisphere, the patient insists he saw nothing at all or only a flash of light. He acts as if he were blind to the left half of the visual field. However, if instead of asking him to *describe* what he saw you ask him to *point*, using his left hand, to a picture or object that matches the one he was shown on the screen, he can do it with no trouble. In such a test, everything indicates that the talking hemisphere (the left) truly did not see the stimulus and does not remember it. The nonverbal hemisphere (the right) *did* see the stimulus, and it can remember and recognize it. Like a deaf-mute, it cannot talk about the object, nor can it write about the object, but it can point out a matching object or picture.

What happens if two different pictures are flashed simultaneously to the left and right visual fields, say a dollar sign to the left and a question mark to the right? If the patient is blindfolded and asked to draw with his left hand what he saw, he reproduces the figure shown on the left, that is, the dollar sign. But if you ask him what he has drawn, he replies without hesitation that it is a question mark. The left hemisphere does not know what the right hemisphere saw and drew. The stimuli in the two halves of the visual field seem to be perceived quite separately in each hemisphere, with little or no cross-influence.

When words are flashed across the whole visual field, the letters on each side of center are perceived and responded to separately. In the "key case" example shown in Figure 16-2, the patient can indicate perception of the word "key" through the minor (right) hemisphere by choosing a key from a collection of objects with his left hand. He can also respond to the word "case" by writing it with his right hand, or saying it aloud. But when asked what kind of case he has in mind, he will say something like "in *case* of fire," or "the *case* of the missing corpse," or "a *case* of beer." Any reference to "key case" by the left hemisphere under these conditions is purely coincidental.

A similar separation in mental awareness is evident when the patient must identify objects by touch with either his right or his left hand. He can easily describe and name objects put into the right hand, orally or in writing. But if the same objects are put into the left hand, he can only make wild guesses. He often seems unaware that anything at all is present. In fact, however, he *is* aware: He will show good perception, comprehension, and memory for objects touched by the left hand if he is allowed to express himself nonverbally, as by finding a matching object with his left hand.

When we first ask the patients to use the left hand for these tests, they complain that they cannot "work with that hand," that the hand is "numb," that they "just can't feel anything or do anything with it," or that they "don't get the message from that hand." If they succeed in finding objects that match the ones they said they could not feel, and if the contradiction is pointed out to them, they make comments like "I was just guessing" and "Well, I must have done it unconsciously."

It should be mentioned that nearly all these signs of the lack of communication between the two hemispheres can be hidden or compensated for in ordinary behavior. A patient's difficulties in identifying objects by touch are not apparent unless he is prevented from using his eyes. In the tests of vision, the picture must appear in one half of the visual field very briefly in order to keep the patient from getting it into the other half of the field by moving his head or eye. Normal, everyday behavior is also favored by the fact that the two hemispheres inhabit the same body. They go the same places, meet the same people, and see and do the same things. Thus they are bound to have many common, almost identical experiences.

Much of the material discussed so far is summarized in Figure 16-3. The left hemisphere of the brain is equipped with the expressive mechanisms for speech and writing and with the main centers for the comprehension and organization of language. This major, or dominant, hemi-

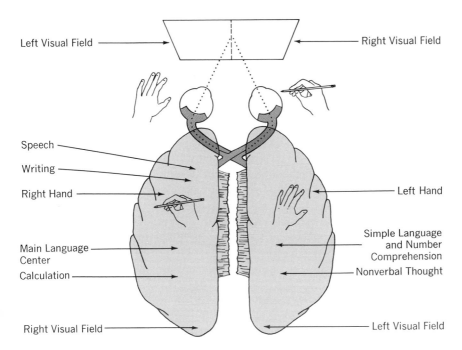

FIGURE 16-3

Schematic outline of the division of certain activities between the brain hemispheres. Note that speech and writing are handled by the dominant left hemisphere, where most language and other symbolic activities are centered.

sphere can communicate its experiences verbally. On the other side is the mute, right hemisphere, which cannot express itself in words but which, through nonverbal responses, can show that it does know things—that mental processes are indeed present, centered around the left visual field and the left side of the body. (Each hemisphere also performs the many cerebral activities, such as hearing and smelling, that are separately and rather fully organized in both halves of the brain.)

The "Unconscious" Minor Hemisphere

One of the main goals of our testing program has been to find out what goes on in the nonverbal, minor hemisphere, which can neither speak nor write. Does it have true conscious awareness, or is it just an unknowing automaton that reacts reflexively or exists in a trancelike state? What kind of mental life is there in this subordinate and unknown half of the human brain—which, like the animal mind, cannot communicate its experiences in words?

With these questions in mind, I will review briefly some of the evidence we have obtained concerning the mental life of the minor hemisphere. First, it is clear from the tests already described that intermodal transfers of information of a kind impossible for monkeys occur readily within the minor hemisphere. When a patient uses blind touch with the left hand to find an item that matches a picture flashed to the minor (right) hemisphere through the left visual field, he shows that he can remember by touch what he saw, even though he cannot describe it.

Other responses suggest that the minor hemisphere has some capacity for ideas, mental associations, and simple reasoning. If we flash a picture of a wall clock to the minor hemisphere and the nearest thing to a matching item that the left hand can find and touch is a toy wrist watch, most patients will choose the watch. It is as if the minor hemisphere is not just matching the physical outlines of the picture but has an idea of a timepiece. Similarly, if a dollar sign is flashed to the minor hemisphere, the patient will search through a collection of items with his left hand and select a quarter or some other coin. If a picture of a hammer is presented, he may come up with a nail or a spike.

The minor hemisphere can also do simple arithmetic. In four out of six patients, the right hemisphere was able to add or multiply two numbers, as long as the answer was less than twenty and could be expressed with the left hand by pointing or other nonverbal means. After the patient had seen his left hand indicate the correct answer, he could give the same answer verbally. The verbal report from the dominant hemisphere could not be made before the left-hand response, however, and if the left hand was wrong the verbal report contained the same error.

It has long been thought by most scientists that the minor hemisphere becomes "word blind" and "word deaf" when it is disconnected from the language centers in the dominant hemisphere, as it is in some stroke victims and other aphasics. In contradiction to this, we find that the disconnected minor hemisphere can comprehend both written and spoken words to some extent, though it cannot express its understanding in words. For instance, when the word "key" was flashed to the left visual field, the patient could find a key in a collection of objects by blind touch with the left hand. If he was asked to identify the object after he had chosen it, his replies showed that he did not know what it was. This means, of course, that the *talking* hemisphere did not know. Since the patient was holding the correct object in his left hand, it is clear that the minor hemisphere must have read and understood the test word.

The patients can also find by blind touch with the left hand an object named aloud by the examiner, again demonstrating comprehension of language by the minor hemisphere. If the patient is asked to find a piece of silverware, he may explore the items before him and pick up a fork. If he is asked what he has picked up, he is just as likely to answer "spoon" or "knife" as "fork." Both hemispheres heard and understood the word "silverware," but only the minor hemisphere knows what the left hand actually found and picked up.

The minor hemisphere shows a capacity for emotion as well as an ability to understand symbols. For example, if a pinup shot of a nude is included in a series of neutral geometric figures being flashed to the left visual field, the patient says that he or she saw nothing, or just a flash of light. However, the appearance of a sneaky grin and perhaps blushing and giggling belies what the talking hemisphere has said. If the patient is asked what all the grinning is about, his replies indicate that the speaking hemisphere has no idea what it was that turned him on. Apparently only the emotional effect gets across, as if the cognitive content has been blocked.

The minor hemisphere also triggers emotional reactions of displeasure in the course of testing. The patient will frown, wince, and shake his head in test situations where the minor hemisphere, which knows the correct answer but cannot speak, hears the major hemisphere making obvious verbal mistakes. The minor hemisphere seems to express genuine annoyance at the incorrect vocal responses of its better half.

Observations like these lead us to suspect that the minor hemisphere is a second conscious entity, characteristically human and running parallel to the dominant stream of consciousness in the major hemisphere. There is no indication that the left hemisphere is concerned about or even aware of the presence of the minor system under ordinary conditions except quite indirectly, as through occasional reactions triggered by the minor side. As one patient remarked after seeing herself make a left-hand response to a problem, "Now I know it wasn't me that did that!"

Let me point out in closing that this has been a somewhat abbreviated and streamlined account of the syndrome of hemisphere deconnection as we understand it at the present time. The more we see of these patients and the more of these patients we see, the more impressed we become with their individual differences and with the qualifications these differences impose on our findings. What the accumulating evidence will show about the outer limits of individual variation and about the existence of an "average" syndrome of hemisphere deconnection remains to be seen.

17

Environmental Stimulation

of the Reproductive System

of the Female Ring Dove

D A L E   L O T T

S U S A N   D .   S C H O L Z

D .   S .   L E H R M A N

In many animal species, stimuli from the outside environment play an essential role in the glandular activity that regulates the reproductive cycle. One such species is the ring dove. Two outside stimuli that are known to affect ovulation and egg-laying in the female ring dove are the presence of a male and exposure to the sounds made by other doves in the breeding colony, both readily available to the female under natural conditions.

Although ovulation normally requires the presence of a male, physical contact between the two doves is not essential. Ovulation has been induced in the laboratory by letting a female see a male that is separated from her by a glass barrier. The male's effect on the

ENVIRONMENTAL STIMULATION OF THE REPRODUCTIVE SYSTEM OF THE FEMALE RING DOVE Adapted from *Animal Behavior* 15 (1967). Used by permission of D. S. Lehrman. This article originally appeared under the title "Exteroceptive stimulation of the reproductive system of the female ring dove (*Streptopelia risoria*)."

female's reproductive system is considerably reduced, however, if he has been castrated; thus it seems that it is not merely the presence of the male but his performance of *courting behavior* that affects the female.

Even if she is in a cage by herself the female will usually lay eggs if, instead of a male mate, she is provided with a mirror so that she can see her reflection. However she will rarely do this unless she can also hear sounds from birds in a breeding colony.

The experiments that yielded these findings (Erickson and Lehrman, 1964; Lehrman, Brody, and Wortis, 1961; Lott and Brody, 1966) show that (1) stimulation from a courting male induces ovarian development when sounds from the colony are also present, and (2) stimulation from the colony can induce ovarian development when a non-courting ring dove is present. The next question that needs to be asked is whether, under natural conditions (in which a female associates with a courting male within the colony milieu), the two stimuli cooperate to produce a higher level of reproductive development than would be produced by either stimulus alone.

In the experiment reported here, we investigated the effects on reproductive development in female ring doves of sounds from the dove colony, with and without stimulation from a courting male. Seventy-two females and seventy-two males, some castrated and some intact, were used. All the birds had previous breeding experience and had produced at least one brood. For the experiment, the seventy-two pairs of doves were placed in soundproof steel chambers, the female on one side of a glass plate and the male on the other. Each chamber was equipped with a small loudspeaker hooked up to a microphone in the adjoining colony room that could be turned on to admit the sounds of other doves.

The female doves were divided into four groups:

Group 1 doves were paired with castrated males and exposed continuously to sound from the colony room.

Group 2 doves were paired with intact males and exposed continuously to sound from the colony room.

Group 3 doves were paired with castrated males but deprived of sound from the colony room.

Group 4 doves were paired with intact males but deprived of sound from the colony room.

Seven days after each pair of doves had been placed in the chamber, the female was removed. An autopsy was performed to determine how much ovarian development had occurred in each bird. If ovulation had not yet taken place, the weight of the oviduct was used to indicate how much preliminary ovarian activity there had been. If ovulation had taken place, we used the location of the egg or eggs and the softness or hardness of the shell to indicate the extent of development. For example, the presence of one egg high in the oviduct showed minimal amount of development beyond ovulation; the presence of one egg in the nest and one high in the oviduct showed a moderate amount; and the presence of two eggs in the nest indicated that the full reproductive cycle had been achieved.

The females placed with intact males and allowed to hear the sounds from the colony room showed considerably fuller ovarian development than did females that had access to one of the stimuli but not both. Females in Group 1, which heard the colony sounds but saw no male courting behavior, and females in Group 4, which saw courting behavior but heard no colony sounds, were stimulated to about the same degree— considerably less than females in Group 2, which received both stimuli, but much more than females in Group 3, which were exposed to castrated males alone.

We can thus conclude that in the normal colony situation stimulation from the bird's mate and from the surrounding colony work together to induce the glandular changes that bring about full ovarian development in female ring doves.

REFERENCES

Erickson, C. J., and Lehrman, D. S. Effect of castration of male ring doves upon ovarian activity of females. *Journal of Comparative and Physiological Psychology* 58 (1964): 164–66.

Lehrman, D. S., Brody, P. N., and Wortis, R. P. The presence of the mate and of nesting material as stimuli for the development of incubation behavior and for gonadotropin secretion in the ring dove (*Streptopelia risoria*). *Endocrinology* 68 (1961): 507–16.

Lott, D. S., and Brody, P. N. Support of ovulation in the ring dove by auditory and visual stimuli. *Journal of Comparative and Physiological Psychology* 62 (1966): 311–13.

Motivation

Motivation is one of the oldest psychological concepts invented by man. It originated so early and has lasted so long because all of us believe that our behavior is directed toward goals. But goals are not always easy to identify on the basis of behavior. When we try to guess a person's motivation from his actions, we often make mistakes. For example, the fact that a classmate fails to appear for a final examination does not tell you much about his intention or help you predict how he will behave the next time a final exam comes up. If he is a close friend and you know a great deal about him and how he has behaved in the past, you may be able to guess his intention accurately. But many actions, no matter how microscopically examined and how minutely described, are misleading as to motivation.

The concept of motivation has a checkered history in modern psychology. Early in the century it was believed that human behavior was powered by internal energy, and that this energy was what pushed people toward goals. Sigmund Freud assumed that a fixed amount of energy was released at birth and directed toward particular sources of gratification. The sources of gratification changed as the person matured—a belief that led to the so-called stage theory of motivation.

But psychologists, unable to measure this mysterious energy, became increasingly dissatisfied with this view of motivation. During the thirties and forties a new approach emerged. Psychologists began to think of motives as behavioral tendencies, as inclinations to move toward a goal. This definition, unlike the energy theory, allowed them to investigate motives by studying behavior. Behavioral studies yielded the lists of motives that appear in most psychology textbooks: People have motives to excel, to affiliate with friends, to dominate others, to gain social approval, and so on. Each of these motives refers to certain behaviors that can be seen and counted.

"The Study of Motivation," by John W. Atkinson, illustrates a behavioral approach to motivation. Atkinson believes that a motive is a tendency to behave in a certain way and that behavior depends on three things: a person's goals, the behavior he has available to help him attain them, and the factors in the immediate environment that determine whether he puts the behavior into action.

Atkinson stresses that we should not think of a motive as a force that pushes a person into action from a state of rest; from the moment a human being is born, he is always behaving, always moving toward some goal—even when he is sleeping. What has to be explained is why he stops chasing one goal and starts pursuing another.

Atkinson presents an important challenge to psychologists: to study the shifts in the balance of conflicting motives that account for a change in a person's behavior. A person who has just awakened has a motive to keep lying in bed; it is opposed by a motive to get up and begin the day. The person gets up at the moment when the motive to begin the day becomes stronger than the motive to stay in bed. As this example implies, a person's behavior is organized in temporal slices. Once he begins a series of actions directed toward a particular goal, he will persist in that behavior until a new motive is aroused. The new motive then competes with the older one. If it wins out, a change in behavior occurs. It is important for psychologists to analyze these points of conflict and change, because they are precisely the points that should reveal the strengths of different motives for an individual at different times.

Instead of viewing a motive as a tendency to behave in a certain way, Jerome Kagan, author of the second selection, regards it as a wish—a mental idea of what one wants. Some motives will lead to behavior; others will not. A child may dream of going to Disneyland or yelling at his mother but make no attempt to gratify either motive, in which case we cannot detect the motives from watching the child's behavior. Moreover, identical behavior can result from different motives. One boy may burn down a school building to experience sexual gratification, another to get even with his teacher. In "Motives and Behavior in the Young Child: Hostility and Affiliation," he discusses the development of two different motives.

When a person finds his goal-directed actions blocked or his standards threatened, he is likely to become angry and to wish that whatever is frustrating him would be hurt or destroyed. When a person cannot predict the future, encounters an unusual event, or notes an inconsistency between his actions and beliefs, he becomes motivated to resolve these uncertainties, perhaps by allying himself with another person. Kagan points out that behavior we call aggressive or dependent is not necessarily aimed at gratifying the motives of hostility or affiliation. Just as burning down a building can serve a sexual, rather than a hostile, motive, so the seeking of close relationships with others can be meant to gratify a desire for power rather than friendship. Since human behavior is ambiguous with respect to the motives it serves, Kagan believes that psychologists must devise ways of measuring motives in their pure form, namely, as wishes.

18

The Study of Motivation

JOHN W. ATKINSON

The study of motivation concerns the factors that incite and direct an individual's activities. Psychologists agree on that much, but on very little more. Theories of motivation and techniques for studying it have changed a great deal since the end of the nineteenth century; in addition, motivation is a concern of a number of different fields of psychology, each of which has its own special language. These facts help account for the confusion that surrounds the terms "motivation" and "motivated behavior" at present, but they do not eliminate our need for a theory that defines, precisely and accurately, what the terms mean. As the following will show, research based on an unclear or unsound concept of what it is we study when we study motivation yields findings whose relevance to a comprehensive view of human behavior is at best limited.

A Common-sense View
of Motivation

A good first step toward a theory of motivation is to inquire into the common-sense view of it, the one we all employ in everyday conversation. Suppose you are asked, for example, why you are reading this book. The question focuses on the direction of your behavior. You have obviously chosen to read the book instead of to do something else. Why?

Your immediate answer will probably contain the word "want," "wish," or "desire." You might say "Because I want to finish the reading assignment" or "Because I wish I knew more about psychology." In other words, you are reading because you want to attain an objective (finishing the assignment or learning more about psychology), and what you are doing is a means to that end. Your answer could include the words "like" or "don't like" instead of "want" or "wish" without much difference in meaning. For example, you might say "I am reading this book because I like psychology" or "I don't like sitting around doing nothing, so I picked up this book."

We want, desire, or like things that are personally gratifying—things that provide satisfaction or pleasure. We dislike and want to turn away from things that are offensive and cause displeasure or resentment. The origins of our impulses to do this or that, whether we call the impulses wants, wishes, or desires, are all motives. That is, they are forces that lie within, rather than outside, the individual and incite him to action.

Action is normally influenced by an *intention*, by a determination to behave in a certain way or to do a certain thing. Intentional behavior is directed toward some conscious objective, or goal. Normally, the goal is to gain some sort of satisfaction or to avoid some sort of displeasure. Were we to pursue this matter further, we could arrive at a more complete common-sense definition of motivation in which the words "want," "decide," and "act" might be the key terms. The individual experiences a want, decides on a course of action, acts.

Sometimes the sequence proceeds smoothly. If a hungry man is presented with a plate of worms and a plate of spaghetti, he will have little trouble deciding which to eat. But sometimes difficulties arise. If a friend were to telephone now and invite you to join him for a movie, your immediate impulse might be to go. But then there might be a fleeting thought of being unprepared for tomorrow's class discussion, or perhaps for tomorrow's quiz. The decision, delayed by conflict, would no longer be easy to make. For some, at least, the movie would lose out. Those people would probably experience the frustration and irritation that usually accompany thwarted wishes.

This is the stuff of which the common-sense view of motivation is made. Motivation has to do with satisfactions and dissatisfactions, with wants that lead to actions, with decisions between alternative actions, with conflicts of interest, with feelings of frustration and feelings of gratification—all of which constantly fill our daily, conscious experience.

The Scientific Study of Motivation

A somewhat more scientific definition of motivation suggests that what we study when we investigate motivation is "how behavior gets started, is energized, is sustained, is directed, is stopped, and what kind of subjective reaction is present in the organism while all this is going on" (Jones, 1955). This definition makes clear, among other things, that motivation is a very large subject. Let us pause for a moment to consider how the study of motivation differs from two other fields of psychology, learning and perception.

Throughout the history of experimental psychology, the problem of learning—that is, how behavior changes as a result of training and practice—and the problem of motivation have been intimately linked. Many important motivational concepts have arisen from analyses of how learning occurs in lower animals. As a result, it is sometimes difficult to separate the two problems, because the treatment of one so often involves the other.

The study of learning is essentially historical in orientation. When learning is examined, the goal is to account for changes in an individual's tendency to behave in a certain way as a direct consequence of *past experience*. By contrast, the primary goal in the study of motivation is to identify and understand the effects of all the important *contemporaneous influences* that determine actions. A tendency to behave in a certain way as the result of prior experience is but one factor to be taken into account in studying motivation; the main interest is the combined effect of all the immediate influences that incite and direct behavior.

When perception is studied, the central goal is to show how the characteristics of a physical stimulus, together with other factors within the individual at the time, influence what he sees, hears, or feels. *What* an individual perceives is important to the study of motivation, but we are not concerned with analyzing the process of perception per se.

In summary, then, the study of motivation takes for granted that tendencies to behave in certain ways can be changed by practice, but it does not include an analysis of how learning occurs. The study of motivation also takes for granted that the individual is sensitive to cues from his environment, but it does not include an analysis of how perception occurs. Rather, the study of motivation concerns how what has been learned in the past and what is momentarily perceived by the individual combine with other factors to determine the direction, vigor, and persistence of behavior at a particular time.

What more specific questions would we expect the scientific study of motivation to deal with? Let us consider a few everyday *wants* that most people are likely to experience at one time or another: want to eat, want to drink, want to be liked, want to get away by myself for a while, want to succeed, want people to do what I say, want to kiss someone. We can substitute the word "like" for the word "want" in these examples without distortion: like to eat, like to drink, like to be liked, and so on. There are also many wants that have to do with averting unpleasantness: want the headache to go away, want to avoid an automobile accident, want to be inside when it rains, want to avoid making a fool of myself. It is clear that many different kinds of things are liked for their apparent satisfaction and that many different kinds of things are disliked for their apparent unpleasantness. One task for a psychology of motivation would be to devise a scheme for the classification of specific wants that seem to have much in common.

Next, let us consider the influence of the *immediate environment* on what we desire. Two specific wants that everyone has experienced are the desire to eat and the desire to succeed. Common sense acknowledges that the strength of certain wants, for example, for food and water, are related to changes in internal, physiological conditions. But why does the desire to eat become stronger after I have entered a restaurant and sniffed the aroma of charcoal-broiled steak? Similarly, why does my desire to succeed vary, becoming stronger, for example, when I am faced with a competitive activity? In both cases, factors in the immediate environment influence the strength of motivation. We should have a conceptual scheme that clarifies the nature of these influences on motivation.

We also need a scheme that treats the matter of *incentives*. Why are some foods preferred to others, even though any will satisfy hunger? Why is the competition sharpened by a good opponent in a tennis or golf match and weakened when one plays with someone who is easily defeated? Different goals seem capable of satisfying the same want, but some are obviously preferred to others. Thus the psychology of motivation should concern itself with the relative attractiveness of different goals that satisfy the same want.

Finally, why do some people have a greater appetite than others? Even when the number of hours since the last meal is the same for two people and attractive food is given to both, one may eat with great relish while the other picks at his meal and shows little enjoyment. In a competitive game, too, some people seem especially eager to win; others seem only moderately interested. There is little question that people differ greatly in the things they are motivated to do and in the strength of particular motives. There are, in other words, important *individual differences* which the psychology of motivation should consider and understand.

To summarize, here are some of the topics we would expect the scientific study of motivation to consider: (1) the kinds of wants people have, (2) the behavior people direct toward things they want or like and away from things they dislike, (3) the factors, both external and internal, that influence the strength of desire and the behavior of a person toward the liked or disliked object, and (4) differences among individuals in the strength of their desires and the strength of their tendency to seek certain things and avoid others.

A New Premise
for the Study of Motivation

The way the topics sketched out above are approached by psychologists will depend on how they view motivation and motivated behavior. That is, it will depend on how motivated behavior is defined and on what theory of motivation is held. Let us consider an important theoretical question raised by recent research on motivation, and especially by Feather's study of achievement-oriented behavior (Feather, 1961).

The traditional view of those who study the persistence of behavior has been that, other things being equal, persistence or lack of persistence is accounted for by the strength or weakness of the organism's tendency to perform the activity in question. Feather's analysis suggests a modification of this view. His study concerned the effects of repeated failure to solve a puzzle on the persistence of his subjects' attempts to do so. He found that he could not predict with any precision when a person would stop working at the puzzle unless he knew something about the strength of the person's desire to do something else. He stated this finding as a principle: An activity persists only as long as the strength of the tendency sustaining it exceeds the strength of the tendency to initiate a new activity. As soon as the strength of the tendency to perform a new activity exceeds the strength of the tendency to continue the activity already in progress, the first activity stops and the second begins. This may seem a fairly obvious point. However, its implications are not immediately obvious, and they are of fundamental importance to the theories on which empirical studies of motivation are based.

As an aid to seeing what Feather's principle means, consider a common situation. Suppose that some children are playing in the living room when their mother calls them from the kitchen, saying that dinner is ready. Their mother will probably have to call several times before one and then another child stops playing and goes to the table. Without the repeated calls, which create a tendency that competes with the tendency to continue playing, the children would play for an indefinite period of time. Eventually one might stop playing and turn to something else—watching television, say. The fact that he stopped playing and started watching television would mean that at the time the change in activity took place the strength of the tendency to watch television exceeded the strength of the tendency to play. The shift in strengths might have occurred because the tendency to play became weaker, or because the tendency to watch television became stronger, or both.

The point is that there are no behavioral vacuums in the life of an individual. Children do not stop behaving when they stop playing, even if what replaces play is not eating dinner or watching TV but merely standing still and looking bored, or even taking a nap. Behavior that appears passive is behavior nonetheless, and it must still be considered an activity.

According to the traditional view, the length of time between a stimulus (such as the mother's call) and a response (such as going to the table) is a measure of the strength of the tendency to display the response. In behavioral terminology, this period of time is called *response latency*. The shorter the period of time is, the stronger the tendency to make the response is assumed to be. Thus the child who gets to the table first when his mother calls "Dinner's ready!" should be the child most strongly motivated to do so, whether by hunger, a desire to obey, or whatever. But is this assumption correct? Might it not be that the child who arrives at the table last is just as hungry and just as eager to be obedient as the one who arrived first, but more interested in his play in the living room?

The persistence of one activity and the initiation of another are two sides of the same problem. A clock is used to measure both, and it measures the same time period for both. If the experimenter's central interest is the duration of the activity in progress, he says he has measured persistence; if his central interest is the initiation of an activity, he says he has measured response latency—that is, the length of time the organism takes to respond to a new stimulus. The terminology differs, but the same period of time is measured in both cases. In order to explain the initiation of a new activity, then, we must know the strength of the tendency sustaining the activity already going on as well as the strength of the tendency to engage in the new activity.

Any theory that attempts to explain the persistence of an activity or the initiation of a new activity without reference to both tendencies must assume to begin with that there is no activity in progress. This assumption of an organism at rest is precisely the mistaken one inherent in contemporary formulations of motivation theory, despite psychologists' universal recognition of the fact that living organisms are constantly behaving. To illustrate, let us refer again to the children playing in the living room when their mother calls them to dinner. Suppose there is a very intent but deaf psychologist in the living room. He is studying the persistence of the children's play activity. In the kitchen is an equally intent but blind psychologist, who is studying the children's responses to the mother's call. The deaf psychologist sees the children playing but does not hear the mother call them to dinner. So, when he observes variations in the persistence of play, he attributes them to factors that he supposes determine the strength of the tendency to play. The situation of the blind psychologist in the kitchen is quite different. He hears the mother call the children but does not see that they are already engrossed in play. Noting that the children arrive in the kitchen at different times, he tries to attribute the variations in response latency to factors that he thinks affect the strength of the tendency to eat (or to obey).

Why do these hypothetical psychologists, and their real-life counterparts, make this kind of mistake? They do so because conventional schemes of thought about behavior restrict the psychologist's attention to the immediate effect of a stimulus or to the response in which he is interested. Contemporary theories of motivation do not encourage one to think of behavior as a continuous stream, with one kind of activity giving way to another and then another until the organism dies. They do not make it apparent that accounting for change of activity is the fundamental problem. Instead, they lead us to think of life as a series of discrete episodes, like events in a track meet, each with a well-defined beginning (the starter's gun), middle, and end, and to think of each episode as if it were separated from others by a period of inactivity in which the subject of study is at rest, passively awaiting the sound of the next gun.

Psychologists attempt to make the conditions of their experiments correspond to this conception of single, goal-directed episodes. They either assume implicitly that the subject is at rest to begin with or try to arrange conditions so that he appears to be. The animal experimenter, for example, usually waits until the rat placed at the starting point of a maze settles down facing the door leading into the maze before he opens the door to provide the stimulus to run. At that time the clock, which in this case is to measure speed (or response latency), is started. The experimenter working with human subjects similarly waits until the conversation between the eager young man and attractive young woman in the back row has stopped, if it is a group experiment, or until the individual subject looks at rest and "ready" before he presents the stimulus for some activity.

The general concept of motivation that prevails at present is not phrased to make experimenters think of doing anything else. The principles with which psychologists attempt to account for motivation have not been formulated in a way that systematically takes into account the activity already in progress when the episode of interest to the researcher is supposed to begin. Hence, he implicitly thinks of the subject at rest when he is not, or tries to arrange things so that he appears to be at rest before the critical stimulus is presented.

What is required is a change in the way that psychologists think about the things that determine a particular action. At least one change of the type I am suggesting has already taken place. In the early days of psychology, it was assumed that a specific act was a response to an immediate environmental stimulus—that behavior consisted of a series of stimulus-response events. Later, it became necessary to view a stimulus-response event as just one incident within a sequence of behavior, a sequence that had a beginning (a state of motivation), a middle (goal-directed activity), and an end (attainment of the goal). Thus the anticipated goal as well as the immediate stimulus came to be recognized as influencing the response.

This is the contemporary view. But, as we have seen, it has its limitations. It assumes that what a person (or animal) is doing *before* the presentation of a stimulus that defines the beginning of a behavior sequence has no effect on the length of time it takes the person to begin the sequence. It also assumes that what the person does *after* a particular sequence has no effect on its duration. The difficulty lies in a failure to appreciate the ramifications of what everyone is quick to acknowledge: that a living organism is constantly active, even when activity superficially appears to have ceased, as when the organism is resting or asleep.

When one pictures a constantly active organism, it becomes apparent that the basic decision the organism must make is not the one usually studied when a rat reaches a choice point in a maze. The fundamental problem for the organism is to decide between continuing an activity already in progress and undertaking some other activity instead. It is this problem of change from one activity to another that is inadequately treated in contemporary concepts of what determines the initiation and persistence of activities. In short, the initiation and the persistence of behavior are two inseparable aspects of a single phenomenon. The critical issue is raised not by separate questions, what causes an activity to start and what causes it to stop, but by a single question: What causes a change in activity?

If we recognize that beginning an activity represents a change in behavior and not the initiation of behavior from a state of rest, how might we state the determinants of the activity? Suppose that a rat has been placed in the start-box of a maze and is exploring one corner of the box. Now the door to the alley into the maze is raised. Our concept of this situation might begin with the assertion that the rat will run into the alley when the strength of the tendency to engage in that activity exceeds the strength of the tendency sustaining the exploratory activity already in progress.

This simple way of describing the change in the rat's activity is similar to Feather's representation of the conditions that must exist if an activity is to stop: it will stop, he said, when the tendency to engage in it becomes weaker than the tendency to do something else. The difference is that Feather's statement focused on the persistence of the old activity, whereas mine emphasizes the change from one activity to another.

The principle I am suggesting agrees with the general assumption of all motivation theories that the stronger of two incompatible tendencies will win out and be expressed in overt behavior. It differs from traditional conceptions in its explicit assertion that the strength of the tendency sustaining an activity is one determinant of any later activity. Most importantly, it recognizes the fact that an organism is always engaging in some activity and never merely awaiting a stimulus with a blank mind and an inactive brain.

REFERENCES

Feather, N.T. The relationship of persistence at a task to expectation of success and achievement related motives. *Journal of Abnormal and Social Psychology* 63 (1961): 552–61.

Jones, M. R., ed. *Nebraska symposium on motivation.* Lincoln: University of Nebraska Press, 1955.

19

Motives and Behavior in the Young Child: Hostility and Affiliation

JEROME KAGAN

Betty is often angry with her mother but rarely talks back and never strikes her. Bill is very jealous of his brother but always friendly with him. John likes his younger sister but sometimes slaps her arm or teases her. As these examples show, hostile motives and aggressive acts do not necessarily go together.

The presence of a motive is no guarantee that a child will try to gratify the motive through direct behavior. Similarly, the presence or absence of a particular behavior cannot be taken to indicate the strength or weakness of a motive. Teasing a brother, behavior that seems to be motivated by hostility, may actually be the product of some other motive, such as a desire to attract the brother's attention.

The Relationship Between Motives and Behavior

Motives are cognitive processes, and their relation to behavior is neither simple nor direct. It is important to distinguish them from biological drives, which are not cognitive processes and are more straightforwardly related to outward behavior. The classic biological drives are hunger, thirst, cold, and pain—states of deprivation or discomfort caused by a disturbance in the basic physiology of the organism. Drives are part of the infant's inborn equipment, with him from birth. Motives, on the other hand, are learned through experience. In simplest form, they are wishes—images or thoughts that represent things a person wants to experience or possess.

What determines whether a motive will produce an act? The first requirement is that a person have available in his repertoire of behavior an action that might serve to gratify the motive. If a six-year-old has a strong desire to control his older brother but has not learned any ways to do it, there will probably be little evidence of the motive in his everyday behavior. On the other hand, if a three-year-old learns that resisting his mother's requests upsets her, he has discovered a tactic he can use when he feels hostile toward her. In this case, the child learns the behavior through direct reward: Whenever the mother indicates how upsetting the child's stubborn resistance is, she unwittingly rewards the behavior and increases the likelihood that it will occur again. The child can also learn responses that gratify motives by watching and imitating other people and through television, books, and the like.

A second factor governing the probability that a motive will lead to behavior is the child's expectation that the action will actually move him toward his goal. A five-year-old who has lived in three foster homes where no one responded to his requests for affection and help is likely to become sullen and withdrawn. His desire for affection may be strong, but his behavior does not reveal it. The lower the child's expectation that a given behavior will lead to the gratification of a motive, the less likely he is to display the behavior.

Anxiety over the behavior itself is also important. In two-year-olds, an aroused motive often leads to an immediate attempt at gratification, because children of this age have not yet learned to postpone or inhibit gratification. In five-year-olds, by contrast, a considerable number of actions are inhibited by guilt or anxiety over parental rejection. The more anxiety the child feels about a behavior, the less likely he is to use it even when a strong motive is aroused.

A final influence on the probability of behavior aimed at gratifying a motive is the immediate situation. A child who feels strong hostility toward his mother while he is sitting in a classroom is not likely to behave in a way that will gratify the motive, though he might behave that way if he were at home.

In sum, the relationship between the existence of a motive and the occurrence of behavior intended to gratify it is complex. When a strong motive is aroused, the probability that a child will make an active attempt to gratify it depends on (1) the child's ability to execute an act that might gratify the motive, (2) his expectation that it will do so, (3) his anxiety over the behavior in question, and (4) the immediate situation.

In this essay I am concerned with the development in the young child of two kinds of motives, hostile motives and affiliative motives, and with the emotions and behavior related to them: anger and aggressive behavior, and anxiety and dependent behavior.

Anger, Hostility, and Aggressive Behavior

ANGER

Under what circumstances does a person become angry? For one thing, he becomes angry in response to frustrating events—events that thwart, block, or threaten his attempts to behave as he wishes or to work toward his goals. Some events do not block activities in progress but merely show a potential for blocking future ones; they are nonetheless frustrating. The central characteristic of frustrating events is that a desired sequence of action cannot take place, and the person must alter his behavior. In such situations a child or an adult normally becomes affectively aroused—angry.

A second set of anger-provoking stimuli are slightly different. These are events that threaten a person's beliefs or values. They imply that his standards are incorrect, invalid, or even immoral. Name-calling is a classic example.

Anger, then, is an affective state aroused when (1) goal-directed or preferred action sequences are thwarted or potentially thwarted, or (2) the standards of the person are threatened by another person or group.

HOSTILE MOTIVES

Anger, an affect, should be distinguished from hostility, a motive. Hostility is a wish to cause pain, distress, or anxiety to another person. Although the affect of anger and the motive of hostility often occur together, they can also take place separately. A five-year-old who cannot open the screen door to enter the house may get angry and stamp his feet on the porch without having hostile wishes toward anyone at that moment. A ten-year-old who is always teased by her brother may think about how she would like to throw him off the roof of the house without being at that time emotionally aroused. One need not have hostile wishes while feeling angry or be angry while entertaining hostile wishes.

The actual situations that are likely to arouse anger change rather dramatically as the child grows. During the first two years of life, re-strictions of the child's natural tendency to explore his environment—his parents' propensity for forcing him to sleep, to stay within fenced areas, and to keep away from fragile objects—often elicit signs of anger. During the preschool years, when the child has more mobility and more freedom to explore his environment, depriving him of specific goals or postponing their attainment are the actions chiefly responsible for eliciting anger, as when parents forbid playing in the dirt, watching television through the dinner hour, and playing too roughly with the baby.

During the school years the child has even more freedom, but by this time he has acquired certain standards regarding, for example, his sex role and his acceptance by other children. Events that violate or threaten these or other standards, as when someone implies that the child has undesirable characteristics or when a person important to the child believes in a value different from the child's, cause anger and hostile wishes toward the per-son seen as the source of the violation or threat. A ten-year-old who believes that good grades require prolonged study feels angry with and hostile toward a child who gets an *A* but rarely studies, because this peer has threatened the child's belief. A nine-year-old who wants to think she is her father's favorite is angry when she sees her eleven-year-old brother receiving more attention. Again, the validity of a belief is threatened.

In sum, restrictions of behavior, interference with progress toward a desired goal, and threats to dearly held values are the major causes of anger and hostility. Whether these will lead to aggressive behavior and what form the behavior takes depend on factors that will be taken up in the following section.

AGGRESSIVE BEHAVIOR

The definition of an aggressive action is the subject of considerable controversy. It can be defined as (1) any behavior that follows from, or is caused by, anger; (2) any action intended to gratify a hostile motive; or (3) any action that causes pain or anxiety to another person, destroys objects, or is extremely vigorous. That is, the definition can focus on the affect, the motive, or the behavior.

There are problems with each of these definitions. For example, according to the third definition (the one most popular in contemporary psychology), if a seven-year-old touches his younger sister's face and accidentally makes her cry, we must call the playful tickling aggressive because it caused distress to another. Similarly, if a child rides his bicycle up and down the driveway with extreme vigor and as a result damages a wheel, the behavior must be called aggressive even though the child did not intend to damage the toy.

A two-criteria definition of aggressive behavior seems more satisfactory than any one of the definitions mentioned above. Aggression is an act that (1) causes pain, anxiety, or distress to another person (or damage to an object), and (2) serves the affect of anger or a hostile wish. The advantage of this definition is that it allows us to exclude acts that unintentionally hurt others and to include acts that appear to be kind but are actually intended to cause anxiety to another.

Consider a family in which the father, an autocratic and rejecting man with only eight years of education, feels threatened by the school success of his sixteen-year-old son, who is planning a career in law. The father becomes upset every time the boy brings home a very good report card or discusses his plans for college. The boy, who feels hostile toward his rejecting father, is gratifying his hostile motive by hard work in school. That is, one of the motives behind his academic involvement is his intention to hurt his father, and the behavior succeeds in doing it. Another example would be a ten-year-old girl who decides to be very obedient to her parents in order to show up her older sister. She is behaving aggressively, even though obedience to one's parents does not seem the sort of behavior that harms another.

In these cases, studying hard and obeying are aggressive acts. It is clear, however, that one cannot call them aggressive without knowing the motives behind them. Most children who study hard or obey their parents do *not* do so out of hostile motivation.

The definition given above, which says that aggression includes only acts that arise from anger or hostility, enables us to avoid a number of common misinterpretations of behavior. For example, boys whose standards of masculinity include roughhousing may push a playmate, grab another's toy, or tease a teacher, but they do not necessarily want to hurt anyone. They may simply be announcing that they are boys. Poking another child is often regarded as an aggressive act, but some boys strike each other on the arm as a greeting and not as an expression of hostility. A child's attempts to get the attention of an adult can be similarly misinterpreted. A three-year-old may get in his mother's way while she is busy in the kitchen in order to obtain her attention, not to cause her distress. A third type of behavior that is not inspired by hostility but may be mislabeled aggressive is very intense or vigorous behavior. In our society, we are prone to consider a loud yell and the vigorous striking of a desk aggressive, though low-intensity versions of these acts are quite acceptable.

The child's tendency to display a genuinely aggressive act—one motivated by anger or hostility as well as causing pain or damage—is determined by at least three factors: (1) the intensity of anger or hostile motivation, (2) the amount of anxiety, guilt, and inhibition associated with the act, and (3) the success with which the act has gratified hostile motives in the past.

The simplest rule maintains that the stronger the hostility or anger, the greater the probability that aggressive behavior will occur. But this does not always hold true. If the child feels anxious or guilty about expressing aggression—if he has been consistently punished for aggressive behavior or has acquired a standard that dictates the inhibition of aggressive acts—he is less likely to react to hostile motives with aggressive behavior. And if a particular aggressive act seems unlikely to succeed in hurting someone, it is also less likely to be performed. Strong motivation is the basic requirement, but minimal anxiety and high expectations that the act will achieve its goal are also necessary before a particular aggressive act will occur.

RESEARCH ON AGGRESSION

Most psychological research on aggression has not been based on the definition of an aggressive act suggested above, partly because the definition requires identifying the intent behind the act. Intention is often very difficult to infer from behavior, and virtually impossible to prove. Therefore, researchers usually label aggressive any action that hurts another or injures property and any act that is vigorous and demands a reaction from another (Patterson, Littman, and Bricker, 1967). As the summary given below shows, most research has concerned behavior only, not the motive or affect at the time of the behavior. Some of the behavior is clearly in the service of hostility and anger, but some probably is not.

Frustrating situations, though they occur very frequently in the daily life of a normal child, often do *not* lead to aggressive behavior (Fawl, 1959). Instead, aggressive behavior is generally learned through the realization that it gets a response—attention from mother, submission from another child—or by watching and copying someone else's behavior. For example, Bandura and Walters (1963) have shown that a child who sees aggressive behavior in another person tends to behave more aggressively thereafter. However, it is likely that many of the imitated behaviors are associated neither with hostile motivation nor with the affect of anger.

In an important study, Patterson, Littman, and Bricker (1967) made continuous observations of four-year-old children at nursery school. Dictating their observations onto magnetic tape, they recorded a total of 2,583 aggressive acts and their consequences. In general, the more structured the nursery school setting, the fewer the aggressive responses. When children were treated permissively, they were apt to behave more assertively. If a particular child's aggressive behavior was successful (that is, if his victim gave up a toy or became passive), the child was likely to increase his aggressiveness. If the behavior was unsuccessful or was met with counteraggression, the child was less likely to behave aggressively in the future. The child who was highly aggressive and assertive at the beginning of the nursery school sessions continued to be aggressive over a period of several months, apparently because his aggressive behavior was successful. In addition, since the aggressive children were generally more active, they were more likely to be targets for aggression and counteraggression. It appears that the typical nursery school contains some very active, aggressive children who also meet the aggression of others and some relatively inactive children who initiate little aggression and do not encounter much aggression from others.

Other studies have shown a relationship between parental punishment and aggressive behavior. In general, boys who are seldom punished for disobedience and boys who are frequently punished display more aggressive behavior than do boys who receive moderate punishment. Boys who receive minimal punishment direct their aggressive behavior toward their parents; those who receive frequent punishment are likely to behave aggressively with other children, perhaps because of the frustrating quality of punishment. Aggressive behavior may also reflect imitation. If a parent often displays aggression to his child in the form of physical and verbal acts that accompany punishment, the child is quite likely to model his own behavior on that of the parent.

The relationship between parental punishment and aggressive behavior in girls is simpler: the more frequent the punishment for aggression, the less aggressive the behavior toward parents or peers. This difference in behavior may be attributed in part to the fact that in our society aggression is not usually regarded as feminine. The models girls choose to imitate are generally not aggressive, and most girls adopt a sex-role standard that calls for the inhibition of aggression. Among girls, therefore, exposure to an aggressive model is less likely to encourage overt aggressive behavior than it is among boys (Bandura, Ross, and Ross, 1963).

Aggressive behavior takes on different meanings at different times in the preschool child's life. A three-year-old who acts aggressively with his peers will not necessarily be a highly aggressive five-year-old. As a matter of fact, he is more likely to be extroverted and "masculine" at five than to be directly involved in aggressive activities such as grabbing toys and hitting. This conclusion comes from a study in which twenty-two boys were observed in a nursery school when they were three and five years of age (Byram, 1966). The boys who were overtly aggressive at age three—that is, who teased their peers, tattled on them, grabbed their toys, and called them names—were rated neither high nor low on similar aggressive behavior at age five. However, they were rated high on extroversion. At age five, the boys who were aggressive at three were more involved in traditionally masculine activities than their classmates who were nonaggressive at three. They were more likely to play cowboys and Indians, to climb, to play with hammers, and to be interested in racing games. They also tended to be more outgoing and to initiate more social contacts with other children.

Thus it appears that a mild degree of aggression at age three is a good predictor of extroversion and masculinity but a poor predictor of aggression at age five. Transformations of this kind are not uncommon during the first six years of life.

Anxiety, Affiliation, and Dependent Behavior

ANXIETY

Anxiety, like anger, is an affect. It is caused by events that create serious uncertainty about the future, such as encounters with unfamiliar situations and people, doubt about the outcome of one's actions, and unclear expectations about such matters as being loved or rejected, passing or failing a test, being robbed on a dark street, functioning effectively away from home.

Under all these circumstances, the person is (1) in an unfamiliar situation or uncertain about the likelihood that something unpleasant may occur, and (2) not sure what response is appropriate to the situation or not able to make the appropriate response. As a result, he is very likely to experience anxiety.

AFFILIATIVE MOTIVES

As with anger, there are often direct and immediate motor responses to anxiety, some learned and others more reflexive. For instance, a person who is anxious may "freeze," or he may tremble. Also, as with anger, there is often a cognitive reaction to anxiety in the form of a motive or wish. Sometimes the wish is that another person would intervene and provide affection, reassurance, advice, or aid. This wish for the supporting intervention of another in order to alleviate or reduce anxiety is called the affiliative motive.

As we have noted, anger and hostility can occur separately. So can anxiety and affiliation. When a child is anxious, he may want to be alone, away from others. Conversely, he may want to be with friends when he is not anxious. However, anxiety and the affiliative motive often occur together, especially in a child who has learned that other people effectively reduce his anxiety.

DEPENDENT BEHAVIOR

Dependent behavior is often defined as behavior directed toward other people for the purpose of obtaining affection, help, and support or establishing close physical or emotional relationships. However, such behavior need not be the product of affiliative wishes or anxiety. For example, a boy who always plays with a particular group of children and rarely plays alone could be motivated by a need for power and dominance rather than by anxiety. A twelve-year-old girl may continually ask her boyfriend or father for help with minor problems because she regards this behavior as feminine, not because she really needs help or feels anxious. An eight-year-old may establish a close relationship with a crippled boy in the neighborhood because he has a motive to help others, not because he wants a new friend to depend on.

Dependency is a large and quite ambiguous concept. As with aggression, it seems best to use a compound definition. Dependent behavior is behavior that (1) establishes close, supportive, and affectionate relationships with other people, and (2) results from anxiety or from an affiliative wish for help, advice, support, or affection.

This definition allows us to reject as dependent any behavior that is characterized by close relationships with others but not caused by affiliative wishes, and to classify as dependent those actions that do not, on the surface, seem to express a desire for help. For example, a seven-year-old who says he is sick will probably receive care and support from his mother, but the announcement of illness does not necessarily serve an affiliative motive. A college student who is anxious and lonely may write a suicide note to a close friend announcing that she plans to take sleeping pills at seven the following evening, but the note, sent twenty-four hours ahead of time, may be a disguised request for help (and thus an instance of dependent behavior) rather than a serious declaration of suicidal intentions.

The probability that a child will behave dependently (as defined above) is determined by the same sorts of things as the probability that aggressive behavior will occur. That is, it is determined by (1) the intensity of anxiety or affiliative motives, (2) the amount of anxiety and guilt about overt dependency, and (3) the degree to which a particular dependent behavior has gratified affiliative motives in the past.

The stronger the motive, the greater the chances that dependent behavior will occur. Dependent overtures toward others will continue, however, only if they are met with positive and helpful support that alleviates anxiety. If a child's open or disguised requests for support are not answered, he will eventually inhibit them and may become cold, aloof, and cynical about the warmth of people in general.

He may also inhibit dependent behavior if he has learned to regard it as childish, inappropriate, or in violation of his sex-role standards. For example, dependent behavior tends to be more stable in girls from age ten to age twenty than in boys because dependency does not violate feminine sex-role standards. A highly dependent preadolescent girl will probably continue to behave dependently as she gets older when she is anxious or buffeted by affiliative wishes. But a dependent ten-year-old boy is likely to be called a sissy and to encounter other signs that his behavior is "unmasculine." Thus dependent responses may disappear from his behavioral repertoire, and he may seem relatively independent as an adult.

RESEARCH ON DEPENDENCY

As with aggression, most investigators of dependency in children have focused on behavior as distinct from motives. However, Rosenthal (1965) has made a study of preschool girls that supports the hypothesis that dependent behavior is likely to occur when a child is anxious. Some of the children in the study were not made anxious; others were made highly anxious by exposure to frightening conditions, including the sound of loud banging on a metal object and a child's high-pitched shrieks. The anxious children were more likely to cling to or stay near the adult in the room than were the children who had not been made anxious.

This result matches a finding of an experiment with adult women, some of whom were told they might be given a strong shock during the experiment and others that they might receive a weak shock (Schachter, 1959). Each woman was asked whether she would prefer to wait alone or with other students for the experiment to start. More women who expected a strong shock chose to wait with others than women who expected a mild shock. Anxiety led both the four-year-old girls and the twenty-one-year-old women to seek proximity to others. The effects resemble those produced when a mother leaves her one-year-old alone. When the mother returns, the child cries and wants to be close to her.

Dependent behavior tends to prevail only if it succeeds in bringing about affiliation. A mother who consistently rewards and rarely punishes dependent behavior produces a highly dependent child. A child reared in an extremely neglectful institutional environment is less likely to behave dependently because dependent actions have not been rewarded (Spitz and Wolf, 1946). Studies with more representative groups of American children (Sears, Maccoby, and Levin, 1957; Kagan and Moss, 1962) reveal that mothers who consistently reward and inconsistently punish dependent actions tend to have children who show a considerable amount of overt dependent behavior. However, maternal acceptance of dependency does not in itself foster dependent actions in the child. If the mother also values and rewards independence, the child inhibits direct dependent overtures toward others.

According to Baumrind and Black (1967), parents who set consistent and firm standards for their children and try to socialize them according to middle-class values have the most independent children. Because the American middle class tends to value responsibility and independence, middle-class parents who take the socialization process seriously urge independence on their children. Young boys who are independent have parents who show consistent discipline, expect mature behavior, encourage independent contacts, and do not restrict or coerce the child. Independent girls have mothers who require obedience and the adoption of maternal values but do not use coercive power.

There are many parallels between the development of aggressive behavior and the development of dependent behavior. The child wants to be helped by and to be close to people, just as he wants to express his anger. However, he may be anxious about punishment, loss of love, or guilt. Such anxiety is more likely to inhibit aggressive behavior in girls, dependent behavior in boys. In both sexes, though, the relationship between motive and response is ambiguous, and motives and behavior change in various ways as a child grows up. These are some of the reasons why trying to understand the development of motive-behavior systems is like trying to decode a complex cryptograph.

REFERENCES

Bandura, A., Ross, D., and Ross, S. A. Vicarious reinforcement and imitative learning. *Journal of Abnormal and Social Psychology* 67 (1963): 601–07.

Bandura, A., and Walters, R. H. *Social learning and personality development.* New York: Holt, Rinehart & Winston, 1963.

Baumrind, D., and Black, A. E. Socialization practices associated with dimensions of competence in preschool boys and girls. *Child Development* 38 (1967): 291–328.

Byram, C. A longitudinal study of aggressive and self-assertive behavior in social interaction. Senior honors thesis, Radcliffe College, 1966.

Fawl, C. L. Disturbances experienced by children in their natural habitats: A study in psychological ecology. Doctoral dissertation, University of Kansas, 1959.

Kagan, J., and Moss, H. A. *Birth to maturity: A study in psychological development.* New York: Wiley, 1962.

Patterson, G. R., Littman, R. G., and Bricker, W. Assertive behavior in children: A step toward a theory of aggression. *Monographs of the Society for Research in Child Development* 32 (1967).

Rosenthal, M. K. The generalization of dependency behaviors from mother to stranger. Doctoral dissertation, Stanford University, 1965.

Schachter, S. S. *The psychology of affiliation.* Stanford: Stanford University Press, 1959.

Sears, R. R., Maccoby, E. E., and Levin, H. *Patterns of child rearing.* New York: Harper & Row, 1957.

Spitz, R. A., and Wolf, K. M. Anaclitic depression: An inquiry into the genesis of psychiatric conditions in early childhood. *The psychoanalytic study of the child*, vol. 1, pp. 313–42. Edited by A. Freud *et al.* New York: International Universities Press, 1946.

Emotion

The concept of emotion, like that of motivation, was formulated a long time ago. Everyone has felt the strong beating of his heart, the tightness in his stomach, and the sweating of his palms that occur when he is insulted, sexually aroused, or confronted by a dangerous animal. Men long ago identified this simultaneous occurrence of strong internal feelings and outside events with a single concept—emotion.

There has been intense controversy among psychologists on several issues related to emotion. One of them is: Is there a different physiological state specific to each emotion? That is, is the physiological arousal that accompanies anger different from the arousal that accompanies joy, depression, or excitement? Some psychologists claim that emotional states are physiologically distinguishable from one another. They believe that a better understanding of the workings of the central nervous system might make it possible to identify specific groups of neurons in the brain that discharge when a person experiences a particular emotion. These psychologists point out, for example, that electrical stimulation of specific areas in the brain of a cat will make the cat behave as if it is in a state of rage.

Other psychologists argue that there are too many subtle differences among human emotions for a distinctive physiological state to accompany each of them. Sadness can take many forms. We have the words "grief-stricken," "mournful," "distraught," "depressed," "lonely," "alienated"—each describing a somewhat different kind of sadness. It is not likely that there are different physiological states to match the feeling described by each of these words.

This line of thought has led to the assumption that there are only a few distinct physiological states that go with emotions. According to this view, physiological arousal alerts a person and forces him to attend to the way he feels. He wants to know why his heart is beating faster, why he feels uncomfortably warm and flushed. To find out, he appraises his situation—the people around him, the events that have just occurred, his thoughts of the moment. Then he "decides"—usually unconsciously—which emotion he feels.

In "How Emotions Are Labeled," Stanley Schachter and Jerome E. Singer describe an experiment supporting this position. Their hypothesis was that if a person is given the drug adrenalin, which causes physiological sensations that duplicate those accompanying strong emotion, his later behavior will depend on his interpretation of his situation. If he knows that his physical symptoms were caused by the adrenalin, he may not feel emotional at all. If he does not know about the adrenalin, he will probably attribute his symptoms to emotion and turn to his social surroundings in an attempt to decide which emotion he feels. Although Schachter and Singer's subjects received the same amount of adrenalin, they felt very different emotions and behaved in very different ways depending on how the people around them were acting.

The second selection, "Fear in Sports Parachutists," by Walter D. Fenz and Seymour Epstein, concerns the specific emotion of fear. Fenz and Epstein studied both the subjective feelings and the physiological reactions of fear in two groups of sports parachutists, novices and experienced jumpers, at various points before and just after a jump. The novices were most afraid (sometimes terrified) just before the jump; the experienced parachutists were less afraid in general, and they felt the greatest fear much earlier. Fenz and Epstein suggest that with experience a parachutist becomes adept at sensing the physiological signs of fear and learns to inhibit his anxiety. He develops a sort of early warning system that helps him gain control of his fear while it is still at a low level and keep it low throughout the jump-run.

20

How Emotions Are Labeled

STANLEY SCHACHTER

JEROME E. SINGER

What it is that allows a person to label and identify his own emotional states has been a problem since the early days of psychology. Most people have the impression that they are subject to many different, and contrasting, emotions—fear, love, hate, joy, anger—but how do they know, on a given occasion, which emotion it is that they feel?

Strong emotion is always accompanied by certain physiological changes. For example, if a person sees a car speeding toward him at an intersection, his muscles tense, his heart races, his palms sweat, and various other signs of excitation in the sympathetic nervous system occur. This fact led William James to suggest, in 1890, that what we call emotion is simply our perception of an aroused physi-

HOW EMOTIONS ARE LABELED   Adapted from *Psychological Review* 69 (1962). Used by permission of Stanley Schachter. This article originally appeared under the title "Cognitive, social, and physiological determinants of emotional state."

ological state within us that has been triggered by external events. In other words, a person who sees a car about to hit him has an automatic physiological response, and he calls that response fear.

Since we are aware of many different emotions, it follows from James' proposition that they should be accompanied by different bodily states. Much research has been done on this point, but the results are inconclusive. Some studies have found *no* differences among the internal physiological changes accompanying different emotions. Others have identified a few differences, but they are at best rather subtle. It is clear that the variety of emotions people experience is by no means matched by an equal variety of internal physiological patterns.

An injection of the drug adrenalin causes physiological changes that are virtually identical with those associated with strong emotion. Adrenalin causes a rise in blood pressure, increases in heart and breathing rates, trembling hands, a flushed face, and other symptoms of physiological arousal. If these physiological changes are what is perceived as emotion, as James suggested, then a person who receives an injection of adrenalin should feel "emotional." However, evidence indicates that he does not. When Marañon (1924) gave adrenalin injections to 210 people and then asked them how they felt, only 29 percent responded by mentioning an emotional state; the rest described their physical symptoms. Furthermore, the "emotional" subjects reported their feelings in a strangely unemotional way. Instead of saying they felt happy, or afraid, or whatever, they said "I feel *as if* I were afraid" and "I feel *as if* I were happy."

It is our theory that emotion is determined not by physiological factors alone but also by cognitive ones. Granting that a pattern of physiological excitation is characteristic of emotional states, we believe that a person identifies, interprets, and labels the state by mentally (though not necessarily consciously) analyzing his immediate situation.

Marañon's subjects probably knew that they had received adrenalin; thus they had available an adequate explanation for the heart palpitations, face-flushing, and other symptoms they felt. If they had not, they might have labeled their feelings by referring to their knowledge of the circumstances they were in. Perhaps some would have decided they were frightened about participating in the experiment while others decided they were elated at being able to do so. In other words, the subjects' cognitive appraisal of the situation might have exerted a steering function, determining with which emotion they associated their physiologically aroused state.

If we assume that emotion requires both a state of physiological arousal and a cognitive appraisal of the situation, and that neither of these alone will induce emotion, we are led to the following propositions:

1. A person who finds himself in a situation in which an emotional re-action is appropriate will react emotionally or describe his feelings as emotions only to the extent that he also experiences a state of physiological excitation.

2. A person who is physiologically aroused and knows why (knows, for example, that he has been given a shot of adrenalin) is unlikely to use some other explanation to label his feelings even if one is available.

3. A person who is physiologically aroused and does not know why (does not know, for example, that he has been given adrenalin) will label and describe his feelings by referring to the cognitive information available to him. Depending on the circumstances, he may decide he feels very happy—euphoric—or very angry.

The Experiment

To test these propositions, we needed an experiment in which (1) some subjects were physiologically aroused and some were not; (2) some of the physiologically aroused subjects were given a completely appropriate explanation of their state and some were not; and (3) the physiologically aroused subjects who were not given an explanation had other information available from which they could produce an explanation themselves.

We asked 185 students at the University of Minnesota to take part in what they thought was a study of the effects of a vitamin supplement on vision. Each student was taken to a private room and told that he would receive an injection of Suproxin, a mild and harmless vitamin supplement. In fact, some students received an injection of adrenalin; others were given a placebo, an injection of completely neutral saline solution that has no physiological effects at all. The injections took care of our first experimental requirement, that some subjects be physiologically aroused and others not.

The next requirement was that some of the aroused subjects be provided with a completely appropriate explanation for their physiological state. We divided the subjects who received the adrenalin into three groups. Some subjects, called the *informed group*, were told that there might be side effects from the Suproxin. "What will probably happen," the experimenter said, "is that your hands will start to shake, your heart will start to pound, and your face may get warm and flushed." The effects were temporary, he continued, and would last only fifteen or twenty minutes. This informed group had completely accurate information about the physical symptoms to expect after the injection.

A second group of subjects, called the *ignorant group*, was told nothing at all about side effects. The experimenter simply said that the injection was mild and harmless and left the room.

The third group, called the *misinformed group*, was included as a control group of sorts. These subjects were told to expect side effects, but the wrong ones. "What will probably happen," said the experimenter, "is that your feet will feel numb, you will have an itching sensation over parts of your body, and you may get a slight headache." None of these symptoms is caused by adrenalin. Our reason for misinforming one group was to make sure that differences in the reactions of the informed and ignorant groups could be attributed to differences in the appropriateness of the available explanations and not merely to the fact that one group was warned to expect symptoms while the other was not.

The subjects who were injected with the neutral saline solution instead of with adrenalin we called the *placebo group*. Like the ignorant group, they were told nothing about side effects. The experimenter simply said that the injection was mild and harmless.

Our final hypothesis was that given a state of physiological arousal for which an adequate explanation has not been provided, a person will describe his feelings by using whatever cognitive cues he can pick up by appraising the situation. Depending on the circumstances, he might come up with any of several emotional labels. To test this hypothesis, we placed some subjects in a situation that suggested anger and some in a situation that suggested euphoria. If our theory was correct, the students who were given adrenalin but not told there would be side effects (the ignorant group) should be more inclined to interpret their feelings as anger or euphoria than both the informed group, which had a better explanation available, and the placebo group, which had not been physiologically aroused by adrenalin. We were especially interested in seeing whether the same physiological state could be given two such different emotional labels as anger and euphoria.

To create the angry and euphoric situations, we used stooges—students who, unbeknownst to our subjects, were actually allies of the experimenter. As soon as a subject had received his injection, the experimenter brought a stooge into the room and introduced him as another participant in the experiment. After the stooge and the real subject had been left alone, the stooge introduced himself again, made a series of comments to break the ice, and then launched into his routine.

If his job was to create a euphoric atmosphere, the stooge began with some mild fooling around. He doodled, then started throwing crumpled balls of paper at the waste basket, saying "two points" occasionally. If the subject did not join in on his own, the stooge threw him a paper ball and said "Here, you try it." From basketball he progressed to making and throwing paper airplanes, then to building a tower of manila folders that

he cheerfully demolished with a makeshift slingshot, and finally to twirling a hula hoop wildly on his arm, chortling such things as "Hey, look
at this—this is great!"

If the stooge's function was to create an angry atmosphere, his routine
was quite different. He began by remarking that he had really wanted to
volunteer for this experiment but that shots were a different matter. "At
least they could have told us about the shots when they called us. You
hate to refuse, once you're already here." Next, he turned to his copy of
a questionnaire that the experimenter had left for all subjects to fill out
while, he said, they waited for the Suproxin to make its way into their
bloodstream. The five-page questionnaire started off innocently enough,
but the questions soon became quite personal and insulting. The stooge,
pacing himself so that he and the subject were always working on the
same question, made a series of increasingly annoyed and complaining
comments. He expressed irritation at a question about childhood diseases,
angrily crossed out a question that asked the respondent to write down
which member of his family came to his mind in connection with such
statements as "does not bathe or wash regularly" and "needs psychiatric
care," and acted generally upset and angry. When he got to question 28,
which said "How many times a week do you have sexual intercourse?
0–1_____2–3_____4–6_____7 and over_____," the stooge snapped,
"The hell with it! I don't have to tell them all this." He sat sullenly for a
moment, then ripped up the questionnaire and stomped out of the room.

Half the subjects in the informed and ignorant groups, who had received adrenalin, and half the subjects who had received the placebo
went through the euphoria sequence with a stooge; the other half went
through the anger sequence. The misinformed subjects, who were given
adrenalin and told to expect a list of incorrect symptoms, went through
the euphoria sequence only. We felt that this would be enough to control
for the possibility that differences among the groups might be due to the
presence or absence of a warning about side effects per se rather than to
the appropriateness of the available explanations.

To summarize there were seven groups of subjects:

Euphoria sequence		*Anger sequence*
1. Informed group	Injected	5. Informed group
2. Ignorant group	with	
3. Misinformed group	adrenalin	6. Ignorant group
4. Placebo group	Injected with saline solution	7. Placebo group

The emotional states of the students in these groups were measured in two ways: through written self-reports in which the subject indicated his mood of the moment, and through behavioral observations made by the experimenter. The self-reports, requested by the experimenter just after the session with the stooge ended, asked the subjects to rate themselves on how good and happy they felt or how angry and annoyed, as well as on a number of dummy questions not related to anger or euphoria. They also included two open-ended questions that asked the subject to describe and account for his physical and emotional feelings. The experimenter's observation of the subject's behavior took place behind a one-way window while the subject was with the euphoric or angry stooge. The experimenter's ratings focused on the extent to which the subject appeared to have picked up the stooge's mood.

Results

After the data had been collected, the first thing we had to find out was whether the adrenalin had succeeded in producing an aroused physiological state in the subjects who received it. For almost all subjects, it did: their pulse rates rose after the injection, and they reported considerably more heart palpitation and tremor of the hands, arms, and legs than did the subjects who were injected with the placebo. Five subjects seemed to be immune to adrenalin; information on them was excluded from our analysis, since for them the necessary experimental conditions had not been established.

EUPHORIA

Next we turned to the question of how the euphoria sequence had affected the moods of the subjects in the various groups. The effects of the sequence are presented in Table 20-1.

A high score on the self-report indicated that a subject reported himself as feeling very happy or good. As we expected, the students in the informed group got the lowest euphoria scores on the self-reports, showing that they were considerably less susceptible to the stooge's mood than were students in the groups that had not received an adequate explanation of the physical sensations caused by the injection. Furthermore, the misinformed subjects (the group that had been told to expect the wrong symptoms) scored themselves almost twice as high on euphoria as the informed subjects did. Thus we can attribute differences between the informed and the ignorant groups to something other than the mere fact that the informed group had its attention directed to side effects—namely, to variations in the appropriateness of the available explanations.

T A B L E 20-1
Did the subjects catch the mood of the euphoric stooges?

Group	Self-report (high scores indicate euphoria)	Participation in euphoric activities	Initiation of euphoric activities
		(high numbers indicate euphoria)	
Informed	.98	12.72	.20
Ignorant	1.78	18.28	.56
Misinformed	1.90	22.56	.84
Placebo	1.61	16.00	.54

The two right-hand columns in Table 20-1 show the observer's ratings of the students' behavior with the stooge. The column headed "Participation in euphoric activities" gives ratings based on how wild the subject's activities were (for example, he got 5 points for hula hooping but only 1 for doodling) and also on how much time he spent at each. The column headed "Initiation of euphoric activities" shows how often the student deviated from the stooge's routine to begin euphoric activities of his own. In both columns, the larger the number, the more euphoric the behavior.

The observer's ratings show the same pattern as the subject's own reports. The subjects who acted least euphoric, showing that they were least susceptible to the stooge's mood, were the ones in the informed group.

There are two rather odd patterns in the data on euphoria that should be noted. First, the misinformed subjects felt and acted more euphoric than the ignorant subjects. Since neither group had been given an adequate explanation of their physical state, why were they not equally likely to pick up the stooge's mood? The answer, which was supported by the subjects' answers to the open-ended questions on the self-reports, seems to be that a fair number of students in the ignorant group (about 25 percent) decided on their own that the shot might be responsible for what they felt. It was apparently harder for students in the misinformed group, who had been told to expect symptoms quite different from what they actually experienced, to come to this conclusion. Therefore they were somewhat more inclined than those in the ignorant group to adopt the alternate explanation provided by the situation with the stooge.

The second strange pattern in the data is that the placebo group felt and acted more euphoric than the informed subjects. The differences were not statistically significant; however, they also appear in the data on anger. We had expected that the placebo group, which had not been physiologically aroused, and the informed group, which had been physiologically aroused but knew why, would be equally unsusceptible to the moods of the stooges.

The most important reason for the difference between the two groups was probably that the injection of saline solution, though it could not *cause* physiological excitation, could not *prevent* it either. The session with the stooges was provocative, and the subjects in the placebo group tended to respond to it. However, the fact that they were less responsive than the misinformed and ignorant subjects suggests that the injection of adrenalin did predispose subjects to feel emotional, whereas the placebo did not.

ANGER

Data on the students who took the annoyingly personal questionnaire with the angry stooges are presented in Table 20-2. We expected higher

TABLE 20-2

Did the subjects catch the mood of the angry stooges?

Group	Self-report (low score indicates anger)	Instances of angry behavior (high number indicates more angry acts)
Informed	1.91	—.18
Ignorant	1.39	2.28
Placebo	1.63	.79

scores on the self-reports, indicating happier and less angry feelings, and fewer instances of angry behavior from the informed group than from the ignorant one. The informed students knew that the injection was responsible for the sensations they felt, and they should therefore have been less likely to search for an explanation in their surroundings.

This expectation was confirmed. The average person in the ignorant group reported himself angrier than the average person in the informed group, and he showed several instances of angry behavior while with the stooge. The observer's ratings of the behavior of subjects in the informed group tended to be slightly negative, showing that many of these subjects failed to catch the stooge's mood at all.

Major Findings

Let us summarize our major findings and examine the extent to which they support our initial propositions. First, we suggested that, given constant cognitive circumstances, a person will react emotionally only to the extent that he experiences physiological arousal. The evidence supports this proposition.

Second, we suggested that a person in a physiologically aroused state for which he has a satisfactory explanation will not be likely to turn elsewhere for an interpretation of his feelings. The evidence strongly supports this proposition. The subjects who were told exactly what to expect from the adrenalin proved relatively immune to the alternate cognitions offered by the stooges.

In the euphoria sequence, the informed subjects reported themselves far less happy than subjects in an identical physiological state who had no knowledge of why they felt as they did; in the anger sequence, the informed subjects neither reported nor showed anger.

Finally, we suggested that a person in a state of physiological arousal for which he has no appropriate explanation will label the state on the basis of the cognitions available to him. Again, the results support this proposition. After the injection of adrenalin, the students who had no explanation for the effects it produced showed, both in their behavior with the stooges and in self-reports on their moods, that they had been easily manipulated into the very different emotional states of euphoria and anger.

What are the implications of these findings? As we noted at the outset, most studies on the physiology of emotion have yielded quite inconclusive results. Most, though not all, indicate no physiological differences among the various emotional states. Since as human beings (rather than as scientists) we have no difficulty identifying, interpreting, and labeling our feelings, the results of these studies have long seemed rather puzzling.

It is conceivable, however, that they should be taken at face value. The many emotional states may indeed be characterized by a high level of physical excitation with few if any corresponding physiological distinctions. Our findings do not rule out the possibility that there are physiological states peculiar to certain emotions or groups of emotions. However, given precisely the same adrenalin-induced activation of the central nervous system, we were able by cognitive means to produce the very different emotions of euphoria and anger. It may be, then, that cognitive factors are major determiners of the various emotional labels that we apply to a common physiological state.

REFERENCE

Marañon, G. Contribution à l'étude de l'action émotive de l'adrénaline [Contribution to the study of the emotional effect of adrenalin]. *Revue Française d'Endocrinologie* 2 (1924): 301–25.

21

Fear in Sports Parachutists

WALTER D. FENZ

SEYMOUR EPSTEIN

For a novice sports parachutist, a parachute jump represents an acute approach-avoidance conflict. On the one hand, there is the excitement and thrill of a new adventure, and on the other, the fear of injury and death. Many jumpers say that their first few jumps were the most terrifying experiences of their lives. Their symptoms, taken out of context, suggest fairly severe mental disorganization. One new parachutist reported that he was amazed at how calm he was before his first jump, until he looked down and saw his knees knocking together. Another failed to jump on the first pass over the target area because he could not decide which foot to use in stepping onto the place he was to jump from. He began to step out

FEAR IN SPORTS PARACHUTISTS Adapted from *Psychosomatic Medicine* 29 (1967). Used by permission of Walter D. Fenz. This article originally appeared under the title "Gradients of physiological arousal in parachutists as a function of an approaching jump."

with one foot, pulled it back, made another abortive attempt with the other foot, and repeated the process. Almost all novice jumpers show some signs of cognitive disruption. They often fail to carry out instructions received during ground training, especially instructions about assuming and maintaining the proper position during the few moments of freefall before the chute opens.

Experienced jumpers, understandably, present an entirely different picture. If they are afraid, they don't show it. They appear to enjoy jumping, and they can carry out highly complex maneuvers before the chute opens, making contact with other jumpers, passing batons, and doing acrobatics. Since a small error could have disastrous consequences, there is little margin for cognitive disorganization.

What allows experienced parachutists to jump in such a relaxed state? An answer to this question could be valuable in understanding failures to cope with stress under other circumstances.

Subjective Fear

In a study we ran in 1965, we had novice and experienced sports parachutists rate the degree of fear they felt at different times before, at, and after a jump (Epstein and Fenz, 1965). The results are summarized in Figure 21-1. The self-ratings do not permit comparison of the amounts of fear felt by the two groups but only of the patterns of fear over time. However, there is no question that the novices felt more afraid shortly before a jump than the experienced jumpers did at any point in the sequence.

In the novice jumpers, fear increased until shortly before the jump and then decreased. Since the decline in the curve is slight, fear was apparently still high at that moment. In the experienced parachutists, fear followed a different pattern. It increased slightly from the week before the jump to the morning of the jump, then declined sharply. In this group, fear was lower at the moment of the jump than at any other time. After the jump it increased again, suggesting an awareness of fear that had earlier been inhibited.

As the graph shows, the peak of anxiety for both groups occurred *before* rather than *at* the time of the jump, which, objectively speaking, is the time of most danger. The essential differences in the fear patterns of the two groups are that the peak occurs earlier for the experienced parachutists and that their fear declines more gradually. It is as if in the experienced jumper both fear and inhibitions against fear begin to rise more rapidly and earlier than they do in the inexperienced jumper, and

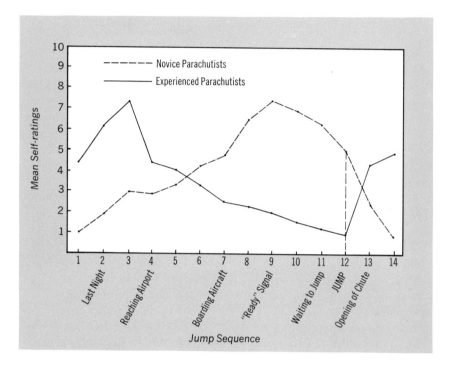

FIGURE 21-1

Self-ratings of fear by novice and experienced parachutists. Each parachutist rated 14 points in the jump sequence on a scale from 1 (the time he felt the least fear) to 10 (the time he felt the most fear).

the inhibitions rise faster than the fear. The result is that the experienced parachutist jumps in a fairly relaxed state; he has apparently acquired a sort of early warning system that helps him cope with the stress of the jump sequence.

Physiological Arousal

The findings of the study on subjective fear raised the question of whether measurements of physiological arousal would parallel the parachutists' own ratings of their fear. It is often assumed that physiological arousal and experienced fear increase together, and that the physiological measurement of arousal provides an index to subjective fear. However, we wondered if that assumption was correct—might it not be possible to inhibit the conscious experience of fear without influencing the physiological changes that accompany the emotion?

In order for physiological arousal to correspond to the self-ratings, experienced parachutists would have to show a continuous decline on such measures as breathing rate, heart rate, and skin conductance (the electrical conduction of the skin, which increases with sweating) during ascent in the aircraft. Novice parachutists would have to show an increase in physiological arousal until shortly before the jump. The major purpose of the study described below was to determine whether fear patterns of experienced and novice sports parachutists measured physiologically correspond to self-rated fear patterns.

Our subjects were ten novice and ten experienced sports parachutists. The novices had made no freefalls and fewer than ten static line jumps—jumps in which the parachutist does not pull his own ripcord but has it pulled for him by the jumpmaster, from the plane. The experienced parachutists had made over one hundred delayed freefalls. In a delayed freefall, the parachutist waits to pull his ripcord until he has had time to execute various maneuvers—acrobatics and the like—while falling through space.

Using automatic equipment similar to that employed in lie detector tests, we recorded the skin conductance, heart rate, and breathing rate of each man before he boarded the plane, throughout the flight, and shortly after landing. We tabulated the data received at each of the following specific points in the sequence.

1. A control day, a day on which the subject did not intend to jump.
2. When the subject got to the airport on the day of a jump.
3. Just before he was checked out to board the plane.
4. Just after boarding.
5. At the beginning of taxiing.
6. At the end of taxiing.
7. During engine warmup just before takeoff.
8. At the end of the engine warmup.
9. During takeoff.
10. Shortly after the plane was airborne.
11. At 1,000 feet.
12. At midpoint altitude.
13. At final altitude, during the jump-run.
14. After the subject had landed.

The midpoint and final altitudes depended on whether an experienced or a novice parachutist was being tested. Novices jump from about 3,000 feet, whereas experienced parachutists jump from much higher altitudes in order to allow for long periods of freefall. Four of the experienced parachutists jumped from 5,200 feet, allowing for a delayed freefall of twenty seconds, and six jumped from 15,000 feet, allowing for a delayed freefall of seventy-five seconds. These differences in altitude had to be taken into account in analyzing the data on heart rates, since heart rate increases with altitude.

A COMPARISON:
EXPERIENCED AND NOVICE JUMPERS

Figure 21-2 presents the findings on the three measures of physiological arousal. The skin conductance, heart rate, and breathing rate of the novice jumpers were highest at final altitude during the jump-run. There was a steady rise before that time and a steady decline thereafter.

For the experienced parachutists, the curves are more complex. Skin conductance increased, as it did in the novices, up to the point of being airborne. At midpoint altitude it started to decrease, and the drop-off continued to the last point recorded after landing. The heart rate of the experienced jumpers, unlike that of the novices, began to level off after they boarded the aircraft. After landing, it showed a slight rise. The breathing rate of the two groups began to differ as soon as the jumpers arrived at the airport. The breathing rate of the novices was higher from then on. Like skin conductance and heart rate, it increased steadily up to final altitude, whereas the breathing rate of the experienced parachutists reached its high point just after takeoff. All ten experienced parachutists breathed more slowly at final altitude than when first airborne, despite the fact that altitude normally leads to slightly faster breathing than usual. After landing, the breathing rate of the experienced parachutists increased from what it had been at the time of the jump.

We were most interested in whether the findings on physiological arousal would parallel the earlier findings on subjective fear—that is, whether the curves in Figure 21-2 would be similar to those in Figure 21-1. For the novices, the curves produced by the physiological measures approximated the curve of self-rated fear: all rose steadily up to the time of the jump. For the experienced parachutists, however, there was a marked difference between the self-ratings and the physiological data. The experienced parachutists' curve of self-rated fear reached its peak on the morning of the jump and declined thereafter. The curves of physiological arousal, by contrast, did not peak until after the subjects were airborne. Thus, during a prolonged period in which the fear that the parachutists felt declined, their physiological excitation continued to increase. This time lag suggests that psychological fear and physiological arousal are distinct concepts.

In the novices, fear and physiological arousal increased together. The reason may be that neither is complicated by inhibition; the novice parachutist has not yet learned ways to control his anxiety effectively. In the experienced jumper, a chain of altering and inhibiting reactions seems to come into play: relatively low levels of stress seem to serve as early warning signals in a system of psychological defenses.

Figure 21-2 offers some evidence that psychological inhibitions against fear help control and lessen physiological arousal. For example, note that the curves for the novice and experienced parachutists, as shown in Figure 21-2, diverge at different points for the three physiological measures. In the experienced group, it appears that the increase in breathing rate is inhibited first, then the increase in heart rate, and last the rise in skin conductance. This order corresponds to the degree to which the reactions

FIGURE 21-2

Three measures of physiological arousal in novice and experienced parachutists.

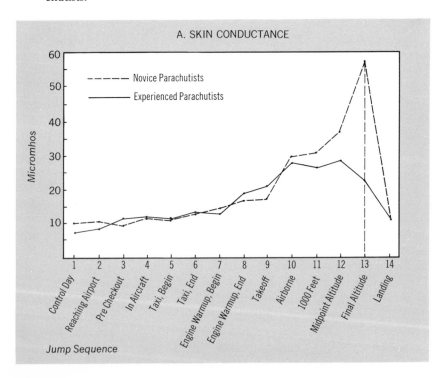

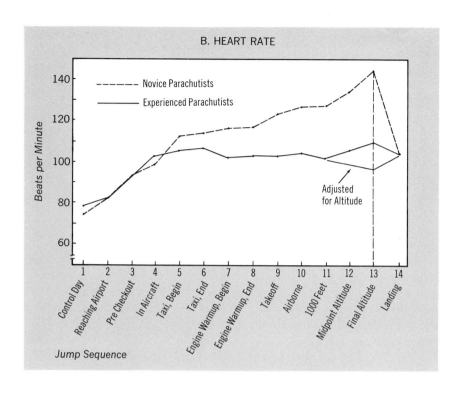

B. HEART RATE

- - - - Novice Parachutists
——— Experienced Parachutists

Beats per Minute

Adjusted for Altitude

Jump Sequence

Control Day | Reaching Airport | Pre Checkout | In Aircraft | Taxi, Begin | Taxi, End | Engine Warmup, Begin | Engine Warmup, End | Takeoff | Airborne | 1000 Feet | Midpoint Altitude | Final Altitude | Landing

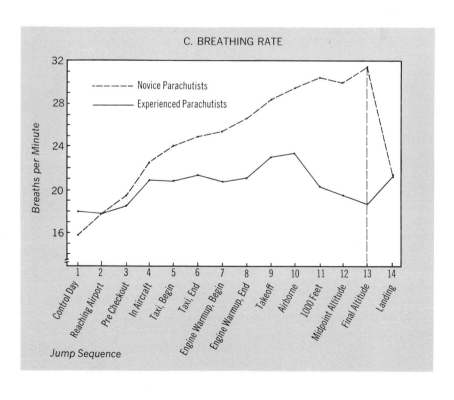

C. BREATHING RATE

- - - - Novice Parachutists
——— Experienced Parachutists

Breaths per Minute

Jump Sequence

Control Day | Reaching Airport | Pre Checkout | In Aircraft | Taxi, Begin | Taxi, End | Engine Warmup, Begin | Engine Warmup, End | Takeoff | Airborne | 1000 Feet | Midpoint Altitude | Final Altitude | Landing

can be recognized and consciously controlled. A person can be aware of an increase in his breathing rate and he can, within limits, vary it at will. An increase in heart rate, while not subject to direct control, can be controlled indirectly. A person who notices that his heart is pounding can try to calm himself by controlling his breathing or directing the content of his thoughts; he may, but need not, do this consciously. Skin conductance, the last measure to show the effects of inhibition, often provides no specific cues and cannot be controlled directly.

The arousal and inhibition of fear demonstrated by the experienced parachutists has some interesting implications for the mastery of anxiety. The early rise in anxiety, together with early and more rapidly rising inhibitions against it, provide the person with increasingly early warnings that stress impends. The warnings allow the person to deal with the stressful situation in advance and while anxiety is still slight, by means of defenses that need not be extreme. In a study of patients about to undergo surgery, Irving Janis (1958) reached a similar conclusion. He noted that the patients who did the "work of worrying" beforehand were less disturbed by the operation than those who did not.

The view that anxiety is inhibited and does not simply fade away is supported by direct observation of parachutists and by the differences between the self-rated and the physiologically measured fear of the experienced parachutists. The behavior of a group of experienced parachutists who faced an unexpected development offers an illuminating example. They were ascending toward an altitude of 12,000 feet when, at 4,000 feet, the airplane developed an engine failure. The jumpers froze, and jumped only after a serious delay. Some of them later acknowledged that the jump was one of the most frightening they had ever made. Apparently they were not able to prepare themselves mentally for jumping under circumstances different from those they were used to.

A second example is provided by two beginning parachutists. On the morning of their first jump both were unusually jovial and convivial. The experimenter at first thought he had encountered two extraordinary first-time jumpers. During training they continued to appear unconcerned, to the dismay of other first-time jumpers in the group. The situation changed dramatically when they boarded the plane. One began vomiting, and the other developed a bad tremor. Both pleaded for the plane to be turned back. It did. As they climbed down from the plane, the parachutists said they were giving up the sport.

These examples suggest the usefulness of mental preparation and worrying ahead of time. It is as if facing the situation in small doses, even if only mentally, serves as an inoculation against being overwhelmed by stress later.

PERSONALITY AND PERFORMANCE
OF THREE EXPERIENCED JUMPERS

For the most part, our study showed a great deal of uniformity within the groups of novice and experienced jumpers. However, there were also some interesting individual differences, which seem to relate to the performance and personality of the jumpers. The reactions of three experienced parachutists will serve to illustrate.

Two parachuting instructors, well acquainted with the three parachutists, were asked to rate them on several factors and to provide a thumbnail sketch of their characteristic reactions when jumping. The first case is that of S. T., a well-known competition jumper. With over five hundred freefalls, he was the most experienced of the three. The second is D. B., who had made more than one hundred and fifty freefalls but was the least experienced of the three. The third is M. A., the only woman jumper among our subjects. Within the short period of less than three months, she had made over two hundred freefalls. The instructors' ratings of these three experienced parachutists are shown in the following table.

TABLE 21-1
Instructors' ratings of three experienced parachutists.

	Instructor A	Instructor B
	S. T.	
Overall performance	Outstanding	Superior
Emotional control	Outstanding	Superior
Consistency of performance	Markedly consistent	Markedly consistent
Activity and talkativeness	Average	Average
Reactions when jumping	Capable, with extremely high skill, highly motivated, a jumper who enjoys jumping; somewhat careless and impulsive, but this affects other aspects of his behavior and not the actual skill he demonstrates in the air.	S. T. seems to be completely confident and outwardly shows no sign of tension during prejump activities in the plane. He seems to be at ease during the jump itself and performs equally well in fun-jumping and competition.

TABLE 21-1   (*Continued*)

D. B.

Overall performance	Poor	Poor
Emotional control	Poor	Poor
Consistency of performance	Slightly erratic	Slightly erratic
Activity and talkativeness	Extremely talkative and overactive	Extremely talkative and overactive
Reactions when jumping	He frequently displays signs of nervousness before making a jump. Has been observed to perform poorly when confronted with unforeseen circumstances. He is below average for his level of experience.	He is less than average as a jumper; a likable fellow but too emotional and a poor performer.

M. A.

Overall performance	Poor	Slightly below average
Emotional control	Superior	Slightly above average
Consistency of performance	Slightly erratic	Slightly erratic
Activity and talkativeness	Markedly quiet and inactive	Markedly quiet and inactive
Reactions when jumping	She seems to have extremely good self-control and a cool head, but her jumping ability itself is very poor, and she does not seem to react well to particular instances of trouble while on the jump-run.	Average female jumper, shows no particular signs of nervousness or stress prior to a jump.

The physiological reactions of the three experienced parachutists during the jump sequence are graphed in Figure 21-3. S. T. follows the pattern of the experienced jumpers (shown in Figure 21-2) more closely than D. B. or M. A. The outstanding characteristic of his record is that by the moment of the jump, in spite of an increase in arousal during the intermediate stages of the flight, his physiological excitation was at or below what it was when he boarded the plane. It is also noteworthy that the curves are relatively smooth, with no temporary reversals in direction.

The record of D. B. provides a striking contrast. His level of arousal was markedly higher and more variable than S. T.'s. Skin conductance, for

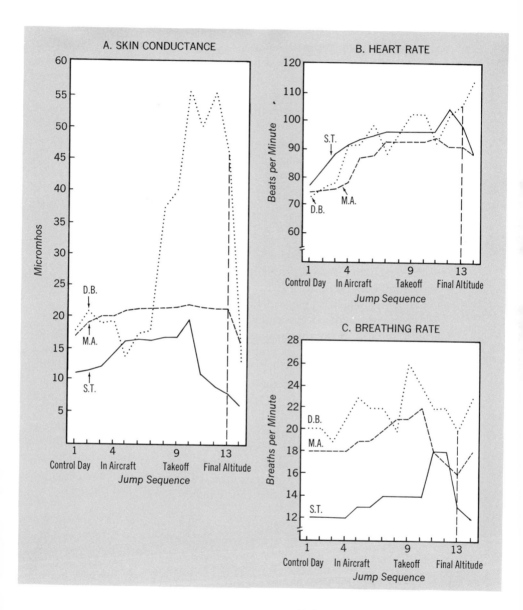

Records of physiological arousal in
three experienced parachutists.

example, followed no specific pattern during the early part of the jump sequence and then, toward the later stages, rose sharply to a level characteristic of a novice. Described by his instructor as hyperactive, poor in emotional control, and erratic in performance, D. B. failed to produce the pattern of the other experienced jumpers on two of the three measures (skin conductance and heart rate), and on all three showed excessive, unstable physiological excitement. It is as if he had a crude control system that first overshot and then undershot, producing an erratic curve.

M. A. showed little change in skin conductance throughout the jump sequence—less in fact, than any other jumper in the study. This corresponds to the observation of the instructors that she was "quiet and inactive." One wonders if the lack of physiological arousal is associated with her failure to respond adequately to crises.

In reviewing these three cases, it seems that the curves for skin conductance correspond more closely with the personality descriptions given by the instructors than do the curves for heart rate and respiration. The "too emotional" D. B. exceeded the others in skin conductance at the time of the jump, which suggests a failure to inhibit fear, and he was very changeable throughout the sequence. (At point 2 his skin-conductance curve is highest of the three jumpers; at point 5, lowest; at point 8, highest again.) M. A.'s curve of skin conductance is remarkably flat, corresponding to her low level of behavioral activity. S. T., the highly skilled competition jumper, follows the overall pattern of the experienced parachutists; his conductance level reached its lowest point at final altitude, during the jump-run.

These three parachutists can be compared to Pavlov's "inhibitory type," "balanced type," and "excitatory type" (Pavlov, 1928). Both the inhibitory type (M. A.) and the excitatory type (D. B.) have performance difficulties, the former as a result of failing to react to new situations and the latter as a result of uncontrolled anxiety.

Summary

The main purpose of the experiment was to determine whether differences in the physiological reactions of experienced and novice parachutists before making a jump would correspond to differences in their subjective ratings of fear. On all three measures of physiological arousal—heart rate, breathing rate, and skin conductance—novices showed increasing anxiety up to the moment of the jump, when they also felt most afraid. Experienced jumpers, by contrast, rated themselves most afraid on the morning of the jump, though their level of physiological arousal did not peak until after they were airborne; by the moment of the jump their arousal had declined to normal levels. It seems that the early rise of subjective fear and the later rise of physiological arousal in the experienced parachutists served as early warning signals that prevented the fear and arousal from becoming excessive.

Not all the experienced jumpers produced the inverted V pattern of physiological arousal that was characteristic of the experienced jumpers as a group. Thus it seems that in addition to repeated exposure to a stressful situation, individual personality factors have a significant influence on a person's reaction to stress and his success in inhibiting it.

REFERENCES

Epstein, S., and Fenz, W. D. Steepness of approach and avoidance gradients in humans as a function of experience: Theory and experiment. *Journal of Experiment Psychology* 70 (1965): 1–12.

Janis, I. L. *Psychological stress.* New York: Wiley, 1958.

Pavlov, I. P. *Conditioned reflexes and psychiatry.* Translated by W. H. Gantt. New York: International Universities Press, 1928.

Symptoms
of Frustration
and Conflict

Life is such that a great many things interfere with a person's pursuit of his goals. Perhaps he wants to get to know someone who obstinately refuses to like him. Or he may want to make friends with someone but be afraid to approach him. Although situations like these, which are frustrating or involve conflicting motives, create anxiety, most people manage to cope with them fairly successfully. If someone you like seems not to like you, you try harder to please, or get angry and tell the person off, or resort to a mild defense mechanism such as rationalization—"Oh well, if I got to know him I probably wouldn't like him anyway." When frustration and conflict are extreme, however, they can cause more anxiety than a person can handle, and the severely disturbed behavior we label "psychotic" may emerge.

Psychotic behavior has not always been interpreted as a psychological problem. Long ago it was taken to mean that a person had been invaded by evil spirits, and only a few hundred years ago American colonists burned "witches" at the stake because they were "possessed by the devil." Later, as the science of medicine advanced, people began to believe that mental illness was caused by a physical defect, perhaps a disease of the nerves. This was the dominant view when Sigmund Freud (1856–1939) began his career as a neurologist in Vienna. Freud's theory of the unconscious maintains that people are totally unaware of some motives that profoundly affect their behavior. This theory is primarily responsible for the present-day view that mental disorders are caused by psychological conflict rather than by physical weakness.

The existence of unconscious motives is such a familiar idea today that it is hard to appreciate the extent to which it revolutionized psychological thought. To demonstrate its importance, let us consider a student who wants to be friends with his teacher but is afraid to try. Suppose that the student, instead of finding the courage to approach the older man or deciding not to bother, begins to act very strangely—to tell his friends that the teacher not only attacks him in class but follows him around the campus, eavesdrops on him and his girl, and even "listens" to his thoughts and intends to kill him. Suppose, in short, that the student develops paranoid delusions of persecution. Three hundred years ago, people might have thought the devil had suddenly taken possession of the young man. Around 1890, they might have thought that an inherited physiological weakness of the nerves had asserted itself. According to Freudian theory, however, the trouble lies in the workings of the student's unconscious mind.

A Freudian interpretation of the student's behavior would probably begin with the assumption that he has unconscious homosexual impulses based on an unresolved Oedipus complex. He is so afraid that his father will retaliate if he tries to take his father's place in his mother's life that he cannot make sexual advances to women and wants to approach men instead. But since homosexuality is forbidden, he turns his love impulses into feelings of hate. These hostile feelings create anxiety, and he makes one more reversal: he transforms his feelings of hostility toward the man he is drawn to into a feeling that the man is hostile toward him. Consciously, the student merely wanted to make friends with the teacher and felt nervous about it. Unconsciously, his line of reasoning went something like this: "I (a man) love him (a man). But that is unacceptable and cannot be true. I do not love him; I hate him. But he is much stronger than I am and would surely destroy me for hating him. So it must not be me who hates him—it's he who hates me. How do I know? Because he *acts* as if he does: he persecutes me. Therefore I am justified in hating him."

In "Psychoanalytic Notes on a Case of Paranoia," Freud describes a man whose delusions of persecution developed in about this way. The case is particularly interesting because the man, Daniel Paul Shreber, suffered from delusions of grandeur as well. He believed he had a mission to redeem the world, and that in order to carry it out he first had to be transformed into a woman. As Freud explains, Shreber's conviction that he must become female began as a kind of self-persecution and only later was aggrandized by the addition of the redeemer idea. This paper is one of Freud's best known, chiefly because it includes Freud's explanation of the relationship between unconscious homosexual wishes and paranoia but also because his analysis of Shreber, whom he never met, is based entirely on Shreber's own written description of his illness.

Paranoia, though fascinating, is an uncommon type of

psychosis. The most common type is schizophrenia, the disorder suffered by well over half the patients now living in mental hospitals. Schizophrenia is unusually resistant to psychoanalytic and other verbal therapies, and certain physiological and biochemical differences between schizophrenics and nonschizophrenics have been identified. Some psychiatrists and psychologists believe that some forms of schizophrenia probably result from an inherited physiological defect that may be potentially controllable with drugs. However, the majority consider schizophrenic behavior a symptom of extreme disturbance in interpersonal relationships.

In "The Ghost of the Weed Garden," R. D. Laing discusses the history and treatment of a schizophrenic patient named Julie. Laing is an existential psychoanalyst: he emphasizes that one must not discount psychotic statements and actions as merely mad but understand the sense in which they are sane when viewed from the patient's standpoint. Julie is terrified that emotional contact with others will lead to her own destruction (and perhaps to theirs). Laing points out the existential truth in her fear of death and explains that she has psychologically killed herself, by removing herself from the world and fragmenting her personality, in order to prevent others from doing an even more thorough job. Thus Laing views the emotional and behavioral isolation of the schizophrenic as a radical defense against an overpowering fear of being destroyed.

Freudian psychoanalysts trace mental disturbance to a person's experiences within his family as a young child and give very little attention to society's contribution to neurosis and psychosis. Recently, a number of psychologists have maintained that the larger social environment is very important in determining both whether a person develops symptoms and what kind. For example, a person with unconscious homosexual impulses may be more likely to become paranoid if he grows up in a puritanical small town than if he is raised in Greenwich Village.

In "A Sociopsychological Investigation of Suicide," Edwin S. Shneidman and Norman L. Farberow analyze the influence of socioeconomic and psychological factors on the suicides of Los Angeles County residents from nine socioeconomic groups. They found that the percentage of the county's suicides in each of the nine groups was about the same as the percentage of the county's population in each group. It is an important finding because it conflicts with two common (though incompatible) beliefs. The first maintains that the poor, since they lack so many advantages and opportunities, are more likely than the rich to kill themselves. The second, based partly on homicide statistics, holds that a man who is going to kill will probably kill himself if he is rich and someone else if he is poor. Although suicide rates do not vary markedly from class to class, suicide victims from different socioeconomic groups seem to destroy themselves for different reasons and to show different emotions at the time of the act. Shneidman and Faberow illustrate these differences in the psychological states of suicide victims by quoting some of the hundreds of suicide notes they analyzed.

22

Psychoanalytic Notes
on a Case of Paranoia

SIGMUND FREUD

The psychoanalytic investigation of paranoia would be altogether impossible if the patients themselves did not tend to betray precisely those things which other neurotics keep hidden as a secret. Since paranoiacs cannot overcome their internal resistances, and since in any case they only say what they choose to say, it follows that this is precisely a disorder in which a written report or a printed case history can take the place of personal acquaintance with the patient. For this reason I think it is legitimate to base analytic inter-

PSYCHOANALYTIC NOTES ON A CASE OF PARANOIA Reprinted from *Complete psychological works of Sigmund Freud*, vol. 12. Revised and edited by J. Strachey. London: The Hogarth Press, 1958. Used by permission of Sigmund Freud Copyrights Limited, the Institute of Psycho-analysis, and The Hogarth Press Limited. This paper also appears in *The Collected Papers of Sigmund Freud*, vol. 3. Edited by E. Jones, M.D. New York: Basic Books, Inc., Publishers, 1959. Used by permission of Basic Books. It originally appeared under the title "Psycho-analytic notes on an autobiographical account of a case of paranoia (*Dementia paranoides*)."

pretations upon the case history of a patient whom I have never seen but who has written his own case history and brought it before the public in print.

I refer to Dr. Daniel Paul Schreber, formerly Senatspräsident in Dresden, whose book, *Denkwürdigkeiten eines Nervenkranken* [Memoirs of a neurotic] was published in 1903. . . .

Case History

"I have suffered twice from nervous disorders," writes Dr. Schreber [in Memoirs of a neurotic], "and each time as a result of mental overstrain. This was due on the first occasion to my standing as a candidate for election to the Reichstag . . . and on the second occasion to the very burden of work that fell upon my shoulders when I entered on my new duties as Senatspräsident . . . in Dresden."

Dr. Schreber's first illness began in the autumn of 1884, and by the end of 1885 he had completely recovered. During this period he spent six months in [Dr. Paul] Flechsig's clinic, and the latter, in a formal report which he drew up at a later date, described the disorder as an attack of severe hypochondria. Dr. Schreber assures us that this illness ran its course "without the occurrence of any incidents bordering upon the sphere of the supernatural.". . .

In June 1893 he was notified of his prospective appointment as Senatspräsident, and he took up his duties on the first of October of the same year. Between these two dates he had some dreams, though it was not until later that he came to attach any importance to them. He dreamed two or three times that his old nervous disorder had come back, and this made him as miserable in the dream as the discovery that it was only a dream made him happy when he woke up. Once, in the early hours of the morning, moreover, while he was in a state between sleeping and waking, the idea occurred to him "that after all it really must be very nice to be a woman submitting to the act of copulation." This idea was one which he would have rejected with the greatest indignation if he had been fully conscious.

The second illness set in at the end of October 1893 with a torturing bout of sleeplessness. This forced him to return to the Flechsig clinic, where his condition grew rapidly worse. The further course of the illness is described in a report drawn up by [one of his doctors]:

> At the commencement of his residence there he expressed more hypo-
> chondriacal ideas, complained that he had softening of the brain, that he
> would soon be dead, etc. But ideas of persecution were already finding
> their way into the clinical picture, based upon sensory illusion which
> . . . later . . . dominated the whole of his feeling and thought. He
> believed that he was dead and decomposing, that he was suffering from
> the plague; he asserted that his body was being handled in all kinds of
> revolting ways; and, as he himself declares to this day, he went through
> worse horrors than anyone could have imagined, and all on behalf of a
> holy purpose. . . . His delusional ideas gradually assumed a mystical and
> religious character; he was in direct communication with God, he was
> the plaything of devils, he saw "miraculous apparitions," he heard "holy
> music," and in the end he even came to believe that he was living in an-
> other world.

It may be added that there were certain people by whom he thought
he was being persecuted and injured and upon whom he poured abuse.
The most prominent of these was his former physician, Flechsig, whom
he called a "soul murderer" . . . . He was moved from [Flechsig's clinic],
and, after a short interval spent in another institution, was brought in
June 1894 to the Sonnenstein Asylum near Pirna, where he remained
until his disorder assumed its final shape.

In the course of the next few years the clinical picture altered . . . .
On the one hand, he had developed an ingenious delusional structure
while, on the other hand, his personality had been reconstructed and now
showed itself, except for a few isolated disturbances, capable of meeting
the demands of everyday life. . . .

Thus the patient's condition had undergone a great change, and he
now considered himself capable of carrying on an independent existence.
He accordingly took appropriate steps with a view to regaining control
over his own affairs and to securing his discharge from the asylum. . . .

The court judgment that gave Dr. Schreber back his liberty summarizes the content of his delusional system in a few sentences: "He believed that he had a mission to redeem the world and to restore it to its
lost state of bliss. This, however, he could only bring about if he were
first transformed from a man into a woman."

For a more detailed account of his delusions as they appeared in their
final shape we may turn to Dr. Weber's report of 1899 [Weber was the
physician in charge of Sonnenstein Asylum]:

> The culminating point of the patient's delusional system is his belief that
> he has a mission to redeem the world, and to restore mankind to their

lost state of bliss. . . . The most essential feature of his mission of re-
demption is that it must be preceded by his *transformation into a
woman*. It is not to be supposed that he *wishes* to be transformed into a
woman; it is rather a question of a "must" based upon the order of
things, which there is no possibility of his evading, much as he would
personally prefer to remain in his own honorable and masculine station
in life. . . . He has a feeling that great numbers of "female nerves"
have already passed over into his body, and out of them a new race of
men will proceed, through a process of direct impregnation by God. . . .

The medical officer lays stress upon two points as being of chief importance: the patient's *assumption of the role of Redeemer*, and his *transformation into a woman*. . . . A study of the *Denkwürdigkeiten* [shows
that] the idea of being transformed into a woman (that is, of being emas-
culated) was the primary delusion, that he began by regarding that act
as a serious injury and persecution, and that it only became related to his
playing the part of Redeemer in a secondary way. There can be no
doubt, moreover, that originally he believed that the transformation was
to be effected for the purpose of sexual abuse and not so as to serve higher
designs. The position may be formulated by saying that a sexual delusion
of persecution was later on converted in the patient's mind into a religious delusion of grandeur. The part of persecutor was at first assigned
to Professor Flechsig, the physician in whose charge he was; later, his
place was taken by God Himself. . . .

The idea of being transformed into a woman was the salient feature
and the earliest germ of his delusional system. It also proved to be one
part of it that persisted after his cure, and the one part that was able to
retain a place in his behavior in real life after he had recovered. "The
only thing which could appear unreasonable in the eyes of other people is
the fact, already touched upon in the expert's report, that I am sometimes
to be found standing before the mirror or elsewhere with the upper portion of my body partly bared, and wearing sundry feminine adornments,
such as ribbons, false necklaces, and the like. This only occurs, I may add,
when I am *by myself* and never, at least so far as I am able to avoid it,
in the presence of other people." The Herr Senatspräsident confesses to
this frivolity at a date (July, 1901) at which he was already in a position
to express very aptly the completeness of his recovery in the region of
practical life. . . .

Before his illness Senatspräsident Schreber had been a man of strict
morals: "Few people," he declares, and I see no reason to doubt his assertion, "can have been brought up upon such strict moral principles as I

was, and few people, all through their lives, can have exercised (especially in sexual matters) a self-restraint conforming so closely to those principles as I may say of myself that I have done." After the severe spiritual struggle, of which the phenomena of his illness were the outward signs, his attitude towards the erotic side of life was altered. He had come to see that the cultivation of voluptuousness was incumbent upon him as a duty, and that it was only by discharging it that he could end the grave conflict which had broken out within him—or, as he thought, about him. Voluptuousness, so the voices assured him, had become "God-fearing" and he could only regret that he was not able to devote himself to its cultivation the whole day long.

Such then, was the result of the changes produced in Schreber by his illness, as we find them expressed in the two main features of his delusional system. Before it he had been inclined to sexual asceticism and had been a doubter in regard to God; while after it he was a believer in God and a devotee of voluptuousness. But just as his reconquered belief in God was of a peculiar kind, so too the sexual enjoyment which he had won for himself was of a most unusual character. It was not the sexual liberty of a man but the sexual feelings of a woman. He took up a feminine attitude toward God; he felt that he was God's wife. . . .

If we now recall the dream which the patient had during the incubation period of his illness, before he had moved to Dresden, it will become clear beyond a doubt that his delusion of being transformed into a woman was nothing else than a realization of the content of that dream. At that time he had rebelled against the dream with masculine indignation, and in the same way he began by striving against its fulfillment in his illness and looked upon his transformation into a woman as a disgrace with which he was threatened with hostile intention. But there came a time (it was in November, 1895) when he began to reconcile himself to the transformation and bring it into harmony with the higher purposes of God: "Since then, and with a full consciousness of what I did, I have inscribed upon my banner the cultivation of femaleness."

He then arrived at the firm conviction that it was God Himself who, for His own satisfaction, was demanding femaleness from him. . . .

Attempts at Interpretation

The study of a number of cases of delusions of persecution have led me as well as other investigators to the view that the relation between the patient and his persecutor can be reduced to quite a simple formula. It appears that the person to whom the delusion ascribes so much power and influence, in whose hands all the threads of the conspiracy converge, is, if he is definitely named, either identical with someone who played an equally important part in the patient's emotional life before his illness or easily recognizable as a substitute for him. The person who is now hated and feared for being a persecutor was at one time loved and honored. The main purpose of the persecution asserted by the patient's delusion is to justify the change in his emotional attitude.

Bearing this point of view in mind, let us now examine the relations which had formerly existed between Schreber and his physician and persecutor, Flechsig. We have already heard that, in the years 1884 and 1885, Schreber suffered from a first attack of nervous disorder, which ran its course "without the occurrence of any incidents bordering upon the sphere of the supernatural." While he was in this condition, which was described as "hypochrondria" and seems not to have overstepped the limits of a neurosis, Flechsig acted as his doctor. At that time Schreber spent six months at the University Clinic at Leipzig. We learn that after his discovery he had cordial feelings toward his doctor. . . .

During the incubation period of his [second] illness, as we are aware (that is, between June 1893, when he was appointed to his new post, and the following October, when he took up his duties), he repeatedly dreamed that his old nervous disorder had returned. Once, moreover, when he was half asleep, he had a feeling that after all it must be nice to be a woman submitting to the act of copulation. The dreams and the fantasy are reported by Schreber in immediate succession and if we also bring together their subject-matter we shall be able to infer that, at the same time as his recollection of his illness, a recollection of his doctor was also aroused in his mind, and that the feminine attitude which he assumed in the fantasy was from the first directed toward the doctor. . . . The exciting cause of his illness, then, was an outburst of homosexual libido; the object of this libido was probably from the very first his doctor, Flechsig; and his struggles against the libidinal impulse produced the conflict which gave rise to the symptoms. . . .

The basis of Schreber's illness was an outburst of homosexual impulse. This hypothesis harmonizes with a noteworthy detail of the case history, which remains otherwise inexplicable. The patient had a fresh "nervous collapse" which exercised a decisive effect upon the course of his illness, at a time when his wife was taking a short holiday on account of her own health. Up till then she had spent several hours with him every day and had taken her midday meal with him. But when she returned after an absence of four days, she found him most sadly altered—so much so, indeed, that he himself no longer wished to see her. "What especially determined my mental breakdown was a particular night, during which I had a quite extraordinary number of emissions—quite half a dozen, all in that one night." It is easy to understand that the mere presence of his wife must have acted as a protection against the attractive power of the men about him and if we are prepared to admit that an emission cannot occur in an adult without some mental concomitant, we shall be able to supplement the patient's emissions that night by assuming that they were accompanied by homosexual fantasies which remained unconscious.

The question of why this outburst of homosexual libido overtook the patient precisely at this period (that is, between the dates of his appointment and of his move to Dresden) cannot be answered in the absence of more precise knowledge of the story of his life. Generally speaking, every human being oscillates all through his life between heterosexual and homosexual feelings, and any frustration or disappointment in the one direction is apt to drive him over into the other. We know nothing of these factors in Schreber's case, but we should draw attention to a somatic factor which may very well have been relevant. At the time of this illness Dr. Schreber was fifty-one years old, and he had therefore reached an age which is of critical importance in sexual development. It is a period at which in woman the sexual function, after a phase of intensified activity, enters upon a process of far-reaching involution; nor do men appear to be exempt from its influence, for men as well as women are subject to a "climacteric" and to the special susceptibility to disease which goes along with it. . . .

Now the father of Senatspräsident Dr. Schreber was no insignificant person. He was the Dr. Daniel Gottlob Moritz Schreber whose memory is kept green to this day by the numerous Schreber Associations which flourish especially in Saxony; and, moreover, he was a *physician.* . . .

We are perfectly familiar with the infantile attitude of boys toward their father; it is composed of the same mixture of reverent submission and mutinous insubordination that we have found in Schreber's relation with his God and is the unmistakable prototype of that relation, which is faithfully copied from it. . . .

Thus in the case of Schreber we find ourselves once again on the familiar ground of the father-complex. The patient's struggle with Flechsig became revealed to him as a conflict with God, and we must therefore construe it as an infantile conflict with the father whom he loved; the details of that conflict (of which we know nothing) are what determined the content of his delusions. None of the material which in other cases of the sort is brought to light by analysis is absent in the present one: every element is hinted of in one way or another. In infantile experiences such as this the father appears as an interferer with the gratification which the child is trying to obtain; this is usually of an autoerotic character, though at a later date it is often replaced in fantasy by some other satisfaction of a less inglorious kind. In the final stage of Schreber's delusion a magnificent victory was scored by the infantile sexual urge; for voluptuousness became God-fearing and God Himself (his father) never tired of demanding it from him. His father's most dreaded threat, castration, actually provided the material for his wishful fantasy (at first resisted but later accepted) of being transformed into a woman. . . .

We must necessarily content ourselves with this shadowy sketch of the infantile material which was used by the paranoiac disorder in portraying the current conflict. [But] perhaps I may be allowed to add a few words with a view to establishing the causes of this that broke out in relation to the feminine wishful fantasy. As we know, when a wishful fantasy makes its appearance, our business is to bring it into connection with some *frustration*, some privation in real life. Now Schreber admits having suffered a privation of this kind. His marriage, which he describes as being in other respects a happy one, brought him no children; and in particular it brought him no son who might have consoled him for the loss of his father and brother and upon whom he might have drained off his unsatisfied homosexual affections. . . . Dr. Schreber may have formed a fantasy that if he were a woman he would manage the business of having children more successfully and he may thus have found his way back into the feminine attitude toward his father which he had exhibited in the earliest years of his childhood. If that were so, then his delusion that as a result of his emasculation the world was to be peopled with "a new race of men, born from the spirit of Schreber"—a delusion the realization of which he was continually postponing to a more and more remote future—would also be designed to offer him an escape from his childlessness. . . .

On the Mechanism
of Paranoia

The knowledge of psychological processes which, thanks to psychoanalysis, we now possess already enables us to understand the part played by a homosexual wish in the development of paranoia. Recent investigations have directed our attention to a stage in the development of the libido which it passes through on the way from autoerotism to object-love. This stage has been given the name of narcissism. What happens is this. There comes a time in the development of the individual at which he unifies his sexual instincts (which have hitherto been engaged in auto-erotic activities) in order to obtain a love-object; and he begins by taking himself, his own body, as his love-object, and only subsequently proceeds from this to the choice of some person other than himself as his object. This halfway phase between autoerotism and object-love may perhaps be indispensable normally, but it appears that many people linger unusually long in this condition and that many of its features are carried over by them into the later stages of their development. What is of chief importance in the subject's self thus chosen as a love-object may already be the genitals. The line of development then leads on to the choice of an outer object with similar genitals—that is, to homosexual object-choice—and thence to heterosexuality. People who are manifest homosexuals in later life have, it may be presumed, never emancipated themselves from the binding condition that the object of their choice must possess genitals like their own and in this connection the infantile sexual theories which attribute the same kind of genitals to both sexes exert much influence. . . .

It is a remarkable fact that the familiar principal forms of paranoia can all be represented as contradictions of the single proposition: "*I* (a man) *love him* (a man)," and indeed that they exhaust all the possible ways in which such contradictions could be formulated.

The proposition "I (a man) love him" is contradicted by . . . delusions of persecution; for they loudly assert: "I do not *love* him—I *hate* him." This contradiction, which must have run in the unconscious, cannot, however, become conscious to a paranoiac in this form. The mechanism of symptom-formation in paranoia requires that internal perceptions—feelings —shall be replaced by external perceptions. Consequently the proposition "I hate him" becomes transformed by *projection* into another one: "*He hates* (persecutes) *me*, which will justify me in hating him." And thus the impelling unconscious feeling makes its appearance as though it were the consequence of an external perception: "I do not *love* him—I *hate* him, because *he persecutes me*." Observation leaves room for no doubt that the persecutor is someone who was once loved. . . .

After this discussion of the unexpectedly important part played by homosexual wishful fantasies in paranoia, let us return to the two factors in which we expected from the first to find the distinguishing marks of paranoia, namely, the mechanism *by which the symptoms are formed* and the mechanism *by which repression is brought about.* . . .

The most striking characteristic of symptom-formation in paranoia is the process of *projection.* An internal perception is suppressed, and instead its content, after undergoing a certain kind of distortion, enters consciousness in the form of an external perception. In delusions of persecution the distortion consists in a transformation of affect; what should have been felt internally as love is perceived externally as hate. . . .

In psychoanalysis we have been accustomed to look upon pathological phenomena as being derived in a general way from repression. If we examine what is spoken of as "repression" more closely, we shall find reason to split the process up into three phases which are easily distinguishable from one another conceptually.

1. The first phase consists in *fixation,* which is the precursor and necessary condition of every "repression." Fixation can be described in this way. One instinct or instinctual component fails to accompany the rest along the anticipated normal path of development and, in consequence of this inhibition in its development, it is left behind at a more infantile stage. The libidinal current in question then behaves in relation to later psychological structures like one belonging to the system of the unconscious, like one that is repressed. . . .

2. The second phase of repression is that of repression proper—the phase to which most attention has hitherto been given. It emanates from the more highly developed systems of the ego—systems which are capable of being conscious—and may in fact be described as a process of "afterpressure." It gives an impression of being an essentially active process, while fixation appears in fact to be a passive lagging behind. What undergo repression may either be the psychical derivatives of the original lagging instincts, . . . or they may be psychical trends which have for other reasons aroused strong aversion. . . .

3. The third phase, and the most important as regards pathological phenomena, is that of failure of repression, of *irruption,* of *return of the repressed.* This irruption takes its start from the point of fixation, and it involves a regression of the libidinal development to that point. . . .

Let us [consider] the question of whether the analysis of Schreber's case throws any light upon the mechanism of repression proper which predominates in paranoia.

At the climax of his illness, under the influence of visions which were "partly of a terrifying character, but partly, too, of an indescribable grandeur," Schreber became convinced of the imminence of a great catastrophe, of the end of the world. Voices told him that the work of the past 14,000 years had now come to nothing and that the earth's allotted span was only 212 years more, and during the last part of his stay in Flechsig's clinic he believed that that period had already elapsed. He himself was "the only real man left alive," and the few human shapes that he still saw—the doctor, the attendants, the other patients—he explained as being "miracled up, cursorily improvised men". . . . He had various theories of the cause of the catastrophe. At one time he had in mind a process of glaciation owing to the withdrawal of the sun; at another . . . Flechsig was the culprit, since through his magic arts he had sown fear and terror among men, had wrecked the foundations of religion, and spread abroad general nervous disorders and immorality, so that devastating pestilences had descended upon mankind. In any case the end of the world was the consequence of the conflict which had broken out between him and Flechsig, or, according to the etiology adopted in the second phase of his delusion, of the indissoluble bond which had been formed between him and God; it was, in fact, the inevitable result of his illness. . . .

A world-catastrophe of this kind is not infrequent during the agitated state in other cases of paranoia. . . . The patient has withdrawn from the people in his environment and from the external world generally. . . . The end of the world is the projection of this internal catastrophe; his subjective world has come to an end since he has withdrawn his love from it. . . .

And the paranoiac builds it up again, not more splendid, it is true, but at least so that he can once more live in it. He builds it up by the work of his delusions. *The delusional formation, which we take to be a pathological product, is in reality an attempt at recovery, a process of reconstruction.* Such a reconstruction after the catastrophe is successful to a greater or lesser extent, but never wholly so; in Schreber's words, there has been a "profound internal change" in the world. But the human subject has recaptured a relation, and often a very intense one, to the people and things in the world, even though the relation is a hostile one now, where formerly it was hopefully affectionate. We may say, then, that the process of repression proper consists in a detachment of the libido from people—and things—that were previously loved. It happens silently; we receive no intelligence of it but can only infer it from subsequent events.

What forces itself so noisily upon our attention is the process of recovery, which undoes the work of repression and brings back the libido again onto the people it had abandoned. In paranoia this process is carried out by the method of projection.

23

The Ghost
of the Weed Garden:
A Study
of a Chronic Schizophrenic

R . D . L A I N G

Julie, at the time I knew her, had been a patient in a ward of a
mental hospital since the age of seventeen, that is, for nine years. In
these years she had become a typically inaccessible and withdrawn
chronic schizophrenic. She was hallucinated, given to posturing and
to stereotyped, bizarre, incomprehensible actions; she was mostly
mute, and when she did speak it was in the most deteriorated schiz-
ophrenese. On admission, she had been diagnosed as suffering from
hebephrenia, a type of schizophrenia common during early adolescence, and given a course of insulin, to no avail. No other specific
attempts had been made to recall her to sanity.

On account of various odd and somewhat alarming things she
said and did when she was seventeen, her parents took her to see a

THE GHOST OF THE WEED GARDEN: A STUDY OF A CHRONIC SCHIZOPHRENIC Adapted
from *The divided self*. London: Tavistock Publications, 1960, and New York:
Pantheon Books, 1969. Copyright © 1969 by R. D. Laing. Used by permission
of the author and the publishers.

psychiatrist. After the interview the psychiatrist recorded that there was nothing particularly unusual about her nonverbal behavior in itself, but that the things she said were enough to establish the diagnosis of schizophrenia. She said the trouble was that she was not a real person; she was trying to become a person. There was no happiness in her life, and she was trying to find happiness. She thought there was an invisible barrier between herself and others. She felt unreal, empty, worthless. She was worried lest she was too destructive, and she was beginning to think it best not to touch anything in case she should cause damage. She had a great deal to say about her mother; her mother was smothering her, she would not let her live, and she had never wanted her. (Since her mother was prompting her to have more friends, to go to dances, to wear pretty dresses, and so on, these accusations seemed palpably absurd.) However, Julie's basic psychotic statement was that a child had been murdered. She was rather vague about the details, but she said she had heard of this from the voice of her brother. (She had no brother.) She wondered, however, if this voice might not have been her own. The child was wearing her clothes when it was killed. The child could have been herself. She had been murdered either by herself or by her mother—she was not sure. She proposed to tell the police about it.

We can see the existential truth in her statements that she is not a person, that she is unreal. Her accusations against her mother, we suspect, must relate to her failure to become a person, but they seem, on the surface, rather wild and far-fetched. However, it is when she says "a child has been murdered" that one's common sense is asked to stretch further than it will go, and she is left alone in a world that no one will share.

It is never easy to obtain an adequate account of a schizophrenic's early life. An investigation into the life of any single schizophrenic is a laborious piece of original research. Discovering the way people in the patient's world have regarded his behavior is as important as having a history of that behavior. In this particular case, I saw the mother once a week over a period of several months and, on a number of occasions, interviewed her father, her sister, who was three years older, and her aunt. Although each had his or her own point of view toward Julie, they all agreed in seeing her life in three basic phases: (1) The patient was a *good*, normal, healthy child, until (2) she gradually began to be *bad*, to do and say things that caused great distress and were on the whole put down to naughtiness or badness, until (3) this went beyond all tolerable limits, so that she could be regarded only as completely *mad*. In the evolution of a psychosis as seen by members of a family, these three phases—good to bad to mad— occur very commonly.

At this point I should like to make one important observation. Julie's parents did not deliberately suppress facts or try to be misleading. On the contrary, both were eager to be helpful. But it is significant that they discounted or denied the obvious possible implications in the facts. I shall now examine the nature of the psychosis, which seemed to begin when Julie was seventeen, by considering her life until then. My account, with the events grouped according to the parents' framework, is given predominantly in the mother's words.

Phase 1: The "Good" Child

In her mother's eyes, Julie was always a "good" child. She was never a demanding baby and was weaned without difficulty. Her mother had no bother with her from the day she took off nappies completely when Julie was fifteen months old. She was never "a trouble"; she always did what she was told.

A really alive baby is demanding, is a trouble, and by no means always does what she is told. It may well be that the baby was never as "perfect" as the mother wanted me to believe, but what is highly significant is that the mother evidently took as expressions of the utmost goodness, health, and normality just those things that I take to be expressions of an inner deadness in the child. None of the adults in Julie's world knew the difference between existential life and death; and the signs of being existentially dead received their highest commendation.

Let us consider each of the mother's statements in turn.

1. Julie was never a demanding baby. She never really cried to be fed. She never sucked vigorously and never finished a bottle. But she was always "whinie and girnie" and did not put on weight very rapidly. "She never wanted for anything, but I felt she was never satisfied."

Here we have a description of a child whose oral hunger and greed have never found expression. Instead of crying lustily and excitedly, sucking energetically, emptying the bottle, and, satiated, falling into contented sleep—all healthy expressions of instinct—she fretted continually, seemed hungry, yet when presented with the bottle sucked desultorily and never satisfied herself.

One of the most important aspects of this account is that the mother was not alarmed that the baby did not cry demandingly or drain the bottle. She regarded Julie's behavior not as an ominous sign of the failure of basic oral instinctual drives to find expression and fulfillment, but solely as a token of "goodness." The combination of the baby's nearly total failure to achieve self-instinctual gratification and the mother's complete unawareness of this failure can be seen repeatedly in the early relationship of schizophrenic children and their mothers.

2. She was weaned without any trouble. It is in feeding that the baby is for the first time actively alive with another person. By the time of weaning the normal infant can be expected to have developed some sense of itself as a being in its own right and some sense of the mother as a separate person. On the basis of these achievements, weaning occurs without much difficulty. The baby at this stage is given to playing "weaning games" in which he drops, say, a rattle, to have it returned to him; drops it again to have it returned; drops it, and so on, interminably. The baby seems here to be playing at an object going away, returning, going away, returning—the central issue of weaning in fact. Moreover, the game usually has to be played *his* way. We find it natural to collude with him in maintaining the impression that he is in control.

Julie's elder sister had played the usual version of this game, and it had exasperated her mother. "I made sure that she [Julie] was not going to play *that* game with me. *I* threw things away and she brought them back to *me*," as soon as she could crawl. It is hardly necessary to comment on the implications of this inversion of roles for Julie's failure to develop any real ways of her own.

She was said to have been precocious in walking (she was just over one year old) and screamed when she could not get to her mother across the room quickly enough. The furniture had to be rearranged because "Julie was terrified of any chairs that came between her and me." Her mother interpreted this as a token of how much her daughter had always loved her. Until Julie was three or four, she "nearly went crazy" if her mother was out of her sight for a moment.

If an individual needs another in order to be himself, he has failed to achieve full autonomy and engages in life from a basically insecure position. Julie could be herself neither in her mother's presence nor in her absence. As far as her mother remembers, she was never out of earshot of Julie until Julie was almost three.

3. She was clean from the moment that nappies were taken off at fifteen months. It is not unusual to find in schizophrenics a precocious development of bodily control. One is often told by parents of schizophrenics how proud they were of their children because of their early crawling, walking, bowel and bladder functioning, talking, giving up crying, and so on. One has to ask, however, how much of the infant's behavior is an

expression of its own will. The question is not how good or how naughty a child is but whether the child develops a sense of being the origin of his own action. The body can perfect its skills and do all that is expected of it without the child's ever acquiring a capacity for genuine self-action. Instead, all action is in almost total compliance and conformity with outside directives. Julie's actions appear to have been trained by her mother, but Julie was not "in" them. This must be what Julie meant when she said she had never become a person.

4. She always did what she was told. There are good reasons for being obedient, but being unable to be disobedient is not one of the best. In the mother's account so far, one is unable to see that she could accept Julie as an independent personality. As a chronic schizophrenic, Julie repeatedly called herself a "tolled bell," or a "told belle." Julie's mother "gave her life" to the tolled bell, but even after twenty-five years, she flatly denied the possibility that this "good," obedient, clean little girl, who so loved her that she nearly went crazy when separated from her by only a chair, had been petrified into a *thing* too terror-stricken to become a person.

Hatred can be expressed in and through compliance. Her mother commended her obedience, but Julie began to carry her obedience to such lengths that it became "impossible." She had a spell, at about the age of ten, when she had to be told everything that was going to happen in the course of the day and what she was to do. Every day had to begin with such a catalogue. If her mother refused to carry out the ritual, she would start to whimper. According to her mother, nothing would stop this whimpering but a sound thrashing. As she grew older, Julie would not use any money she was given. Even when encouraged to say what she wanted, to buy a dress by herself, or to have friends like other girls, she would not express her own wishes; she had to have her mother along to buy her clothes, and she showed no initiative in making friends. She would never make a decision of any kind.

Phase 2: The "Bad" Child

From about fifteen her behavior changed, and the "good" girl became "bad." At this time also, her mother's attitude toward her began to change. She had earlier thought it right and proper that Julie should be with her as much as possible, but now she began to urge Julie to get out

more, to have friends, to go to the movies and even to dances, and to have
boy friends. All these things Julie "obstinately" refused to do. Instead, she
would sit and do nothing, or wander the streets, never telling her mother
when she would be back. She kept her room extravagantly untidy. She
continued to cherish a doll that her mother felt she should have "grown
out of." We shall return to this doll later. Julie's diatribes against her
mother were endless and always on the same theme: she would accuse her
mother of not having wanted her, of not letting her be a person, of
never having let her breathe, of having smothered her. She swore like a
trooper. Yet to other people she could be charming—when she wanted
to be.

So far we have considered only the relationship between Julie and her
mother. It is the thesis of this study that schizophrenia is a possible outcome of more-than-usual difficulty in being a whole person with others
and of not sharing the common-sense (that is, the community-sense) way
of experiencing oneself in the world. Despite the importance of the first
year of life, the nature of the milieu in which the child exists throughout
its infancy, childhood, and adolescence may still have great effect one
way or the other. At these subsequent stages, the father and other significant persons can play a decisive role in the child's life, either in direct
relation with the child or, indirectly, through effects on the mother.

Julie's sister, three years older, was a rather forthright, assertive married woman, though not without femininity and charm. According to her
mother, she had been difficult from birth: demanding and always "a
trouble." That is, she seems to have been a relatively normal child of
whom her mother never much approved. But they appeared to get on
well enough (though Julie's sister claimed the mother had "done everything for Julie, and Julie was always her favorite"). The sister regarded
her mother as a rather dominating person if one did not stand up to her.
It was quite clear that this sister had achieved autonomy early, but if one
cared to look closely into the sister's personality, there were many neurotic elements to be found. Julie, however, had built into her scheme of
phantoms a big sister who was one of the few predominantly good figures
in her world, a "Sister of Mercy."

The father said he had not much to tell me, because he had "withdrawn
himself emotionally" from the family before Julie was born. But he
played a more obviously significant part. In his wife's eyes, he was a
"sexual beast." In his, she was cold and unsympathetic. They spoke to
each other no more than was absolutely necessary, and he found sexual
satisfaction elsewhere. However, neither built into their many accusations
against each other any allegations about mistreating their daughters. The

father thought his wife useless to him, but "to be fair to her," he confessed, "she was a good mother. I have to grant her that." He did not attempt to win the children to his side, since he did not need their support.

The mother, however, did not hesitate to misrepresent her husband to her daughters, and she piled up innumerable instances of injustices. The elder sister, seeing faults on both sides, tried not to favor either and took the middle way. If she had to, though, she took her mother's side against her father as well as against Julie. Julie refused to collude openly with her mother against her father.

It is remarkable that despite the radical disruption of the relationship between husband and wife, in at least one respect they maintained a collusion. Both accepted Julie's false self as good and rejected every other aspect of her as bad. But in the "bad" phase, a corollary to this was perhaps even more important. Not only did they reject as bad all of Julie apart from the compliant, lifeless shadow that passed in their eyes for a real person, they completely refused to "take to heart" any of Julie's reproaches against them.

Both Julie and her mother were at this time desperate people. Julie in her psychosis called herself Mrs. Taylor. What does this mean? Julie explained, "I'm tailormade. I'm a tailored maid; I was made, fed, clothed, and tailored." Such statements are psychotic not because they may be untrue but because they are cryptic: they are often quite impossible to fathom unless the patient decodes them. Yet Julie's statement is very cogent, for it gives in a nutshell the reproaches she was making against her mother when she was fifteen and sixteen. Her "ranting and raving" and her "badness" were the same thing. The most schizophrenic factor at this time must have been not simply Julie's attack on her mother, or even her mother's counterattack, but the complete absence of anyone in her world who could or would see some sense in her point of view, whether it was right or wrong.

When her mother said she was bad, Julie felt herself murdered. It was the negation of any autonomous point of view on her part. Her mother was prepared to accept a compliant, false self, to love a shadow, and to give it anything. She even tried to order the shadow to act as if it were a person. But she never recognized the real, disturbing presence in the world of a daughter with her own possibilities. The existential truth in Julie's delusions was that her own true possibilities were indeed being smothered, strangled, murdered.

She began to convert existential truth into physical fact; she became deluded. She began by accusing her mother of having, in an existential sense, never let her live; she ended by talking and acting as if her mother had, in a legal sense, murdered an actual child. It was quite clearly a relief to the family when they could pity her and no longer have to vindicate themselves by condemning her.

Phase 3: The "Mad" Child

Julie's basic accusation was that her mother was trying to kill her. When she was seventeen, an incident occurred that probably triggered the transition from "bad" to "mad." This episode was related to me by the sister.

Until the age of seventeen, Julie had a doll, which she had owned from infancy. She dressed it and played with it in her room—no one quite knew in what way; her play with the doll, which she called Julie Doll, was a secret part of her life. Her mother grew more and more insistent that she give up the doll as she became "a big girl." One day the doll was gone. It was never known whether Julie had thrown it out or her mother had put it away. Julie accused her mother. Her mother denied that she had done anything to the doll and said that Julie must have lost it. Shortly after this, Julie was told by a voice that a child wearing her clothes had been beaten to a pulp by her mother. She proposed to report this crime to the police. It was at this point that psychiatric care was sought.

The Ghost of the Weed Garden

Julie's self-being had become so fragmented that she could best be described as living a death-in-life existence in a state approaching chaotic nonentity. In Julie's case, the chaos and lack of identity were not complete. With her, one had for long periods an uncanny feeling of being in the presence of another person and yet a feeling that there was no one there. Even when what was said seemed to be an expression of someone, the fragment of a self behind the words was not Julie. There might be someone addressing me, but in listening to a schizophrenic it is very difficult to know who is talking and whom one is talking to. Listening to Julie, I often felt as if I were doing group psychotherapy with one patient. I was confronted with a jumble of quite disparate attitudes, feelings, and expressions of impulse. Julie's intonations, gestures, and mannerisms changed their character from moment to moment. It seemed that I was in the presence of various fragments, or incomplete elements, of different personalities in operation at one time. This impression was strengthened, though hardly made less confusing, by the fact that Julie seemed to speak of herself in the first, second, or third person. The overall unity of her being had broken up into several partial assemblies, or partial systems, each with its own little stereotyped personality. However, even this state of near-chaotic nonentity was by no means irreversible or fixed in its disintegration. Sometimes she would marvelously come together again and display a most pathetic realization of her plight. But she was terrified of these moments of integration for various reasons. They caused her intense anxiety; and she seemed to remember and dread the process of disintegration as an experience so awful that unintegration, unrealness, and deadness were a refuge.

Thus Julie's personality was characterized by lack of unity and by division into partial systems. Each partial system had recognizable features and distinctive ways of its own; by following them through, many features of her behavior became clearer. All her life seemed to go on in the present moment. The absence of a total experience of her being as a whole meant that she lacked a unified experience on which to base a clear idea of the boundary of her being. Each partial system seemed to have its own focus or center of awareness, its own very limited memory and limited ways of structuring percepts, its own drives, its own tendency to preserve its autonomy, and its own special dangers that threatened its autonomy. She would refer to these diverse systems as "he" or "she," or address them as "you."

Along with the tendency to perceive aspects of her own being as not-her went a failure to discriminate between what objectively was not-her and what was her. She might, for instance, feel that rain on her cheek was her tears. William Blake in *Prophetic Writings* describes a tendency to become what one perceives, and in Julie all perception seemed to threaten confusion with the object. She spent much of her time exercising herself with this difficulty. "That's the rain. I could be the rain." "That chair . . . that wall. I could be that wall. It's a terrible thing for a girl to be a wall."

Almost every act of perception appeared to involve a confusion of self with not-self. The ground for this confusion was prepared by the fact that since large aspects of her person were partially outside her self, it was easy to confuse those split-off aspects of her being with other people. For example, she confused conscience with her mother and her mother with conscience.

To love was therefore very dangerous. To like = to be like = to be the same as. If she likes me, she is like me; she *is* me. Thus Julie said she was my sister, my wife, she was a McBride. I was life, and she was the Bride of Life. She developed my mannerisms, and she had the Tree of Life inside her, she was the Tree of Life. Or again:

> If she is thinking thoughts a, b, c, and
> I express closely similar thoughts a^1, b^1, c^1, then
> I have stolen her thoughts.

The completely psychotic expression of this was to accuse me of having her brains in my head.

In one of the simplest instances of the operation of two partial systems, she would issue an order and proceed to obey it. She did this continually, under her breath, out loud, or by hallucinations. For instance, there was a peremptory bully who was always ordering her about. The same peremptory voice would make endless complaints to me about "this child": "This child is a wicked child; this child is wasted time; this child is just a cheap tart. You'll never do anything with this child. . . ." It would be appropriate to call this partial system a cruel internal mother. Basically an internal female persecutor, it contained in concentrated form all the cruelty that Julie ascribed to her mother.

Two other partial systems could be readily identified. One fulfilled the role of an advocate on Julie's behalf to me. Acting as a protector or buffer against persecution, "she" frequently called Julie her little sister. We may refer to this system as her kind sister. The third partial system was an entirely good, compliant, propitiating little girl. When this system spoke, Julie said, "I'm a good girl. I go to the lavatory regularly." Finally, as I remarked earlier, there were periods of precarious sanity when, in a pathetically scared, barely audible tone, Julie seemed to be more nearly speaking in her own person than at any other time.

Let us now consider these various systems operating together. (The examples I give are of her more coherent utterances.)

> I was born under a black sun. I wasn't born, I was crushed out. It's not one of those things you get over like that. I wasn't mothered, I was smothered. She wasn't a mother. I'm choosey who I have for a mother. Stop it. Stop it. She's killing me. She's cutting out my tongue. I'm rotten, base. I'm wicked. I'm wasted time. . . .

She starts by talking to me in her own person, leveling the same accusations against her mother that she had persisted in for years but in a particularly clear and lucid way. The "black sun" appears to be a symbol of her destructive mother. It was a frequently recurring image. Thus the first six sentences are spoken sanely, but suddenly Julie appears to be subject to some terrifying attack, presumably from the cruel mother. She breaks off: "Stop it, stop it." Addressing me briefly again she exclaims, "She's killing me." Then follows a defensive denigration of herself, couched in the same terms as her cruel mother's condemnations of her, "I'm rotten, base. I'm wicked. I'm wasted time. . . ."

Accusations against her mother were always liable to bring on some such catastrophic reaction. On a later occasion she made her usual accusations against her mother, and the cruel mother interrupted with her customary accusations against "that child." I interrupted these remarks to say, "Julie's frightened of being killed by herself for saying these things." The diatribe ended, and she said very quietly, "Yes, that's my conscience killing me. I've been frightened of my mother all my life and always will be. Do you think I can live?" This relatively integrated statement makes clear the remaining confusion of her conscience and her real mother.

> This child doesn't want to come here, do you realize that? She's my little sister. This child does not know about things she shouldn't know about.

Here her "big sister," her protector, is speaking, making clear to me that Julie is innocent and ignorant and, therefore, blameless and not responsible. The big sister system was very knowing and responsible, rather patronizing though kindly and protective. However, she is not in favor of Julie's growing up; she is always speaking for the little sister. She wishes to maintain the status quo.

> This child's mind is cracked. This child's mind is closed. You're trying to open this child's mind. I'll never forgive you for trying to open this child's mind. This child is dead and not dead.

The implication of the last sentence is that, by remaining in a sense dead, Julie can be in a sense not dead, but if she takes responsibility for being alive, then she may really be killed.

However, this sister could also say:

> You've got to want this child. You've got to make her welcome. . . . You've got to take care of this girl. I'm a good girl. She's my little sister. You've got to take her to the lavatory. She's my little sister. She doesn't know about these things. That's not an impossible child.

This big sister had experience, knowledge, a sense of responsibility, and reasonableness, in contrast to the little sister's innocence, ignorance, irresponsibility, and waywardness. We see here that Julie's schizophrenia consisted not of the absence of a center for her personality, but of an overall lack of integration. This big sister could speak in a reasonable, sane, and balanced way, but it was not Julie who was speaking. Her real sanity depended not on being able to speak sanely in the person of a big sister, but on achieving an integration of her own total being. Schizophrenia is betrayed by Julie's reference to herself as a third party and by the sudden intrusion of the little sister while the big sister is speaking: "I'm a good girl."

When Julie did present words or actions to me as her own, the self she offered was completely psychotic. However, one must be prepared to paraphrase her statements into sane speech before one can attempt to understand the experience of this self. In using the term "self" in this context, I do not mean to imply that this was her *true* self, only that this system seemed to be a rallying point around which integration could occur. It appeared as the really mad kernel of her being, the central aspect of her that, so it seemed, had to be maintained chaotic and dead lest she be killed. I shall attempt to characterize the nature of this self not only by its direct statements but also by its statements that appeared to originate in other systems.

When Julie elaborated on the statement that she had the Tree of Life inside her, she said that the apples of the tree were her breasts, that she had ten nipples (her fingers), that she had "all the bones of a brigade of the Highland Light Infantry." She had, all at one time, everything she could think of, and anything she wanted she had immediately. Thus she could be anyone, anywhere, anytime. "I'm Rita Hayworth, I'm Joan Blondell. I'm a Royal Queen. My royal name is Julianne." But since she was anyone she cared to mention, she was no one. "I'm thousands. I'm an in divide you all. I'm a no un" (i.e., a nun; a noun; no one single person).

Being a nun had many meanings. One of them was contrasted with being a bride. She usually regarded me as her brother and called herself my bride or the bride of "leally lovely lifely life." Of course, since life and I were sometimes identical for her, she was terrified of Life, or me. She was afraid that Life would mash her to pulp, burn her heart with a red-hot iron, cut off her legs, hands, tongue, breasts. Notwithstanding having the Tree of Life inside her, she generally felt that she was the Destroyer of Life. It was understandable, therefore, that she was terrified that life would destroy her. Life was usually depicted by a male or phallic symbol, but what she seemed to wish for was not simply to be a male herself but to have a heavy armament of the sexual equipment of both sexes, all the bones of a brigade of the Highland Light Infantry and ten nipples, and so on.

She was born under a black sun.
She's the occidental sun.

She always insisted that her mother never wanted her and had crushed her out in some monstrous way rather than give birth to her normally. Her mother had "wanted and not wanted" a son. She was "an occidental sun," an accidental son whom her mother out of hate had turned into a girl. The rays of the black sun scorched and shriveled her. Under the black sun she existed as a dead thing.

> I'm the prairie.
> She's a ruined city.

The only living things in the prairie are wild beasts; rats infest a ruined city. Her existence was depicted in images of utterly barren, arid desolation. This existential death, this death-in-life, was her prevailing mode of being in the world.

> She's the ghost of the weed garden.

In this death there was no hope, no future, no possibility. Everything had happened. There was no pleasure, no source of possible satisfaction or possible gratification, for the world was as empty and dead as she.

> The pitcher is broken, the well is dry.

She was utterly pointless and worthless. She could not believe in the possibility of love anywhere.

> She's just one of those girls who live in the world.
> Everyone pretends to want her and doesn't want her. I'm just leading the life now of a cheap tart.

Yet, Julie did value herself, if only in a phantom way. There was a belief and, however psychotic a belief it was, it was still a form of faith in something of great value in herself, in something of great worth deeply lost or buried inside her, still undiscovered by herself or by anyone. If one could go deep into the depths of the dark earth, one would discover "the bright gold." If one could get fathoms down one would discover "the pearl at the bottom of the sea."

24

A Sociopsychological
Investigation of Suicide

EDWIN S. SHNEIDMAN
NORMAN L. FARBEROW

Perhaps the most familiar approach to suicide is a sociological one, in which an investigator divides a city (or country) into socioeconomic regions, tabulates the number of suicides that occur in each region, and discusses the relationship between socioeconomic factors and suicide rates. This approach is valuable, but it has an important disadvantage, especially for those who wish to reduce suicide rates: it provides no information about the psychological states of suicide victims, which are personal and individual.

In the study described below, we examined suicide from a psychological as well as a sociological point of view. Our purpose was to identify the relationships between the psychological characteristics of people who commit suicide and the sociological facts of their

A SOCIOPSYCHOLOGICAL INVESTIGATION OF SUICIDE Adapted from *Perspectives in personality research*. Edited by H. P. David and J. C. Brengelmann. New York: Springer Publishing Company, 1960. Used by permission of E. S. Shneidman and the publisher.

lives, such as wealth. Do all suicides, regardless of socioeconomic class, show similar psychological tendencies, or do their psychological characteristics vary in some systematic way with socioeconomic class?

The suicides we studied included 768 residents of Los Angeles County whose deaths were certified as suicide by the County Coroner's Office in 1957. From the Coroner's Office we obtained certain basic information about each suicide victim, such as age, sex, race, marital status, and home address. Next, we used the home addresses to divide the suicides into nine socioeconomic groups, ranging from "most advantaged suburban group" to "least advantaged apartment (and rooming house) group." The groups were based on analysis of 1950 census data by the Los Angeles Welfare Planning Council. The council had divided Los Angeles County into one hundred geographic areas, analyzed the social, economic, and cultural characteristics of each area, and then classified the areas into the nine groups. Somewhat to our surprise, the percentage of the county's *population* in each of the nine socioeconomic groups was very similar to the percentage of *suicides* in each group. Thus suicide seems to be neither the malady of the rich nor the scourge of the poor; rather, it is "democratically" distributed across the society.

For psychological information, we turned to the coroner's file of suicide notes. Of the 768 people who committed suicide in Los Angeles County in 1957, 278 (36 percent) left one or more notes; the total number of suicide notes for 1957 was 361. To increase the reliability of the study, we also analyzed the 339 suicide notes on file for 1956 and the 248 on file for 1958, bringing the total number of notes examined to 948.

Each note was read by a psychologist who knew nothing about the person who had written it (and nothing about the purpose of the study). He looked for five things: the relationship between the suicide and the person to whom he addressed the note (spouse, friend, etc.); the reason given for the suicide (ill health, financial difficulty, rejection, etc.); the emotional content of the note (anger, sorrow, love, etc.); any other topics mentioned (insurance, funeral arrangements, etc.); and the basic aim of the note (reason for the suicide, emotional expression, practical instructions, etc.).

Analysis of Suicide Notes

When we examined the relationship between these psychological data and the socioeconomic group to which each person belonged, we found significant differences among the groups on two of the five psychological factors analyzed: the reason given for the suicide and the emotional content of the note. There were differences among the groups in both the kind of reason given and the frequency with which a reason was given. Similarly, there were differences in the kind of emotion expressed and in the frequency with which an emotion was expressed. The findings, which are summarized in Table 24-1, are discussed and illustrated below.

1. Most Advantaged Suburbs. The residents of four wealthy suburban areas make up this socioeconomic group. La Canada and La Crescenta are typical examples. Almost all the residents are white and live in single-family houses on large lots, many with swimming pools. This group includes a smaller percentage of widowed and divorced people than most other groups. It accounts for 5 percent of the county's population and 4 percent of its suicides.

People in this group tend to give reasons for their suicides, but the reason is seldom ill health, rejection, or financial difficulty. Instead, people say they are "tired of life," "can't go on," and "see no point in living." The suicides in this wealthy group do not consider themselves deprived; on the contrary, they seem almost to have been overwhelmed by life's riches.

Here are two sample notes. (Identifying details such as names have been changed here and elsewhere but the notes are reproduced verbatim.)

No funeral. Please leave the body to science.

WILLIAM SMITH

I'm sorry. Don't bother with a post. It's sodium cyanide. At 11:12.

2. Most Advantaged Residential Communities. Typical of the fourteen areas in this group, which tend to be somewhat older than the communities in the first group, are Pacific Palisades, Westwood, and Brentwood. Fine houses, spacious yards, good schools, and elaborate recreational facilities abound. Virtually all the residents are white. The group includes 16 percent of the county's population and 17 percent of its suicides.

The notes written by members of this group are strikingly uninformative about the psychological state of the note-writer. They show no particular emotion and seldom cite a reason for the suicide. The most one can say about the reasons given is that they rarely concern health, rejection, or loneliness. Many financially independent and successful people in their forties belong to this group, and that fact may help explain the apparent absence of a need to communicate with others about the suicidal act.

TABLE 24-1

People from different social classes seem to be about equally prone to suicide, as the close correspondence between the percentages in columns 1 and 2 shows. However, social class does affect the frequency with which note-writers give reasons for their suicides and express emotion, and also the particular reason given and emotion shown. The ways the notes from each socioeconomic group differed from those of the nine groups as a whole are indicated below.

Socioeconomic group	Percentage of population	Percentage of suicides*	Reason given for suicide				Emotion expressed			
			None	Ill health	Rejection	Tired of life	None	Absolution	Self-depreciation	Affection
1. Most advantaged suburbs	5	4	Rare			Frequent				
2. Most advantaged residential communities	16	17		Rare	Rare					
3. Most advantaged apartment areas	4	6		Frequent				Frequent		
4. Moderately advantaged suburbs	21	12		Rare			Rare			
5. Moderately advantaged natural communities	31	31	Rare		Frequent				Rare	Frequent
6. Moderately advantaged apartment areas	7	11			Rare				Rare	Frequent
7. Least advantaged rural areas	2	1	(excluded from analysis)							
8. Least advantaged industrial communities	10	9					Frequent			Rare
9. Least advantaged apartment areas	4	5	Frequent				Frequent			Rare

* Percentages do not add to 100 because addresses of some suicides were not known.

Here are two sample notes:

Don't take life too seriously. You'll never get out of it alive anyway.

MARY ADAMS

[On Beverly Hilton Hotel stationery] Nobody to blame. Call YO 1-2345.

3. Most Advantaged Apartment Areas. This group includes five apartment-house areas, among them Wilshire North, inhabited by mainly professional people. There are few non-whites, few children, and more divorced and widowed people than in most other groups. With 4 percent of the population, this group has 6 percent of the county's suicides, of which an unusually large percentage are women.

With 22 suicides per 100,000 people, this group has the highest suicide rate of the nine. (The average for Los Angeles County is 14; the national average is 9.8.) Group 6, moderately advantaged apartment areas, has the second highest rate, 21 per 100,000. Group 9, least advantaged apartment areas, is third with 19 per 100,000. Thus the three apartment areas have high suicide rates in common. However, the psychological content of the notes left by members of the three groups does not seem to be similar.

Suicide notes written by people from this group have two outstanding characteristics. First, they often cite ill health (physical disability, symptoms, pain) as a reason for suicide. Second, the emotion expressed tends, more often than for any other group, to concern guilt, absolution, forgiveness. The notes convey an impression of considerable dependence for existence on the body and its functioning, of self-centeredness, and of attempts to assuage psychological conflicts through self-blame and rationalizations based on physical pain.

Notes left by members of this group have more in common with those of the less advantaged groups, discussed below, than with those of Groups 1 and 2. A typical note follows:

To all my friends:
Please forgive me and thanks for all your kindness.
My courage has run out. In the face of poor health, deserted by my sisters, and persistent cruelty of my husband I have no further reason to keep fighting.
All my life I have tried to be decent. I have worked hard to make a marriage out of puny material. To be deserted at such a time of my life is too disillusioning and too harsh. It is more than I can bear. I just feel that those who should be close to me are like "rats deserting a sinking ship." Therefore I do not want any of them (my sisters or my husband) near me in death or to have any part of my possessions.

But I do appreciate the goodness and the kindness of my friends, my doctors and my lawyer—it kept me going up to this point.

Goodbye and try to remember me at my best.

4. Moderately Advantaged Suburbs. This group includes thirteen suburban communities, such as Reseda and Encino. Although there are some older estates, most homes are tract houses. The residents, almost none of whom belong to minority groups, are chiefly young white-collar and skilled workers and their families. The suicide rate in this group is low: with 21 percent of the population, the group accounts for only 12 percent of the suicides.

Most notes give some reason for the suicide and express some emotion. In contrast to Group 3, however, the reason is rarely ill health and the emotion is usually not related to guilt or self-blame. Instead, the emotions stressed are affection and love (idealization of others, praise, defense of others); their converse, hostility, is often strongly implied. The typical person in this group is about thirty-five, very much involved in his interpersonal relationships, and undergoing considerable conflict over love and hate. This group and the next (Group 5) are probably those who could have been helped most by psychotherapy.

The following is a sample suicide note:

> Ann:
> Here is the note you wanted giving you power of attorney for the house and everything else (including all of *your* bills).
> I hope that my insurance will get you out of the whole mess that you got us both in.
> This isn't hard for me to do because it's probably the only way I'll ever get rid of you, we both know how the California courts only see the women's side.
> My only hope is that you can raise Junior to be as honest and as good as he is right now.
> I think that Junior and Betty and George are really the only things in the world that I'll miss. Please take good care of them.
>
> Good luck,
> PAUL
>
> P.S. I love you Junior, and thank you Betty for all you've done for me and Junior.
>
> Love,
> DADDY

5. Moderately Advantaged Natural Communities. This group, the largest of the nine, includes thirty-four of the one hundred geographic areas in Los Angeles County, 31 percent of the population, and 31 percent of the suicides. Fully built up, mainly with small but fairly new one-family houses, the communities that make it up are the "little cities" of greater Los Angeles, such as Alhambra. Most residents are married and white.

The dominant reason for suicide in this group seems to be rejection (not being understood, feelings of loneliness and isolation, loss of love). The notes show very little affection toward the addressees and the note-writers seem very angry—possibly, in view of their suicides, with themselves.

Here are two notes written by the same person:

Dear Carol:

Be sure you hold fast to what you think you have now. I go with no bitterness toward you, only pity and love.

I pray this example will be the means of you going forward in life in the right way. Take good care of Junior and love him, do not vent your spite out on him when things do not go your way. Here are my car keys. If Dad will grant my one wish this car is yours.

MOTHER

This ten dollars is from what I earned last week, part of it I mean. Nothing to do with Dad's money. I've left him $70 more than he would have done for me if the shoe had been on the other foot.

Dear Ted:

Please do not have a lot of hypocrisy such as burial etc. Give my carcass to a hospital or cremate it.

If you have a spark of honesty in you and you love our son try and arrange for him to live with Bob and Carol where he will be happy and raised in a decent home. He will never be happy with you.

Here's what money I've left. I've sent Henry's to him and I've left Carol ten dollars out of it, what I earned last week.

Goodbye and God bless you.

ALICE

6. Moderately Advantaged Apartment Areas. These eight areas, typified by Southeast Hollywood, have a high population density and limited space. The residents include many older people, few children, and a small number of nonwhites. The group accounts for 7 percent of the population and 11 percent of the suicides. A large percentage of them, compared to other groups, are unmarried.

In this group, reasons for suicide are offered about as often as in other groups, and they differ from those given by other groups only in that rejection is seldom mentioned. Below are two sample notes:

Dear Joan.

I am so sick and disgusted can't get well so do the best you can. So sorry can't take it no longer. Cremate my body no flowers no minister. Just cremate me the least expense. My all my love to all of you.

ED

Phil.

I'm sorry but I had this all made out and decided when you called. A hell of a day today. Thanks for the call. But call Peter.

JOHN

7. *Least Advantaged Rural Areas.* This group consists of just one geographic area, an unincorporated region near Norwalk that includes only 2 percent of the population and 1 percent of the suicides. It was therefore excluded from our analysis.

8. *Least Advantaged Industrial Communities.* San Pedro, on the Los Angeles harbor, is typical of the fourteen areas in this group. Population density is moderate; there are many multiple dwellings, a fairly large minority population, and a smaller-than-average percentage of single people. The group includes 10 percent of the population and 9 percent of the suicides in the county.

Except for Group 9, notes left by people from this group show less emotion than those from any other group. The absence of affection is especially striking. The notes emphasize instructions, usually to relatives, about material possessions, disposing of the remains, and notifying people of the death. They tend to be matter-of-fact directives concerning the material aspects of a hard existence.

Two examples follow:

To whom it may concern:

I live at 100 Main Street, Los Angeles, California. In case of extreme emergency, please notify my daughter, Judy C. Jones, Box 100, San Diego, California. In my apartment there is a letter to her giving all necessary instructions about what to do with my affairs. I have a checking account with the National Bank, 1st Street Branch, Los Angeles. It is my wish that all of my friends listed in my address book be notified. I am a Protestant. Belong to no lodges now. My apartment rent is paid to the 15th of next month.

ROGER B. CLARK

James:

BE ALERT . . . CLOSE THE DOOR . . . NOW HEAR THIS. . . . BE ALERT.

By the time you read this, I shall have *disposed* of *myself*. (I can only guess your reaction. If its bad, massage your crotch and breath deeply.)
FINISH READING:

I felt better when I decided, several weeks ago. Too many adjustments to make. Ten years ago may have been able to do it. Too rigid now. Too many crystallizations. Too late to utilize the recently acquired revelation that many years ago, fear of world obstructed and stunted natural drives and imagination. Just the one fear was enough. World as total. Not individuals as such. What complete jerks make up this world.

First, check in my room. I may have goofed. If I did, I'll kill myself. That's a joke. Come on relax. You have things to do.

If you want to avoid Mom knowing (boy, am I burdening you) . . . get hold of the police and tell them to cooperate, to *quietly* come and take me to city facility. I should have passed out from strangulation about five hours ago, so only necessary to cart me away.

Pull this off!! To ease your mind, tell Pop. Then both of you tell Mom I took off and you don't know where—say Merchant Marine.

The V.A. can bury me. Pop has my papers. They ship me out out of town don't bother to go. In fact don't bother anyway. It's incredibly stupid the way people mourn the dead. My only regret is that I didn't have the world by the balls. If you don't, *you* suffer. Remember that.

You may doubt this letter, James. Satisfy your curiosity, but don't immediately hate me for imposing on you. Get things done. You can even stay home from work. I could have gone away and done it. But for once, let this ass hole family be practical. I would have taken my car—but now you have it.

If (I hate that word) I am dead, pull yourself together and do the things I said.

So help me if you go into the bathroom during the night and read this before you are supposed to, I'll kill you. Two cars and all.

9. Least Advantaged Apartment Areas. The Central Avenue area is typical of the seven neighborhoods in this group. Older houses have been converted into rooming houses and apartments; many buildings are run-down; industry and business have encroached substantially on housing areas. The population, which is dominated by minority groups (blacks, Mexican-Americans, Chinese, Japanese), is declining. At present the group includes 4 percent of the people in the county. It accounts for 5 percent of the suicides, an unusually high percentage of them unmarried.

These notes, even more than those from Group 8, tend neither to give reasons for the suicide nor to express emotion, especially affection. They contain instructions about workaday details—things for people to do, to get, to fix, to put right. Many of the notes are addressed to no one. They seem intended for the world at large, a world the victim has found harsh and unrewarding.

A sample note follows:

> My name is José B. Sanchez. In case of my death I am leaving everything I have in this room to Mr. Miguel A. Fuentes. His address is 145 Elm Street, Los Angeles, California, WU 5-4321.
>
> J.B.S.

Conclusions

Many studies that cut across social status have shown a relationship between psychological behavior and socioeconomic class. Kinsey's investigations of sexual behavior (1948, 1953), for example, made it clear that socioeconomic factors play an important part in the demonstration of emotion. In some socioeconomic groups, the expression of emotion (physical, verbal, or both) is accepted, while in others it is frowned on. Studies of alcoholics reveal similar social-class differences in behavior, and Hollingshead and Redlich's work (1958) on mental illness demonstrates that the form taken by emotional maladjustment varies with social class.

Our results are in line with the findings of such studies. They indicate that if one knows the socioeconomic class of a suicidal person, one also knows something about the reasoning and the emotions behind the suicidal impulses. The differences are by no means clear-cut or comprehensive enough to allow us to map out a suicide-prevention program based on social class, but they do suggest some questions. Why should people in Group 1, with all the material advantages, be "tired of life"? Is there really more physical sickness in Group 3 and if not, why the stress on it? What is the significance of the love-hate conflicts in Group 4 and the feeling of rejection in Group 5? As for Groups 8 and 9, what conclusions can be drawn from the apparent shortage of close one-to-one relationships and from the suicides' difficulties in expressing emotion, or in finding someone to express it to? Why is the suicide rate in Groups 3, 6, and 9, the three apartment-house groups, higher than average?

Questions like these need answers, but their general import is clear. Suicides, those enigmatic acts of total self-destruction, are neither wholly psychological nor wholly social. They must be viewed as a mixture of the two—as sociopsychological phenomena.

REFERENCES

Hollingshead, A. B., and Redlich, F. C. *Social class and mental illness.* New York: John Wiley and Sons, 1958.

Kinsey, A. C., Pomeroy, W. B., and Martin, C. E. *Sexual behavior in the human female.* Philadelphia: Saunders, 1953.

Kinsey, A. C., Pomeroy, W. B., and Martin, C. E. *Sexual behavior in the human male.* Philadelphia: Saunders, 1948.

Psychotherapy

Centuries ago, when insanity was thought to be caused by evil spirits, holes were sometimes bored in people's heads to let the evil spirits out. During the last century, people whose behavior was so disturbed that they could not get along in daily life were committed to insane asylums, where they were treated more like prisoners than like patients. Similarly, little help was available for less severely disturbed people—the ones who then were said to suffer from constitutional weaknesses and today might be called neurotic. Doctors sometimes suggested a change of scene or a long ocean voyage to "calm the nerves" of the rich; the poor, who did not visit doctors for their nerves, simply got along on their own as best they could.

Some mental hospitals today resemble prisons more than treatment centers, and people with psychological problems still are more likely to get help if they have money than if they do not. However, psychosis and neurosis are now thought of as problems that are at least potentially solvable, and a wide variety of effective treatments —drug therapy, group therapy, individual therapy—is available.

The most important psychotherapeutic movement of the century, individual analytic therapy, began with Sigmund Freud and psychoanalysis. (The picture on the preceding page shows the couch in Freud's office.) Psychoanalysis and the analytic therapies derived from it differ in significant ways, but they all have a common goal and a common overall method: to identify and deactivate the basic cause of the patient's symptoms by means of conversation between therapist and patient about the patient's anxieties and conflicts. R. D. Laing's "The Ghost of the Weed Garden" in the preceding part is an excellent example of the analytic approach, though unusual in that analysis is seldom undertaken with schizophrenic patients like Julie. In general, analytic therapy is more effective with neurotics than with psychotics, and it seems to work best with patients who are both intelligent and articulate.

Even for an intelligent, articulate, only moderately neurotic person, however, analytic therapy is not guaranteed to work, and it is an expensive, time-consuming method of treatment. Over the past forty years or so, psychologists and psychiatrists have devoted much effort to finding surer, more efficient ways of helping people with psychological problems. One major new approach, behavior therapy, has grown out of B. F. Skinner's work with operant conditioning. The behavioral approach differs from the analytic chiefly in that it ignores basic causes and concentrates on outward behavior. Behavior therapists see their job as education rather than "cure": from the therapist's point of view the patient has acquired certain bad habits (symptoms, in analytic terminology); he must break the bad habits and learn more desirable ones.

Behavior therapy is sometimes criticized as superficial and simplistic. Its opponents say, for example, that a person who gets rid of one set of bad habits will simply develop another, perhaps less obvious, set unless the underlying reason for the neurotic behavior is removed. In reply, advocates of the behavioral approach ask for empirical evidence that symptom-substitution really does occur and insist that the question of whether unconscious conflicts remain is academic if a person's behavior changes for the better.

In actual practice, therapy directed at changing outward behavior and therapy directed at analyzing underlying conflicts may be less incompatible than they seem, because they appear to work best with different kinds of patients and problems. The first selection, "Behavior Modification in a Mental Hospital," describes the use of reinforcement techniques to change the behavior of psychotics who probably could not have been reached at all by analytic methods. The second selection, "Treatment of Insomnia by Relaxation Training," reports a training program for more or less normal people whose problems did not seem severe enough to warrant long-term analytic therapy.

Teodoro Ayllon and Jack Michael, authors of "Behavior Modification in a Mental Hospital," taught the ward nurses at a mental hospital in Canada to use reinforcement techniques to change the behavior of their patients. The goals of therapy were very specifically defined; Ayllon and Michael were not trying to cure the patients but to show what reinforcement techniques can do. In three cases, the nurses succeeded in reducing the frequency of undesirable behavior: Lucille's visits to the nurses' office, Helen's constant senseless talk, and four men's habit of stuffing their clothes with magazines and trash. In the fourth case, they increased the frequency of a desirable behavior that rarely occurred: Mary's eating on her own. In this case, behavior therapy was so successful that Mary could be released from the hospital.

In "Treatment of Insomnia by Relaxation Training," Michael Kahn, Bruce L. Baker, and Jay M. Weiss describe a training program in which college students troubled by insomnia were taught specific techniques for relaxing. Kahn and his colleagues gave special attention to symptom-substitution, but their subjects did not seem to replace insomnia with some other behavior problem. The project illustrates the promising results that a narrowly focused therapeutic program can have with a troublesome, though by no means incapacitating, problem such as insomnia.

25

Behavior Modification
in a Mental Hospital

TEODORO AYLLON
JACK MICHAEL

A person is usually admitted to a mental hospital because his behavior represents a withdrawal from normal social functioning, is
dramatically different from his usual ways of acting, or is dangerous
to himself or to others. The staff of the hospital assumes that the
patient has a mental disease and that his symptoms will not disappear
until the basic illness has been diagnosed and treated. The main goal
of the doctors and nurses, therefore, is to discover the mental flaw
that presumably underlies the patient's disturbing and dangerous behavior.

During his stay at the hospital the patient may behave in annoying
and disrupting ways, which are usually regarded as further symp-

BEHAVIOR MODIFICATION IN A MENTAL HOSPITAL Adapted from *Journal of the
Experimental Analysis of Behavior* 2 (1959). Used by permission of Teodoro
Ayllon. This article originally appeared under the title "The psychiatric
nurse as a behavioral engineer."

toms of his basic difficulty. Sometimes the behavior is identical with that which led to the patient's hospitalization; at other times it seems to originate and develop at the hospital. A patient may refuse to eat, dress, bathe, walk from room to room by himself, or interact with other patients. He may hit, pinch, spit, upset chairs, scrape paint from the walls, hoard various items, stuff paper in his mouth or ears, or constantly try to get the nurses' attention. Such behavior, if it occurs often, can engage the full energies of the ward nurses and postpone, sometimes permanently, efforts by the nurses to deal with the patient's so-called basic problem.

At present, no systematic approach to such problems is available to ward nurses. Psychiatrists and psychologists may interpret the behavior for the nurses or the nurses may construct their own interpretations, but the interpretations seldom suggest any specific remedial action. From the point of view of modern behavior theory, however, a patient's behavior can be considered the result of elements in his environment rather than a manifestation of his mental disorder. Thus the behavior can be changed by manipulating the environment—by reinforcing desirable behavior and withdrawing reinforcement from undesirable behavior.

The research described here was an attempt to discover and manipulate environmental factors in order to bring about more normal behavior in a group of patients at Saskatchewan Hospital, in Weyburn, Saskatchewan. Saskatchewan Hospital houses about fifteen hundred psychiatric patients. Of the nineteen we worked with, fourteen had been classified as schizophrenic and five as mentally defective. Except for one woman who had been in the hospital only seven months, all the patients had been hospitalized for several years. None of them received psychotherapy, electroconvulsive therapy, or any other kind of individual treatment during the course of our work with them.

The psychiatric nurses at Saskatchewan Hospital bear most of the responsibility for patients in their wards. The nurses control mail, visitors, ground passes, leaves, and, usually after consultation with a psychiatrist, discharge. The psychiatrists on the staff do not give orders but simply offer advice when the nurses ask for it. Each patient in our experimental group was referred to Dr. Ayllon, then clinical psychologist at the hospital, by the nursing staff. The reason for the referral was that the patient had a persistent behavior problem—not the most serious problems encountered in psychiatric hospitals, but ones that had persisted despite various attempts to remedy them. Dr. Ayllon designed and supervised an operant-conditioning program which was carried out by the nurses.

Pretreatment studies indicated that what maintained undesirable behavior in most of the patients was attention or social approval from the nurses. Thus instructions to the nursing staff emphasized the giving and withholding of social reinforcement, as follows:

> Reinforcement is something you do for or with a patient, for example, offering candy or a cigarette. Any way you convey attention to a patient is reinforcing. Patients may be reinforced if you answer their questions, talk to them, or let them know by your reaction that you are aware of their presence. The common-sense expression "pay no attention" is perhaps closest to what must be done to discourage the patient's behavior. When we say "do not reinforce a behavior," we are actually saying "ignore the behavior and act deaf and blind whenever it occurs."

The following cases are representative of the behavior problems we tried to solve and the ways we tried to solve them. The first three problems—Lucille's visits to the nurses' office, Helen's psychotic talk, and Harry, Joe, Tom, and Mac's hoarding of magazines and trash—concerned frequent behavior that we hoped to reduce or eliminate. The fourth problem, Mary's reluctance to eat, concerned infrequent behavior that we wished to strengthen. In general, the time required to change behavior ranged from six to eleven weeks.

Lucille

Lucille's frequent visits to the nurses' office interrupted and interfered with their work. Lucille had been doing this for two years. The nurses' response was usually to tell Lucille she should not spend her time in their office and often to take her by the hand and pull her back into the ward. Because Lucille was classified as mentally defective, the nurses had resigned themselves to her behavior. As one of them put it, "It's difficult to tell her anything because she can't understand—she's too dumb."

The nurses were told not to give Lucille any reinforcement for entering the office. By the seventh week of treatment, the number of times a day she came to the office had declined from sixteen to two, and the program was terminated.

Helen

Helen was described by one psychiatrist as a delusional patient who "feels she must push her troubles onto somebody else, and by doing this feels she is free." For at least three years her conversation had been largely psychotic, centering on her illegitimate child and the men she claimed were always pursuing her. It was the nurses' impression that Helen had nothing else to talk about. Some of them said they listened to Helen's psychotic talk in an effort to get to the "root of her problem"; others said they did not listen but simply nodded and remarked, "Yes, I understand," or some such, hoping Helen would proceed to another topic. These reports suggested that the nurses' attention maintained the psychotic talk.

The nurses were instructed to pay no attention to Helen's psychotic talk and to reinforce all sensible talk. As Figure 25-1 shows, the relative frequency of Helen's psychotic talk decreased markedly during the first nine weeks of treatment. During the tenth week, however, it increased again, apparently because Helen had begun talking to a social worker who was reinforcing the behavior. As the patient herself said to one nurse, "Well, you're not listening to me. I'll have to go and see Miss ——— [the social worker] again, because she told me that if she would listen to my past she could help me." Two other instances of bootleg reinforcement for Helen's psychotic talk, one by a hospital employee and one by a group of volunteers, also came to light. These occurrences, impossible to avoid, indicate some of the difficulties in long-term control over verbal behavior.

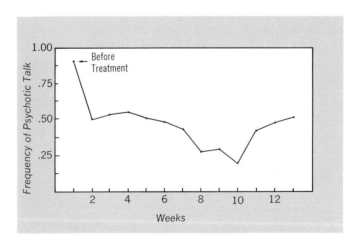

FIGURE 25-1

Helen: Extinction of psychotic talk.

Harry, Joe, Tom, and Mac

For five years, Harry, Joe, Tom, and Mac, mentally defective patients in the same ward, had collected papers, rubbish, and magazines and carried them around inside their clothing. The most serious offender was Harry, whose hoarding resulted in skin rashes. He carried so much trash so persistently that the nurses routinely dejunked him several times a day and before he went to bed.

An analysis of the situation indicated that the hoarding was probably maintained by the nurses' attention and by the actual scarcity of printed matter in the ward. We advised the nurses to withhold social reinforcement for hoarding and also to flood the ward with magazines. We expected that a large supply of magazines would decrease the patients' hoarding behavior much as animals stop hoarding food when they are satiated.

The results for all four patients were the same: a gradual decrease in hoarding. After nine weeks, the program was terminated. The number of magazines Joe, Tom, and Mac kept in their clothing simply declined, as expected. Harry, after four days of the program, no longer carried the rubbish or magazines in his clothing but kept a stack of magazines on his lap while sitting in the dayroom instead. This improvement has been maintained for at least six months.

Mary

Mary was admitted to the hospital because she claimed that her food was poisoned and refused to eat. During the next seven months she was spoonfed by the nurses in a room next to the dining room. She was more or less indifferent to attention from the nurses and had little social contact with other patients. She seemed to care only for the neat and clean appearance of her clothing.

The treatment program involved a combination of escape-and-avoidance conditioning. All spoonfeeding by a nurse was to involve some spilling of food. Mary could escape the messiness by feeding herself after the first spilling, or she could avoid it by feeding herself the entire meal. Social reinforcement, such as conversation, was to be given whenever Mary did feed herself.

We hoped that once self-feeding began to occur with some regularity, it would come under the control of the environmental factors that maintain it in most people, such as convenience and social stimulation at meal time. The program ultimately resulted in complete self-feeding, which has been maintained for over ten months.

Mary was observed for eight days before treatment began. During that time she ate five meals on her own, was spoonfed twelve, and refused to eat seven. At this time she was very thin and weighed only 99 pounds.

The instructions given to the nurses were:

> Continue spoonfeeding the patient but from now on do it in such a careless way that the patient will have a few drops of food fall on her dress. Be sure not to overdo the food dropping, since what we want to convey to the patient is that it is difficult to spoonfeed a grown-up person and not that we are mean to her. What we expect is that the patient will find it difficult to depend on your skill to feed her. You will still be feeding her, but you will simply be less efficient in doing a good job of it. As the patient likes having her clothes clean, she will have to choose between feeding herself and keeping her clothes clean, or being fed by others and risking getting her clothes soiled. Whenever she eats on her own, be sure to stay with her for a while (three minutes is enough), talking to her or simply being seated with her. We do this to reinforce her eating on her own. In the experience of the patient, people become nicer when she eats on her own.

Thus, during treatment, a nurse would start to feed Mary and then carelessly drop some food on her dress. This continued until Mary took the spoon or until the nurse had spoonfed the entire meal. The behavior the patient adopted included (1) reaching for the spoon after a few drops of food had fallen on her dress, (2) eating completely on her own, (3) closing her mouth so that spoonfeeding was impossible, and (4) being spoonfed the entire meal. During the early stages of treatment the most frequent behavior was the first, but after a while Mary ate on her own immediately.

The number of meals per week that were spoonfed over the eight weeks of treatment and the number that were self-fed are shown in Figure 25-2. Mary's relapse in the fifth week, after she had been eating well for two weeks, was quite unexpected. No reasonable explanation is suggested by a study of her daily records, but it was rumored that someone had told her the food spilling was not accidental. However, the failure to feed herself lasted only about five days.

The success of the program led to Mary's discharge. Although nothing specific had been done to deal with her claims that the food was poisoned, they stopped when she began to eat on her own. When she left the

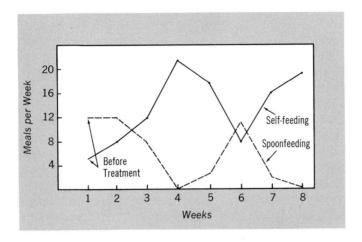

FIGURE 25-2
Mary: Escape-and-avoidance conditioning of self-feeding.

hospital she weighed 120 pounds, a gain of 21 pounds over her weight before treatment began.

Comments

In general, the results of the program at Saskatchewan Hospital were good. They show, first of all, that the behavior of psychotic patients can change in response to changes in the external environment. In addition, the research brought to light a number of specific and general difficulties that can be attacked and, we hope, overcome in future projects.

One major problem is the lack of laboratory recording and programing apparatus, which is unquestionably more reliable than nurses. For the most part, however, the nurses' failures in carrying out instructions did not seriously damage the effectiveness of the program. One way to reduce errors in observation is to deal only with behavior that is unambiguous and easy to identify. A better way, perhaps, is to continue to refine the principles and techniques of behavioral analysis so that subtle as well as obvious forms of behavior can be described, observed, and modified with precision.

Before the study began, we wondered about the acceptability of our approach to the hospital staff. This turned out not to be a serious difficulty. The nurses and psychiatrists who were familiar with reinforcement programs were given questionnaires and interviews to determine their attitudes toward this type of work. The results indicate a mildly favorable reception in general, with some enthusiastic support from both nurses and psychiatrists.

Two sources of possible misunderstanding between the experimenters and the nurses should be pointed out. First, if no dramatic behavior such as violent acts or suicide attempts had been recently reported, nurses often denied having any problems when asked about difficulties in the wards. Problems also went unrecognized because they were considered an inevitable result of the patient's illness and therefore unsolvable. Since most nurses attributed a patient's behavior to his illness or his age, little effort was made to seek out and change environmental factors that might be maintaining the behavior.

Second, even after behavior had been modified, it was not uncommon to hear nurses remark "So what? She's still psychotic." Once a problem had been eliminated, its previous importance seemed to be forgotten, so that other undesirable aspects of the patient's behavior looked more important. In general, the nurses' specific expectations were unclear or unverbalized, and they tended to be less than satisfied with anything but total "cure."

Finally, an objection often raised against the approach we used is that the behavior changes may be only temporary. It is true that permanent elimination of ward behavior problems requires permanent elimination of the environmental factors that shape and maintain them. The standard clinical belief that favorable change will be permanent only if "properly accomplished" probably rests on a faulty evaluation of the role of environmental factors in controlling behavior—certainly it is not based on any actual accomplishments in the field of mental health.

26

Treatment of Insomnia
by Relaxation Training

MICHAEL KAHN
BRUCE L. BAKER
JAY M. WEISS

The exact cause of insomnia is not known, but whatever its origins may be, it seems to require a high level of tension in the large muscles. This fact suggests that it may be possible to short-circuit insomnia by teaching insomniacs a form of behavior that is incompatible with tension—relaxation.

We therefore undertook a study whose primary purpose was to determine whether relaxation training alone would relieve insomnia. The program was based on the technique of autogenic training developed by Schultz and Luthe (1959). A secondary purpose of the study was to find out whether the autogenic technique could be used effectively for home relaxation training. Another secondary aim was to see whether symptom substitution would occur. Some psychologists argue that a patient's "underlying problem" must be

TREATMENT OF INSOMNIA BY RELAXATION TRAINING Adapted from *Journal of Abnormal Psychology* 73 (1968). Used by permission of Michael Kahn.

treated rather than an isolated aspect of his behavior, and we wanted to know whether, if our subjects' insomnia improved, they would develop other "symptoms" to take its place.

Several weeks before the final exam period, an article appeared in the Yale college newspaper reporting that we planned to conduct an experiment with simple relaxation therapy that might lessen insomnia and increase study efficiency. The article said we would like to hear from volunteer subjects who suffered insomnia and suggested that the relaxation techniques might be particularly useful during exam week, an especially difficult time for insomniacs. Seventeen students responded. Two were women from the graduate school; the other fifteen were men, three graduate students and twelve undergraduates.

Before the program began, one of us talked to each subject about the project. We stressed its experimental nature and asked the subjects to be as objective as possible throughout. We also obtained a biographical sketch of each subject, a detailed account of his insomnia—its history and the form it took—and a description of any other problems the subject had such as disturbances in personal relationships, trouble with his studies, and physical illness.

All the subjects were chronic insomniacs. Practically every night they had trouble falling asleep, a difficulty that dated back several years at least. The other problems most frequently reported were nervousness, study inefficiency, and difficulties in interpersonal relationships.

For training, the subjects were divided into three groups, each led by one of us. Half-hour training sessions were held twice a week for two weeks. The first session took place a few days after the initial interview. In each group the leader briefly described the history and details of autogenic training. Then the subjects were instructed to lie comfortably on mattresses with their eyes closed and to visualize themselves in a peaceful situation, for example, lying on a beach, while thinking the words, "I am at peace." This instruction was alternated with another, involving a given limb: for example, "My right arm is heavy." The leader said the instructions aloud— "I am at peace; my right arm is heavy. My right arm is heavy; I am at peace"—for thirty to forty-five seconds and then asked the subjects to say the same thing silently for an additional thirty to forty-five seconds. The first session consisted of four such trials; between the trials, the leader answered questions.

At the end of the first session, the subjects were asked to practice the technique at home three times a day, using three one-minute trials, with short breaks in between. They were also asked to use the technique for five or ten minutes after going to bed. Each subject was given a notebook to record the results of the practice sessions and his success in getting to sleep at night.

At the beginning of the next three training sessions, we talked briefly about how the training was progressing and about any difficulties the subjects were having with it. Other problems were avoided. The subjects then practiced four trials, as in the first session. The instructions were gradually extended to include both arms and legs, and warmth as well as heaviness.

Several days after the last training session, near the end of the exam period, the subjects were interviewed again. We asked how often they were using the method, whether their insomnia had changed, and whether there had been any change in old problems or any evidence of new ones. We explained that new problems sometimes crop up when an old one becomes less severe, and the subjects were encouraged to mention anything that was bothering them, whether they thought it important or not. We stressed again that we were interested simply in finding out about this method and that negative effects were as important as positive ones.

During this postinterview, each subject was asked to compare his insomnia in the week just past with his insomnia in the week just before the study. Of the thirteen subjects who were available at the time eleven reported improvement and two reported no improvement. The two who reported no improvement said their insomnia was better than it usually was during exams, but not better than it had been the week before the study.

We also asked some specific questions about sleeping patterns. In the interview before the program began, ten subjects had specified the amount of time it usually took them to get to sleep; in the postinterview, all ten reported shorter times. Before training, it took the average subject fifty-two minutes to get to sleep, whereas the median after training was twenty-two minutes. The maximum time to get to sleep on any one night also decreased for all thirteen subjects, though four of them still reported a maximum of over an hour. There was no consistent change in total hours slept.

None of the thirteen subjects reported any new problems. Twelve said some old problems had improved; the thirteenth, whose insomnia was worse, said the problems he had reported earlier were also worse. Table 26-1 shows the problems specified by at least two subjects in the interview that preceded training, and the changes with treatment. The most consistent change was a decrease in nervousness or tension.

Two follow-up questionnaires were sent to the subjects later on. The first went out during the summer about two and a half months after the

TABLE 26-1

Problems reported in the interview before training and changes reported in the interview after training.

Problem	Number of subjects reporting	Better	Same	Worse
Insomnia	13	11	1	1
Nervousness, tension, anxiety	8	7	1	0
Study inefficiency	7	1	6	0
Interpersonal relationships	7	2	3	2
Stomach difficulties	5	1	3	1
Daytime fatigue	3	3	0	0
Poor concentration	3	3	0	0
Occupational choice	3	2	1	0
Family problems	3	1	2	0
Depression	2	1	1	0
Academic difficulties	2	1	1	0

end of the training program, and the second about eleven months after training. They covered the same material as the postinterview.

On the first follow-up questionnaire, many subjects reported a further decline in insomnia, though some attributed it to lack of pressure and not to relaxation training. Of the thirteen subjects who replied to the questionnaire, only one had relapsed: he felt increased stress in his life and said he found the training only slightly helpful. Seven other subjects were still having trouble getting to sleep, although generally much less trouble than before the study, and all were using the method sometimes. Five subjects said it now took them less than ten minutes to get to sleep, and only one of them was continuing to use the relaxation technique.

Though many subjects also reported gains in their other problems, two said they had developed new ones. One had an aching leg from a pulled ligament, apparently a nonpsychological symptom. The other had an occasional, but persistent, muscle twitch that had started about three weeks after he began the exercises. It is probably relevant that suffering seemed to be an integral part of this subject's life. Throughout the study, he stressed the sacrifices he had to make in college, and at the postinterview he said his insomnia was unchanged, although he also reported amounts of time before sleep that were half what he reported in the pretraining interview.

Twelve subjects responded to the second follow-up questionnaire, sent out eleven months after training. All but one said his insomnia was better than before treatment; the median "average time getting to sleep" was fifteen minutes. Most subjects were no longer using the technique, although several said it was comforting to know that they had a method available in case insomnia returned.

In evaluating these findings two questions arise: Did the subjects really improve, and if so, why? It is hard to be sure about the first question because, as in any self-report study, the subjects may have tended to tell us what they thought we wanted to hear. In spite of our emphasis on the exploratory nature of the research and on the importance of negative results, the subjects' reports might indicate more success than was actually realized. If that were so, the reports should indicate increased study efficiency as well as relief from insomnia, since the original newspaper article suggested that study efficiency as well as insomnia might be helped. But as Table 26-1 shows, though all but two subjects had less trouble with insomnia, only one of the seven for whom study efficiency was a problem reported any improvement. And although the subjects reported less nervousness, fatigue, and inability to concentrate—all problems likely to arise from an inability to relax—there was no general improvement in interpersonal relationships or in academic difficulties. Thus there seems to have been no general tendency for subjects to comply with suggested outcomes or to report all possible desirable results.

As to the second question—what actually accounted for the subjects' improvement—we cannot be sure. The data indicate that relaxation training is effective in relieving insomnia. But aspects of the program other than the training itself, or outside circumstances, may have contributed. Until studies are made that control for such possibilities, one cannot conclude that relaxation training was the crucial factor. However, it seems fair to say that our results are at least encouraging.

REFERENCE

Schultz, J. H., and Luthe, W. *Autogenic training*. New York: Grune & Stratton, 1959.

Measuring Personality
and Intelligence

Although diagnosing personality is usually thought to be the job of the clinical psychologist, all of us try to "figure out" other people every day. We try to tell from a person's facial expression whether he is angry or friendly; from the way he is standing whether he is interested or bored; from his tone of voice whether he is steady or skittish. In "The What and Why of Personality Assessment," Robert R. Holt discusses the ways we informally assess personality in daily life, before briefly describing the more formal assessment techniques used in clinical settings, in schools and businesses, and in behavioral research.

A formal assessment technique with which almost everyone has had first-hand experience is the IQ test. IQ tests were unknown before the early 1900's, when Alfred Binet, a psychologist, was asked to devise a test that would help educators in Paris decide which children to admit to the public schools and which to exclude because they would not profit from instruction. Binet made up a set of test questions that measured the intellectual talents that lead to good performance at school, such as reading skills, a good memory for verbal concepts, a rich vocabulary, and an ability to deal with abstract ideas. Test items measuring these same abilities make up today's IQ tests, and IQ tests still predict success at school.

To define intelligence as what IQ tests measure—namely, skills that help a child do well at school—is to define it rather narrowly. On the average, lower-class children and children from ethnic minorities score lower on IQ tests and do less well at school than middle-class, white children. Both from a common-sense standpoint and in view of experimental evidence, however, it is highly unlikely that middle-class children are more intelligent. A broader definition of intelligence is clearly needed.

Many psychologists now think that intelligence should be regarded as a trait that permits adaptation to the culture. They compare intelligence to a set of physical characteristics that allows an animal to adapt to its environment. A frog does well in a pond but poorly in a desert; an iguana is well adapted to the desert but would die in a pond. Neither species is physically superior to the other, though the frog would seem to be if an iguana were placed with it in a pond. Middle-class children learn to use language and manipulate ideas in ways that tend to help them fit into middle-class culture—the dominant one in the United States. Lower-class children learn the same skills, but only to the extent that their culture overlaps with the dominant one; in addition, they learn other skills that middle-class children are less likely to have and which, as yet, are not measured by standard IQ tests.

The second and third selections, though they make the traditional assumption that intelligence is measured by IQ tests, also suggest the extent to which IQ is culturally determined because they relate IQ-test scores to personality traits and behavior valued by the middle class. "Mental Growth and Personality Development," by Lester W. Sontag, Charles T. Baker, and Virginia L. Nelson, is based on a long-term study of a group of children, most of them middle class, who were given intelligence tests at frequent intervals throughout childhood and early adolescence. Between kindergarten and fifth grade, some children's IQ's rose considerably; some gradually declined. An analysis of other information on the children's personalities showed a strong correlation between certain personality traits and the direction of IQ change. For instance, children who scored higher on IQ tests with increasing age tended to be aggressive, independent, and competitive—especially at school—whereas children whose IQ's declined tended to be passive, dependent, and noncompetitive. Since the personality traits that make for increases in IQ-test scores are the same ones that are likely to motivate a child to work hard at school, these findings broaden our understanding of the close relationship between high IQ and scholastic success.

"The Discovery and Encouragement of Exceptional Talent" is Lewis M. Terman's classic description of one of the most important psychological investigations of the century. In the early 1920's, Terman identified a group of about fifteen hundred children in California who had IQ-test scores of 140 or over, which put them in the "genius" range. Terman and his staff studied the personality traits and general performance of the children through adolescence and into adulthood. They found that, as adults, their high-IQ subjects were more creative and more likely to excel in intellectual vocations than adults in a control group chosen without reference to IQ. They were also apparently better adjusted and happier: fewer had been divorced and fewer had psychoses and other psychological difficulties.

The Terman study refuted the common beliefs that gifted children are one-sided and that "geniuses" tend to be maladjusted, unhappy people. It also indicates the intimate connection between high IQ and success in American middle-class society, as represented by scholastic and professional achievement. The question yet to be answered is whether the children in Terman's genius group would have been as successful and happy if they had lived in a culture that placed less value on the skills IQ tests measure.

27

The What and Why
of Personality Assessment

ROBERT R. HOLT

In the first and basic sense, personality assessment is an *informal* process, used by everyone to understand and describe people. It is also a scientific and professional specialty, the *formal* discipline of analyzing and measuring personalities. Both kinds of assessment will be discussed here. Although the formal assessment of personality is young both as a science and as a profession—still very much a skill or even an art—studying it helps sharpen one's capacity to size people up informally. And the professional psychologist can improve his own results by investigating how the good natural judge of men operates.

THE WHAT AND WHY OF PERSONALITY ASSESSMENT Adapted from *Personality: Dynamics, development, and assessment* by I. L. Janis, G. F. Mahl, J. Kagan, R. R. Holt. Copyright © 1969 by Harcourt Brace Jovanovich, Inc. Used by permission of Robert R. Holt and the publisher.

What Is Personality?

The basic fact on which the whole psychology of personality is founded is that people behave in organized, recognizable ways. At least two levels of organization, or patterning, can be distinguished: the *trait* and the *personality*. When we use adjectives to describe someone's behavior, we are talking about traits. To say that a person is clever implies not just a single clever remark on his part, since almost everyone occasionally says something delightfully witty. Rather, it implies that clever acts and sayings are a feature of the person's behavior that recurs with some regularity. Thus, a trait is a simple behavioral pattern, a disposition to behave in a certain way. And a working definition of personality, for the purposes of assessment, is that it is a pattern of traits.

However, a person cannot be described by merely listing his traits. Two people can have the same traits but very different personalities, just as two weavers can make different designs out of identical batches of threads. The uniqueness of pattern arises in part because the same traits have different strengths in different people. Suppose that both Henry and Herbert are to some degree strong, friendly, tidy, anxious, and effeminate, but friends notice that Henry is very strong and very effeminate, about average in friendliness, and not particularly tidy or anxious, whereas Herbert is very friendly and very anxious, about average in effeminacy, and not very tidy or strong. These imaginary men can also be used to illustrate *causal* patterning. Because of his effeminacy, Henry has concentrated on keeping down anxiety by building up his muscles, at the expense of cultivating friendships. Though Herbert's effeminacy is slightly above average, it is unrelated to his anxiety, which arises instead from a fear of being rejected that leads him to be unusually friendly to others. Traits may conflict with one another. Ambition, for instance, sometimes gets in the way of friendliness, and a person who is both ambitious and friendly may behave somewhat ruthlessly one day and more sociably the next. Traits differ not only in strength and in the ways they interact but in the degree to which a person is conscious of them. Out of these and other relationships, the unique pattern of personality is made.

What Are the Uses of Informal Assessment?

In order to interact with people in even the simplest ways, we have to be able to understand them and to predict what they will do. Most of the time it is fairly easy to do so, because much behavior is conforming and a great deal of the patterning in personalities is determined by society and culture. Nevertheless, it is a happy fact that no one conforms completely to social norms (including laws, customs, and other standards of conduct). If we are to know what to expect from a person, one of the first things we must learn is the extent of his conformity and conventionality.

ASSESSING NONCONFORMITY

There are three principal types of nonconformity to major social norms: criminal, psychotic, and creative nonconformity. Nonconformists who are poorly socialized and narrowly self-seeking often break laws and other norms because they think they can do what they want and get away with it. Of course, everyone has *some* antisocial tendencies, but people differ tremendously in this respect. Clearly, honesty or integrity is one of the first things we look for, consciously or not, in sizing a person up.

If you saw someone driving down the wrong side of the street or taking a short cut across a busy airfield, you might be tempted to yell, "What's the matter, are you crazy?" Sometimes such a nonconformist is, for a psychotic person loses touch with the social reality of norms and may behave in ways that endanger himself and others. Hence the extent to which someone is in touch with reality is another basic quality that we assess.

These two fundamental decisions about other people—whether they are reasonably ethical and reasonably sane—are usually tacit. We are not aware of making them and probably could not explain how we do so, but someone has only to raise the issue for us to be quite emphatic in our judgments.

When people deplore the conformity of modern life, they are usually deploring the lack of *creative* nonconformity. This kind of nonconformity involves a questioning of norms and an attempt to improve on them. Sometimes the questioning is more negativistic and rebellious than constructive, and violent disagreement can arise about what constitutes improvement. For example, many people would be reluctant to call social and political rebellion creative, especially in their own time and place, though they might be willing to grant that, historically, progress has sometimes required revolutionary change. In the long run, society's most valuable members are those who contribute new ways of doing things. In assessing personalities, we must therefore try to distinguish creative nonconformists from destructive nonconformists. In some cases the three forms of nonconformity are intricately combined. Raskolnikov, the central character in Dostoevsky's novel *Crime and Punishment*, was a psychotic who considered his murder of an old woman pawnbroker and her sister an act of creative nonconformity.

ASSESSING OTHER INDIVIDUAL DIFFERENCES

There is a great deal of individual variation within the general framework of social norms, and in most situations, one wants to know a good deal more about a person than the extent to which he can be expected to behave like most other people. One reason to assess these differences is the need to know how others will respond. All kinds of decisions at every level of human enterprise hinge directly on this matter. For example, your strategy in any kind of competitive situation (love, war, business, play) will be determined by your evaluation of your opponent—his probable aggressiveness, courage, wiliness, tractability, and intelligence.

If you are looking for someone to marry, it is not much help to know that many members of the opposite sex would make satisfactory spouses. You want to find a person with the combination of qualities that is best for you. The same reasoning holds in finding a good adviser, choosing a secretary, or seeking a compatible business partner. Although everyone is subject to the same general laws of behavior, there is a great range in ability, disposition, emotional make-up, and so on. One would be crippled in interpersonal relationships without some ability to assess individual differences in personality.

In these few examples it should be apparent that informal assessment is the rule. Even though computer dating is quite popular, it would be highly inappropriate to try to use formal procedures of assessment in serious courtship or in business competition. However, it is sometimes appropriate to supplement informal assessment with formal procedures, as when a business firm uses stenographic and typing tests as well as interviews to choose its employees.

SELF-ASSESSMENT

Perhaps the most important, and surely the most interesting and popular, subject of informal assessment is oneself. As soon as self-awareness is possible, a child begins to evaluate himself and to form expectations about what he can do compared to others. The self-assessing process is closely connected with ambitions, ideals, and aspirations, as well as with feelings of self-respect, inferiority, shame, guilt, and pride. Learning more about both informal and formal methods of assessing personality can help a person know himself better, though it cannot be guaranteed to do so.

The fact that informal assessment begins as soon as a child starts to form expectations and concepts about himself, his parents, his playmates, and other people indicates how involuntary and essentially nonverbal an operation it is. In part, informal assessment is the building up of expectations on the basis of experience. There is little basic difference between learning to recognize a mother's face and learning to recognize her quick temper.

A process of tacit knowing of people that is less rational than building up expectations but fundamental to informal assessment is *empathy*. As usually defined, empathy is a process of feeling what another person feels, but exactly how it happens is still unclear. It has been repeatedly observed, however, that a very young baby will grow tense and restless if his mother is anxious when she holds him; this process has been called *emotional contagion*. In one experimental demonstration, two groups of mothers and babies were observed at a clinic where the children had been brought for routine injections. Some of the mothers were given preliminary instructions that emphasized the possible dangers and difficulties surrounding the injection; the others were given neutral instructions. More mothers in the first group became noticeably anxious, and more of their babies cried *before* getting their shots.

Empathy, the mature version of emotional contagion, makes it possible for a person to know some things about another on short acquaintance. The main information empathy provides is emotional: it can tell us how friendly or hostile, tense or relaxed, interested or bored, open or defensive, hopeful or bitter, self-confident or doubtful a person feels; how much he enjoys life; and even how sick he is. Empathy cannot always provide this information, and it does not work for everybody to the same extent or with the same accuracy. But the fact that so much information can be picked up by this effortless opening of oneself to impressions of another person makes it an important part of informal assessment. It seems to be at the center of what is commonly called intuition.

Effective informal assessment presupposes that you care about people. It is likely that the more interested you are in other human beings as individuals, the better you will be at assessing them. The objective ideal of a completely mechanized assessment will be impossible until computers can be taught to feel, to judge, and to care about people. Having an interest in a person and a desire to get to know him is, then, the first step in informal assessment. Next, we obtain immediate impressions through empathy. Finally, we continue to observe his behavior until we notice invariances in it—persistent, recognizable trends.

THE PLACE OF INFORMAL ASSESSMENT
IN MODERN PSYCHOLOGY

There has been a curiously antipsychological tradition within the discipline of psychology, which makes a kind of fetish of skepticism toward or opposition to informal assessment. According to this view, intuition, empathy, and judging personality from facial or bodily expression are all unscientific mysticism.

A few psychologists held out against this opinion from the beginning. Most psychoanalysts were unaffected by it, though many of them were a little too impressed with Freud's theories as a short cut to understanding by means of formulas and not aware enough of his own practice, which relied on his intuitive feelings about people, enriched by a deep literary culture. In recent years, the tide has begun to turn. Social psychologists have begun to elucidate the processes by which people form impressions of one another, and the superobjectivists have simmered down as it has become apparent that no scientist actually works in the ways they had described. There is a large element of skill or art in scientific theorizing and experimenting, which must be recognized and respected before we can begin the laborious job of studying scientific inquiry and formulating parts of it into explicit rules. All psychologists can agree that a science of human behavior must eventually establish lawful relationships by objective methods, but in discovering psychological principles (as opposed to nailing them down in scientific laws) and in applying them to everyday life, we should not hesitate to use empathy and to rely on our feelings.

What Are the Uses of Formal Assessment?

Those who are involved in formal assessment supplement the tacit processes of informal assessment by a number of technical procedures for obtaining data about people and reaching conclusions about them. Even within the field of personality assessment there are those who try to eliminate all human judgment and other nonmechanical processes from their work; typically they rely on "objective" tests. They often deny that they make any use of the intuitive methods of the ordinary man. But they continue to rely on them anyway because they must, if only to recognize when an "objective" finding is so implausible as to indicate that the system has broken down.

The techniques of gathering data in formal assessment include interviewing, testing, obtaining personal documents, such as autobiographies and letters, and making observations in specially controlled situations. Formal assessment is undertaken for the most part by five types of professional people: psychologists of several specialized kinds, psychiatrists, personnel workers, social workers, and guidance counselors. (To a lesser degree, anthropologists, criminologists, and sociologists also assess personalities.) Three of the more important areas in which the work goes on are described below.

CLINICAL SETTINGS

Clinical settings include hospitals, mental-health clinics, and private offices of psychodiagnosticians and psychotherapists of various kinds, including psychoanalysts. People being assessed in these settings suffer from personal problems and difficulties in living that are often called mental illnesses, emotional disorders, or types of psychopathology.

The focus of assessment in clinical settings is diagnosis: finding out just what is wrong with the person and measuring the qualities that are relevant to helping him so that the most effective plan of treatment may be devised. A private practitioner of psychotherapy or psychoanalysis may conduct a diagnostic assessment by means of a single, unstructured interview, relying on empathic impressions and other methods of informal assessment.

In institutional clinical settings such as hospitals for severely disturbed people, the task of assessment is often divided up among clinical psychologists, social workers, and psychiatrists. The psychologist concentrates on administering and interpreting tests; the social worker conducts interviews, obtaining a social history from the person and his family; and the psychiatrist may supplement his own interviewing with physical or laboratory tests. All this information is brought together in case conferences, where the members of the clinical team construct a picture of the personality pattern—how the person got that way, his assets and liabilities, and his future prospects. Then they plan what to do to help him. A similarly elaborate assessment is sometimes used to gauge the effects of treatment, although more commonly the patient is merely retested and reinterviewed by one person.

EDUCATIONAL AND VOCATIONAL SELECTION

Whenever they can, educational institutions and businesses select from a large group of applicants the ones likely to do best on the task in question. Thus students who may already have been carefully tested and advised to apply to, let us say, medical schools find themselves subjected to further assessment by an application form, requests for transcripts of grades and letters of recommendation, and often more tests and personal interviews. Similarly, an employer may have a personnel department, where specialized workers (who are sometimes industrial psychologists) screen and evaluate applicants for each job.

RESEARCH

Many kinds of psychological research, whether conducted in university, government, or commercial laboratories or research centers, require some use of formal assessment procedures. For example, suppose you were interested in studying the possibility that high school drop-outs who are intelligent enough to handle the academic work stop school at least in part because of something about their personalities. If you happened to know a drop-out personally, you would already have some ideas about what he was like from your informal assessment of him, which would probably suggest leads for systematic study. Perhaps you know that he had constant battles with his parents and suspect that the struggle interfered with his schoolwork. You might be right, and yet there are others who stay in school despite similar family crises. To settle the question you would have to get information on performance in school and on relationships with parents from a representative sample of people who drop out of school and people who do not. You would probably use a focused interview or a test, or both. Groups of students who are alike in intelligence but differ on dropping out could then be compared on the quantitative measures or scores obtained from the systematic assessment. Thus you could check on the validity of your initial idea about the effect of the family fights on schoolwork.

Both informal and formal assessment go on in many different settings for many different purposes, and they focus on many different aspects of personality. No one set of abilities is relevant to any and all jobs, and no single set of personality characteristics is looked for in each and every new acquaintance. However, the general principles described above are useful no matter what personality traits a particular assessment enterprise concerns.

28

Mental Growth
and Personality Development

LESTER W. SONTAG
CHARLES T. BAKER
VIRGINIA L. NELSON

The research described below concerns the relation of certain personality traits to increases or decreases in IQ during a child's first ten years of life. It is based on the files of 140 children, participants since birth in an extensive longitudinal study carried out at the Fels Research Institute, in Yellow Springs, Ohio. These particular 140 children, from eighty-nine different families, were selected from the total group of Fels children not because of their personalities or their IQ's but simply because their files contained a full series of Stanford-Binet intelligence test scores and a relatively complete set of other records concerning their lives from infancy through age ten.

We studied two separate periods, the preschool period (ages four and one-half to six) and the early school years (ages six to ten). One

MENTAL GROWTH AND PERSONALITY DEVELOPMENT Adapted from *Monographs of the Society for Research in Child Development* 23 (1958). Used by permission of L. W. Sontag.

experimenter tabulated increases and decreases in IQ scores during these periods. Another experimenter, who had no knowledge of the children's IQ scores, read the central file on each child, which consisted of several hundred pages of narrative and objective information. Using a seven-point scale, he rated each child at age six and at age ten on the following personality characteristics:

1. Emotional independence from parents. This was a rating of the child's attempt to gain satisfaction from peers or from solitary pursuits rather than by turning for warmth and approval to one or both parents.

2. Aggressiveness in peer relationships. Low ratings went to children who were characteristically quiet and passive in play and in group situations with other children.

3. Self-initiated behavior. A low score indicated that the child seemed overly conforming to external demands; he was well behaved at home and seldom or never a disciplinary problem to his parents.

4. Socialization. Children given low ratings on this scale were characteristically withdrawn in group situations.

5. Friendliness. A low score indicated repeated hostile behavior; a high score, warmth and friendliness toward peers and adults.

6. Problem-solving behavior. A low score meant that the child tried to avoid responsibility for problem-solving or shift it to another person, as by soliciting the help of adults or by asking other children to complete projects for him; a high score indicated that the child made repeated efforts of his own to overcome obstacles in learning and other situations.

7. Anticipation of reward. This scale was an attempt to measure the child's ability to endure a lapse of time between behavior and reward. A low rating meant that the child had little tolerance for delays in gratification and that he favored behavior likely to bring immediate rewards.

8. General competitiveness. A child received a low rating on this scale if he tended to withdraw from competitive situations at nursery school or elementary school and in play at home. Some children with low ratings had indicated distrust of their own abilities to teachers; by contrast, children who rated high on this scale were apt to express realistic self-confidence in a number of areas.

9. Femininity (girls only). With this rating the experimenter tried to separate girls who seemed to derive great satisfaction from being considered pretty, dainty, or charming from girls who tended to compete in more masculine or neutral activities such as sports, scholastic attainment, and class leadership.

10. Sibling rivalry. This was a rating of the amount of friction between brothers and sisters initiated by the child being rated.

11. Anxiety. The anxiety scale indicated the child's general level of emotional comfort and freedom of movement in various situations. Children rated low in anxiety tended to be poised, self-assured, even-tempered: observers might have noted in their reports that the child "takes physical accidents, difficulties, or disappointments in his stride." A high rating meant that the child showed a particular pattern of behavior that reflected upsetting situations or specific fears.

12. Scholastic competition (age ten only). This rating was based on the child's competitiveness in the academic aspects of school work.

13. Independence in scholastic achievement (age ten only). This rating showed whether the child sought scholastic achievement out of self-motivation or because he wanted to gain the approval of parents and teachers by conforming to their wishes.

14. Parental emphasis on school achievement (age ten only). A high rating meant that one or both parents put heavy emphasis on the importance of the child's doing well at school, and that the child responded with high scholastic achievement.

An examination of the children's IQ scores at ages four and one-half, six, and ten allowed us to identify two groups for each age period: those whose mental growth was faster than average (that is, those whose IQ scores were higher at six than at four and one-half or higher at ten than at six) and those whose mental growth was slower than average. For each age period there were 35 children whose IQ's had risen. Boys tended to gain more than girls at all ages, but the tendency was less pronounced during the preschool years than later on.

After the children had been rated for the personality traits described above, we used statistical analysis to find out which traits, if any, would distinguish children whose IQ's had risen from four and one-half to six or from six to ten from children whose IQ's had fallen. At age six, only one personality characteristic clearly distinguished the two IQ change groups: independence from parents. The children whose IQ's had increased during the preschool years tended to be independent; those whose scores were lower at six than at four and one-half tended to show more emotional dependence on their parents.

At age ten, a much larger cluster of personality traits was associated with changes in IQ. Children whose IQ's were higher at ten that at six were rated high in independence, aggressiveness, self-initiation, problem solving, anticipation of reward, competitiveness, scholastic competition, and independence in scholastic achievement. The group whose IQ's were lower at ten than at six received significantly lower ratings on these traits than did the accelerated-IQ group.

A knowledge of personality traits seems to have value not only in predicting IQ change but in understanding the nature of mental growth. A child who is emotionally dependent during the preschool years is likely to show a decline in IQ later on, whereas a preschool child who develops modes of behavior characterized by aggressiveness, self-initiation, and competitiveness seems to have laid the groundwork for acceleration in mental growth. During the first few years of elementary school, rapid mental growth is closely associated with a cluster of personality traits whose common element is the need for achievement.

As the child develops characteristic ways of handling interaction with other children and with adults, his behavior seems to generalize to new learning situations. Thus the basic motives for behavior that affect the child's adjustment in a variety of life situations also operate in the development of intellectual ability, enhancing or diminishing the child's motivation to learn new things. This conclusion is consistent with an increasingly prevalent view of child development, which regards intelligence less as an ability that develops separately from other traits than as just one aspect of the personality as a whole.

29

The Discovery
and Encouragement
of Exceptional Talent

LEWIS M. TERMAN

I have often been asked how I happened to become interested in mental tests and gifted children. My introduction to the scientific problems posed by intellectual differences occurred well over fifty years ago when I was a senior in psychology at Indiana University. I was asked to prepare two seminar reports, one on mental deficiency and one on genius. Up to that time, despite the fact that I had studied teaching at college and had taught school for five years, I had never so much as heard of a mental test. The reading for those two reports opened up a new world to me, the world of Galton, Binet, and their contemporaries.

Then I entered Clark University, where I spent considerable time reading about mental tests and precocious children. Child prodigies,

THE DISCOVERY AND ENCOURAGEMENT OF EXCEPTIONAL TALENT Adapted from *American Psychologist* 9 (1954). Used by permission of the American Psychological Association.

I soon learned, were in bad repute. The prevailing belief was that they were usually psychotic or otherwise abnormal and almost sure to burn themselves out quickly or to develop postadolescent stupidity. "Early ripe, early rot" was a slogan frequently encountered. By the time I reached my last year of graduate school, I had decided to find out for myself how precocious children differ from the mentally backward and chose as my doctoral dissertation an experimental study of the intellectual processes of fourteen boys, seven of them picked as the brightest and seven as the dullest in a large city school. The experiment contributed little or nothing to science, but it contributed a lot to my future thinking. Besides selling me completely on the value of mental tests as a research method, it offered an ideal escape from the kind of laboratory work that I disliked and was more than ordinarily inept at.

Exceptional Talent
and Achievement

In the spring of 1921, I launched an ambitious study that required the participation of close to 1,500 children with IQ's of 140 or higher. The average IQ of the group was about 150, and 80 children had scored 180 or higher. The purpose of the project was, first of all, to find out what traits characterize children with high IQ's, and second, to follow them for as many years as possible to see what kind of adults they would become. The more important results can be stated briefly: children with IQ's of 140 or higher are appreciably superior to children in general in physique, health, and social adjustment; markedly superior in moral attitudes as measured by either character tests or trait ratings; and vastly superior in their mastery of school subjects as shown by a three-hour battery of achievement tests. In fact, the typical child in the group had mastered the school subjects to a point about two grades beyond the one in which he was enrolled (some had progressed three or four grades beyond), and his achievement in the different subjects was so general that it refutes completely the traditional belief that gifted children are usually one-sided. I take some pride in the fact that not one of the major conclusions we drew in the early 1920's regarding the traits that are typical of gifted children has been overthrown in the three decades since then.

Results of thirty years' follow-up of these subjects, by field studies in 1927–28, 1939–40, and 1951–52 and by mail follow-up at other dates, show that the incidence of mortality, ill health, insanity, and alcoholism is in each case below that for people of corresponding age in the general population, that the great majority are still well adjusted socially, and that the delinquency rate is but a fraction of what it is for the population as a whole. Two forms of our difficult Concept Mastery Test, devised especially to reach into the stratosphere of adult intelligence, have been administered to all members of the group who could be visited by the field assistants, including some 950 tested in 1939–40 and more than 1,000 in 1951–52. On both tests they scored on the average about as far above adults in general as they had scored above children in general when we selected them. Moreover, in the twelve-year interval between the two tests, 90 percent increased their intellectual stature as measured by this test. "Early ripe, early rot" simply does not hold for these subjects. So far, no one has developed postadolescent stupidity!

As for schooling, close to 90 percent entered college and 70 percent graduated. Of those graduating, 30 percent were awarded honors and about two-thirds went on to graduate work. The educational record would have been still better but for the fact that a majority reached college age during the Depression. In their undergraduate years, 40 percent of the men and 20 percent of the women earned half or more of their college expenses.

The achievement of the group to midlife is best illustrated by the case histories of the 800 men, since only a minority of the women had professional careers. By 1950, when the men were about forty, they had published 67 books (46 in the fields of science, arts, and the humanities and 21 books of fiction). They had published more than 1,400 scientific, technical, and professional articles; over 200 short stories, novelettes, and plays; and 236 miscellaneous articles on a great variety of subjects. They had also authored more than 150 patents. The figures on publications do not include the hundreds of news stories, editorials, and columns by journalists; nor do they include the hundreds, if not thousands, of radio and TV scripts.

The 800 men include 78 who have taken a Ph.D. degree or its equivalent, 48 with medical degrees, 85 with law degrees, 74 who are teaching or have taught in a four-year college or university, 51 who have done basic research in the physical sciences or engineering, and 104 who are engineers but have done only applied research or none. Of the scientists, 47 are listed in the 1949 edition of *American Men of Science*. Nearly all of these numbers are from ten to thirty times as large as would be found for 800 men of corresponding age picked at random from the general population.

The follow-up of these gifted subjects has proved beyond question that tests of "general intelligence" given as early as six, eight, or ten years tell a great deal about the ability to achieve both at that time and thirty years later. Such tests do not, however, enable us to predict what direction the achievement will take, and least of all do they tell us what personality factors or what accidents of fortune will affect the actual use of exceptional ability. Granting that both interest patterns and special aptitudes play important roles in the making of a gifted scientist, mathematician, mechanic, artist, poet, or musical composer, I am convinced that to achieve greatly in almost any field special talents have to be backed up by a lot of the kind of general intelligence, called Spearman's g (for general) factor, that requires an ability to form many sharply defined concepts, to manipulate them, and to perceive subtle relationships between them—in other words, the ability to engage in abstract thinking.

Our original plan was to investigate superior ability not only by identifying and following gifted subjects from childhood onward but by proceeding in the opposite direction and tracing mature geniuses back to their childhood. A study using the second method, begun just a year after our study using the first, resulted in Catherine Cox's magnum opus, *The Early Mental Traits of Three Hundred Geniuses* (1926). Cox and her assistants amassed more than six thousand pages of biographical data that seemed relevant to the early mental development of three hundred geniuses. Three psychologists read the data and then estimated for each subject the IQ that would be necessary to account for his intellectual behavior at various ages.

The average estimated IQ for the three hundred geniuses was 155, with many as high as 175 and several as high as 200. Estimates below 120 occurred only when there was little biographical evidence about the early years. As one of the three psychologists who examined the evidence and made the ratings, I think Cox's main conclusion is fully justified: "The genius who achieves highest eminence is one whom intelligence tests would have identified as gifted in childhood."

Special attention was given the geniuses who at some time or other in childhood had been labeled backward, and in every one of these cases the facts clearly contradicted the legend. One of them was Oliver Goldsmith, of whom his childhood teacher reportedly said, "Never was so dull a boy." The fact is that little Oliver was writing clever verse at seven and was reading Ovid and Horace at eight. Another was Sir Walter Scott, who at seven not only read widely in poetry but was using correctly in his written prose such words as "melancholy" and "exotic." Other alleged childhood dullards included a number who disliked the usual diet of Latin and Greek but had a natural talent for science. Among these were the celebrated German chemist Justus von Liebig, the great English anatomist John Hunter, and the naturalist Alexander von Humboldt, whose name is scattered so widely over the maps of the world.

In the cases just cited one notes a tendency for the direction of later achievement to be foreshadowed by the interests and preoccupations of childhood. Very marked foreshadowing was noted for more than half the group, none at all for less than a fourth. Macaulay, for example, began his career as historian at the age of six with what he called a "Compendium of Universal History," filling much paper before he lost interest in the project. Ben Franklin before the age of seventeen had displayed nearly all the traits that characterized him in middle life: scientific curiosity, unorthodox religious opinions, wit and buffoonery, political and business shrewdness, and an ability to write. At eleven, Pascal was so interested in mathematics that his father thought it best to deprive him of books on this subject until he had first mastered Latin and Greek. Pascal secretly proceeded to construct a geometry of his own. At fourteen, Leibnitz was writing on logic and philosophy and was composing what he called "An Alphabet of Human Thought." He relates that at this age he took a walk one afternoon to consider whether he should accept the "doctrine of substantial forms."

Similar foreshadowing is disclosed by the case histories of my gifted subjects. A 1954 study of the scientists and nonscientists among the eight hundred gifted men showed many highly significant differences between the early interests and social attitudes of those who became physical scientists and those who majored in the social sciences, law, or the humanities. Those in medical or biological sciences usually rated somewhere between the physical scientists and the nonscientists on such variables.

What I especially want to emphasize, however, is that both the evidence of early mental development of historical geniuses and that obtained by follow-up of gifted subjects selected in childhood point to the conclusion that the capacity to achieve far beyond the average can be detected early in life by a well-constructed test heavily weighted with items that measure the ability to think abstractly. It remains to be seen how much more specific the prediction of future achievement can be made by getting, in addition, measures of other abilities.

Educational Acceleration

I have always stressed the importance of early discovery of exceptional abilities. Its importance is now highlighted by the facts disclosed in Harvey Lehman's monumental studies of the relationship between age and creative achievement (1953). The striking thing about his age curves is how early in life the period of maximum creativity is reached. In nearly all fields of science, the best work is done between ages twenty-five and thirty-five, and rarely later than forty. The production of lesser works usually reaches a peak five to ten years later; this is true in some twenty fields of science, in philosophy, in most kinds of musical composition, in art, and in literature of many varieties. The lesson in Lehman's statistics is that young people of high achievement potential should be well trained for their life work before too many of their most creative years have passed.

This raises the issue of educational acceleration for the gifted. It seems that educators are more opposed to acceleration now than they were thirty years ago. The lockstep seems to have become more and more the fashion, notwithstanding the fact that practically everyone who has investigated the subject favors acceleration. Of my gifted group, 29 percent managed to graduate from high school before the age of sixteen and one-half (62 of these before fifteen and one-half), but I doubt if so many would be allowed to do so now. The other 71 percent graduated between sixteen and one-half and eighteen and one-half. We have compared the accelerated with the nonaccelerated on numerous case-history variables. The two groups differed very little in childhood IQ, their health records are equally good, and as adults they are equally well adjusted socially. More of those who accelerated graduated from college, and on the average nearly a year and a half earlier than did the others; they averaged higher in college grades and more often remained for graduate work. Moreover, the accelerated married on the average seven-tenths of a year earlier, have a trifle lower divorce rate, and score just a little higher on a test of marital happiness.

Since 1951 the Ford Fund for the Advancement of Education has annually awarded some four hundred college scholarships to gifted students who are not over sixteen and one-half years old, are a year or even two years short of high school graduation, and show good evidence of ability to do college work. Three-quarters of them are between fifteen and one-half and sixteen and one-half at the time of college entrance. A dozen colleges and universities accept these students and are keeping close track of their success. A summary of their records for the first year shows that they not only get higher grades than their classmates, who average about two years older, but are equally well adjusted socially and participate in as many extracurricular activities. The main problem the boys have is in finding girls to date who are not too old for them. Some of them have started a campaign to remedy the situation by urging that more of these scholarships be awarded to girls.

The facts I have given do not mean that all gifted children should be rushed through school just as rapidly as possible. If that were done, a majority of those with IQ's of 140 could graduate from high school before the age of fifteen. I do believe, however, that such children should be promoted rapidly enough to permit college entrance by the age of seventeen at the latest and that a majority would be better off to enter at sixteen. The exceptionally bright student who is kept with his age group finds little to challenge his intelligence and all too often develops habits of laziness that later wreck his college career. I could give you some choice examples of this in my gifted group. In the case of a college student who is preparing for a profession in science, graduation at twenty instead of the usual twenty-two means two years added to his professional career; the two years saved could be used for additional training beyond the doctorate, if that were deemed preferable.

Learned and Wood (1938) have shown by objective achievement tests in some forty Pennsylvania colleges how little correlation there is between a student's knowledge and the number of months or years of his college attendance. They found some beginning sophomores who had acquired more knowledge than some seniors near their graduation. They found similarly low correlations between the number of course units a student had in a given field and the amount he knew in that field. Some with only one year of Latin had learned more than others with three years. And, believe it or not, they even found boys just graduating from high school who had more knowledge of science than some college seniors who had majored in science and were about to begin teaching science in high schools. The sensible thing to do, it seems, would be to quit crediting the individual high school or the individual college and begin crediting the individual student.

The Influence of Society

However efficient our tests may be in discovering exceptional talents, and whatever the schools may do to foster those discovered, it is the society that will decide, by the rewards it gives or withholds, what talents will come to flower. In Western Europe during the Middle Ages, the favored talents were those that served the Church by providing the priests, the architects of its cathedrals, and the painters of religious themes. A few centuries later the same countries experienced a renaissance that included science and literature as well as the arts. Although presumably there are as many potential composers of great music as there ever were, and as many potentially great artists as in the days of Leonardo da Vinci and Michelangelo, I am reliably informed that in this country today it is almost impossible for a composer of *serious* music to earn his living except by teaching, and that the situation is much the same, though somewhat less critical, with respect to artists.

The talents most favored in the United States today are those that can contribute to science and technology. One may regret that the spirit of the times is not equally favorable to the discovery and encouragement of potential poets, prose writers, artists, statesmen, and social leaders.

But in addition to the overall spirit of the times, there are localized climates that favor or hinder the encouragement of given talents in particular colleges and universities. I especially have in mind two recent investigations of the differences among colleges in the later achievement of their graduates. One (Knapp and Goodrich, 1952) dealt with the undergraduate origin of 18,000 scientists listed in the 1944 edition of *American Men of Science*. Some of the results were surprising, not to say sensational. The institutions that were most productive of future scientists were not the large universities but the small liberal arts colleges. Reed College topped the list with 132 scientists per thousand male graduates. The California Institute of Technology was next with 70. Kalamazoo College was third with 66, Earlham fourth with 57, and Oberlin fifth with 56. Only a half-dozen of the large universities were in the top fifty with 25 scientists or more per thousand graduates.

The second study (Knapp and Greenbaum, 1953) was a rating of educational institutions according to the proportion of their graduates who received certain awards at the graduate level during a six-year period. The roster of awardees included 7,000 students who had graduated from 377 colleges and universities. This study differed from the former in that it dealt with recent graduates in a variety of fields, the social sciences and the humanities as well as the physical and biological sciences. In this study the large universities made a better showing than in the first, but still only a dozen of them are in the top fifty institutions in the production of men who are good bets. In the top ten, the University of Chicago is third, Princeton is eighth, and Harvard is tenth; the other seven in order of rank are Swarthmore (1), Reed (2), Oberlin (4), Haverford (5), California Institute of Technology (6), Carleton (7), and Antioch (9).

The causes of these differences are not entirely clear. Scores on aptitude tests show that the intelligence of students in a given institution is by no means the sole factor, though it is an important one. Other important factors are the quality of the school's intellectual climate, the proportion of able and inspiring teachers on its faculty, and the amount of conscious effort that is made not only to discover but also to motivate the most gifted. The influence of motivation can hardly be exaggerated.

Nonintellectual Influences on Success

I have alluded several times to the fact that achievement in school is influenced by many things other than the sum total of intellectual abilities. The same is true of success in life. In closing I will briefly discuss an attempt we made a dozen years ago to identify some of the nonintellectual factors that have influenced life success among the men in my gifted group. Three judges, working independently, examined the records (to 1940) of the 730 men who were then twenty-five years old or older, and rated each on life success. The criterion of "success" was the extent to which a subject had made use of his superior intellectual ability, little weight being given to earned income. The 150 men rated highest for success and the 150 rated lowest were then compared on some two hundred items of information obtained from childhood onward. How did the two groups differ?

During the elementary school years, the A's and the C's (as we called them) were almost equally successful. The average grades were about the same, and average scores on achievement tests were only a trifle higher for the A's. Early in high school the groups began to draw apart in scholarship, and by the end of high school the slump of the C's was quite marked. The slump could not be blamed on extracurricular activities, for these were almost twice as common among the A's. Nor was much of it due to difference in intelligence. Although the A's tested on the average a little higher than the C's both in 1922 and 1940, the average score made by the C's in 1940 was high enough to permit brilliant college work, and in fact was equaled by only 15 percent of our highly selected Stanford students. Of the A's, 97 percent entered college and 90 percent graduated; of the C's, 68 percent entered but only 37 percent graduated. Of those who graduated, 52 percent of the A's but only 14 percent of the C's graduated with honors. The A's were also more accelerated than the C's in school; on the average they were six months younger on completing the eighth grade, ten months younger at high school graduation, and fifteen months younger at graduation from college.

The differences between the educational histories of the A's and C's reflect to some degree the differences in their family backgrounds. Half of the A fathers but only 15 percent of the C fathers were college graduates, and twice as many A siblings as C siblings graduated. The estimated number of books in the A homes was nearly 50 percent greater than in the C homes. As of 1928, when the average age of the subjects was about sixteen years, more than twice as many C parents as A parents had been divorced.

Interesting differences between the groups were found in the childhood data on emotional stability, social adjustments, and various personality traits. Of the twenty-five traits on which each child was rated by parent and teacher in 1922, the only trait on which the C's averaged as high as the A's was general health. The superiority of the A's was especially marked in prudence, self-confidence, perseverance, desire to excel, leadership, popularity, and sensitiveness to approval or disapproval. By 1940 the difference between the groups in social adjustment and all-round mental stability had greatly increased and showed itself in many ways. By that time four-fifths of the A's had married but only two-thirds of the C's, and the divorce rate was twice as high for the C's as for the A's. Moreover, the A's made better marriages; their wives on the average came from better homes, were better educated, and scored higher on intelligence tests.

But the most spectacular differences between the two groups came from three sets of ratings, made in 1940, on a dozen personality traits. Each man rated himself on all the traits and was rated on them by his wife if he had a wife, and by a parent if a parent was still living. Although the three sets of ratings were made independently, they agreed unanimously on the four traits in which the A and C groups differed most widely. These were persistence in the accomplishment of ends; integration toward goals, as contrasted with drifting; self-confidence; and freedom from inferiority feelings. These closely parallel the traits that Cox found to be especially characteristic of the 100 leading geniuses in her group. Their three outstanding traits she defined as persistence of motive and effort, confidence in their abilities, and strength or force of character.

There was one trait on which only the parents of our A and C men were asked to rate them; that trait was common sense. As judged by parents, the A's were again superior. We are still wondering what self-ratings by the subjects and ratings of them by their wives on common sense would have shown if we had been impudent enough to ask for them.

Everything considered, there is nothing in which our A and C groups present a greater contrast than in drive to achieve and in all-round mental and social adjustment. Our data do not support the Lange-Eichbaum theory (1932) that great achievement usually stems from emotional tensions that border on the abnormal. In our gifted group, success is associated with stability rather than instability, with the absence rather than the presence of disturbing conflicts—in short, with well-balanced temperament and with freedom from excessive frustrations. The Lange-Eichbaum theory may explain a Hitler, but hardly a Churchill; a Joseph McCarthy, possibly, but not a Jefferson or a Washington.

At any rate, we have seen that intellect and achievement are far from perfectly correlated. To identify the internal and external factors that help or hinder the fruition of exceptional talent, and to measure the extent of their influences, are surely among the major problems of our time. These problems are not new; their existence has been recognized by countless men from Plato to Francis Galton. What is new is the general awareness of them caused by the manpower shortage of scientists, engineers, moral leaders, statesmen, scholars, and teachers that the country must have if it is to survive. These problems are now being investigated on a scale never before approached, and by a new generation of workers in several related fields. Within a couple of decades vastly more should be known than we know today about our resources of potential genius, the environmental circumstances that favor its expression, the emotional compulsions that give it dynamic quality, and the personality distortions that can make it dangerous.

REFERENCES

Cox, C. C. The early mental traits of three hundred geniuses. *Genetic studies of genius*, vol. 3. Edited by L. M. Terman. Stanford: Stanford University Press, 1926.

Knapp, R. H., and Goodrich, H. B. *Origins of American scientists*. Chicago: University of Chicago Press, 1952.

Knapp, R. H., and Greenbaum, J. J. *The younger American scholar: His collegiate origins*. Chicago: University of Chicago Press, 1953.

Lange-Eichbaum, W. *The problem of genius*. New York: Macmillan, 1932.

Learned, W. S., and Wood, B. D. The student and his knowledge. *Carnegie Foundation Advanced Teaching Bulletin*, no. 29 (1938).

Lehman, H. C. *Age and achievement*. Princeton: Princeton University Press, 1953.

Human Development

The importance of what happens to a person in childhood —particularly early childhood—has not always been recognized. In the past it was generally believed that young infants were passive, insensitive creatures that required only food and shelter and could neither relate to nor learn from their environment. No one seriously believed that experiences during the first year of life could be very important in shaping psychological growth.

The facts, however, turn out to be quite different. In "Visual Perception in Infancy," Robert L. Fantz demonstrates that a newborn baby, though totally unable to move around in his environment, is already actively exploring it with his eyes. Moreover, babies seem to have inborn tendencies that make them prefer looking at patterns to looking at plain, unpatterned surfaces or open spaces. The preference operates independently of color and brightness, often thought to be the first qualities infants notice. A baby's preference for patterns is useful in helping him learn to recognize the human face and to identify objects he will have to avoid when he begins to crawl and walk. In the third month of life, Fantz shows, the baby begins to show a preference for new patterns rather than familiar ones—another apparently inborn tendency that contributes to his eventual knowledge of the environment.

How strongly experiences in the early months of life can affect a child's psychological and even physical development is demonstrated in "Teddy and Larry: A Comparison of an Institutionalized and a Family-raised Infant," an excerpt from a book by Sally Provence and Rose C. Lipton. Teddy's and Larry's development was studied from birth to the age of eighteen months. Larry, reared in his own home by a mother who spent considerable time holding him, playing with him, and talking to him, developed into an active, robust, well-coordinated child who showed a "zest for life." Teddy, brought up in an institution where there was far less opportunity for affection and attention from a caretaker, seemed to deteriorate instead of to progress. He began well, but his scores on standard tests of infant development declined as time went on. His eager, active approach to the world gradually disappeared; by eighteen months, his outstanding qualities were his soberness, forlorn appearance, and lack of animation.

In "Birth to Maturity," Jerome Kagan and Howard A. Moss describe a long-term study in which a group of children were observed at frequent intervals from birth until their mid-twenties. The study casts considerable light on the question of whether adult personality and behavior can be predicted from traits developed and demonstrated in childhood.

The Kagan-Moss study shows that even before puberty the child has developed many traits that are likely to persist into adulthood. A ten-year-old who values achievement is likely to strive for achievement as an adult; a ten-year-old whose behavior shows considerable spontaneity is likely to be a spontaneous adult. A ten-year-old girl who is passive and dependent often becomes a passive, dependent woman. A boy who is passive and dependent, however, is much less likely to show the same traits in adulthood. The reason is that childhood traits tend to continue into adult life if they accord with the traditional roles of the sexes in our society but may be abandoned if they violate traditional sex roles. Our society encourages passive and dependent behavior by girls and women, but a boy who behaves that way will probably be teased by his friends and chastised by his parents and teachers for acting "unmasculine." Social pressure, his own observations of the people around him, what he learns from movies and books—all combine to persuade him that men are supposed to be active and aggressive.

The message of the Kagan-Moss study is that there is a momentum in human behavior that makes childhood experiences important in shaping adult life. Once a person learns and begins to display a certain kind of behavior, he is likely to continue to do so unless some change in his environment—for example, pressure to abandon behavior considered inappropriate to his sex—forces him to revise his strategy. A ten-year-old child might be compared to a ball that is rolling down a hill. The ball will keep going in the same direction unless its course is altered by a rock or a tree. Thus adult personality and behavior can be predicted quite accurately, though by no means perfectly, from the traits of a ten-year-old.

One factor that is important in determining a child's outlook on life, and therefore his adult personality, is the extent to which he believes he has a chance of success—some degree of control over his environment and his fate. Robert Coles's "Like It Is in the Alley" is an intimate and revealing study of Peter, a nine-year-old black boy who lives with his widowed mother, a brother, and three sisters in a Boston ghetto. Like many children who have grown up in such a deprived and often hostile atmosphere, Peter has already given up on the future. He views the world as treacherous and has no hope of ever changing it or finding anything better.

Peter's sense of futility is matched by that of his mother; indeed, it may spring in part from his mother's attitude toward life. One of the most unfortunate aspects of the problems of poverty and the ghetto, Coles implies, is that they tend to be self-perpetuating. Mothers in this situation tend to be immobilized by their own feelings of hopelessness. Since they despair of ever being able to help their children toward a better life, they may not invest as much time and energy in teaching and interacting with their children as middle-class mothers usually do. In view of what is known about the importance of early stimulation and experience and the continuing effect of many traits developed before the age of ten, it seems obvious that society cannot solve the problem of poverty unless the apathy and expectations of failure characteristic of ghetto families are somehow dispelled.

30

Visual Perception
in Infancy

ROBERT L. FANTZ

Casual observation of an infant during his early months of life indicates, first of all, that he is helpless. His movements are uncoordinated, and he can make few responses to objects or situations. Second, the infant receives, and often appears to respond to, sensory stimulation. In particular, he seems to look at his surroundings throughout most of his waking hours.

Thus the infant has two points of contact with his environment: motor output and sensory input. Common sense might suggest that he spends most of his first few months receiving information about his surroundings via his senses, that he learns something from the experience, and that he uses what he has learned later on, when he begins to explore, manipulate, and control his environment in more

VISUAL PERCEPTION IN INFANCY Adapted from *Annals of the New York Academy of Sciences* 118 (1965): art. 21, pp. 793–814. Copyright © 1965 by the New York Academy of Sciences. Used by permission of the author and the publisher. This article originally appeared under the title "Visual perception from birth as shown by pattern selectivity."

active ways. However, this is not the view put forth in most prevailing theories of child development. Gesell (1949), for example, says that visual development cannot take place until the infant's physiological equipment has matured to a point where he can use it actively. Similarly, many behaviorists assume that since behavior is learned through the reinforcement of overt actions, the child who is too young to act does not learn.

Those of us who favor the former view, that the infant does receive and learn from sensory information well before he can act on it, face a methodological difficulty. Active behavior can be observed directly, but the reception of sensory input can only be inferred from the infant's subsequent reactions, if any. To study sensory stimulation, one must therefore take advantage of the limited response capacities that young infants do have.

For example, even a newborn infant seems to explore his surroundings visually, looking at some things longer than others. Under carefully con-

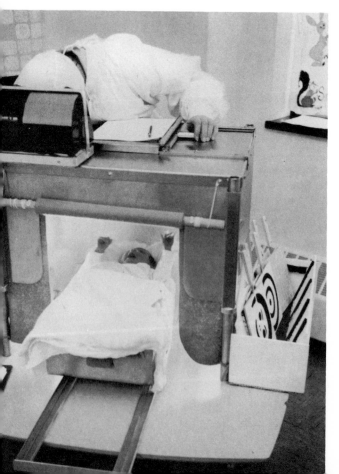

FIGURE 30-1

A newborn infant in a "looking chamber." The observer has slid a picture into the ceiling of the chamber and will note the amount of time the infant spends looking at it.

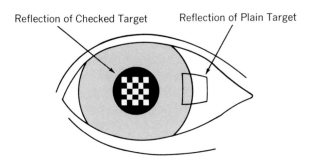

Reflection of Checked Target   Reflection of Plain Target

FIGURE 30-2
The observer can tell what an infant in a "looking chamber" is looking at by watching the reflections in the pupil of the infant's eye. In this drawing, the visual stimuli are a pair of pictures, one checked and one plain. The fact that the checked picture is reflected in the infant's pupil shows that he is looking at that picture.

trolled conditions, an experimenter can tell not only what the infant is looking at but which aspect of it has caught his attention. This method, called the *visual preference method,* is the one used in the research on infants' visual abilities described below. An infant is placed in a "looking chamber" like the one shown in Figure 30-1 and shown a series of visual stimuli—pairs of pictures, for instance. As Figure 30-2 illustrates, the experimenter can tell which picture the infant is looking at by which is reflected in his pupil, and he keeps track of the amount of time the infant spends gazing at each. If the pictures are identical in all respects but one (for instance, the same in color, size, and brightness, but different in pattern), then any statistically significant differences in the amount of time the infant devotes to the two pictures can be attributed to the one element that varies.

Can Infants See Patterns?

To find out whether infants see a difference between patterned and nonpatterned surfaces, we showed the six targets pictured at the top of Figure 30-3 to a group of 119 infants, ranging in age from newborn to six months old. The five patterned targets were made by gluing black, three-quarter-inch squares onto white poster board; the sixth target was a square of gray paper of the same brightness (measured by reflected light) as the patterned targets.

Figure 30-3 shows the average time spent looking at each target by the

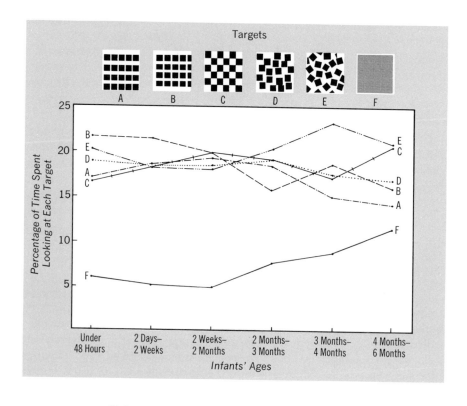

FIGURE 30-3

When infants were shown the six targets pictured above, even newborns spent more time looking at the patterned targets than at the gray one.

infants at various ages. At all ages, they spent considerably more time looking at the patterned squares than at the gray one. The differentiation among the five patterns was less marked (though newborns tended to favor pattern B, whereas older infants looked longest at pattern E and spent least time on A and B). The low response to gray, especially pronounced in very young infants, indicates that infants have the visual capacity to distinguish between patterns and nonpatterns at birth. It gives no support to the idea that the ability to see patterns and the tendency to look at them develop only through maturation or experience after birth.

This finding is especially interesting in view of some recent neurological research by Hubel and Wiesel (1962). Electrical recordings of single nerve cells in the visual area of animal brains show that a particular cell may respond to one type of pattern, such as an illuminated slit or a dark bar, but have no response to other patterns or to light. This seems to indicate an unlearned neural mechanism for pattern discrimination. If such a mechanism does exist, it could account for the high interest shown even by newborn infants in the five patterned targets of Figure 30-3.

Patterns versus Color and Brightness

Visual perception involves more than the ability to tell the difference between patterns and nonpatterns. It implies the use of that ability in behavior. During the early months of life, visual ability cannot be used to direct motor responses (it takes the infant some time to learn to reach toward, touch, and grasp things), but it might be used to direct the visual exploration of the environment. To determine whether this is so, one must identify the visual features that an infant gives special attention to and ask whether his choices seem to pave the way for later, more mature uses of vision.

The experiment with the patterned and nonpatterned targets indicates not only that infants can tell the difference between patterns and nonpatterns but that they prefer looking at patterns. That preference was shown again in another study (Fantz, 1963), in which the targets differed in color and brightness as well as in pattern. The stimuli were six disks, three patterned and three plain but bright or colored. The responses, summarized in Figure 30-4, show that both newborn and older infants devote considerably more time to patterned targets than to plain ones, despite brightness of color. More than half the infants in each group looked longest at the face; no infant looked longest at the white, yellow, or red disk. This finding contradicts the traditional belief that color, brightness, and size are the first things infants are attracted to, and that the perception of forms is secondary and learned.

If we consider how vision is actually used, the infants' tendency to pay attention to patterns makes good sense. An infant who looked only at unpatterned surfaces or open spaces, no matter how bright or colored, would learn little about his environment. A child can crawl or walk without bumping into things and falling off edges largely because he notices variations in surface patterning or contouring that indicate an obstacle or drop-off in the path ahead (Gibson, 1950). Objects are recognized largely by means of the configuration produced by fine details, edges, curved surfaces, texture, and shading (Fantz, in press), rather than by color, brightness, size, or external outline, which often vary with lighting, distance, and viewing angle. The patterning of a face and head, for example,

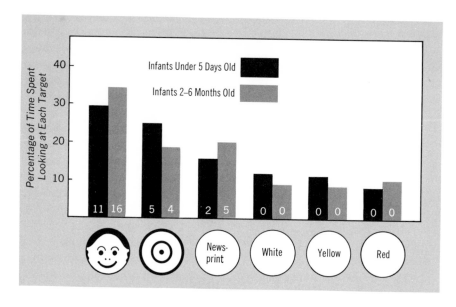

FIGURE 30-4

The height of the bars shows the amount of time infants spent looking at each of the six targets; the number at the bottom of each bar indicates how many infants looked longest at each target. Both newborn and older infants seem to prefer patterns to bright or colored, but unpatterned, targets.

is the surest way for an infant (or an adult) to tell a human being from some other object. Finer perceptions of facial patterns allow the viewer to recognize a particular person, and still finer discriminations inform him of that person's mood and emotional reactions.

Using vision to orient oneself in space, to recognize objects, and to tell one person from another requires attention first to patterns as a general class and then to the specific types of pattern that provide the most constant cues for behavior. The infant's unlearned preference for patterned visual targets may be the necessary starting point for this developmental process.

Faces as Patterns

In the world of the helpless infant, the human being is a very important object. Many observers have noted the high attention value of the human face, but most of them have attributed it to the fact that faces move, or to their brightness or shininess. We have studied infants' interest in three other attributes of faces and heads: complex patterning, the particular complex pattern formed by facial features, and solidity (depth).

To investigate the possibility that infants are attracted to the complex patterning of faces, we used the six head-shaped pictures shown in Figure 30-5. The two ovals on the left are presumably most like real faces in complexity, while the plain white and gray ovals on the right are least like faces. When we showed these six figures to fifteen infants less than a week old, they showed a strong preference for the more complex, facelike patterns. This was expected, given our earlier findings on infants' preferences for abstract patterns. It simply illustrates how a general interest in patterns may be useful to the infant by directing his attention to objects that are important to him.

The two faces on the left of Figure 30-5, one with normally placed features and one with scrambled features, were equally attractive to newborn infants. At later ages, infants showed some preference for the normally arranged features, though it was never pronounced. The preference for the normal face was most consistent in infants two to three months old; at that age they also showed a consistent preference for the eyelike spots to the off-center spots in the middle pair of ovals.

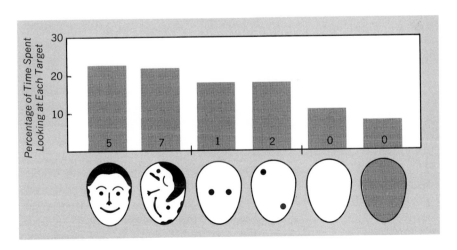

FIGURE 30-5

When infants were shown these six facelike targets, they looked longest at the two complex patterns on the left. The number of infants who spent most time looking at a given target is indicated inside each bar.

Another characteristic of the human head that might interest the infant is its solidity. When we showed our infants a solid model of a human head and a similar flat form, both painted white, a strong preference for the solid head appeared quite suddenly in infants two months old. They looked longer at the solid head, whether they were tested with both eyes open or only one, suggesting that it is the *patterning* of solid objects, rather than depth cues (which require the use of both eyes), that makes them more interesting to infants than flat forms.

The fact that even newborn infants pay more attention to facelike configurations than to other targets does not imply that infants recognize people as people. Neither does the appearance of preferences for other visual characteristics of faces later on, since these characteristics are shared by many objects that are not faces. However, the visual preferences of the young infant do assure him, under normal rearing conditions, of many opportunities to study people visually. An interest in the visual characteristics that human beings possess, like an interest in visual elements that will help the child recognize objects and move around among them, constitutes a primitive knowledge of the environment that serves as a foundation for later knowledge acquired through experience.

Familiar Patterns versus New Ones

An increased responsiveness to people, developing from the infant's unlearned attraction to their intrinsic visual characteristics and from the experience the attraction leads to, is one useful outcome of early visual perception. Another is illustrated in the final experiment, which concerns responsiveness to familiar patterns and novel ones.

The targets in this experiment were eleven photographs, all complex but otherwise quite different. They were shown in pairs to infants of various ages. For each infant, one picture was used as a "constant pattern." It was paired in turn with each of the other pictures (the "novel patterns"), so that the infant saw it ten times in all. Infants less than two months old were as likely to gaze at the familiar picture the tenth time they saw it as the first. Older infants, however, showed a decreasing interest in the familiar picture, apparently recognizing and becoming bored with it after repeated exposures. Their high responsiveness to the novel pictures can be seen as an unlearned interest in unfamiliar visual patterns.

The satiating effects of familiarity, like other changes in visual preference discussed here, may be helpful to the infant in the visual exploration of the environment. The infant's inborn tendency to look at patterns serves to concentrate his attention on patterned parts of the environment, which include such important objects as people. The very young infant is not very discriminating about which patterns he looks at, but discrimination develops with time. For example, the older infant prefers solidity to flatness and thus turns his attention to objects rather than to flat surfaces. Finally, a decreased interest in patterns that are already familiar encourages the infant to become acquainted with new visual objects.

It can be concluded that the perception of patterns is possible from birth and that visual experience with important parts of the environment begins in the early months of life. The visual world of the infant is patterned and organized. It is selectively explored in the only way possible for the helpless but visually active child. Early visual preferences help direct visual exploration and lay the groundwork for more active exploration of the environment later on, supporting the priority of perception over action in the development of behavior.

REFERENCES

Fantz, R. L. Pattern discrimination and selective attention as determinants of perceptual development from birth. *Perceptual development in children.* Edited by A. H. Kidd and J. L. Rivoire. New York: International Universities Press, forthcoming.

Fantz, R. L. Pattern vision in newborn infants. *Science* 140 (1963): 296–97.

Gesell, A., Ilg, F. L., and Bullis, G. E. *Vision: Its development in infant and child.* New York: Harper & Brothers, 1949.

Gibson, J. J. *The perception of the visual world.* Boston: Houghton Mifflin, 1950.

Hubel, D. H., and Wiesel, T. N. Receptive fields, binocular interaction, and functional architecture in the cat's visual cortex. *Journal of Physiology* 160 (1962): 106–54.

31

Teddy and Larry: A Comparison

of an Institutionalized

and a Family-raised Infant

S A L L Y   P R O V E N C E
R O S E   C .   L I P T O N

In the thirteenth century, Frederick II, Emperor of the Holy
Roman Empire, directed an experiment in child development that
did not turn out as he expected:

> He wanted to find out what kind of speech and what manner of
> speech children would have when they grew up if they spoke to
> no one beforehand. So he bade foster mothers and nurses to suckle
> the children, to bathe and wash them, but in no way to prattle with
> them or to speak to them, for he wanted to learn whether they
> would speak the Hebrew language, which was the eldest, or Greek,
> or Latin, or Arabic, or perhaps the language of their parents, of
> whom they had been born. But he labored in vain, because the

TEDDY AND LARRY: A COMPARISON OF AN INSTITUTIONALIZED AND A FAMILY-RAISED
INFANT Adapted from *Infants in institutions* by Sally Provence and Rose C.
Lipton. Copyright © 1962 by International Universities Press. Used by permis-
sion of Sally Provence, Edgar L. Lipton, and the publisher.

children all died. For they could not live without the petting and joyful faces and loving words of their foster mothers (Ross and McLaughlin, 1949).

In the seven hundred years since that bit of data on the importance of maternal care was obtained, many other observers have studied what happens to young children who grow up without normal mothering. It has become clear that the family is the setting in which babies are most likely to receive the treatment that makes for good development and that institutional living, with the characteristic lack of adequate maternal care, has a damaging effect. An infant's needs are multiple and complex, and it is difficult—perhaps impossible—to meet them under conditions of group care.

Tremendous differences exist among mothers and families, of course. Sometimes an infant receives excellent care; in other cases he is subjected to extreme neglect and abuse. As might be expected from the vast number of possible combinations of babies with individual traits and predispositions and mothers with unique ways of mothering, infants cared for by their mothers show infinite variations in development. Despite all the variations, however, babies raised at home are still more like one another than they are like infants raised in institutions.

To illustrate the contrast between institutionalized and family-raised infants, we shall describe two babies, Teddy and Larry, in some detail. Both were subjects in a large research study comparing the development of seventy-five institutionalized infants with that of seventy-five infants who lived at home. We first met Teddy, the institutionalized infant, when he was between two and three weeks old. Larry, the family-raised infant, was known to us from birth. The differences between the two infants are typical of, though somewhat less extreme than, the differences found more generally between the two groups.

We selected Teddy for detailed description because he was the "best" of the institutionalized group: his development during the first year of life was less severely retarded than that of the rest. On the other hand, Larry, the family-raised baby, was an average, middle-of-the-road fellow— by no means the best developed of his group. By discussing the best of the institutional group and an average child from the family-raised group we hope to communicate, without danger of exaggeration, the differences in development shown by infants who had adequate maternal care and infants who did not.

Both infants weighed eight pounds at birth and were healthy, vigorous newborns. Their scores over the next eighteen months on two standard development tests, the Gesell Scale and the Viennese Scale, are shown in Figure 31-1.

FIGURE 31-1

Larry and Teddy were given two standard tests of infant development many times during their first eighteen months. As the scores show, Larry's development was about average for his age, but Teddy fell farther and farther behind as time went on.

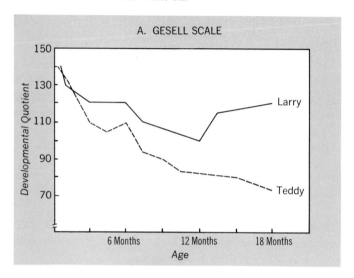

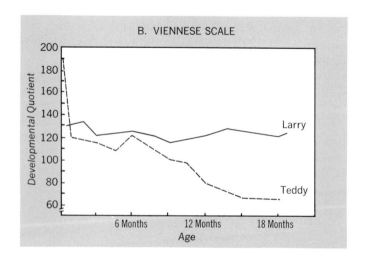

Teddy

We first examined Teddy when he was twenty days old. At that time he was a well-nourished, husky-looking baby who was taking adequate amounts of formula feeding. His physical development was somewhat advanced, and some of the reflex responses of a newborn child were beginning to be replaced by more mature forms of behavior. Teddy was visually alert, had a good loud cry, and looked robust and vigorous.

For several months, though his development showed the same kind of retardation that characterized the other infants in the institution, Teddy's performance on tests and his general behavior and responsiveness were less severely impaired than were the other children's. It is not completely clear why Teddy did better than the other institutionalized infants. However, there are two possibilities. First, his biological endowment may have been favorable, as is suggested by the signs of good maturation during the earliest months. Second, Teddy posed a feeding problem: he frequently lost the nipple of his propped bottle and cried. Since he had a loud voice, he was usually heard and attended to. The attendants were not always happy with him and considered his protests something of a nuisance, but they nevertheless had more contact with him than with most other babies in the ward.

Examined at six months, Teddy was still doing reasonably well. He was a husky, attractive infant with a moderately strong drive toward motor activity. His interest in the test materials at that time was greater than that of the other institutionalized infants, and he functioned at a higher level. There was no sign of anxiety toward strangers. He accepted us with a friendly, amiable smile, and at times actively initiated contact by smiling at or reaching toward one of us. The attendant told us that she could not prop his bottle as she could for the other infants because Teddy tended to lose it from his mouth; then he would yell loudly, and she had to go to him and hold the bottle for a few minutes. He was often placed in a small canvas bouncing chair so that he would be less noisy.

At six months Teddy scored 108 on the Gesell Scale and 122 on the Viennese Scale, as shown in Figure 31-1. The high score on the Viennese Scale was due particularly to his activity in seeking social contact and to his good motor development. However, his performance on the tests was below average for his age: when a toy was taken away from him, he did not protest or try to get it back and he showed no signs that he could tell the difference between familiar and unfamiliar people or between the nursing bottle and a doll. His language development was especially poor, about six weeks behind that of the average six-month-old. Although he made various sounds—grunts, growls, and some spontaneous babbling—he seldom vocalized in the service of social contact. Unlike most children his age, he showed no tendency to imitate the facial expressions and sounds made by adults.

Teddy could grasp objects well enough, but he did not use his hands as skillfully as his physical development suggested he should have. When placed on his hands and knees or held in a sitting position on someone's lap, he rocked. He seemed rather stiff and not at all cuddly when held. He had some interest in motor activity and could change his position by pivoting or rolling, but he showed less interest in exploring his hand with his mouth and vice versa than he had some weeks earlier.

Teddy gave the impression at six months that he was developing fairly well for his age, better than the other institutionalized babies, but some signs of retardation were already apparent. They grew more dramatic during the second half of the first year. We examined Teddy at thirty-two weeks, thirty-eight weeks, forty-five weeks, and fifty-five weeks, and found him becoming gradually but steadily more retarded. He was less active in his approaches to people and was not as responsive to them. His interest in toys diminished markedly, as did his interest in solving problems appropriate to babies of his age. He was not playful and became increasingly listless and inexpressive. Although his weight gain was adequate, he looked less vigorous, robust, and active; he often had a runny nose.

Teddy was changing. At forty-five weeks (ten months), his score on the Gesell Scale was 87; on the Viennese Scale, 99. The changes in appearance, mood, and reactions to people since his examination at thirty-eight weeks were even more marked than the decline in the test scores. Moreover, many of the things he was able to do he did only briefly and after much effort on the part of the examiner. He was solemn-faced, unsmiling, and miserable looking. His nose was being wiped as the examiner approached, a procedure at which he cried woefully but without trying to avoid it or push the nurse's hand away. The staff still considered him a "smart little boy" compared to the others in his nursery, but he looked strikingly different from an infant in his own family. Here are a few detailed observations made at the time:

> When several cubes were presented, he looked at them, leaned forward, and reached toward them with his right hand. He tentatively grasped one and quickly released it. Then, since he failed to approach the cubes for a time, I put a cube in his hand; he accepted it readily. Next he took a cube from my hand, looking at me as if suspicious. Finally he smiled tentatively in response to my smile and my efforts to interest him in the

other cubes. His movements seem very inhibited, as if he cannot move or use anything vigorously. . . . He often holds his arms quite still, in a "frozen" position, until a toy is placed in his hand.

He could sit, pull himself up to a standing position, and creep a short distance on all fours. He did little creeping, however, and a lot of rocking. He could approach and grasp toys and had the ability to hold two at once. However, he regularly discarded one, focusing his interest on a single object. He showed some displeasure when a toy was taken away but accepted substitutes easily. He made no effort to recover a hidden toy. When upset, he seemed more easily comforted by being given a toy than by direct contact with an adult, even a "familiar" adult. Having a toy in hand seemed to be more important to him than any attraction to the specific qualities of a toy.

It was more difficult to induce him to imitate an adult than at the time of last contact. He did not make the playful responses to social games such as peek-a-boo and pat-a-cake that are usual in children of his age. He showed no awareness of the meaning of an adult's gesture to pick him up, though he showed some enjoyment in being picked up.

Teddy's soberness, his forlorn appearance, and his lack of animation were outstanding. When he was unhappy, he now cried in a way that sounded neither demanding nor angry—just miserable. His capacity for protest, shown earlier in connection with losing the bottle, was much diminished. He did not turn to adults to relieve his distress or to involve them in a playful or pleasurable interchange. He made no demands. The active approach to the world, which was one of the encouraging aspects of his earlier development, had vanished. When an adult made active and persistent efforts to be sociable, he became somewhat more responsive and animated, but only briefly.

Two observers well described the impression Teddy made at this time. One said, "The light in Teddy has gone out." The other said, "If you crank his motor, you can get him to go a little; he can't start on his own."

Larry

Larry, a full-term eight-pound infant, was the second child in his family. As a newborn he was attractive, husky, mature, and moderately active, and he had a lusty cry. Breast-fed for the first six months and then gradually weaned to a cup, Larry gained weight rapidly. For the first three to four months he was somewhat fretful at night, and his mother soothed him by holding and nursing him.

At one month he was large and well-nourished-looking, visually alert, and beginning to develop a social smile. At seven weeks, when first tested, he was doing well. There was some hand-to-mouth activity; he was visually perceptive and attentive; and he responded to adults with much smiling, cooing, and vocalizing. Although his movements were not very active, they gave the impression of strength and good organization. He adapted well to holding and reacted to being placed in a feeding position with increased sucking. His mother held him comfortably and securely. Her pleasure in him was obvious, though she had some complaints about him.

At twenty weeks Larry was socially responsive and interested in the toys used for testing. His hand-to-mouth movements were well organized and purposeful. He vocalized to people and also spontaneously, to toys and to himself. He played with his hands, rubbed his face, touched his body. He mouthed the toys as well as his hands. He was large, well proportioned, and moderately active.

His test performance was good, both quantitatively and qualitatively. He was smiling and attentive to the examiner but frequently turned to his mother, who sat nearby, looking at her and often smiling and "talking" to her. An interchange between Larry and his mother was described by one of the observers; part of it is included here because it demonstrates some of the differences in the experiences of Teddy and Larry.

> Larry was placed on the examining table by his mother, who undressed him in preparation for the physical examination; he reached up to her face and touched it. After she had removed his shirt, she bent over him, rubbed her nose and mouth on his abdomen and chest, nuzzling into him, kissing him and biting him gently. He chortled and gurgled with increased excitement, pulling at her hair which rubs across his nose and mouth. Dorothy, his two-year-old sister, had been playing with toys in the room and tried to get her mother's attention by calling her two or three times. Mrs. D. lifted her face briefly and with a somewhat peremptory "put the toys back" returned to her play with Larry. This play lasted perhaps two minutes, after which the pediatrician started the physical examination. Larry, now quiet, smiled and reached toward the pediatrician when his abdomen was palpitated and gurgled as if he enjoyed the stimulation.

When examined at the age of twenty-seven weeks, Larry was described as a large, well-proportioned infant with a charming smile. His developmental quotient on the Gesell Scale was 120; on the Viennese Scale, 124.

There were no deficits in his performance on the test at this age level in any area. He clearly distinguished between familiar and unfamiliar people, and he showed some anxiety toward strangers. In spite of the anxiety he was able to adapt to the test situation without difficulty and became interested in and responsive to the examiner. He turned fairly often to look at his mother, and his most intense smile was to her. His mood was a happy one.

Still partially breast-fed, he was taking solids well and some milk from a cup. He could feed himself a cookie or cracker. He was up on all fours and attempting to creep. He was interested in the test materials. If he lost a toy, he would search for it. He would initiate contact with adults and imitate their facial expressions and sounds. He often put his hands—and even his feet—into his mouth.

Larry was examined again at thirty-six, forty-three, forty-eight, and fifty-five weeks, and he continued to progress well. At forty-three weeks he was a robust, vigorous infant; his score on the Gesell Scale was 103, and on the Viennese Scale, 114. By forty-eight weeks his gross motor development was well organized; he crept well and pulled himself up to a standing position. He also used his motor equipment effectively, both to pursue a toy or a person and to avoid things he found unpleasant. His fine motor skills were also well developed. He could handle two objects simultaneously with ease, and he showed a capacity to stay interested in both. He showed an interest in the test materials, and in exploring and inspecting the external world generally. When a toy was hidden behind a solid screen, he succeeded in finding it.

Social contact with the examiner interested Larry, who participated in games such as pat-a-cake, peek-a-boo, and bye-bye with pleasure. He had a large repertoire of sounds, which he used to express a variety of feelings, and he used "mama" and "dada" specifically as names for his parents. A brief excerpt from Larry's record illustrates the impression he made at forty-eight weeks:

> He is still attractive, vigorous, and friendly, but there is a change in Larry and it is difficult to know what factors contribute to this impression. He seems more mature and less of an infant. Certainly his motor skill contributes to this, as does the fact that he is less chubby, and body proportions have changed somewhat. However, the predominant change is in his facial expression, which is more intense, purposeful, and self-directed. . . . There is considerable mouthing and banging of toys. He bangs with large vigorous swings and seems to enjoy not only the motion but the sound. His movements are well coordinated and graceful. There is no noticeable hesitancy about approaching new objects or giving up the old, though he looks after them and tries to retrieve them if no substitute is given. This increased interest and impression of self-directed activity is accompanied by something that makes one think he has a zest for life.

In the following months Teddy and Larry looked increasingly different from each other in their development. And the differences between them were characteristic of the differences between the other family-raised and institutionalized infants we studied. By the time they were eighteen months old, their scores on the two standard development tests had diverged sharply. However, the scores do an imperfect job of conveying the difference between the two children. The contrast between them in their relationships with people and in their use of developing skills to relate to the people, objects, and events around them was striking and provides the most vivid demonstration of the impact of maternal deprivation.

REFERENCE

Ross, J. B., and McLaughlin, M. M., eds. *A portable medieval reader.* New York: Viking, 1949.

32

Birth to Maturity

JEROME KAGAN
HOWARD A. MOSS

Many childhood behaviors have short lives and are replaced or dropped long before maturity. Fear of the dark, for example, is associated with a specific period in the development of the child, and we are not surprised when it vanishes from the behavioral scene. However, people have long believed that many adult motives, attitudes, and behaviors originate during childhood and, once established, become permanent parts of an individual's behavioral repertoire. This belief is supported by various private recollections and personal reports, but more substantial evidence has been difficult to come by. The only way to discover which childhood behaviors are marked for future use and which will be lost along the way is through systematic longitudinal studies, in which the behavior of a

BIRTH TO MATURITY Adapted from *Birth to maturity: A study in psychological development*. New York: Wiley, 1962. Used by permission of Jerome Kagan and the publisher.

given group of children over a long period of time is observed, recorded, and analyzed.

The investigation summarized here, which was carried out at the Fels Research Institute, in Yellow Springs, Ohio, is one such study. It is based in part on longitudinal data concerning the personality development of eighty-nine children, forty-five girls and forty-four boys, who from birth through early adolescence participated in a long-term research project at the institute, and in part on follow-up data regarding their personalities as young adults. The purpose of the investigation was to compare the two sets of data in an attempt to relate the functioning of the child to the psychological status of the adult or, in more technical terms, to study the selective stability of behavior from childhood through early adulthood.

Subjects and Methods

The eighty-nine subjects in our investigation had joined the Fels project between 1929 and 1939. They came from sixty-three families, all white and most of them middle class. About three-fourths of the parents were high school graduates and almost half had attended college. The fathers included roughly equal numbers of laborers, farmers, small businessmen, white-collar workers, and professionals. In religious background, fifty-three families were Protestant, nine were Catholic, and one was Jewish.

ASSESSMENT: BIRTH THROUGH ADOLESCENCE

The children were interviewed, observed, and tested repeatedly over the years from birth through the mid-teens. Table 32-1 summarizes the information obtained for a typical child in the sample. The narrative summaries of observations of the child at home, in school, and at the institute proved to be the richest and most accurate source of data on the child's personality development.

We divided this material into four age periods: birth to age three, three to six, six to ten, and ten to fourteen. These divisions roughly correspond to important developmental periods. The first three years include infancy and early social training. Years three to six, the preschool years, involve the child's first contacts with children his own age and his early attempts to become less dependent on his parents. The next four years call for adjustment to school, the establishment of interests and skills, and the development of friendships with other children of the child's own sex. During the preadolescent years, ten to fourteen, heterosexual interests

TABLE 32-1

Summary of longitudinal information obtained on a typical child.

Type of information	Setting and method of recording	Typical frequency
1. Observation of child and mother	(a) Half-day observation of child and mother in home. Observations summarized in narrative style.	Twice yearly from birth to age 6. Annually from age 6 to 12.
	(b) Observation of child in Fels Experimental Nursery School and Day Camp; half-day sessions for 3 weeks. Observations summarized in narrative style and numerical ratings.	Twice yearly from age 2½ to 5. Annually from age 6 to 10.
	(c) Interview with child. Interview summarized in narrative style.	Annually from age 6 to 12.
	(d) Interview with mother with narrative summary.	Annually from child's birth to adolescence.
	(e) Observation of child in school with narrative summary.	Twice yearly from 1st to 8th grade.
2. Personality tests	(a) Selected stimuli from the Thematic Apperception Test.	Every third year from age 8½ to 17½.
	(b) Rorschach Test.	Every third year from age 8½ to 17½.
	(c) Minnesota Multiphasic Personality Inventory.	Once during adolescence—age 17.
	(d) Kuder Preference Record.	Once during adolescence—age 17.
3. Mental development tests	(a) Gesell Development Schedule.	6, 12, 18, and 24 months.
	(b) Merrill-Palmer Infant Test.	18, 24, and 30 months.
•	(c) Stanford-Binet Intelligence Test.	2½, 3, 3½, 4, 4½, 5, 6, 7, 8, 9, 10, 11, 12, and 14 years.
	(d) Wechsler-Bellevue IQ Test.	Age 13 and 17.
	(e) Primary Mental Abilities Test.	Age 17.
4. Mental testing of mother and father	Otis IQ Test.	One administration.

develop, vocational choice begins to emerge, and modes of defensive reaction to anxiety-arousing situations are firmly established.

We had decided to organize the investigation around four major classes of behavior: behavior related to motives, anxiety, defenses against anxiety, and social interaction. Within those general classes, we constructed forty-eight specific variables, on which each child was to be rated by means of a seven-point rating scale. These ratings were made by Howard Moss. He read each child's file and rated all children at birth to age three, three to six, six to ten, and ten to fourteen, in that order. These four sets of ratings became our primary source of historical data on the children.

The files on which the ratings were based did not include test information, and it should be stressed that Dr. Moss had no knowledge of any subject's performance on any test. Nor was he acquainted with their psychological status as adults. Special precautions were taken to insure that he would learn nothing about the subjects except what he read in the narrative reports.

ASSESSMENT: EARLY ADULTHOOD

From July 1957 through October 1959, seventy-one of the eighty-nine subjects for whom longitudinal ratings had been made participated in an adult assessment program. It had two parts, an interview and a formal testing schedule. On the basis of the tape-recorded interviews, each adult was rated on variables similar to those used for childhood behavior. The testing program included a modified ink blot task, selected cards from the Thematic Apperception Test, a self-rating inventory, conceptual sorting tasks, a task involving the recognition of slides flashed briefly on a screen, the Wechsler-Bellevue IQ Test (Form I), and measures of reactivity of the autonomic nervous system. The interviews always took place before the series of tests, and they were conducted by Jerome Kagan. At the time of the interview, he had no knowledge of any longitudinal or test information on the subjects. This precaution insured that the childhood data would influence neither the interview itself nor later evaluations of the adults.

Thus the ratings based on longitudinal childhood data and the ratings based on adult interviews were completely independent of each other. Since the primary purpose of the research was to relate child and adult personality dispositions, this independence was mandatory.

Selected Results

When all the data had been collected, tabulated, and analyzed, we found that some of our hunches about the continuity of behavior from childhood to adulthood were verified; others were clearly refuted. Equally important were unexpected discoveries that suggested leads for future research and had implications for educational practices. We cannot summarize all the results here, but there are several conclusions that should be singled out for attention.

THE INFLUENCE OF SEX TYPING

The most dramatic and consistent finding of the study was that many of the behaviors exhibited by the child during the period from six to ten years of age, and a few from the period three to six, were moderately good predictors of related behavior during early adulthood. Passive withdrawal from stress, dependence on family, ease of anger-arousal, involvement in intellectual mastery, social anxiety, sex-role identification, and sexual behavior in adulthood were each related to reasonably similar behavioral tendencies during the early school years. Figure 32-1 summarizes the stability of these seven classes of responses from childhood to adult-

FIGURE 32-1

Continuity of behavior from childhood to adulthood.

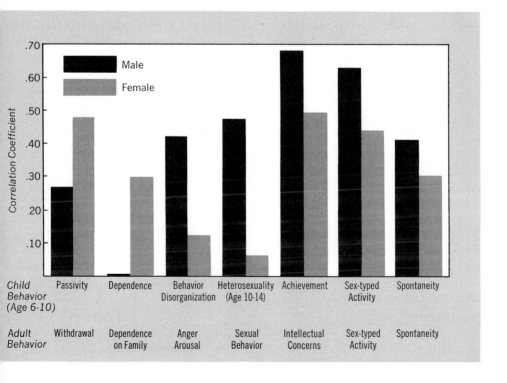

hood. These results offer strong support to the popular notion that many characteristics of the adult personality begin to take form early in childhood.

However, it should be noted that the degree of continuity in all seven response classes was strongly influenced by traditional standards of masculinity and femininity. For example, passive girls were more likely to become passive adults than were passive boys, whereas angry boys were more likely than angry girls to become hostile adults. In our culture passive and dependent behavior are subject to consistent cultural disapproval for men but not for women. Direct aggressive retaliation, frequent sexual behavior, and a low threshold for anger, on the other hand, are frowned on in females; males are given greater license in these areas. It is not surprising, therefore, that childhood passivity and dependency were related to passive and dependent behavior during adulthood in women but not in men, and that childhood rages and frequent dating during preadolescence predicted adult aggressive and sexual predispositions, respectively, in men but not in women.

Some families did not consciously attempt to mold the children in strict accordance with traditional sex-role standards, but the children apparently responded to social pressure from outside the family. Aggressive and sexually active girls learned to inhibit direct expression of aggressive and sexual behavior; dependent boys gradually stopped making dependent overtures to others.

Intellectual mastery and the adoption of sex-typed interests are approved for both sexes, and both types of behavior showed considerable continuity in males and females from the early school years through adulthood. In some cases, even preschool behavior was related to a similar disposition in adulthood. For example, the preschool girl's involvement in achievement tasks successfully predicted her concern with intellectual mastery in adulthood.

Some forms that childhood behavior took during adulthood seemed to be determined in part by the sex-role appropriateness of the childhood behavior. Passivity in boys predicted noncompetitiveness, sexual anxiety, and social apprehension in adult men, but not direct dependent overtures to parents or love objects. A tendency toward rage reactions in young girls predicted intellectual competitiveness, masculine interests, and dependency conflict in adult women, but not direct expression of aggression. It appears that a childhood behavior is likely to lead to similar behavior in adulthood only when the early behavior fits traditional sex roles. When it conflicts with sex-role standards, the motive is more likely to be expressed later through substitute behaviors that are socially more acceptable than the original ones.

The relevance of sex-role identification in directing behavioral choices is supported by investigations indicating that the child begins to differentiate masculine and feminine characteristics and activities, as defined by his culture, at a very early age. Even three-year-olds are aware of the different interests and appearances of males and females. Comprehension of the world is much like a game of twenty questions in which the child tries to understand new experiences by categorizing them, broadly at first and then by successively narrow labels. One of the first questions a child asks about an object or activity seems to be whether it is masculine or feminine. Having determined the answer to that question, he adjusts his behavior accordingly. One of us recalls a conversation between his three and one-half year old daughter (D) and a female college student (S):

D: What are you studying?
S: Psychology, for your daddy.
D: Are you going to be a psychologist?
S: Yes.
D: Are you going to be a mother?
S: Yes, I think so.
D (*after a puzzled pause*): Well, you can't be
    a psychologist and a mother too.

Social-class membership places constraints on the behavior the child sees as suitable for one of his sex. An interest in art and music, for example, is more acceptable to middle-class than to lower-class men, and vocational aspirations are, of course, strongly influenced by social class. Thus knowledge of the sex and social class of a child allows one to make a strikingly large number of predictions about his future interests, goals, vocational choice, and tendencies regarding dependent, aggressive, sexual, and mastery behavior. The face that a person shows the world depends to a large extent on what he thinks the world expects from one of his sex and social class.

The preceding discussion assumes that many people are motivated to behave in ways that fit an idealized model of the "masculine" man or the "feminine" woman. This assumption locates both the goals of motives and the incentive to move toward them in the cognitive system of the individual rather than in the outside world. Psychologists in the behavioral tradition, by contrast, define both the conditions that create motives (and drives) and the rewards that gratify them primarily in terms of external events. For example, they might say that rejection arouses a motive whose goal is the receipt of love. Although we do not deny the usefulness or validity of this orientation, it seems necessary to acknowledge a need, perhaps unique to human beings, to act and believe in ways that fit previously established, internal standards. Each person has a mental picture of the person he would like to be and the goals he would like to reach—an idealized model of himself. Any behavior or belief that increases the discrepancy between the person's perception of himself as he is and his picture of himself as he wants to be provokes anxiety and is likely to be shunned; any behavior that seems to bring the actual and the idealized selves into closer correspondence is pleasing and likely to be practiced.

It would appear that the desire to be an ideal male or an ideal female, as defined by the individual, is an essential part of every man's model of himself. An important determinant of the acceptability, and thus of the occurrence, of a given behavior is its position on a cognitive dimension ranging from "highly masculine" to "highly feminine."

THE EARLY SCHOOL YEARS: A CRITICAL PERIOD

Some adult behavior—especially withdrawal (in women), involvement in task mastery, social spontaneity, and the adoption of sex-typed interests—has clear antecedents in the individual's behavior from age six to ten, but the relation of adult behavior to behavior before age six is far less clear. This suggests that important changes in the child's behavioral organization take place between the ages of six and ten. The significant events of this period include: (1) identification with parents and attempts to adopt the parents' values and imitate their behavior; (2) the realization that mastering intellectual skills is both a cultural requirement and a source of satisfaction; and (3) the establishment of relationships with other children. The last experience forces the child to accommodate himself, at least to some degree, to the values and expectations of his peers. In some children, this strengthens tendencies toward dominance, social spontaneity, and positive self-evaluation; in others, such as those whose peers reject them, it can lead to social anxiety, social submission, and a sense of ineffectiveness. Some children in the latter group try to compensate by developing their competence in areas that do not require interaction with other children. Those who are unable to do that continue to anticipate failure when faced with challenges of various sorts.

The first four years of contact with the school and with other children seem to crystallize behavioral tendencies that some children maintain through young adulthood. Children who display intense strivings for mastery between ages six and ten are likely to maintain this behavioral posture; on the other side of the coin, withdrawal from anticipated failure, especially among girls, grows rapidly during the early school years once it has begun. These findings have implications for educational practices. For example, selecting bright, highly motivated fourth graders for special educational programs involves little risk that the children will suddenly stop trying. Similarly, children who tend to withdraw from tasks during the first few grades are likely to continue to do so, and remedial or therapeutic intervention should probably take place earlier than it usually does at present.

THE SLEEPER EFFECT

The bombardment of atomic nuclei or the reaction of hydrochloric acid with a base leads to effects that are immediate—sometimes even too fast to measure. In psychological development, however, the effects of specific early experiences are often not evident until long periods of time have passed. For instance, the assumption that a good relationship between mother and infant is necessary for the development of satisfactory interpersonal relationships cannot be verified until the child is six or seven and beginning to have relationships with other children and adults.

One way to detect a time lag between cause and effect is to find a stronger relationship between one variable measured early and another measured late in development than between similar variables measured closer together in time. This set of circumstances—which we have called the "sleeper effect"—came up twice in our material. For boys, passivity and fear of bodily harm during the period from birth to age three and a tendency toward minimal body movement from three to six were each better predictors of love-object dependence in adulthood than were later assessments of these childhood variables. In the second case of the "sleeper effect," certain maternal practices during the first three years of life were more closely related to the child's preadolescent and adult behavior than were evaluations of similar parental practices in later childhood. These findings require different explanations.

Passivity and fear of harm in the young boy are probably less disguised during the preschool years than at later ages. As he grows up, the boy learns to inhibit the open expression of passivity and fear as immature, disapproved behavior. Thus an assessment of predispositions to passivity and anxiety about bodily harm based on behavior at age six is likely to be less sensitive than one based on behavior at age two or three. During the earlier period the child's defenses are weaker, and he is less able or less strongly motivated to prevent immature, anxiety-based reactions. However, a hidden predisposition to passivity may remain during the school years and gain expression, perhaps in behavior that is not obviously passive, during adolescence and adulthood.

The reasons for the "sleeper effect" of certain behaviors by mothers are more complicated. A highly critical maternal attitude toward daughters before the age of three predicted adult achievement behavior, but a critical maternal attitude toward daughters from three to six and from six to ten showed a negligible relation to achievement behavior in adult women. Similarly, maternal protection of a daughter during infancy predicted adult withdrawal from stress, but protectiveness from three to six and from six to ten showed no relation to adult withdrawal.

One explanation for these results rests on the fact that the nature of the interaction between mother and child becomes more reciprocal with time. That is, the degree to which the child's actions have the power to change the mother's behavior increases with the child's age: a six-year-old is more likely to produce a major change in his mother's behavior toward him than is a two-year-old.

Beginning at the child's birth, if not before, a mother typically establishes expectations as to what her child should be like and what standards his behavior should meet. The greater the discrepancy between her expectations and her evaluation of the child's behavior, the greater the likelihood that she will exert pressure of some sort on the child in an attempt to bring his behavior into line with her expectations. During infancy the child's "personality" is fairly ambiguous, and the discrepancy between the mother's standard and what she perceives in the child is necessarily small. The mother sees the child as she would like to see him; he is primarily an object to be acted upon. Her behavior toward the infant, therefore, is relatively uncontaminated by the child's own behavior. With a ten-year-old, things are likely to be different. To illustrate, a mother's concern with the intellectual achievement of her two-year-old (dissatisfaction with his verbal development, for example) is likely to be based primarily on her own needs and values, whereas a critical attitude toward the academic performance of a ten-year-old may be based on the fact that he is failing in school. Similarly, encouragement of independence in or overprotection toward a ten-year-old may be newly developed reactions to a child's excessive dependence or fragile defenses. Excessive permissiveness or protectiveness toward a three-year-old, on the other hand, probably reflects fundamental maternal attitudes.

Mothers who were hypercritical during the first three years were usually dissatisfied with their daughters' intellectual development and lack of autonomy. These mothers often resented the child's dependency and rewarded mastery and independence. When the child began to achieve intellectually and to behave more independently at age nine or ten, the mother became less critical: the girl's adoption of the traits valued by the mother led to a decrease in the mother's criticism of the child. Thus the high correlation between maternal hostility or protection during infancy and adult behavior in women could be due to the fact that these practices during the first three years, by comparison to similar practices at age ten, are a more sensitive index of the mother's basic attitudes toward the child and therefore of her more lasting effect on the child's developing behavior.

The maternal behaviors that showed the "sleeper effect" most clearly were protection and hostility toward infant daughters. An extremely protective attitude was characteristic of mothers who wished to infantilize their children. A critical attitude was characteristic of mothers who wanted early autonomy and independence for their daughters. The daughters of these two types of mothers developed personalities that realized their mothers' expectations. The daughters of protective mothers were, as adults, passive, afraid of social interaction, noncompetitive, and involved in traditional feminine interests. Those of critical mothers gained independence from the family at an early age and retained this orientation through adolescence into adulthood.

Without a longitudinal research design, it is difficult to pair up causes and effects that are separated by time. Longitudinal research taxes even a scientist's capacity to tolerate delay of gratification, but we believe the results of our investigation demonstrate the value of continuous study of the developing child. We need more standard measures, more rigorous theory, and perhaps a series of five- to ten-year longitudinal studies aimed at specific developmental hypotheses. With these advantages we should become more adept at wresting from nature the secrets of human development.

33

Like It Is in the Alley

R O B E R T   C O L E S

"In the alley it's mostly dark, even if the sun is out. But if you
look around, you can find things. I know how to get into every
building, except that it's like night once you're inside them, because
they don't have lights. So, I stay here. You're better off. It's no good
on the street. You can get hurt all the time, one way or the other.
And in buildings, like I told you, it's bad in them, too. But here it's
o.k. You can find your own corner, and if someone tries to move in
you fight him off. We meet here all the time, and figure out what
we'll do next. It might be a game, or over for some pool, or a coke
or something. You need to have a place to start out from, and that's
like it is in the alley; you can always know your buddy will be
there, provided it's the right time. So you go there, and you're on
your way, man."

LIKE IT IS IN THE ALLEY   Reprinted from *Dædalus* (Fall, 1968). Used by permission of the author.

Like all children of nine, Peter is always on his way—to a person, a place, a *"thing"* he wants to do. *"There's this here thing we thought we'd try tomorrow,"* he'll say; and eventually I'll find out that he means there's to be a race. He and his friends will compete with another gang to see who can wash a car faster and better. The cars belong to four youths who make their money taking bets, and selling liquor that I don't believe was ever purchased, and pushing a few of those pills that *"go classy with beer."* I am not completely sure, but I think they also have something to do with other drugs; and again, I can't quite be sure what their connection is with a "residence" I've seen not too far from the alley Peter describes so possessively. The women come and go—from that residence and along the street Peter's alley leaves.

Peter lives in the heart of what we in contemporary America have chosen (ironically, so far as history goes) to call an urban ghetto. The area was a slum before it became a ghetto, and there still are some very poor white people on its edges and increasing numbers of Puerto Ricans in several of its blocks. Peter was not born in the ghetto, nor was his family told to go there. They are Americans and have been here *"since way back before anyone can remember."* That is the way Peter's mother talks about Alabama, about the length of time she and her ancestors have lived there. She and Peter's father came north *"for freedom."* They did not seek out a ghetto, an old quarter of Boston where they were expected to live and where they would be confined, yet at least some of the time solidly at rest, with kin, and reasonably safe.

No, they sought freedom. Americans, they moved on when the going got *"real bad,"* and Americans, they expected something better someplace, some other place. They left Alabama on impulse. They found Peter's alley by accident. And they do not fear pogroms. They are Americans, and in Peter's words: *"There's likely to be another riot here soon. That's what I heard today. You hear it a lot, but one day you know it'll happen."*

Peter's mother fears riots too—among other things. The Jews of Eastern Europe huddled together in their ghettos, afraid of the barbarians, afraid of the goyim, but always sure of one thing, their God-given destiny. Peter's mother has no such faith. She believes that *"something will work out one of these days."* She believes that *"you have to keep on going, and things can get better, but don't ask me how."* She believes that *"God wants us to have a bad spell here, and so maybe it'll get better the next time—you know in Heaven, and I hope that's where we'll be going."* Peter's mother, in other words, is a pragmatist, an optimist, and a Christian. Above all she is American: *"Yes, I hear them talk about Africa, but it don't mean anything to us. All I know is Alabama and now it's in*

*Massachusetts that we are. It was a long trip coming up here, and some-
times I wish we were back there, and sometimes I'd just as soon be here,
for all that's no good about it. But I'm not going to take any more trips,
no sir. And like Peter said, this is the only country we've got. If you come
from a country, you come from it, and we're from it, I'd say, and there
isn't much we can do but try to live as best we can. I mean, live here."*

What is "life" like for her over there, where she lives, in the neighborhood she refers to as *"here"?* A question like that cannot be answered by
the likes of me, and even her answer provides only the beginning of a
reply: *"Well, we does o.k., I guess. Peter here, he has it better than I did,
or his daddy. I can say that. I tell myself that a lot. He can turn on the
faucet over there, and a lot of the time, he just gets the water, right away.
And when I tell him what it was like for us, to go fetch that water—we'd
walk three miles, yes sir, and we'd be lucky it wasn't ten—well, Peter, it
doesn't register on him. He thinks I'm trying to fool him, and the more
serious I get, the more he laughs, so I've stopped.*

*"Of course it's not all so good, I have to admit. We're still where we
were, so far as knowing where your next meal is coming from. When I go
to bed at night I tell myself I've done good, to stay alive and keep the
kids alive, and if they'll just wake up in the morning, and me too, well
then, we can worry about that, all the rest, come tomorrow. So there you
go. We do our best, and that's all you can do."*

She may sound fatalistic, but she appears to be a nervous, hardworking,
even hard-driven woman—thin, short, constantly on the move. I may not
know what she "really" thinks and believes, because like the rest of us
she has her contradictions and her mixed feelings. I think it is fair to say
that there are some things that she can't say to me—or to herself. She is a
Negro, and I am white. She is poor, and I am fairly well off. She is very
near to illiterate, and I put in a lot of time worrying about how to say
things. But she and I are both human beings, and we both have trouble—
to use that word—"communicating," not only with each other, but with
ourselves. Sometimes she doesn't tell me something she really wants me to
know. She has forgotten, pure and simple. More is on her mind than information I might want. And sometimes I forget too: *"Remember you
asked the other day about Peter, if he was ever real sick. And I told you
he was a weak child, and I feared for his life, and I've lost five children,
three that was born and two that wasn't. Well, I forgot to tell you that
he got real sick up here, just after we came. He was three, and I didn't
know what to do. You see, I didn't have my mother to help out. She
always knew what to do. She could hold a child and get him to stop crying, no matter how sick he was, and no matter how much he wanted food,
and we didn't have it. But she was gone—and that's when we left to come*

up here, and I never would have left her, not for anything in the world. But suddenly she took a seizure of something and went in a half hour, I'd say. And Peter, he was so hot and sick, I thought he had the same thing his grandmother did and he was going to die. I thought maybe she's calling him. She always liked Peter. She helped him be born, she and my cousin, they did."

Actually, Peter's mother remembers quite a lot of things. She remembers the "old days" back South, sometimes with a shudder, but sometimes with the same nostalgia that the region is famous for generating in its white exiles. She also notices a lot of things. She notices, and from time to time will remark upon, the various changes in her life. She has moved from the country to the city. Her father was a sharecropper and her son wants to be a pilot (sometimes), a policeman (sometimes), a racing-car driver (sometimes), and a baseball player (most of the time). Her husband is not alive. He died one year after they all came to Boston. He woke up vomiting in the middle of the night—vomiting blood. He bled and bled and vomited and vomited and then he died. The doctor does not have to press very hard for "the facts." Whatever is known gets spoken vividly and (still) emotionally: *"I didn't know what to do. I was beside myself. I prayed and I prayed, and in between I held his head and wiped his forehead. It was the middle of the night. I woke up my oldest girl and I told her to go knocking on the doors. But no one would answer. They must have been scared, or have suspected something bad. I thought if only he'd be able to last into the morning, then we could get some help. I was caught between things. I couldn't leave him to go get a policeman. And my girl, she was afraid to go out. And besides, there was no one outside, and I thought we'd just stay at his side, and somehow he'd be o.k., because he was a strong man, you know. His muscles, they were big all his life. Even with the blood coming up, he looked too big and strong to die, I thought. But I knew he was sick. He was real bad sick. There wasn't anything else, no sir, to do. We didn't have no phone and even if there was a car, I never could have used it. Nor my daughter. And then he took a big breath and that was his last one."*

When I first met Peter and his mother, I wanted to know how they lived, what they did with their time, what they liked to do or disliked doing, what they believed. In the back of my mind were large subjects like "the connection between a person's moods and the environment in which he lives." Once I was told I was studying "the psychology of the ghetto," and another time the subject of "urban poverty and mental health." It is hoped that at some point large issues like those submit themselves to lives; and when that is done, when particular but not unrepresentative or unusual human beings are called in witness, their concrete medical history becomes extremely revealing. I cannot think of a better way to begin knowing what life is like for Peter and his mother than to hear the following and hear it again and think about its implications: *"No sir, Peter has never been to a doctor, not unless you count the one at school, and she's a nurse I believe. He was his sickest back home before we came here, and you know there was no doctor for us in the county. In Alabama you have to pay a white doctor first, before he'll go near you. And we don't have but a few colored ones. (I've never seen a one.) There was this woman we'd go to, and she had gotten some nursing education in Mobile. (No, I don't know if she was a nurse or not, or a helper to the nurses, maybe.) Well, she would come to help us. With the convulsions, she'd show you how to hold the child, and make sure he doesn't hurt himself. They can bite their tongues real, real bad.*

"Here, I don't know what to do. There's the city hospital, but it's no good for us. I went there with my husband, no sooner than a month or so after we came up here. We waited and waited, and finally the day was almost over. We left the kids with a neighbor, and we barely knew her. I said it would take the morning, but I never thought we'd get home near suppertime. And they wanted us to come back and come back, because it was something they couldn't do all at once—though for most of the time we just sat there and did nothing. And my husband, he said his stomach was the worse for going there, and he'd take care of himself from now on, rather than go there.

"Maybe they could have saved him. But they're far away, and I didn't have the money to get a cab, even if there was one around here, and I thought to myself it'll make him worse, to take him there.

"My kids, they get sick. The welfare worker, she sends a nurse here, and she tells me we should be on vitamins and the kids need all kinds of check-ups. Once she took my daughter and told her she had to have her teeth looked at, and the same with Peter. So, I went with my daughter, and they didn't see me that day, but said they could in a couple of weeks. And I had to pay the woman next door to mind the little ones, and there was the carfare, and we sat and sat, like before. So, I figured, it would take more than we've got to see that dentist. And when the nurse told us we'd have to come back a few times—that's how many, a few—I thought that no one ever looked at my teeth, and they're not good, I'll admit, but you can't have everything, that's what I say, and that's what my kids have to know, I guess."

What *does* she have? And what belongs to Peter? For one thing, there is the apartment, three rooms for six people, a mother and five children. Peter is a middle child with two older girls on one side and a younger sister and still younger brother on the other side. The smallest child was born in Boston: *"It's the only time I ever spent time in a hospital. He's the only one to be born there. My neighbor got the police. I was in the hall, crying I guess. We almost didn't make it. They told me I had bad blood pressure, and I should have been on pills, and I should come back, but I didn't. It was the worst time I've ever had, because I was alone. My husband had to stay with the kids, and no one was there to visit me."*

Peter sleeps with his brother in one bedroom. The three girls sleep in the living room, which is a bedroom. And, of course, there is a small kitchen. There is not very much furniture about. The kitchen has a table with four chairs, only two of which are sturdy. The girls sleep in one big bed. Peter shares his bed with his brother. The mother sleeps on a couch. There is one more chair and a table in the living room. Jesus looks down from the living room wall, and an undertaker's calendar hangs on the kitchen wall. The apartment has no books, no records. There is a television set in the living room, and I have never seen it off.

Peter in many respects is his father's successor. His mother talks things over with him. She even defers to him at times. She will say something; he will disagree; she will nod and let him have the last word. He knows the city. She still feels a stranger to the city. *"If you want to know about anything around here, just ask Peter,"* she once said to me. That was three years ago, when Peter was six. Peter continues to do very poorly at school, but I find him a very good teacher. He notices a lot, makes a lot of sense when he talks, and has a shrewd eye for the ironic detail. He is very intelligent, for all the trouble he gives his teachers. He recently summed up a lot of American history for me: *"I wasn't made for that school, and that school wasn't made for me."* It is an old school, filled with memories. The name of the school evokes Boston's Puritan past. Pictures and statues adorn the corridors—reminders of the soldiers and statesmen and writers who made New England so influential in the nineteenth century. And naturally one finds slogans on the walls, about freedom and democracy and the rights of the people. Peter can be surly and cynical when he points all that out to the visitor. If he is asked what kind of school he would *like*, he laughs incredulously. *"Are you kidding? No school would be my first choice. They should leave us alone, and let us help out at home, and maybe let some of our own people teach us. The other day the teacher admitted she was no good. She said maybe a Negro should come in an give us the discipline, because she was scared. She said all she wanted from us was that we keep quiet and stop wearing her nerves down, and she'd be grateful, because she would retire soon. She said we were becoming too much for her, and she didn't understand why. But when one kid wanted to say something, tell her why, she told us to keep still, and write something. You know what? She whipped out a book and told us to copy a whole page from it, so we'd learn it. A stupid waste of time. I didn't even try, and she didn't care. She just wanted an excuse not to talk with us. They're all alike."*

Actually, they're all *not* alike, and Peter knows it. He has met up with two fine teachers, and in mellow moments he can say so: *"They're trying hard, but me and my friends, I don't think we're cut out for school. To tell the truth, that's what I think. My mother says we should try, anyway, but it doesn't seem to help, trying. The teacher can't understand a lot of us, but he does all these new things, and you can see he's excited. Some kids are really with him, and I am, too. But I can't take all his stuff very serious. He's a nice man, and he says he wants to come and visit every one of our homes, but my mother says no, she wouldn't know what to do with him, when he came here. We'd just stand and have nothing to talk about. So she said tell him not to come, and I don't think he will, anyway. I think he's getting to know."*

What is that teacher getting to know? What *is* there to know about Peter and all the others like him in our American cities? Of course Peter and his friends who play in the alley need better schools, schools they can feel to be theirs, and better teachers, like the ones they *have* in fact met on occasion. But I do not feel that a reasonably good teacher in the finest school building in America would reach and affect Peter in quite the way, I suppose, people like me would expect and desire. At nine Peter is both young and quite old. At nine he is much wiser about many things than my sons will be at nine, and maybe nineteen. Peter has in fact taught me a lot about his neighborhood, about life on the streets, about survival: *"I get up when I get up, no special time. My mother has Alabama in her. She gets up with the sun, and she wants to go to bed when it gets dark. I try to tell her that up here things just get started in the night. But she gets mad. She wakes me up. If it weren't for her shaking me, I might sleep until noon. Sometimes we have a good breakfast, when the check comes. Later on, though,* before *it comes, it might just be some coffee and a slice of bread. She worries about food. She says we should eat what she gives us, but sometimes I'd rather go hungry. I was sick a long time ago, my stomach or something—maybe like my father, she says. So I don't like all the potatoes she pushes on us and cereal, all the time cereal. We're supposed to be lucky, because we get some food every day. Down South they can't be sure. That's what she says, and I guess she's right.*

"Then I go to school. I eat what I can, and leave. I have two changes of clothes, one for everyday and one for Sunday. I wait on my friend Billy, and we're off by 8:15. He's from around here, and he's a year older. He knows everything. He can tell you if a woman is high on some stuff,

or if she's been drinking, or she's off her mind about something. He knows. His brother has a convertible, a Buick. He pays off the police, but Billy won't say no more than that.

"In school we waste time until it's over. I do what I have to. I don't like the place. I feel like falling off all day, just putting my head down and saying good-bye to everyone until three. We're out then, and we sure wake up. I don't have to stop home first, not now. I go with Billy. We'll be in the alley, or we'll go to see them play pool. Then you know when it's time to go home. You hear someone say six o'clock, and you go in. I eat and I watch television. It must be around ten or eleven I'm in bed."

Peter sees rats all the time. He has been bitten by them. He has a big stick by his bed to use against them. They also claim the alley, even in the daytime. They are not large enough to be compared with cats, as some observers have insisted; they are simply large, confident, well-fed, unafraid rats. The garbage is theirs; the land is theirs; the tenement is theirs; human flesh is theirs. When I first started visiting Peter's family, I wondered why they didn't do something to rid themselves of those rats, and the cockroaches, and the mosquitoes, and the flies, and the maggots, and the ants, and especially the garbage in the alley which attracts so much of all that "lower life." Eventually I began to see some of the reasons why. A large apartment building with many families has exactly two barrels in its basement. The halls of the building go unlighted. Many windows have no screens, and some windows are broken and boarded up. The stairs are dangerous; some of them have missing timber. (*"We just jump over them,"* says Peter cheerfully.) And the landowner is no one in particular. Rent is collected by an agent, in the name of a "realty trust." Somewhere in City Hall there is a bureaucrat who unquestionably might be persuaded to prod someone in the "trust"; and one day I went with three of the tenants, including Peter's mother, to try that "approach." We waited and waited at City Hall. (I drove us there, clear across town, naturally.) Finally we met up with a man, a not very encouraging or inspiring or generous or friendly man. He told us we would have to try yet another department and swear out a complaint, and that the "case" would have to be "studied," and that we would then be "notified of a decision." We went to the department down the hall, and waited some more, another hour and ten minutes. By then it was three o'clock, and the mothers wanted to go home. They weren't thinking of rats anymore, or poorly heated apartments, or garbage that had nowhere to go and often went uncollected for two weeks, not one. They were thinking of their children, who would be home from school and, in the case of two women, their husbands who would also soon be home. *"Maybe we should come back some other day,"* Peter's mother said. I noted she didn't say *tomorrow,* and I realized that I had read someplace that people like her aren't precisely "future-oriented."

Actually, both Peter and his mother have a very clear idea of what is ahead. For the mother it is *"more of the same."* One evening she was tired but unusually talkative, perhaps because a daughter of hers was sick: *"I'm glad to be speaking about all these things tonight. My little girl has a bad fever. I've been trying to cool her off all day. Maybe if there was a place near here, that we could go to, maybe I would have gone. But like it is, I have to do the best I can and pray she'll be o.k."*

I asked whether she thought her children would find things different, and that's when she said it would be *"more of the same"* for them. Then she added a long afterthought: *"Maybe it'll be a little better for them. A mother has to have hope for her children, I guess. But I'm not too sure, I'll admit. Up here you know there's a lot more jobs around than in Alabama. We don't get them, but you know they're someplace near, and they tell you that if you go train for them, then you'll be eligible. So maybe Peter might someday have some real good steady work, and that would be something, yes sir it would. I keep telling him he should pay more attention to school, and put more of himself into the lessons they give there. But he says no, it's no good; it's a waste of time; they don't care what happens there, only if the kids don't keep quiet and mind themselves. Well, Peter has got to learn to mind himself, and not be fresh. He speaks back to me, these days. There'll be a time he won't even speak to me at all, I suppose. I used to blame it all on the city up here, city living. Back home we were always together, and there wasn't no place you could go, unless to Birmingham, and you couldn't do much for yourself there, we all knew. Of course, my momma, she knew how to make us behave. But I was thinking the other night, it wasn't so good back there either. Colored people, they'd beat on one another, and we had lot of people that liquor was eating away at them; they'd use wine by the gallon. All they'd do was work on the land, and then go back and kill themselves with wine. And then there'd be the next day—until they'd one evening go to sleep and never wake up. And we'd get the Bossman and he'd see to it they got buried.*

"Up here I think it's better, but don't ask me to tell you why. There's the welfare, that's for sure. And we get our water and if there isn't good heat, at least there's some. Yes, it's cold up here, but we had cold down there, too, only then we didn't have any heat, and we'd just die, some of us would, every winter with one of those freezing spells.

"And I do believe things are changing. On the television they talk to you, the colored man and all the others who aren't doing so good. My boy

Peter, he says they're putting you on. That's all he sees, people 'putting on' other people. But I think they all mean it, the white people. I never see them, except on television, when they say the white man wants good for the colored people. I think Peter could go and do better for himself later on, when he gets older, except for the fact that he just doesn't believe. He don't believe what they say, the teacher, or the man who says it's getting better for us—on television. I guess it's my fault. I never taught my children, any of them, to believe that kind of thing; because I never thought we'd ever have it any different, not in this life. So maybe I've failed Peter. I told him the other day, he should work hard, because of all the 'opportunity' they say is coming for us, and he said I was talking good, but where was my proof. So I went next door with him, to my neighbor's, and we asked her husband, and you know he sided with Peter. He said they were taking a few here and a few there, and putting them in the front windows of all the big companies, but that all you have to do is look around at our block and you'd see all the young men, and they just haven't got a thing to do. Nothing."

Her son also looks to the future. Sometimes he talks—in his own words —"big." He'll one day be a bombardier or "*something like that.*" At other times he is less sure of things: "*I don't know what I'll be. Maybe nothing. I see the men sitting around, hiding from the welfare lady. They fool her. Maybe I'll fool her, too. I don't know what you can do. The teacher the other day said that if just one of us turned out o.k. she'd congratulate herself and call herself lucky.*"

A while back a riot excited Peter and his mother, excited them and frightened them. The spectacle of the police being fought, of white-owned property being assaulted, stirred the boy a great deal: "*I figured the whole world might get changed around. I figured people would treat us better from now on. Only I don't think they will.*" As for his mother, she was less hopeful, but even more apocalyptic: "*I told Peter we were going to pay for this good. I told him they wouldn't let us get away with it, not later on.*" And in the midst of the trouble she was frightened as she had never before been: "*I saw them running around on the streets, the men and women, and they were talking about burning things down, and how there'd be nothing left when they got through. I sat there with my children and I thought we might die the way things are going, die right here. I didn't know what to do: if I should leave, in case they burn down the building, or if I should stay, so that the police don't arrest us, or we get mixed up with the crowd of people. I've never seen so many people, going in so many different directions. They were running and shouting and they didn't know what to do. They were so excited. My neighbor, she said they'd burn us all up, and then the white man would have himself one less of a headache. The colored man is a worse enemy to himself than the white. I mean, it's hard to know which is the worst."*

I find it as hard as she does to sort things out. When I think of her and the mothers like her I have worked with for years, when I think of Peter and his friends, I find myself caught between the contradictory observations I have made. Peter already seems a grim and unhappy child. He trusts no one white, not his white teacher, not the white policeman he sees, not the white welfare worker, not the white storekeeper, and not, I might add, me. There we are, the five of us from the 180,000,000 Americans who surround him and of course 20,000,000 others. Yet, Peter doesn't really trust his friends and neighbors, either. At nine he has learned to be careful, wary, guarded, doubtful, and calculating. His teacher may not know it, but Peter is a good sociologist, and a good political scientist, a good student of urban affairs. With devastating accuracy he can reveal how much of the "score" he knows; yes, and how fearful and sad and angry he is: *"This here city isn't for us. It's for the people downtown. We're here because, like my mother said, we had to come. If they could lock us up or sweep us away, they would. That's why I figure the only way you can stay ahead is get some kind of deal for yourself. If I had a choice I'd live someplace else, but I don't know where. It would be a place where they treated you right, and they didn't think you were some nuisance. But the only thing you can do is be careful of yourself; if not, you'll get killed somehow, like it happened to my father."*

His father died prematurely, and most probably, unnecessarily. Among the poor of our cities the grim medical statistics we all know about become terrible daily experiences. Among the black and white families I work with—in nearby but separate slums—disease and the pain that goes with it are taken for granted. When my children complain of an earache or demonstrate a skin rash I rush them to the doctor. When I have a headache, I take an aspirin; and if the headache is persistent, I can always get a medical check-up. Not so with Peter's mother and Peter; they have learned to live with sores and infections and poorly mended fractures and bad teeth and eyes that need but don't have the help of glasses. Yes, they can go to a city hospital and get free care; but again and again they don't. They come to the city without any previous experience as patients. They have never had the money to purchase a doctor's time. They have never had free medical care available. (I am speaking now of Appalachian whites as well as southern blacks.) It may comfort me to know that every American city provides some free medical services for its "indigent," but Peter's mother and thousands like her have quite a different view of things: *"I said to you the other time, I've tried there. It's like at City Hall, you wait and wait, and they pushes you and shove you and call your name, only to tell you to wait some more, and if you tell them you can't stay there all day, they'll say 'lady, go home, then.' You get sick just trying to get there. You have to give your children over to people or take them all with you; and the carfare is expensive. Why if we had a doctor around here, I could almost pay him with the carfare it takes to get there and back for all of us. And you know, they keep on having you come back and back, and they don't know what each other says. Each time they starts from scratch."*

It so happens that recently I took Peter to a children's hospital and arranged for a series of evaluations which led to the following: a pair of glasses; a prolonged bout of dental work; antibiotic treatment for skin lesions; a thorough cardiac work-up with the subsequent diagnosis of rheumatic heart disease; a conference between Peter's mother and a nutritionist, because the boy has been on a high-starch, low-protein, and low-vitamin diet all his life. He suffers from one attack of sinus trouble after another, from a succession of sore throats and earaches, from cold upon cold, even in the summer. A running nose is unsurprising to him—and so is chest pain and shortness of breath, due to a heart ailment, we now know.

At the same time Peter is tough. I have to emphasize again *how* tough and, yes, how "politic, cautious and meticulous," not in Prufrock's way, but in another way and for other reasons. Peter has learned to be wary as well as angry; tentative as well as extravagant; at times controlled and only under certain circumstances defiant: *"Most of the time, I think you have to watch your step. That's what I think. That's the difference between up here and down in the South. That's what my mother says, and she's right. I don't remember it down there, but I know she must be right. Here, you measure the next guy first and then make your move when you think it's a good time to."*

He was talking about *"how you get along"* when you leave school and go *"mix with the guys"* and start *"getting your deal."* He was telling me what an outrageous and unsafe world he has inherited and how very carefully he has made his appraisal of the future. Were I afflicted with some of his physical complaints, I would be fretful, annoyed, petulant, angry—and moved to do something, see someone, get a remedy, a pill, a promise of help. He has made his "adjustment" to the body's pain, and he has also learned to contend with the alley and the neighborhood and *us*, the world beyond: *"The cops come by here all the time. They drive up and down the street. They want to make sure everything is o.k. to look at. They don't bother you, so long as you don't get in their way."*

So, it is live and let live—except that families like Peter's have a tough time living, and of late have been troubling those cops, among others. Our cities have become not only battlegrounds, but places where all sorts of American problems and historical ironies have converged. Ailing, poorly fed, and proud Appalachian families have reluctantly left the hollows of eastern Kentucky and West Virginia for Chicago and Dayton and Cincinnati and Cleveland and Detroit, and even, I have found, Boston. They stick close together in all-white neighborhoods—or enclaves or sections or slums or ghettos or whatever. They wish to go home but can't, unless they are willing to be idle and hungry all the time. They confuse social workers and public officials of all kinds because they both want and reject the city. Black families also have sought out cities and learned to feel frightened and disappointed.

I am a physician, and over the past ten years I have been asking myself how people like Peter and his mother survive in mind and body and spirit. And I have wanted to know what a twentieth-century American city "means" to them or "does" to them. People cannot be handed questionnaires and asked to answer such questions. They cannot be "interviewed" a few times and told to come across with a statement, a reply. But inside Peter and his brother and his sisters and his mother, and inside a number of Appalachian mothers and fathers and children I know, are feelings and thoughts and ideas—which, in my experience, come out casually or suddenly, by accident almost. After a year or two of talking, after experiences such as I have briefly described in a city hall, in a children's hospital, a lifetime of pent-up tensions and observation comes to blunt expression: *"Down in Alabama we had to be careful about ourselves with the white man, but we had plenty of things we could do by ourselves. There was our side of town, and you could walk and run all over, and we had a garden you know. Up here they have you in a cage. There's no place to go, and all I do is stay in the building all day long and the night, too. I don't use my legs no more, hardly at all. I never see those trees, and my oldest girl, she misses planting time. It was bad down there. We had to leave. But it's no good here, too, I'll tell you. Once I woke up and I thought all the buildings on the block were falling down on me. And I was trying to climb out, but I couldn't. And then the next thing I knew, we were all back South, and I was standing near some sunflowers—you know, the tall ones that can shade you if you sit down.*

"No, I don't dream much. I fall into a heavy sleep as soon as I touch the bed. The next thing I know I'm stirring myself to start in all over in the morning. It used to be the sun would wake me up, but now it's up in my head, I guess. I know I've got to get the house going and off to school."

Her wistful, conscientious, law-abiding devoutly Christian spirit hasn't completely escaped the notice of Peter, for all his hardheaded, cynical protestations: *"If I had a chance, I'd like to get enough money to bring us all back to Alabama for a visit. Then I could prove it that it may be good down there, a little bit, even if it's no good, either. Like she says, we had to get out of there or we'd be dead by now. I hear say we all may get killed soon, it's so bad here; but I think we did right to get up here, and if we make them listen to us, the white man, maybe he will."*

To which Peter's mother adds: *"We've carried a lot of trouble in us, from way back in the beginning. I have these pains, and so does everyone around here. But you can't just die until you're ready to. And I do believe something is happening. I do believe I see that."*

To which Peter adds: *"Maybe it won't be that we'll win, but if we get killed, everyone will hear about it. Like the minister said, before we used to die real quiet, and no one stopped to pay notice."*

Two years before Peter spoke those words he drew a picture for me, one of many he has done. When he was younger, and when I didn't know him so well as I think I do now, it was easier for us to have something tangible to do and then talk about. I used to visit the alley with him, as I still do, and one day I asked him to draw the alley. That was a good idea, he thought. (Not all of my suggestions were, however.) He started in, then stopped, and finally worked rather longer and harder than usual at the job. I busied myself with my own sketches, which from the start he insisted I do. Suddenly from across the table I heard him say he was through. Ordinarily he would slowly turn the drawing around for me to see; and I would get up and walk over to his side of the table, to see even better. But he didn't move his paper, and I didn't move myself. I saw what he had drawn, and he saw me looking. I was surprised and a bit stunned and more than a bit upset, and surely he saw my face and heard my utter silence. Often I would break the awkward moments when neither of us seemed to have anything to say, but this time it was his turn to do so: *"You know what it is?"* He knew that I liked us to talk about our work. I said no, I didn't—though in fact the vivid power of his black crayon had come right across to me. *"It's that hole we dug in the alley. I made it bigger here. If you fall into it, you can't get out. You die."*

He had drawn circles within circles, all of them black, and then a center, also black. He had imposed an X on the center. Nearby, strewn across the circles, were fragments of the human body—two faces, an arm, five legs. And after I had taken the scene in, I could only think to myself that I had been shown *"like it is in the alley"*—by an intelligent boy who knew what he saw around him, could give it expression, and, I am convinced, would respond to a different city, a city that is alive and breathing, one that is not for many of its citizens a virtual morgue.

Social
Psychology

One of the basic differences between men and animals is that men have beliefs and attitudes that guide their actions. Man's behavior is strongly influenced by what he believes, and what he believes is strongly influenced by the beliefs and actions of others around him. Some beliefs and attitudes are learned during early childhood and tend to last a long time; others are specific to particular occasions. Two important concerns of social psychology are how attitudes are learned and how they control behavior in various situations.

One might think that the current American near-obsession with sex would have led to a homogenization of attitudes toward sexuality and to a corresponding uniformity in patterns of sexual behavior, but it has not. In "Patterns of Sexual Behavior in Three Ethnic Groups," Bernard Rosenberg and Joseph Bensman point out that members of the American middle class who consider themselves regrettably inhibited sometimes make up romantic fantasies about the free, joyful sexual expressiveness of the so-called culture of poverty. They describe a series of interviews with adolescent boys from three ethnic groups living in urban ghettos: Appalachian whites in Chicago, Puerto Ricans in New York, and blacks in Washington, D.C. The sexual behavior and attitudes of the three groups, they found, differ considerably from those of the middle class, but no more than they differ from each other. Many of the boys in all three groups had a surprising amount of misinformation about the basic facts of reproduction, and their behavior and attitudes showed a considerable amount of hostility and fearfulness. Their sex lives seem to have little of the spontaneous, Garden-of-Eden quality for which the middle class longs.

In "Bystander 'Apathy,' " Bibb Latané and John M. Darley describe an ingenious series of experiments based on the behavior of witnesses to the murder of Kitty Genovese several years ago in New York. In the middle of the night, Miss Genovese was attacked repeatedly and finally killed, while thirty-eight of her Kew Gardens neighbors watched in fascination from their apartment windows. They did nothing to help. At the time, most people attributed the unresponsiveness of the witnesses to "alienation" and to the loss of a "sense of community" brought on by life in a large city. The evidence gathered by Latané and Darley suggests that although a person is less likely to help in an emergency if other people are present, he does not fail to act because of apathy or a vague sense of alienation. Instead, a person is less likely to interpret an event as an emergency when he is part of a group than when he is alone. Furthermore, if he does recognize the event as an emergency, he feels less personal responsibility for intervening. The insight this series of experiments offers into the helping behavior of people in groups is badly needed, especially in a society where the population grows denser every day.

34

Patterns of Sexual Behavior
in Three Ethnic Groups

BERNARD ROSENBERG
JOSEPH BENSMAN

Like speech, dress, manners, and a score of other practices, sexual conduct has always been class-bound. For example, the Victorian double standard, which prescribed chastity and fidelity for women but allowed premarital and extramarital sex for men, was mainly an upper-middle-class phenomenon. Similarly, the revolt against it seems to have liberated mostly members of the middle class from sexual repression, or at least from the idea of it. And as Theodore Dreiser noted in his novels, the blue-collar working class has long been identified with prudery and sexual hypocrisy.

Romantic writers, artists, and social scientists, searching for "genuine" or "natural" sexuality, have often idealized peasants, primitive

PATTERNS OF SEXUAL BEHAVIOR IN THREE ETHNIC GROUPS Adapted from *Annals of the American Academy of Political and Social Science* (March, 1968). Used by permission of the authors and the American Academy of Political and Social Science. This article originally appeared under the title "Sexual patterns in three ethnic subcultures of an American underclass."

islanders, and others who—when viewed from a safe distance—look sexually spontaneous, unalienated, and free and easy in all their ways. Are there such groups of people within our own society? And do they form, perhaps, a single "culture of poverty"?

The discussion that follows is based on interviews with a number of adolescent boys and a few girls living in impoverished areas in three cities, Chicago, New York City, and Washington, D.C. In Chicago, almost all the subjects were Appalachian whites; in New York, Puerto Ricans; in Washington, blacks. The three groups had very different backgrounds, though all consisted largely of recent migrants from other parts of the United States (including Puerto Rico). We found that their sexual patterns, as revealed by overt behavior and attitudes and reflected in the language used to describe them, differ from those of the American middle class, but no more sharply than they differ from one group to another.

Chicago

Dating is often thought to be a general American phenomenon, part of the "standard" courtship pattern. In our samplings, however, only the Appalachian whites were consistently familiar with the word. Their dating practices were similar in some ways to those of their middle-class counterparts, but there were also some important differences. The telephone, for instance, played no great part in their activities, as it does among more privileged adolescents, but the automobile was central. (Neither is used much by lower-class Puerto Ricans or blacks.)

The Chicago boys would go to great lengths to get a car, sometimes stealing one in order to commit other crimes. They had a great deal more physical mobility than any other economically deprived group we have studied. In a crisis occasioned, say, by the impregnation of a girl (not a rare occurrence), they often took to the road, ranging widely over Illinois and nearby states. The automobile liberated them, up to a point, not only from their constricted neighborhood but from the city as a whole. They also used the car as a "portable bedroom," at drive-in movies, for example.

Two or three couples often went to a drive-in, a bowling alley, or a roller-skating rink together. This preference for double-dating is superficially similar to early dating patterns among middle-class adolescents, but the reasons behind it are quite different. A strong streak of violence ran through the sex lives of the Appalachian whites in our sample, and the presence of another couple offered protection: "I like to go out with other couples because it's better when you travel together. When you're alone, there's always other guys trying to start trouble." Having someone else along might also prove useful later on:

> I was going with a girl. She was sixteen. She squealed on me, and they tried to get me on statutory rape. And, oh, she gave them a big, long story, trying to get me into a lot of trouble. But there was another kid along with me on the date. And she claimed that he held her down and that I held her down. But this boy's stories matched and hers didn't. Otherwise, I would have been sunk.

Boys showed a measure of respect to the girls they dated—who might, after all, become their wives—but they treated other girls and older women as sexual objects. The following statement is an apt, though somewhat extreme, illustration of the puritanical distinction between "good" girls and "bad":

> I consider a girl you go out with and a girl you have intercourse with two different kinds of girls. There's a girl I date. I like to hold hands with her, and make out with her, kiss her, but that's as far as I want to go with any girl I take out. If I like the girl, I don't want to mess her up. But then, there is the other girls I just don't care about because they give it to the other guys—which means they don't care too much for theirselves.

Asked whether he still considered girls decent if they had intercourse with him, another Chicago boy said:

> It's a matter of how hard I have to work. If I have to work real hard I think a lot of them. If they give it to me right off I think they're pigs.

Unquestioning submission to male authority was expected of a wife, however.

> "What if you married a girl who talked back to you? What would you do?"
> "Shut her up."
> "How?"
> "Well, I'd fix her where she wasn't able to talk much."

The usual answer to the question "What would you do if the woman you married was unfaithful?" was "Beat the shit out of her." (Appalachian girls in Chicago stressed the necessity of female adjustment in marriage. They hoped for husbands who would not be unfaithful, would not drink, would be "nice," and would "work hard.") Thus the possibility of violence is always present, after marriage as well as before and with "good" girls as well as "bad." It is revealing that the word the Chicago adolescents typically used for the sex act was "cut."

New York City

Among Puerto Rican adolescents in New York, the word "cutting" is not used. Instead there is "scheming"—a word that has mildly conspiratorial instead of sadistic overtones. "Scheming" stands for everything from kissing to intercourse; it is secret, exploitative, and pleasurable, but seldom brutal.

Scheming begins at parties, called sets, held in someone's apartment or in a vacant apartment on the block. Twenty or so boys and girls meet, play records, dance, drink beer and whisky more or less moderately, smoke cigarettes and pot more or less immoderately, and, under dim colored lights, begin to scheme. Soon a man steps outside with his girl and schemes in the hallway, or at her place if no one is home, or on a rooftop. And:

> "If you got a really good friend, and the girl is willing, if she's really bad off or something, you know what she will do? She'll pull the train."
> "Pull the train?"
> "Yes, that's what we call it: pulling the train. You take one chance. Then another guy takes a chance. You know."
> "Usually, how many guys are there?"
> "Two."
> "Not like ten guys with one girl?"
> "Oh, depends on what kind of girl . . . I been in a situation with about six guys."

"Pulling the train" was not a common occurrence in the New York Puerto Rican group. Sets were. Informal parties semi-secretly arranged by those who go to them, they provided a way to get away from official organizations and affairs sponsored by benevolent adults. They were a place to prepare for scheming, which usually meant private and clandestine sexual activity. Most boys were willing to boast about sexual conquests, but they were reluctant to name names and thus "cause trouble" for themselves or their girl friends. Sets, which people begin going to at about age fifteen, were considered somewhat illicit. They sometimes become pot parties or sex parties, and either one, if publicized, can lead to unpleasantness.

Washington, D.C.

Boy-girl relationships among the poor blacks we studied in Washington were neither as car- and movie-centered as in the Chicago white group nor as party-centered as in the New York Puerto Rican group. In Washington, the school, despite its deficiencies, was much more important than one would have supposed. Young people attended school dances now and then, met classmates formally and informally, and "went out" with one another. Soon there was sex play and, in many cases, sexual intercourse.

Relationships tended to begin at school. Here, too, the "facts of life" were transmitted most frequently and most effectively. Only in the Washington sample did high school children use technical (though sometimes garbled) scientific terms for the sex act and the sex organs. They described human reproduction as it had been explained to them by their biology teachers:

> We had it in school. I know how the sperms come down, when a boy is having sex relations with a girl; they meet in the egg, go up through the vagina, stay in the womb and grow month after month. And then after a period of time, the woman have a baby.

And:

> Well, I know the process of starting—I mean, you have to have two unions, I mean a fusion of, uh, male and female, between the two organs. I mean the vulva and the, um, penis. And, um, it takes a union of sperm and meeting with the egg. And after that, I know the situation of —what do you call it?—the embry—yeah, embry—and that's the first stage of the child. . . . And the food which the child receives comes from the navel of the mother. It's connected to the child, I believe mouth-to-navel, something like that. And after a nine-month period, the child's supposed to be born.

These teen-agers showed a degree of sophistication not found in their counterparts from New York and Chicago, where sexual knowledge was more likely to be gotten in colloquial language from peers than from the classroom. In all three groups it was rare for children to seek information about sex from their parents or for parents to offer it. One girl in Washington, the mother of two illegitimate children, said that she had matured early and at age twelve had been followed home from school by one man and propositioned by another. Although her mother knew of both incidents, she did not talk to the girl about them, and the daughter observed, "I just could not bring myself to look up at my mother and ask her what was happening." Her knowledge of sex came from experience with "fellows" and from other girls and her older sister.

On the other hand, one boy in the Washington group had been encouraged by his father to become the sex partner of an older woman:

> She [the older woman] came down to see my sister, and she started liking me. She started paying my way to the movies and all that. So my father told me to go on and do it. So I did. . . . He say, "I know you going to do it when I ain't around." So he gave me a protector, and I go on and do it. . . . I ain't never used the protection, though.

Birth Control, Pregnancy, and Marriage

Although he might confuse protection against venereal disease with protection against pregnancy, the average black adolescent from the Washington group knew more about contraception than the average adolescent in the New York or Chicago group. He more often recognized and used such terms as contraceptive, diaphragm, coil, prophylactic, and rubber, because he more often knew what they meant. However, neither he nor his girl friend was much inclined to use any of these devices. A minority in all three groups favored contraception; it might be said that the blacks understood best, and the Puerto Ricans least, just what it was that they declined to use.

All three groups tended to see sexual fulfillment as a physical release in which the female is a necessary but unequal partner. Feelings of emotional and material responsibility were not much in evidence; neither was their opposite, pure joy in unrestrained sexuality. Among the Chicago whites, there was a degree of egocentricity unequaled in New York or Washington. Here is an extreme but not atypical example:

> "Do you ever use contraceptives?"
> "Nope."
> "How about women? Do they ever use anything?"
> "Nope."
> "Are you afraid of what might happen?"
> "Nope. They can't touch me. I'm under age."

When this boy comes of age, his concern with legal jeopardy will probably lead him to prefer sexual relations with older women so that he can avoid possible charges of statutory rape. Told by the interviewer about diaphragms and how they work, he strongly objected to the idea on the ground that they "might get in my way." Another boy, explaining why he never uses a condom (or anything else), said "I tried it once. It's like riding a horse with a saddle instead of bareback."

Besides interfering with pleasure, contraceptives cost money. The Appalachian whites in Chicago were markedly more reluctant to spend money on contraceptive frills than were the Puerto Ricans in New York or the blacks in Washington, although the poverty of the three groups was about equal. One boy explained this indirectly, as follows:

> Oh, I've used them a couple of times. Like one time, a broad got all worried, and she told us to lay off. . . . We had her pants off and everything. She asked me if I didn't have some rubbers. Uh-uh. "Get off." I had to wait a little longer. I didn't have any money, either.

How much responsibility does a boy feel if his girl becomes pregnant? The Puerto Ricans of New York and the blacks of Washington felt some; the whites of Chicago, virtually none. In the Chicago group, there was a minimum of anxiety about the consequences of sexual intercourse. Most boys were unconcerned about whether their partners used a contraceptive—"I don't care if they do or not"—and poorly informed about what girls might do to protect against pregnancy:

> Well there's with the hot water, like that. Then, there's, they press on their stomach someplace . . . on some cords, usually when you get done, the girl has to go to the bathroom. She goes in, she presses here and there, and it all comes out. They claim that's one of the best ways.

Asked "What's stopping you from knocking up girls?" one Chicago boy answered,

> "Nothing. I've got four kids, maybe five. Two here in Chicago, two in Wisconsin, and when I left Wisconsin I heard there was one more."
> "Do you support any of them?"
> "Shit no. I just take off."

The New York Puerto Rican boy was as unlikely as the Chicago Appalachian boy to use a contraceptive but less able to "take off." He worried about the possibility that a girl might become pregnant by him, not usually because he felt a direct responsibility to her (which would require a kind of socialization and internalization of standards evident among neither "good" nor "bad" boys) but because the parents might make him marry her. Unwanted marriage brought about by pregnancy was a nightmare of the New York group. When we asked the Puerto Ricans whether they would marry the girl if not forced to, most of them said no. When we asked if they would support the baby, though, they usually said yes—even if they had to quit school to do it, although "that would be pretty bad."

There was a qualitative difference among the groups on the matter of responsibility that we wish to point up. The following exchange can be identified as involving a Puerto Rican boy, not an Appalachian or a black:

"Do you try to avoid getting a girl pregnant or don't you care?"
"I try to avoid it."
"Suppose you did, and she found out where you lived?"
"I'd have to marry the broad."
"Would you like that?"
"No, that's a hell of a mess."

Another boy simply said that if you get a girl pregnant, "You've got to marry her." Note that both boys left implicit why you have got to.

Given the unpopularity of contraception, one would expect abortions to be common. If so, most boys in Chicago felt that it was no business of theirs. In New York, the attitude was different: "If I liked the girl enough I would marry her, *or something.*" This boy said he would still feel obligated if he didn't like the girl so much, but he would not arrange for an abortion: "That would mess her up too much. . . . Some ladies, they just do it to get money out of it; they don't really do it to help a person at all."

The difference in warmth, involvement, and concern for the woman, while it should not be exaggerated, was present no matter what tack we took. The Puerto Rican boys, despite the myth of *machismo* (the need for constant and dramatic assertions of masculinity), did not preen themselves on their virility. Most of them said it was not right to talk to other guys about girls they had schemed with, although some did talk about "street girls," whose well-known promiscuity made it impossible to take pride in having "scored" with them. Similarly, the reaction to betrayal in the New York group was a mild one. Violent assault on a girl might occur if she was suspected of having told the police about stealing or fighting, but not for sexual defections. When they occur, "I tell her not to do that again," or "I walk away," or "I call it quits." In this realm, as elsewhere, *fatalismo* apparently counts for more than *machismo*.

If early marriage ensues, it is accepted in a spirit best described as resignation. However, the Puerto Rican boys protested with great vehemence that it was the thing they wished above all to avoid. Often referring to unsatisfactory family relations from their own experience, they said they wanted to marry late or never. Pointing to others around them, they spoke out against too many people marrying too soon, having too many children. Most of their own trouble and that of others in the ghetto, they said, began when some young man fathered a child he did not want.

With a mixture of envy and indignation, middle-class people often assume that the sex lives of their socioeconomic inferiors are dominated by pure, free sensual pleasure. This assumption is unwarranted. The Puerto Ricans in our New York group stressed sensual pleasure somewhat more than the other two groups, but even they were more interested in collective fun, in the set itself, than in pure hedonism. Furthermore, they enjoyed scheming partly because it is an act of rebellion against authority. In any class, defiance is a tacit acknowledgment that a coercive culture exists to be resisted.

The cultural origins of the three groups are totally different, but all three now live in urban ghettos where, to varying degrees, they are shut off from middle-class society. The Appalachian whites in Chicago and the Washington blacks are in most ways slightly less "middle-class" in behavior than the Puerto Ricans in New York. Many people in Appalachia have had no contact with outsiders since the pre-Revolutionary settlement of this country. For lower-class blacks, isolation may have begun with the capture of their ancestors in Africa and continued through slavery and segregation. It is hardly surprising that these groups have developed standards for sexual behavior that differ from those of the middle class. What is less obvious, and therefore more important to note, is that middle-class fantasies about uninhibited sexual joy among members of a "culture of poverty" are equally foreign to people who are historically, socially, and personally alienated from the so-called mainstream of American society.

35

Bystander "Apathy"

BIBB LATANÉ

JOHN M. DARLEY

On a March night in 1964, in Kew Gardens, Queens, Kitty Genovese was set upon by a maniac as she came home from work at
3 A.M. Thirty-eight of her neighbors came to their windows when
she cried out in terror. None came to her assistance. Her assailant
took over half an hour to murder her, but no one even so much as
called the police.

The story became the journalistic sensation of the decade. "Apathy,"
cried the newspapers. "Indifference," said columnists and commenta-
tors. "Moral callousness," "dehumanization," "loss of concern for
our fellow man," added preachers, professors, and other sermonizers.

Although it is true that witnesses to emergencies often do nothing
to save the victims, "apathy," "indifference," and "unconcern" are

BYSTANDER "APATHY" Adapted from *American Scientist* 57 (1969). Used by
permission of Bibb Latané. Fuller details of these experiments and related research can be found in Latané and Darley, *The unresponsive bystander*. New
York: Appleton-Century-Crofts, 1970.

not accurate descriptions of their reactions. The thirty-eight witnesses to Kitty Genovese's murder did not merely glance at the scene and turn away. Instead, they continued to stare out their windows—caught, fascinated, distressed, but unwilling to act. Their behavior was not helpful, but neither was it indifferent or apathetic. It was like crowd behavior in many emergencies—car accidents, drownings, fires, and attempted suicides. All attract substantial numbers of people who watch in helpless fascination.

In such situations, there are strong forces that urge people to act, including sympathy for the victim and various social norms concerning people's obligation to help each other. However, strong counterforces also exist. The basic characteristic of an emergency is that it involves threat or harm, certainly to the victim and possibly to those who try to help him. A second characteristic of emergencies is that they are highly unusual events, different from the normal course of life and also from each other. For this reason, people have little personal experience with handling them. In addition, little second-hand wisdom on the subject is available. One might get through a formal dinner party by using manners gleaned from old Fred Astaire movies, but it is difficult to cope with a genuine emergency by relying on "Charge!" "Women and children first!" and "Quick, get lots of hot water and towels!" Third, emergencies are sudden and unforeseen, and they require instant action. The bystander has no opportunity to plan in advance or to consider his alternatives in a leisurely fashion. Faced with a situation that offers at least some risks and few positive rewards, unable to rely on past experience or learning, and denied the time for planning and careful consideration, the bystander to an emergency is in an unenviable position. It is perhaps surprising that anyone should intervene at all.

Approaching the matter from a different angle, one can ask what has to go on in the mind of a bystander before he acts. Suppose an emergency is actually taking place. A middle-aged man, walking down the street, has a heart attack. He stops short, clutches his chest, and staggers to the nearest building wall, where he slowly slumps to the sidewalk in a sitting position. Before coming to the man's assistance, a passerby must make a series of decisions that can be schematized as follows:

1. He must *notice* that something is happening.
2. He must *interpret* the event, deciding that something is clearly and urgently wrong. (Perhaps the man slumped on the sidewalk is a drunk who neither wants nor can use help.)
3. He must *assume personal responsibility* for giving assistance. (Perhaps help is already on the way; perhaps someone else in the crowd is a doctor and will come forward.)

4. He must *decide how to help.* (Should he himself go to the man, or should he call a doctor or the police? What are the first-aid rules? Where is the nearest telephone?)

In the course of making these decisions, an individual bystander is likely to be considerably influenced by the decisions he perceives other bystanders to be making. If all the other onlookers seem to regard an event as non-serious and the proper behavior as nonintervention, perhaps they are right. One must ask, of course, why the group would remain inactive in the face of an emergency. One reason is that each bystander, while he watches the reactions of the others, is aware that the others are also watching him. In our society, men are supposed to remain poised and collected under stress and women are supposed to leave the handling of crises to men. It is not hard to see how a group of people, trying to follow these rules and simultaneously watching the behavior of others for cues, might be led (or misled) to define the situation as less critical than each would if alone. In addition, the presence of other people may affect a person's assessment of the costs and rewards of nonintervention. When only one bystander is present, it is clear that only he can act or fail to act. When there is a group, responsibility is diffused over all its members.

Let us examine some experiments that bear on these two points: the interpretation of a situation as an emergency and the decision to undertake personal responsibility for handling it. Our theory is that both are more likely when a bystander is alone than when he is part of a group.

Interpreting the Event

EXPERIMENT 1: WHERE THERE'S SMOKE, THERE'S (SOMETIMES) FIRE

In this experiment, fifty-eight Columbia students (all men) agreed to submit to an interview about "some of the problems involved in life at an urban university." While they waited to be called for the interview, they filled out a preliminary questionnaire in a small waiting room. Some subjects waited alone; others waited with two confederates of the experimenter; still others waited with two subjects who, like themselves, had no knowledge of the real purpose of the experiment.

Soon after the subjects began working on the questionnaires, a stream of whitish smoke began to puff into the room through a wall vent at irregular intervals. The experiment lasted until a subject left the room to report the smoke or, if he did not, for six minutes after he first noticed it. The question was, what effect would the presence of other people have on the likelihood that a subject would report the smoke and on his speed in doing so?

The typical subject who was alone in the waiting room behaved very reasonably. Shortly after the smoke appeared, he glanced up from the questionnaire, noticed the smoke, looked startled, and went through a brief period of indecision. Soon he went to the vent and investigated. He hesitated again, then finally walked out of the room and calmly reported the smoke to the experimenter. Eighteen of the twenty-four people tested alone reported the smoke, most of them within two minutes of noticing it.

The behavior of subjects who went through the experiment with two confederates of the experimenter (who had been told to act indifferent to the "emergency"—to stare at the smoke, shrug, and return to their questionnaires) was dramatically different. Of the ten subjects in this group, only one ever reported the smoke—10 percent, as compared to 75 percent of the subjects who worked alone. The other nine stayed in the room, worked doggedly on their questionnaires, and waved the fumes away. In the third group, which consisted of twenty-four students working in threes, only three subjects reported the smoke within the six-minute experimental period, and two of them waited more than four minutes to do so.

Interviewed later, all the subjects who did not report the smoke said they had rejected the idea that it came from a fire. They hit upon an astonishing variety of other explanations, all of which assumed the smoke not to be dangerous. Many thought it was steam or air-conditioning vapor; several thought it was smog purposely pumped in to simulate an urban environment; two (from different groups) actually thought it was "truth gas" filtered into the room to induce them to answer the questionnaire accurately. Predictably, a few decided that "it must be some sort of experiment" and stoically endured the discomfort rather than overreact. Despite the obviously inhibiting effects of other bystanders, the subjects almost invariably claimed that they had paid little or no attention to the reactions of others in the room.

EXPERIMENT 2: A LADY IN DISTRESS

Our second experiment was designed to see whether the inhibiting effects of a group also operate when the danger is not to the bystander himself, as in the smoke-filled room, but to another person. We also added a new variable: some bystanders were strangers; others knew each other.

The subjects, again Columbia undergraduates, waited in a room alone, with a friend, or with a stranger to participate (they thought) in a market research study. As they waited, they heard the attractive young woman who had guided them to the testing room climb onto a chair in the next room, then fall and apparently injure herself. There was a loud crash and a scream (from a tape recorder) as the chair supposedly collapsed. "Oh, my God, my foot . . . I . . . can't move . . . it. Oh . . . my ankle," the woman moaned. "I . . . can't get this . . . thing . . . off me." She cried and moaned for about a minute longer, but the cries got more subdued and controlled. Finally she muttered something about getting outside, knocked over the chair as she pulled herself up, and thumped to the door, closing it behind her as she left. The incident took just over two minutes in all.

Of the students who heard the accident while alone in the waiting room, 70 percent offered to help the victim before she left the room. By contrast, there were responses from only 7 percent of the subjects who waited with a passive confederate of the experimenter and 13 percent of those who waited with another subject they did not know. When friends waited together, at least one person intervened in 70 percent of the pairs. Although this percentage is the same as that for subjects who waited alone, the response rate for pairs is actually lower than that for single individuals. Allowing for the fact that twice as many people are free to act when pairs are involved, there would have to be a response from at least one person in 91 percent of the pairs to equal a response from 70 percent of the subjects who were alone.

The groups ranked the same on speed as they did on response rate. Subjects who were alone acted fastest; then pairs of friends; then pairs of strangers. Subjects whose partners had been told to act passive responded most slowly of all.

When those who did not intervene were interviewed later, most of them said they were not sure what had happened but had decided it was not too serious. Some said they thought other people would or could help, and three said they did not want to embarrass the victim. None of them felt they had behaved callously or immorally. Their behavior was generally consistent with their interpretation of the situation, and they almost uniformly maintained that, in a "real" emergency, they would be among the first to help. Interestingly enough, the subjects whom the results showed to have been *most* influenced by the presence of another person, those paired with passive confederates of the experimenter, were those *least* aware of or willing to admit to having been influenced. Asked to rate the influence of their partners, 14 percent of the subjects with passive confederates, 30 percent of the paired strangers, and 70 percent of the paired friends checked "moderate" or more.

How can we account for the fact that strangers inhibit intervention more than friends? It may be that people are less afraid of possible embarrassment in front of friends and also that friends are less likely than strangers to misinterpret each other's behavior. When strangers overheard the accident, they seemed noticeably concerned but confused. They often glanced furtively at each other, apparently anxious to discover the other's reaction yet unwilling to betray their own concern. Friends, on the other hand, seemed better able to convey their concern nonverbally, and they were also more inclined to discuss the incident and arrive at a mutual plan of action.

EXPERIMENT 3: THE CASE OF THE STOLEN BEER

Perhaps, we thought, there are circumstances under which people are more likely to intervene when others are present than when they are alone. For instance, when there is a criminal, the presence of potentially risk-sharing allies might make intervention more likely.

To test this possibility, two Columbia undergraduates staged a series of "robberies." During a two-week period in 1968, they "stole" a case of beer from the Nu-Way Beverage Center in Suffern, New York, a total of ninety-six times. The proprietor was always out of the room when the robbery took place but returned shortly thereafter. Half the time the robbery occurred while one customer was in the store; half the time there were two witnesses.

Of the single witnesses, 65 percent reported the theft to the proprietor. From this one would predict (adjusting for the fact that a pair includes two people) that at least one person in 87 percent of the pairs would mention the robbery. Only 56 percent of the pairs did.

In three very different situations, then, the same effect has been observed. People are less likely to take a socially responsible action if other people are present than if they are alone. The effect holds whether the situation involves general danger, the victim of an accident, or a criminal against whom a group could unite. The results also support the argument advanced earlier to account for the inhibiting effect of a group. Bystanders tend to be led by other bystanders to interpret the situation as less serious than they would if alone, and to hesitate to take action because they do not believe a dangerous situation really exists.

Assuming the Responsibility

But what happens when a person *does* know, perhaps because a victim makes it very clear, that an emergency exists? In that case, the observer must still decide whether he himself should intervene. The decision will presumably be based on an assessment of the costs and rewards of action and inaction.

The presence of other people can alter the costs and rewards of intervention chiefly by reducing the cost to any one person of not acting. A bystander who is alone bears all the responsibility for mishandling the situation. If he fails to act, he is the one who feels all the guilt and gets all the blame. If others are present, they share the responsibility. If, as in the Genovese case, the members of a group cannot watch each other closely, each person also has the option of assuming that "somebody else must be doing something."

EXPERIMENT 4: "I NEED HELP"

In this experiment, we needed to create a clear-cut emergency in which each observer was prevented from communicating with any other observers he believed to be present. We recruited about one hundred introductory psychology students from New York University to take part in an unspecified experiment required for the courts. (Although all the subjects were women, a variation of the basic experiment run with subjects of both sexes showed no sex differences in the rate or speed of responses. Coping with emergencies is often thought to be the duty of men, especially when women are present, but this study showed no evidence that this is the case.)

Each subject was ushered into a room of her own and told, over an intercom, that she was to participate in a discussion of the kinds of personal problems faced by normal college students in a high-pressure urban environment. To avoid embarrassing anyone, the experimenter continued, the subjects would converse over the intercom instead of face-to-face, and the experimenter would not listen to the discussion itself but only get the students' reactions to it later on, by questionnaire.

The plan for the discussion was that each person would talk in turn for two minutes, presenting her problems to the group. Next, each person in turn would comment on what others had said, and finally there would be a free discussion. A mechanical device regulated the discussion, switching on only one microphone at a time.

The discussion started with the future "victim" speaking first. He said he found it difficult to get adjusted to New York and to his studies. Very hesitantly and with obvious embarrassment, he mentioned that he was prone to seizures, particularly when studying hard or taking exams. The other people, including the one real subject, took their turns and discussed similar problems (minus the proneness to seizures). The subject talked last in the series, after the last prerecorded voice.

When it was again the victim's turn to talk, he made a few relatively calm comments, and then, growing increasingly loud and incoherent, he continued:

> I er um I think I I need er if if could er er somebody er er er er er er er give me a little er give me a little help here because er I er I'm er er h-h-having a a a a real problem er right now and I er if somebody could help me out it would it would er er s-s-sure be sure be good . . . because er there er er a cause I er I uh I've got a a one of the er sei-----er er things coming on and and and I could really er use some help so if somebody would er give me a little h-help uh er-er-er-er-er c-could somebody er er help er uh uh uh (*choking sounds*) . . . I'm gonna die er er I'm . . . gonna die er help er er seizure er (*chokes, then quiet*).

Some subjects were led to believe that the victim was the only other person taking part in the discussion. Others thought the group consisted of three people (the subject, the victim, and one other person); others thought there were six in the group. In some of the three-person groups, the two subjects were friends; in others they were strangers. We thought that knowing the victim might also affect a person's tendency to help, so we arranged for some subjects from six-person groups to encounter a student posing as the future victim in the hall, where they chatted for about a minute before the experiment began.

All the subjects who reported the emergency did so within three minutes after the victim's seizure began. Of those who thought they alone knew of the victim's plight, 85 percent reported it before the victim had stopped pleading for help and the remaining 15 percent did so shortly thereafter. Of the subjects who thought they were part of a six-person group, only 62 percent ever reported the trouble.

Subjects who thought the discussion group consisted of themselves, the victim, and a friend responded significantly faster than those who thought the third member of the group was a stranger. In fact, they responded with about the same speed as subjects who believed that they alone knew of the emergency, suggesting that responsibility does not diffuse across friends.

Subjects who had met the victim were faster to report his distress than other subjects from six-person groups. Some said later that they had actually pictured him in the grip of the seizure; no one who had not met the victim said this. Apparently the ability to visualize a specific distressed individual increases the likelihood of helping him.

Whether or not they intervened, subjects did believe the fit was genuine and serious. "My God, he's having a fit," many said to themselves (and we overheard via their microphones). Others gasped or simply said "Oh." One subject said to herself, "It's just my kind of luck, something has to happen to me!" Several spoke aloud of their confusion: "Oh, God, what should I do?"

Those who failed to report the emergency showed few signs of the apathy and indifference thought to characterize unresponsive bystanders. When the experimenter came into the room to end the experiment, subjects who had not responded often asked about the victim: "Is he being taken care of?" "He's all right, isn't he?" Many showed physical signs of nervousness, such as trembling hands and sweating palms. They seemed somewhat *more* emotionally aroused than did the subjects who reported the situation, who did so rather uncertainly but without panic.

It is not our impression that the nonresponders had decided *not* to act; rather, they were still in a state of indecision. This distinction may be academic for a victim, since he gets no help in either case, but it is an extremely important one for understanding the causes of inaction. The fit created a conflict of the avoidance-avoidance type. On the one hand, subjects wanted to avoid the guilt and shame they would feel if they did not help the person in distress. On the other hand, they wanted to avoid making fools of themselves by overreacting, ruining the experiment by leaving their intercoms, and destroying the anonymous nature of the situation, which the experimenter had said was important. Subjects who thought they alone could help were able to resolve the conflict quickly. For those who thought other bystanders were present, however, the cost of not helping was reduced and the conflict was harder to resolve. As their emotional behavior showed, they did not choose not to respond; instead, they were still vacillating between two negative alternatives when the experiment ended.

As in the earlier experiments, we asked all subjects whether the presence or absence of other bystanders had entered their minds while they listened to the victim. We asked the question every way we knew how: subtly, directly, tactfully, rudely. The answer was always the same. The subjects had been aware of the presence of other bystanders, but they did not think it had influenced them in any way. Once again, this denial was in contradiction to the findings of the experiment.

Safety in Numbers?

In these four experiments, bystanders in groups were less likely to intervene in an emergency than if they were alone. The behavior of the other bystanders and the relationships among them seem to be important.

A stranger who has been "programed" not to react is the most inhibiting; a neutral stranger next; and a friend the least. We have suggested two reasons for inaction by a group: the *apparent* lack of concern on the part of others may lead each person to interpret the situation as less serious than he would otherwise, and the presence of others may diffuse the responsibility for coping or not coping with the situation. In a particular emergency, both processes could operate, although the diffusion of responsibility should play a role only to the extent that social influence is unsuccessful in leading people to downgrade the seriousness of the event.

"There's safety in numbers," according to an old adage, and modern city dwellers seem to believe it. They shun deserted streets, empty subway cars, and lonely walks in dark places. While it may be true that a person is less likely to *become* a victim if he stays with the crowd, our experiments call into serious question the belief that he is more likely to receive help if many people are present. In fact, the opposite seems to be true: the fewer people who are available to take action, the better.

Although the results of these studies may shake our faith in "safety in numbers," they may also help us begin to understand the frightening incidents in which crowds have heard but not answered a call for help. They suggest that the immediate social environment is more important in determining a person's reaction to an emergency than such vague cultural or personality concepts as "apathy" and "alienation due to urbanization." They also help explain why the failure to intervene seems more common in large cities than in rural areas. When an emergency arises in a large city, a crowd is likely to gather; the members of the crowd are likely to be strangers; and it is likely that none of them will know the victim. These are exactly the conditions that, in our experiments, led to the fewest attempts to help.